The Address of the Eye

The Address of the Eye

A PHENOMENOLOGY OF
FILM EXPERIENCE

Vivian Sobchack

PRINCETON UNIVERSITY PRESS

PRINCETON, NEW JERSEY

Library of Congress Cataloging-in-Publication Data

Sobchack, Vivian Carol.
The address of the eye : a phenomenology of
film experience / Vivian Sobchack.
p. cm.
Includes bibliographical references and index.
ISBN 0-691-03195-9 : $35.00
1. Motion pictures—Philosophy. I. Title.
PN 1995.S54   1992
791.43'01—dc20   91-21402   CIP

This book has been composed in Linotron Palatino

Princeton University Press books are
printed on acid-free paper, and meet the guidelines
for permanence and durability of the Committee
on Production Guidelines for Book Longevity
of the Council on Library Resources

Printed in the United States of America by
Princeton University Press, Princeton, New Jersey

1 2 3 4 5 6 7 8 9 10

1 2 3 4 5 6 7 8 9 10
(Pbk.)

TO RICHARD L. LANIGAN

FOR TEACHING ME WHAT I ALWAYS

ALREADY KNEW

As soon as we see other seers . . . henceforth,
through other eyes we are for ourselves fully visible. . . . For the first time, the seeing that I am is for
me really visible; for the first time I appear to myself
completely turned inside out under my own eyes.

MAURICE MERLEAU-PONTY
The Visible and the Invisible

A being which is not the object of another being . . .
presupposes that *no* objective being exists. . . . To be
sensuous, i.e., to be real, is to be an object of sense,
a *sensuous* object, and thus to have sensuous objects
outside oneself, objects of one's sense perceptions.

KARL MARX
Early Writings

Contents

Figures

Preface

WHEN I BEGAN writing this book about the embodied nature and dialectical structure of the film experience, two theoretical paradigms and approaches had dominated the American enterprise of cinema studies for some time. There were, of course, significant and historical reasons for the appeal of both Lacanian psychoanalysis and neo-Marxism. The major project of most film theorists in the 1980s was to dynamize the rigorous structuralism that had changed the field of film studies in the 1970s, to temporalize its formal abstractions, and to bring it into animated engagement with an increasingly contentious and fractured social world. Both psychoanalysis and Marxism—one concerned with the "interior" and the other with the "exterior" of human existence—attempt to theorize not merely the structure but also the dynamics of, respectively, the social subject and the objective social formation.

Once seen as theoretically incommensurable, in their poststructuralist manifestations psychoanalysis and Marxism have seemed to become increasingly compatible, particularly as both have converged in a mutual recognition of the originary nature and productive function of language and discourse in constituting the libidinal "economy" of the "self" and the political "unconscious" of the social formation. Indeed, achieved through a correspondent focus on language as constitutive of both psychic and social life, this seeming complementarity between Lacanian psychoanalysis and neo-Marxism has promised a comprehensive—and dialectical—theory of cinematic representation that would subtend the gap between "interiority" and "exteriority," between psychic and social formation and their expression. Thus, in a situation akin to the crises of relevance experienced in many other academic disciplines, by embracing these two theoretical paradigms, cinema studies was able to move (without a loss of "scientific" rigor) from static, abstract, and formal description of its objects of study to more dynamic, functional, and historical description.

Given this profound transformation of the structuralist enterprise and its animated turn toward the social world, the new linguistically and discursively oriented forms of psychoanalysis and Marxism were (and still are) regarded as particularly responsive to the remedial and revisionary projects of a contemporary film theory and analysis that sees social reform as much a part of its work as formal description. It is not accidental that Lacanian psychoanalysis was taken up by feminist film theorists who used it both to explore the gendered structure of cinematic spectatorship and to disclose the patriarchal functions of classical Hollywood narrative. It is also hardly coincidental that neo-Marxist theory was taken up by radical theorists bent not only on transforming a previously "neutral" and monolithic film History into invested and multiple histories, but also on exposing the ideological information of cinematic representation as it has emerged from the dynamics of a capitalist, corporate American industry.

Within this theoretical context, writing a book on the "phenomenology" of the film "experience" was both a lonely and suspect enterprise. First, "experience" seems a mushy, soft, term—a remainder (and reminder) of the sloppy liberal humanism that retrospectively characterized cinema studies before it was informed by the scientific methods and technically precise vocabularies of structuralism and semiotics. Second, although nearly all contemporary critical theory and its linguistic and discursive concerns were European in origin, "existential phenomenology" was not numbered among film theory's Continental imports. Indeed, little understood and even less read, "phenomenology" was loosely conceived and associated with a multitude of precontemporary sins. It was regarded as idealist, essentialist, and ahistorical. It was also seen as extremely naive, making claims about "direct" experience precisely at a moment when contemporary theory was emphasizing the inaccessibility of direct experience and focused on the constitutive processes and mediating structures of language.

On the one hand, phenomenology was connected primarily to Edmund Husserl and to his goal of getting to the "essence" of "the things themselves" through the process of "bracketing" all psychic, social, and scientific presuppositions held about them—a project that seemed completely antithetical to those of contemporary cinema studies. Phenomenology's relevance and legitimacy were further (and quite properly) undermined by the Husserlian notion of the "transcendental ego," anathema to theorists looking to bridge the gap between metaphysics and the dynamic social world of fractious and fragmented concrete subjects. On the other hand, phenomenology was also tainted for cinema studies by its connection to French Catholicism. Paradoxically, it was charged with being both a form of transcendental, religious "mysticism" (evidenced by the work of film theorists Amédée Ayfre and Henri Agel) and a form of "naive realism" (evidenced by the work of André Bazin who apotheosized the cinema's capacity for "revelation" of the "real" world).

In this context, my own discovery of Maurice Merleau-Ponty's existential phenomenology and my elaboration of its special focus on the radical semiosis of the lived-body as a practical method for describing the existential structure of cinematic vision might seem perverse. If so, however, I would argue that this perversity is profound. That is to say, my move to phenomenology emerges not from my desire to exercise transcendental phenomenology's capacity for describing "essences" or demonstrating "universal" structures, but rather from my desire to cry out my *inherent qualification* of the world of essences and universals, to allow for my *existential particularity* in a world I engage and share with others. In this regard, although what follows is not an overtly feminist work, it is written by a woman who has felt constrained by contemporary theoretical analysis, who wants to speak of more possibilities than either psychoanalytic or Marxist theory currently allows. Even—or, perhaps, especially—because it has grounded and circumscribed feminist film theory, neo-Freudian psychoanalysis has not exhausted my experience, although it has often exhausted my patience. I refuse to be completely contained within its structures and described by its terms. Psychoanalysis is fine, perhaps, for disclosing the "unconscious" of patriarchal texts and the power and constitutive nature of an experienced "lack," but it is not so fine for describing the pleasure and plenitude of an experience that includes—but is also in *excess* of—"sexual difference." Thus, refusing its psychoanalytic meaning, my "perverse" turn away from *accepted analysis* and toward a thick and *radical description* of experience is a turn toward articulating not only another kind of bodily being, but also a healthy and adult polymorphousness, a freedom of becoming.

My critical embrace of existential phenomenology also reflects my sense of the limitations of contemporary Marxist film theory. However accurately it seems to describe certain aspects of and social relations within my world, however persuasively it has teased out the ideological objectives of the cinematic "apparatus" and its representations, it has not yet fully accommodated to its vocabulary the embodied experience of labor, alienation, engagement, and transformation I have every time I go to the movies—or elsewhere. Attempting a synthesis of subject and object in a concrete and constantly changing social world, contemporary Marxist theory has still tended to neglect the embodied experience I live as "mine." Although, in his early work, Marx wrote, "To be sensuous, i.e., to be real, is to be an object of sense, a sensuous object . . . ," Marxism has tended to focus less on the *sensuous objectivity of subjective being* than it has on the *sensible being of objects*.[1] As Scott Warren suggests, "the ignorance and destruction of subjectivity has generally characterized Marxism in our century."[2]

I would argue that in the final analysis (indeed, perhaps as a result of the "objective" process of analysis), both psychoanalytic and Marxist film theory in most of their current manifestations have obscured the dynamic, synoptic, and lived-body situation of both the spectator and the film—ironically, in this context, as they have respectively emphasized the *sexual* and *material* economy of the sign and the signifying subject. A libidinal theory of the subject based on sexual difference and unconscious, prerational experience, psychoanalytic theory has performed its own sexual objectifications that mutilate the simultaneous integrity, mutability, and sensuous materiality of the lived-body subject and dissect, abstract, and fetishize certain body parts as if they had a life of their own, as if they determined or were the whole of a person. A rational philosophy of history grounded in objective, concrete, social praxis, contemporary Marxism (if not Marx) has neglected the prereflective, prerational, libidinal life of the body-subject and has elided certain experienced aspects of concrete praxis—losing Marxism's original dialectical power by obscuring the sensuous materiality of the lived-body subject and by objectifying and reducing material existence to "materialism" and sensuous experience to "commodity fetishism."

Thus, without denying the power and utility of both psychoanalytic and Marxist film theory as they are presently applied to cinema, and with a clear sense that Marx's dialectical materialism has much more in common with existential phenomenology than is currently recognized within cinema studies, I want to begin again. That is, I want to mistrust what has become the certain ground, the *premises*, of contemporary film theory and to interrogate certain widely held

[1] Karl Marx, "Economic and Philosophical Manuscripts," in *Early Writings*, trans. Rodney Livingstone and Gregor Benton (New York: Vintage Books, 1975), p. 390.

[2] Scott Warren, *The Emergence of Dialictical Theory: Philosophy and Political Inquiry* (Chicago: Univ. of Chicago Press, 1984), p. 110.

assumptions about the nature of film and the intelligibility and significance of spectatorship and the film experience. To do so, however, I must interrogate vision—vision as it is embodied, vision as it
is performed, vision as it signifies, vision as it radically entails a
world of subjects and objects to make sense of them and of itself as
it is lived.

More formally, the task of *The Address of the Eye: A Phenomenology
of Film Experience* is to describe and account for the origin and locus
of cinematic signification and significance in the experience of vision
as an embodied and meaningful existential activity. My study here is
less theoretical than it is empirical. Or, rather, if it is theoretical, it is
radically—materially—so, grounding itself in an interrogation and
description of the experiential phenomenon of sensing, enworlded
bodies that can see and be seen. Given this task, both the philosophical reflection and eidetic method of existential phenomenology best
provide me the basis and means to develop an existentially grounded
and radical semiotics and hermeneutics capable of describing the origins of cinematic intelligibility and the signifying activity of embodied vision. Although I will devote later pages to a general introduction to phenomenology (and, most importantly, to Merleau-Ponty's
existential turn on Husserlian transcendental phenomenology), some
comments are in order to prepare the reader for this present work—
if not for the possibly unfamiliar philosophical vocabulary of phenomenology, then for the particular intersection of my project and
my prose style.

Prereflective experience is neither verbal nor literary, and yet the
goal of phenomenology is to describe experience. Experience comes
to description in acts of reflection: consciousness turning reflexively
on itself to become conscious of consciousness. And it is in reflection
that experience is given formal significance, is spoken and written.
Too often, however, language—particularly theoretical language—is
used to banish and disavow experience. On the other side, experience would banish language as inadequate to it, or so both romantics
and antitheoretical activists would have it. Experience, nonetheless,
seeks and is fulfilled by language even as language and experience
are categorically incommensurable. This is something that all marginalized peoples recognize. They desire a "new" language that will articulate the specificity of their experience, and they struggle to find
the grounds from which they can speak it. Certainly, the highly codified language of official culture has been seen to appropriate, con-

strain, and transform experience different from its own, whether that of women, people of color, or the differently abled. But the unreflective language of everyday life also constrains us; its usage is habitual and sedimented, and we tend to no longer listen to a language that first arose from—within—experience and was vital in a profoundly dialectical way.

For me, part of the appeal of phenomenology lies in its potential for opening up and destabilizing language in the very process of its description of the phenomena of experience. That is, not only does phenomenology allow us a place from which to speak, the unique and always social ground of our lived-body situation, but it also allows us to reinvent language, to objectively relocate its intersubjective origins in existential experience. Its rigorous method of reflection renews language, reaffirming it as rooted in the existential and embodied significance of being. Its descriptive activity brings to consciousness not only the structures of experience, but also their becoming in language. The following work, therefore, is marked by a prose style that insists on interrogating "ordinary" language as it interrogates "ordinary" experience. This involves frequent hyphenation in order to force a certain form of attentiveness to what we say but hardly hear, a certain heretical recognition of the general *adequacy* of language to experience. In this regard, except insofar as all language is metaphorical or as it is specifically identified in this present work, I do not use metaphor. (For example, the term *film's body* in this work is meant to be empirical, not metaphoric.) My prose is also engaged in serious punning and in a kind of dialectical play, inversions and parallelisms underscored in order to model and highlight in language the transitivity and reversibility experienced in subject-object relations in general, and vision in particular. It is my hope these peculiarities will be more illuminating than irritating.

While the task of this book is to describe the origin, locus, and existential significance of cinematic vision and the film experience, its goal is broader. In literally "fleshing out" contemporary film theory, I hope to restore to reflection about the cinema the existential experience of the medium's openness and the spectator's freedom. This restoration means neither to deny the constraints and institutions of convention nor the binds of culture and the bounds of historical consciousness. It does, however, wish to suggest that "openness" and "freedom" are not merely the naive conceptions of liberal humanism, but possible daily performances of both films and the people who make and watch them.

In this regard, Merleau-Ponty is worth quoting at length. At a time when theorists describe contemporary American culture as undergoing a simultaneous and related crisis of representation and crisis of the "real," his eloquence, I hope, will charge the less eloquent and more technical pages to follow with political urgency and hope:

> What then is freedom? To be born is both to be born of the world and to be born into the world. The world is already constituted, but also never completely constituted; in the first case we are acted upon, in the second we are open to an infinite number of possibilities. But this analysis is still abstract, for we exist in both ways *at once*. There is, therefore, never determinism and never absolute choice. . . . We are involved in the world and with others in an inextricable tangle.
>
> The choice we make of our life is always based on a certain givenness. . . . I am a psychological and historical structure, and have received, with existence, a manner of existing, a style. All my actions and thoughts stand in relationship to this structure. . . . The fact remains that I am free, not in spite of, or on the hither side of, these motivations, but by means of them. For this significant life, this certain significance of nature and history which I am, does not limit my access to the world, but on the contrary is my means of entering into communication with it. It is by being unrestrictively and unreservedly what I am at present that I have a chance of moving forward; it is by living my time that I am able to understand other times, by plunging into the present and the world, by taking on deliberately what I am fortuitously, by willing what I will and doing what I do, that I can go further. I can miss being free only if I try to bypass my natural and social situation by refusing to take it up. . . . Nothing determines me from outside, not because nothing acts upon me, but, on the contrary, because I am from the start outside myself and open to the world.[3]

Freedom is thus attained and lived within history and culture, not in impossible escape attempts from them. And, insofar as it, too, is embodied and enworlded and has a "manner of existing," a style, "the address of the eye" (whether human or cinematic) is both constrained in its being and yet free to realize and make visible in action the possibilities of becoming other than what it is.

[3] Maurice Merleau-Ponty, *Phenomenology of Perception*, trans. Colin Smith (London: Routledge and Kegan Paul, 1962), pp. 453–456.

Acknowledgments

THE PROJECT that became this book was conceived at the University of Southern Illinois at Carbondale where, long ago, I studied in the Department of Speech Communication (which offers a unique emphasis on phenomenology and the philosophy of language and communication). I thank the members of that department for their much needed moral and financial support, and the Graduate Division at SIU for awarding me the Dissertation Research Fellowship that supported the beginning of this present work. Much more recently, my work has been supported by the institution where I now teach: the University of California, Santa Cruz. Research and writing have been regularly funded through grants from both the Faculty Senate Research Committee and the Arts Division Faculty Research Committee.

At various times, colleagues in the cinema studies community have had occasion to respond to the manuscript. In this regard, I particularly want to express my deep gratitude to Dudley Andrew and Peter Brunette for their careful, critical, and appreciative readings. I have taken their comments most seriously. Thanks and apologies also go to Joanna Hitchcock of Princeton University Press, an immensely gracious editor who possesses boundless patience.

Finally, I should like to thank three people whose critical intelligence, support and love, whose passion for what, after all, was *my* project, enabled me to write this book: Richard L. Lanigan, a mentor in the most rigorous and nurturing sense of the term and the person to whom this work is dedicated; Bill Pietz, an astute critic and loving source of support, who first understood the *material* in what I was writing; and Paige Baty, a true friend and colleague, who, provoked by the manuscript, shared invaluable editorial suggestions and many glasses of wine with me during wonderful evenings of exciting and far-ranging talk. Becoming would not have been as precious an adventure without the company of these three.

The Address of the Eye

Phenomenology and the Film Experience

> In a sense the whole of philosophy . . . consists in
> restoring a power to signify, a birth of meaning, or a
> wild meaning, an expression of experience by
> experience, which in particular clarifies the special
> domain of language. And in a sense . . . language is
> everything, since it is the voice of no one, since it is
> the voice of the things, the waves, and the forests.[1]

WHAT ELSE IS A FILM if not "an expression of experience by experience"? And what else is the primary task of film theory if not to restore to us, through reflection upon that experience and its expression, the original power of the motion picture to signify? However, when Maurice Merleau-Ponty wrote the above lines shortly before his death in 1961, it is unlikely that the cinema was in his thoughts. Rather, his overarching concern was with the living exchange of perception and expression, with the sensuous contours of language, with meaning and its signification born not abstractly but concretely from the surface contact, the fleshly dialogue, of human beings and the world together making sense sensible. Yet it is precisely this emphasis on the material and carnal foundations of language that makes the above fragment of *The Visible and the Invisible* particularly relevant to the semiotic and hermeneutic questions posed by the medium of cinema. The passage suggests not only the primordial and unprivate nature of language, but also the physically concrete "reversibility" of perception and expression that constitutes both the moving picture and our experience of it.

More than any other medium of human communication, the moving picture makes itself sensuously and sensibly manifest as the expression of experience by experience. A film is an act of seeing that makes itself seen, an act of hearing that makes itself heard, an act of physical and reflective movement that makes itself reflexively felt

[1] Maurice Merleau-Ponty, *The Visible and the Invisible*, ed. Claude Lefort, trans. Alphonso Lingus (Evanston, IL: Northwestern University Press, 1968), p. 155.

and understood. Objectively projected, visibly and audibly expressed before us, the film's activity of seeing, hearing, and moving signifies in a pervasive, primary, and embodied language that precedes and provides the grounds for the secondary significations of a more discrete, systematic, less "wild" communication. Cinema thus transposes, without completely transforming, those modes of being alive and consciously embodied in the world that count for each of us as *direct* experience: as experience "centered" in that particular, situated, and solely occupied existence sensed first as "Here, where the world touches" and then as "Here, where the world is sensible; here, where I am."[2]

In an unprecedented way, the cinema makes visible and audible the primordial origins of language in the reversibility of embodied and enworlded perception and expression. However, as Merleau-Ponty points out in a continuation of the passage quoted above, "What we have to understand is that there is no dialectical reversal from one of these views to the other; we do not have to reassemble them into a synthesis: they are two aspects of the reversibility which is the ultimate truth."[3] That is, the reversibility of perception and expression is neither instantiated as a thought nor synthesized from discrete and separate acts of consciousness. It is *given* with existence, in the simultaneity of subjective embodiment and objective enworldedness. Using the term *chiasmus* to name this reversibility ("the ultimate truth"), Merleau-Ponty characterizes it as that "unique space which separates and reunites, which sustains every cohesion."[4] That unique space is both the lived-body and the experienced world.

Indeed, the cinema uses *modes of embodied existence* (seeing, hearing, physical and reflective movement) as the vehicle, the "stuff," the

[2] This manner of reference to the "centering" of embodied existence is used frequently within the context of phenomenological inquiry but has a slightly different emphasis than that currently used to discuss—and disparage—the notion of the "centered subject." For phenomenological usage, see particularly Maurice Merleau-Ponty, *Phenomenology of Perception*, trans. Colin Smith (London: Routledge and Kegan Paul, 1962); Erwin Straus, *The Primary World of the Senses: A Vindication of Sensory Experience*, trans. Jacob Needleman (London: The Free Press of Glencoe, Collier-Macmillan, 1963); and Richard M. Zaner, *The Problem of Embodiment: Some Contributions to a Phenomenology of the Body*, 2d ed. (The Hague: Martinus Nijhoff, 1977).

[3] Merleau-Ponty, *The Visible and the Invisible*, p. 155.

[4] Maurice Merleau-Ponty, "Eye and Mind," trans. Carleton Dallery, in *The Primacy of Perception*, ed. James M. Edie (Evanston, IL: Northwestern University Press, 1964), p. 187.

substance of its language. It also uses the *structures of direct experience* (the "centering" and bodily situating of existence in relation to the world of objects and others) as the basis for the structures of its language. Thus, as a symbolic form of human communication, the cinema is like no other. At the end of his two-volume *Esthétique et psychologie du cinéma* (and sounding very much like Merleau-Ponty), Jean Mitry articulates both the medium's privileged nature and the problem it poses for those who would discover the "rules" governing its expression and grounding its intelligibility:

> These [cinematic] forms are . . . as varied as life itself and, furthermore, as one hasn't the knowledge to regulate life, neither has one the knowledge to regulate an art of which life is at one and the same time the subject and object.
>
> Whereas the classical arts propose to signify movement with the immobile, life with the inanimate, the cinema must express life with life itself. It begins there where the others leave off. It escapes, therefore, all their rules as it does all their principles.[5]

In a search for rules and principles governing cinematic expression, most of the descriptions and reflections of classical and contemporary film theory have not fully addressed the cinema as life expressing life, as experience expressing experience. Nor have they explored the mutual possession of this experience of perception and its expression by filmmaker, film, and spectator—all *viewers viewing*, engaged as participants in dynamically and directionally reversible acts that reflexively and reflectively constitute the *perception of expression* and the *expression of perception*. Indeed, it is this mutual capacity for and possession of experience through common structures of embodied existence, through similar modes of being-in-the-world, that provide the *intersubjective* basis of objective cinematic communication.

Insofar as the embodied structure and modes of being of a film are

---

[5] Jean Mitry, *Esthétique et psychologie du cinéma*, vol. 2 (Paris: Editions Universitaires, 1965), pp. 453–454. My translation from the following: "Les formes . . . sont . . . aussi variées que la vie elle-même et, pas plus qu'on ne saurait réglementer la vie, on ne saurait réglementer un art dont elle est à las fois le sujet et l'objet.

Tandis que les arts classiques se proposent de signifier le mouvement avec de l'immobile, la vie avec du non-vivant, le cinéma, lui, se doit d'exprimer la vie avec la vie elle-même. Il commence là où les autres finissent. Il échappe donc à toutes leurs règles comme à tous leurs principes."

like those of filmmaker and spectator, the film has the capacity and competence to signify, to not only *have* sense but also to *make* sense through a unique and systemic form of communication. Indeed, to the extent that any film can and does signify in some fashion to a viewer who is communicatively competent (that is, already aware that perception is expressible), and that any film—however abstract or "structural-materialist"—presupposes that it will be understood *as* signification, as conveying meaning beyond the brute material presence of light and shadow on a plane surface, the cinema assumes and assures its own intelligibility (even if it assumes and assures no single interpretation).[6] That intelligibility is also assumed by filmmaker and spectator. The film experience, therefore, rests on the mutual presupposition of its intersubjective nature and function, based on the intelligibility of embodied vision. Its significance emerges from a shared belief and from shared evidence that the substance and structure of cinematic perception and expression (however historically and culturally qualified) are inherently able to "reflect the universality of specific scopes of experience."[7]

This presupposition remains to be explored in the following chapters. Yet, immediately, it indicates that any semiotics and hermeneutics of the cinema must return to radically reflect on the origins of cinematic communication in the structures and pragmatics of existential experience. Such a semiotics and hermeneutic enterprise, undertaking this radical turn toward existence and away from secondary and abstract formulations, becomes a *semiotic phenomenology*—taking, as it does, signification and significance as immanent, as given with

[6] What is suggested here is that even at its most abstract and materially reflexive, the cinema is not understood as *merely* its brute material unless it is *secondarily* coded as such. Thus, in "structural-materialist" films, the materiality of the film is, and must be, *signified* in order to be understood on a material basis. In sum, the young infant (not yet communicatively competent because only preconscious of its own production of vision as both a viewing view/moving image) sees the play of light and shadow and color of *any* film as only its brute materiality, whereas the communicatively competent, self-conscious viewer sees *no* film in that manner, unless it is secondarily coded as materially significant. That is, to the baby the film is not yet a film, but to the mature viewing subject, the film is always *more* than its material presence and play before it can be seen as anything *less*.

[7] Jürgen Habermas quoted in T.A. McCarthy, "A Theory of Communicative Competence," in *Critical Sociology*, ed. Paul Connerton (London: Penguin Books, 1976), p. 472. On "communicative competence," see also Jürgen Habermas, *Communication and the Evolution of Society*, trans. Thomas McCarthy (Boston: Beacon Press, 1979).

6

existence.[8] Such a phenomenology of human meaning and its representation attempts to describe, thematize, and interpret the structures of communication as they radically emerge in the structures of being. This phenomenology's aim, however, is not to arrive at "essential" and proscriptive categories but to address the "thickness" of human experience and the rich and radical entailments of incarnate being and its representation. To accommodate itself to experience, its method is responsively dialectical and informed by no particular *telos*.

The aim of this simultaneously empirical and philosophical study, then, is to serve as a prolegomenon to a lived logic of signification in the cinema. The focus here will center on the radical origin of such a logic in lived-body experience, that is, in the activity of embodied consciousness realizing itself in the world and with others as both visual and visible, as both sense-making and sensible. The entailment of incarnate consciousness and the "flesh" of the world of which it is a part will be described as the basis for the origination of the general structures of cinematic signification, structures that are themselves produced in the performance of specific modes of existential and embodied communication in the film experience (that is, in the activity of vision intersubjectively connecting film and spectator with a world and each other).

In no way is the following effort meant to deny the extra-cinematic, empirical, and contingent conditions that limit and affect the specific shape of actual (not merely possible) cinematic communication, systematically distorting it either spontaneously or willfully for ideological, rhetorical, and poetic purpose. Indeed, as indicated in the Preface, this study itself is necessarily situated within and distorted by its own theoretical context; and, so situated, it must always and necessarily entail the ideological, rhetorical, and poetic in-formation of its own historicity. Nonetheless, what follows is not intended as remedial. This is no idealist attempt to "cure" cinema or to uncritically embrace the "critical theory" of the Frankfurt school in general (or

---

[8] This relation between existential phenomenology and semiotics is first made explicit and recognized as a "semiotic phenomenology" in Richard L. Lanigan, *Speaking and Semiology: Maurice Merleau-Ponty's Phenomenological Theory of Existential Communication* (The Hague: Mouton, 1972), pp. 51–96. This relation is summarized: "Existential phenomenology posits the *sign as given*, not as the synthetic product of a phenomenalism (or objective principium) or the synthetic product of an existentialism per se (or subjective principium)." (p. 75)

7

Habermas in particular).[9] It does not take as its focus the exposure of "distorted" cinematic communication and, in fact, refuses the idealism that yearns for communication (an *existential* phenomenon) made completely rational, somehow "purged" of historical and cultural prejudice or "distortion," somehow "cleansed" of the contingencies and specificity of biased existence that make communication not only necessary but also possible.[10] Similarly, although this study must be informed necessarily by rhetorical force and poetic linguistic praxis, it is not intended as a rhetoric or poetics of cinematic communication. Rather, its phenomenological project is to radically reflect upon the general structures that always emerge particularly and contingently as the entailment of the lived-body and the world in cinematic acts of perception and expression. These primary structures, founded in existence and constitutive of conscious experience, produce themselves in the world as a systemic "cinematic communicative competence," against which the secondary (but always present) notion of systematic "distortion" can be identified and, indeed, from which it can be constituted as ideology, rhetoric, and poetics.

THE EMBODIED AND ENWORLDED EYE:
PERCEPTION AND EXPRESSION

When we sit in a movie theater and perceive a film as sensible, as making sense, we (and the film before us) are immersed in a world and in an activity of visual being. The experience is as familiar as it is intense, and it is marked by the way in which significance and the act of signifying are *directly* felt, *sensuously* available to the viewer. The embodied activity of perception and expression—making sense and signifying it—are given to us as modalities of a single experience

---

[9] For a general yet thorough introduction to the "critical theory" of the Frankfurt school and Habermas, see David Held, *Introduction to Critical Theory: Horkheimer to Habermas* (Berkeley: Univ. of California Press, 1980). Held summarizes my own reservations about critical theory and its utopian idealism when, in a closing section on critical theory's "unresolved problems," he asks: "How can the possibility of critique be sustained, if the historical contextuality of knowledge is recognized? Or, to put the question somewhat differently, how can critical theory at once acknowledge its historicality and yet be critical?" (p. 398)

[10] "Systematically distorted communication" is a concept used by Habermas and relates to his theory of communicative competence. See Jürgen Habermas, "Systematically Distorted Communication," in *Critical Sociology*, pp. 348–362.

of being in the presence of and producing meaning and diacritical value. What we look at projected on the screen—whether Merleau-Ponty's "the things, the waves, and the forests," or only abstract lines and colors—addresses us as the expressed perception of an anonymous, yet present, "other." And, as we watch this expressive projection of an "other's" experience, we, too, express our perceptive experience. Through the address of our own vision, we speak back to the cinematic expression before us, using a visual language that is also tactile, that takes hold of and actively grasps the perceptual expression, the seeing, the direct experience of that anonymously present, sensing and sentient "other."

Thus, the film experience is a system of communication based on bodily perception as a vehicle of conscious expression. It entails the visible, audible, kinetic aspects of sensible experience to make sense visibly, audibly, and haptically. The film experience not only *represents* and reflects upon the prior direct perceptual experience of the filmmaker *by means of* the modes and structures of direct and reflective perceptual experience, but also *presents* the direct and reflective experience of a perceptual and expressive existence *as* the film. In its presence and activity of perception and expression, the film transcends the filmmaker to constitute and locate its own address, its own perceptual and expressive experience of being and becoming. As well, the film experience includes the perceptive and expressive viewer who must *interpret* and *signify* the film *as* experience, doing so through the very same structures and relations of perception and expression that inform the indirect representational address of the filmmaker and the direct presentational address of the film. As a communicative system, then, what is called the "film experience" uniquely opens up and exposes the inhabited space of direct experience as a condition of singular embodiment and makes it accessible and visible to more than the single consciousness who lives it. That is, direct experience and existential presence in the cinema belong to both the film and the viewer. (As noted, the filmmaker's presence in that experience is indirect and only re-presented.[11])

[11] The term *filmmaker* is used here and throughout (except where otherwise stipulated) as naming not a biographical person and his or her style or manner of being through cinematic representation (a focus found in Gilles Deleuze's *Cinema 1: The Movement-Image* and *Cinema 2: The Time-Image*), but rather the concrete, situated, and synoptic presence of the many persons who realized the film as concretely visible for vision. Thus, the term is also not equivalent to the textual function identified as the

As perception-cum-expression that can be perceived by another, as a communication of the experience of existence that is publicly visible, the anonymous but centered "Here, where *eye (I) am*" of the film can be doubly occupied. "Decentered" as it is engaged by an other in the film experience, it becomes the "Here, where *we see*"—a *shared* space of being, of seeing, hearing, and bodily and reflective movement performed and experienced by both film and viewer. However, this "decentering," this double occupancy of cinematic space, does not conflate the film and viewer. The "Here, where eye (I) am" of the film retains its unique situation, even as it cannot maintain its perceptual privacy. Directly perceptible to the viewer as an anonymous "Here, where eye am" simultaneously available as "Here, where we see," the concretely embodied situation of the film's vision also stands *against* the viewer. It is also perceived by the viewer as a "There, where I am not," as the space consciously and bodily inhabited and lived by an "other" whose experience of being-in-the-world, however anonymous, is not precisely congruent with the viewer's own. Thus, while space and its significance are intimately shared and lived by both film and viewer, the viewer is always at some level aware of the double and reversible nature of cinematic perception, that is, of perception *as* expression, of perception as a process of *mediating* consciousness's relations with the world. The viewer, therefore, shares cinematic space with the film but must also negotiate it, contribute to and perform the constitution of its experiential significance.

Watching a film is both a direct and mediated experience of direct experience as mediation. We both perceive a world *within* the immediate experience of an "other" and *without* it, as immediate experience mediated by an "other." Watching a film, we can see the seeing as well as the seen, hear the hearing as well as the heard, and feel the movement as well as see the moved. As viewers, not only do we spontaneously and invisibly perform these existential acts directly for and as ourselves in relation *to* the film before us, but these same acts are coterminously given to us *as* the film, as mediating acts of perception-cum-expression we take up and *invisibly perform* by appropriating and incorporating them into our own existential performance; we

---

"implied author" in Wayne C. Booth, *The Rhetoric of Fiction* (Chicago: Univ. of Chicago Press, 1961), pp. 71–76.

watch them as a *visible performance* distinguishable from, yet included in, our own.

The cinema thus transposes what would otherwise be the invisible, individual, and intrasubjective privacy of direct experience as it is embodied into the visible, public, and intersubjective sociality of a language of direct embodied experience—a language that not only refers to direct experience but also uses direct experience as its mode of reference. A film simultaneously has sense and makes sense both for us and before us. Perceptive, it has the capacity for experience; and expressive, it has the ability to signify. It gives birth to and actualizes signification, constituting and making manifest the primordial significance that Merleau-Ponty calls "wild meaning"—the pervasive and as yet undifferentiated significance of existence as it is lived rather than reflected upon. Direct experience thus serves double duty in the cinema. A film presents and represents acts of seeing, hearing, and moving as both the *original structures of existential being* and the *mediating structures of language*. As an "expression of experience by experience," a film both constitutes an original and primary significance in its continual perceptive and expressive "becoming" and evolves and regulates a more particular form of signification shaped by the specific trajectory of interests and intentions that its perceptive and expressive acts trace across the screen.

The spontaneous and constitutive significance, the "wild meaning" that grounds the specificity and intelligibility of cinematic communication is itself grounded in and borne by embodied existence in its relation to and within a world. Having the bodily capacity to perceive and express and move in a world that exists both for us and against us, we are, as Merleau-Ponty points out, "condemned to meaning."[12] From the first, we are engaged in a living dialogue with a world that sufficiently exceeds our grasp of it as we necessarily intend toward it, a world in which we are finitely situated as embodied beings and yet always informed by a decisive motility. Thus, the need and power to signify are synonymous with embodied existence in the world. As evoked by the passage that opens this chapter, that original need and power are first encountered everywhere and in everything, neither ascribable to a single source nor consciously differentiated in their range or application. Before the ascriptions, differences, and systems of exchange articulated in and by what we call

---

[12] Merleau-Ponty, *Phenomenology of Perception*, p. xix.

"natural language" (the discrete instrumentality and systematic objectification of experience abstracted from experience for general use), we are always first immersed in the more primordial language of embodied existence.

This primordial language is not systematic and regulative but systemic and constitutive, arising in the process of being-in-the-world and in the living reversibility of perception and expression exercised by the lived-body as it materially and finitely shares the "flesh" of the world it inhabits. That is, both the *material nature* and the *finite situation* of embodied existence always already constitute a *diacritical system* that primordially signifies through the lived-choices of existential movement and gesture. From the first, embodied existence inflects and reflects the world as always already significant. Thus, long before we consciously and voluntarily differentiate and abstract the world's significance for us into "ordinary language," long before we constrain "wild meaning" in discrete symbolic systems, we are immersed in language as an existential system. In the very movement of existence, in the very activity of perception and its bodily expression, we inaugurate language and communication.

The moving picture, too, perceives and expresses itself wildly and pervasively before it articulates its meanings more particularly and systematically as this or that kind of signification, that is, as a specific cinematic trope or figure, a specific set of generic configurations, a specific syntactical convention. Indeed, before it is fragmented and dissected in critical and theoretical analyses, before the reified shorthand of formalist, realist, semiotic, structuralist, neo-Marxist, and psychoanalytic terminology abstracts aspects of the cinema's "wild meaning" into discrete codes governed by montage, mise-en-scène, syntagmatic categories, binary and oppositional structures, and particular ideological and poetic pathologies, a film makes sense by virtue of its very ontology. That is, its existence emerges embodied and finitely situated. It comes into being (becomes) as an ongoing and unified (if always self-displacing) situation of perception and expression that *coheres* in relation to the world of which it is a material part, but in which it is also materially and diacritically differentiated. As a medium that articulates the unified, if ever-changing, experience of existence, that expresses the original synonymity of existence and language, of perception and its expression, the cinema is a privileged form of communication. A film is given to us and taken up by us as perception turned literally inside out and toward us as expression. It presents and represents *to* us and *for* us and *through* us the very modes and structures of being as language, of being as a system of primary and secondary mediations through which we and the world and others significantly communicate, constituting and changing our meanings from the moment of our first lived gesture. Thus, in its modalities of having sense and making sense, the cinema quite concretely returns us, as viewers and theorists, to our senses.

What is suggested by this general, philosophically inflected, and preliminary description of the structure that is the film experience is that cinematic "language" is grounded in the more original pragmatic language of embodied existence whose general structures are common to filmmaker, film, and viewer. Even though the film differs from the other two in the material and mode of its embodiment, for each "the perceiving mind is an incarnated mind."[13] It is this mutuality of embodied existence and the dynamic movement of its perceptual and expressive relations with and in the world that provide the common denominator of cinematic communication. Situated, finite, and—by virtue of being a body—"centered" in a world, embodied existence is constituted as and marked by the intrasubjective and intersubjective exchange between perception and expression. In a film, as in our direct and immediate experience, perception functions as a modality of expression, and expression as a modality of perception, both aspects of a synoptic "reversibility" and lived "directionality" that is the movement of existence, both thus subject to directional reversals that allow them to appear as either spontaneously prereflective and "operational" or as reflective and reflexive.

As two modalities of significant and signifying existence, perception and expression are interwoven threads, the woof and warp that together form a seamless and supple fabric, the whole cloth of existential experience from which specific forms of signification can be fashioned to instrumentally suit specific functions. Thus, in a film as in life, perception and expression—having sense and making sense—

[13] Maurice Merleau-Ponty, "An Unpublished Text by Maurice Merleau-Ponty: A Prospectus of His Work," trans. Arleen B. Dallery, in Merleau-Ponty, *The Primacy of Perception*, p. 3. The use of the word *mind* here may seem problematic to the reader at this point, because the attribution of mind to a film (i.e., a consciousness) is yet to be demonstrated and seems at first highly unlikely. However, as shall be discussed at great length, insofar as the consciousness of another as well as of oneself is known in its manifest form as *embodied intentionality*, then a human and a film can both be said to articulate consciousness, or, in this instance, "mind."

do not originally oppose each other and are not separated or differentiated as distinctly binary constructs and practices. Rather, they are complementary modalities of an original and unified experience of existence that has long been fragmented and lost to those interested in the ontology of the cinema and its structures of signification.

FILM THEORY AND THE OBJECTIFICATION OF EMBODIED VISION

The reversibility of cinematic perception and expression is the "enabling structure" of cinematic communication.[14] In semiotic terms, it constitutes what Umberto Eco calls an "s-code": the system-code that "makes a situation comprehensible and comparable to other situations, therefore preparing the way for a possible coding correlation."[15] Without such a systemic exchange of cinematic perception and expression (one comparable to and comprehensible as such an exchange in the human situation), other secondary and more systematic cinematic coding correlations would not be possible and comprehensible. There could be no narrative codes, no codes of subjective vision, no editorial codes, and their like. Nonetheless, the cinematic system-code constituted by the exchange and reversibility of perception and expression has been almost completely neglected by the respective analytic and synthetic emphases of classical and contemporary film theory.[16]

Three metaphors have dominated film theory: the *picture frame*, the *window*, and the *mirror*.[17] The first two, the frame and the window,

[14] The phrase "enabling structure" is borrowed from Wolfgang Iser, *The Act of Reading: A Theory of Aesthetic Response* (Baltimore, MD: The Johns Hopkins Univ. Press, 1978), p. 230. The reader is also directed to Iser's discussion of "negativity" (pp. 225–231), which parallels Merleau-Ponty's discussion of reversibility or the "chiasm" in *The Visible and the Invisible*, pp. 130–155.

[15] Umberto Eco, *A Theory of Semiotics* (Bloomington: Indiana Univ. Press, 1979), pp. 40, 43–44.

[16] In the following paragraphs, I thematize the work of traditional and contemporary film theorists too numerous to cite. The reader unfamiliar with the field who wishes to follow the arguments advanced here is urged to seek out specific theorists and their texts with the help, perhaps, of J. Dudley Andrew, *The Major Film Theories: An Introduction* (New York: Oxford Univ. Press, 1976) and *Concepts in Film Theory* (New York: Oxford Univ. Press, 1984). Andrew's two volumes are hardly exhaustive (and occasionally exclusive), but they do provide a place to begin.

[17] This formulation was first emphasized in Charles F. Altman, "Psychoanalysis and

represent the opposing poles of classical film theory, while the third, the mirror, represents the synthetic conflation of perception and expression that characterizes most contemporary film theory. What is interesting to note is that all three metaphors relate directly to the screen rectangle and to the film as a static *viewed object*, and only indirectly to the dynamic activity of viewing that is engaged in by both the film and the spectator, each as *viewing subjects*. The exchange and reversibility of perception and expression (both in and as the film and spectator) are suppressed, as are the intrasubjective and intersubjective foundations of cinematic communication.

Most often identified with the binary poetics of a sufficiently opposed but necessarily linked *formalism* and *realism*, classical film theory has argumentatively and analytically severed expression from perception in its inquiries into the "true nature" or ontology of the cinema. That is, cinematic "language" (here we might think of montage) and cinematic being (and here of mise-en-scène) have been contrasted categorically and set against each other as opposing poles of a single, digital, two-valued system—each, in opposing the other, affirming it by implication and dependent upon it by necessity. The formalists, seeking to transform and restructure the "brute" referentiality and "wild" meaning of cinematic images into personally determinate and expressive signification (hence the metaphor of the frame), acknowledge the camera's perceptive nature as they celebrate the artist's triumph over it. On the other side, the realists, seeking to reveal and discover the world's expression in all its "wild" meaning

---

Cinema: The Imaginary Discourse," *Quarterly Review of Film Studies* 2 (August 1977), pp. 260–264. Examples of other metaphors that have not had the same impact as the three mentioned here are the film as *dream* and the film as *consciousness*. The metaphor of dream tends to intertwine itself with the metaphor of the frame insofar as it is personal, subjective, autonomous, and connected with the artist/filmmaker; however, it is also connected with the metaphor of the mirror insofar as it is a deceptive structure needing disclosure and decoding or deconstruction in the psychoanalytic situation. See Janet Jenks Casebier and Allan Casebier, "Selective Bibliography on Dream and Film," *Dreamworks* 1 (Spring 1980), pp. 88–93, and John Michaels, "Film and Dream," *Journal of the University Film Association* 32 (Winter-Spring 1980), pp. 85–87. The metaphor of consciousness is to be distinguished from the thrust of the present study insofar as consciousness in this work is 1) not considered apart from its embodiment in a person and 2) not used as a metaphor but to denote an empirical function of being. Consciousness as a metaphor for film, however, can be found throughout George W. Linden, *Reflections on the Screen* (Belmont, CA: Wadsworth, 1970), and it provides a focal point for Bruce Kawin, *Mindscreen: Bergman, Godard, and First-Person Film* (Princeton, NJ: Princeton Univ. Press, 1978).

(hence the metaphor of the window), acknowledge the camera's expressive nature in its selective and shifting vision, even as they celebrate the medium's perceptual purity and openness. For the most part, however, this dependence on and suppression of one of the necessary conditions for the existence of a film has not been overtly articulated as the infrastructure that binds formalism and realism into a single theoretical system.[18] Instead, the emphasis has been on a dual poetics—one valorizing cinematic expression and the other, cinematic perception.

Opposing each other, both formalist and realist arguments converge in their assumption that meaning is located in the text as a significant object, and in their assumption of that text's transcendence of its origin and location either in the world or in persons. The metaphor of the frame is emblematic of the *transcendental idealism* that infuses classical formalism and its belief in the film object as *expression-in-itself*—subjectivity freed from worldly constraint. In contrast, the window as metaphor is emblematic of the *transcendental realism* that informs realist film theory and its belief in the film object as *perception-in-itself*—objectivity freed from entailment with the prejudicial investments of human being. The first belief leads to the formalist celebration of what phenomenology criticizes as "subjective psychologism," the second to the realist celebration of what it decries as "objective empiricism."[19]

In an attempt to correct this tidy theoretical opposition and its contradiction by actual cinematic practice, contemporary theorists have tended to synthesize perception and expression, categorically collapsing and confusing them in an analogue relation in which they are distinguishable only by degree, not by modality. The nature of film

[18] One of the earliest explicit statements of this systemic interdependence appears in Jean-Luc Godard, "Montage My Fine Care," in *Godard on Godard*, trans. Tom Milne (New York: Viking Press, 1972), pp. 39–41. It also pervades Mitry's many discussions of editing throughout both volumes of his *Esthétique et psychologie du cinéma*. Also of relevance here is a subtle and nuanced overview of the history and practice of literary theory (with references to film theory) found in Catherine Belsey, *Critical Practice* (New York: Methuen, 1980), particularly her use of the term "expressive realism" to nominate the single theoretical system that opposes and differentiates itself as formalism and realism.

[19] For basic description and phenomenological critique of the limitations of "subjective psychologism" and "objective empiricism," see the preface to Merleau-Ponty, *Phenomenology of Perception*, pp. vii–xxi. This preliminary discussion is deepened in Chapters 1–3, pp. 3–51.

is considered as neither perceptive nor expressive. Rather, both modalities of existential experience are conflated as a synthesis of the *refractive*, *reflexive*, and *reflective* (hence the metaphor of the mirror). Drawing primarily upon linguistically oriented psychoanalytic and neo-Marxist paradigms (the former already privileging the metaphor of the mirror for its own purposes), the resultant theories of cinematic communication have emerged not as a celebratory poetics, but as a critical rhetoric, charging cinematic communication with some equivalent to sophistry.

That is, contemporary theory (most of it feminist and/or neo-Marxist in approach) has focused on the essentially deceptive, illusionary, tautologically recursive, and coercive nature of the cinema, and on its psychopathological and/or ideological functions of distorting existential experience. Such theory elaborately accounts for cinematic representation but cannot account for the originary activity of cinematic signification. Thus, it is hardly surprising, if poignant, that, attempting to liberate female spectatorship and spectators of color from linguistically determined psychic structures and colonial discursive structures, psychoanalytically based feminist film theory and ideologically based film theory so often bemoan the impossibility of a "new" language to express the specificity of their excluded experience and the lack of an uncolonized "place" from which to speak. Articulated in various ways and amid a number of highly sophisticated arguments, what contemporary film theory stresses and decries in its variations on the metaphor of the mirror is the totalitarian transcendence of either psychic or ideological structures over the signifying freedom of individual viewers in their concrete, contingent, existential situation. As perception and expression are confused with each other in the deceptive processes of the cinematic apparatus and the seamless and conventional unfolding of a privileged (if reviled) "classical narrative cinema," the possibility of dialogic and dialectical communication is suppressed and the film experience is seen as grounded in a false and sophistic rhetoric that essentially distorts the possibility of any "real" communication.

Thus, the metaphor of the mirror entails a critical judgment of the cinema that is as damning as it is descriptive. It condemns the very ontological being of cinema as substitutive (rather than expansive) and deceptive (rather than disclosing). It reflects the viewer only to point to his or her subjection to signs and meanings produced by an always already dishonest and subjugating "other." Idealist in its uto-

17

pian longings for liberatory signification while losing itself in a labyrinth of representation, contemporary film theory is informed by a
transcendental determinism—based on the belief in the film object as
mediation-in-itself. In the one instance, signification and significance
are seen as always predetermined by apparatus and ideology; the
film object as it is experienced invisibly and rhetorically interpellates
the spectator and speaks the culture, producing cinematic language
and its norms of usage as a *given*. In the other instance, signification
and significance are predetermined by psychic structures; the camera's and spectator's vision are confused and bound together in a
false and distorted primary identification that cannot be denied, only
disavowed. In sum, in most contemporary theory, viewing in the cinema leads to no good—or, at best, to the remedial practice of demys-
tifying the cinema's material, structural, and ideological pathology
and, at worst, to a pleasure that is guilty and must be adjudged "perverse."

In most of its classical and contemporary articulations, then, film
theory has focused not on the *whole correlational structure* of the film
experience, but has abstracted and privileged only one of its *parts* at
a time: expression-in-itself, perception-in-itself, and mediation-in-itself, respectively. Although the next section of this chapter will introduce the reader to phenomenology as the philosophy and research
procedure that informs the remainder of this study, film theory's abstraction and fragmentation of the correlational structure that is the
film experience can be criticized against the main phenomenological
theme of *intentionality*: the invariant, pervasive, and immanent correlational structure of consciousness. Intentionality is "the unique
peculiarity of experiences 'to be the consciousness *of* something.' "[20]
That is, the act of consciousness is never "empty" and "in-itself," but
rather always intending toward and in relation to an object (even
when that "object" is consciousness, reflexively intended). The invariant correlational structure of consciousness thus necessarily entails the *mediation* of an *activity* and an *object*. If we substitute the specificity of the film experience as a reversible structure correlating the
activity of perception and expression and commuting one to the
other, the whole of the structure could, and later will more elaborately, be mapped as follows: *the perception* (act of consciousness)

[20] Edmund Husserl, *Ideas: General Introduction to Pure Phenomenology*, trans. W. R.
Boyce Gibson (New York: Collier Books, 1962), p. 223.

of (mediation) *expression* (object of consciousness) *and/as the expression* (act of consciousness) *of* (mediation) *perception* (object of consciousness). In relation to my previous thematization of classical and contemporary film theory, formalist theory can be linked to a focus on the cinematic *expression* (of perception)—perception here represented as the suppressed part of the entire relation; realist theory to a focus on the cinematic *perception* (of expression)—expression here represented as the suppressed part of the entire relation; and contemporary theory to a focus on the mediating copula (perception) *of* (expression)—with perception and expression represented as the suppressed part of the entire relation.

Whatever their respectively different foci, classical and contemporary film theory have pursued their inquiry into the nature of cinematic signification sharing three crucial and largely uninterrogated presuppositions. First, film theory has presupposed *the act of viewing.* Certainly, there have been some considerations of the anatomical, mechanical, and psychic aspects of vision that characterize and differentiate the human and camera eye.[21] As well, a major portion of contemporary film theory dwells on the psychoanalytic aspects of the spectator's visual engagement with the cinema. Nonetheless, film theory has generally assumed as given the act of viewing in its totality, that is, as *the constituting condition of the film experience* in each and all of its aspects and manifestations, and as the nexus of communication among the filmmaker, film, and spectator.

Second, film theory has presupposed the cinema's and spectator's *communicative competence.* Discussions of cinematic codes and their entailments are all based on the assumption that a film is intelligible as the imaging and expression of experience—something that "counts" and has a particular kind of significance above the random projection and play of brute light and shadow. That is, although film theory has attempted to describe and explain cinematic signification or "language" in great detail, it has assumed the cinema's power to signify and the spectator's power to see this signification as signifi-

[21] See, for example, Barbara Anderson, "Eye Movement and Cinematic Perception," *Journal of the University Film Association* 32 (Winter-Spring 1980), pp. 23–26. As well, most contemporary introductory aesthetics and histories contain mechanical and anatomical dissections of the camera and process of human vision and "perception." For a brief but comprehensive example, see the first two chapters in George Wead and George Lellis, *Film: Form and Function* (Boston: Houghton Mifflin, 1981), pp. 3–53.

cant. It has assumed *the fundamental intelligibility of the film experience*. Whether fragmenting its analyses of cinematic semiosis into a syntactics (primarily revealed in the formalist emphasis on structuring), a semantics (primarily revealed in the realist emphasis on content), or a pragmatics (primarily revealed in the contemporary theorist's emphasis on relational functions), film theory has assumed rather than accounted for the film experience's intrasubjective and intersubjective nature and its transitive function or performance.

Third, film theory has presupposed that a film is a *viewed object*. Whether it has been considered the aesthetic and expressive object of the formalist; the empirical and perceptive object of the realist; or the cultural, rhetorical, and reflexive object of the contemporary theorist; the film has been regarded as merely, if complexly, a vehicle through which meaning can be represented, presented, or produced; a visible object in the manner of the frame, the window, and the mirror. That a film, as it is experienced, might be engaged as something *more* than just an object of consciousness is a possibility that has not been entertained.

These three presuppositions have informed almost all film theory and directed its fragmented course and conclusions. That the act of viewing constitutes cinematic communication, that communication occurs, and that the communication is effected by a viewed object on a viewing subject (despite contemporary theory's objectification of the viewing subject as the predicate of cinematic vision)—these are the givens of the film experience and the ground upon which various theories of film base themselves and from which they proceed.

However, these presuppositions are themselves open to investigation and, indeed, require it if we are to understand the original power of the cinema to signify, its genesis of meaning and ability to communicate, its "expression of experience by experience." In this regard, both classical and contemporary theory have provided us only partial descriptions and abstract formulations that have detached cinematic signification from its origin in concrete sense and significance. As Dudley Andrew points out:

> We can speak of codes and textual systems which are the results of signifying processes, yet we seem unable to discuss that mode of experience we call signification. More precisely, structuralism and academic film theory in general have been disinclined to deal with the "other-side" of signification, those realms of pre-formulation where

sensory data congeals into "something that matters" and those realms of post-formulation where that "something" is experienced as mattering. Structuralism, even in its post-structural reach toward psychoanalysis and intertextuality, concerns itself only with that something and not with the process of its congealing nor with the event of its mattering.[22]

Previous discussion has introduced the exchange or reversibility of perception and expression in the film experience as the commutative basis for the emergence of cinematic signification and significance. Focus on this exchange is a focus on both the process that constitutes "something that matters" and the "event of its mattering." It points to and describes the radical and existential ground for both a theory of sign production and a theory of meaning as they are always entailed in the lived-body experience. Thus, relative to cinema, the *existential and embodied act of viewing* becomes the paradigm of this exchange of perception and expression. That is, the act of viewing provides both the necessary and sufficient conditions for the commutation of perception to expression and vice-versa. It also communicatively links filmmaker, film, and spectator by means of their respective, separate, and yet homeomorphic existential performance of a shared (and possibly universal) competence: the capacity to localize and unify (or "center") the invisible, intrasubjective commutation of perception and expression and make it visible and intersubjectively available to others.

Filmmaker, film, and spectator all concretely use the agency of visual, aural, and kinetic experience to express experience—not only to and for themselves, but also to and for others. Each engaged in the visible gesture of viewing, the filmmaker, film, and spectator are all able to commute the "language of being" into the "being of language," and back again. Dependent upon existence and embodiment in the world for its articulation as an activity, the act of viewing as the commutation of perception and expression is both an intrasubjective and intersubjective performance equally performable by filmmaker, film, and spectator.

This suggests, therefore, the possibility that a film may be considered as more than a merely visible object. That is, in terms of its performance, it is as much a *viewing subject* as it is also a *visible* and *viewed*

---

[22] J. Dudley Andrew, "The Neglected Tradition of Phenomenology in Film Theory," *Wide Angle* 2, No. 2 (1978), pp. 45–46.

object. Thus, in its existential function, it shares a privileged equivalence with its human counterparts in the film experience. This is certainly *not* to say that the film is a *human* subject. Rather, it is to consider the film a *viewing* subject—one that manifests a competence of perceptive and expressive performance *equivalent* in structure and function to that same competence performed by filmmaker and spectator. The film actualizes and realizes its ability to localize, unify (or "center") the "invisible" intrasubjective exchange or commutation between the perception of the camera and the expression of the projector. As well, it makes this exchange visible and intersubjectively available to others in the expression of its perception—in the visible commutation between the perceptive language of its expressive being (the prereflective *inflection* of its "viewing view" as the *experience of consciousness*) and the expressive being of its perceptive language (the *reflection* of its "viewed view" as the *consciousness of experience*).

In the act of vision, the film transcends its existence as a merely visible object reducible to its technology and mechanisms, much as in similar acts of vision, the filmmaker and spectator transcend their existence as merely visible objects reducible to their anatomy and physiology. All are not merely objects for vision, but also subjects of vision. Thus, Merleau-Ponty's description of the structured, centered, inherent "co/herence" of human experience in the world as not only for others, but also for itself, seems just as applicable to the *visual being* of the *visible film*:

> Just as . . . when I walk round an object, I am not presented with a succession of perspective views which I subsequently co-ordinate thanks to the idea of one single flat projection, . . . so I am not myself a succession of "psychic" acts, nor for that matter a nuclear *I* who brings them together into a synthetic unity, but one single experience inseparable from itself, one single "living cohesion," one single temporality which is engaged, from birth, in making itself progressively explicit, and in confirming that cohesion in each successive present. . . . The primary truth is indeed "I think," but only provided we understand thereby "I belong to myself" while belonging to the world. . . . Inside and outside are inseparable. The world is wholly inside and I am wholly outside myself.[23]

The intrasubjective or implicit (what in phenomenological terms shall later be explored as the "introceptive") and the intersubjective or

---

[23] Merleau-Ponty, *Phenomenology of Perception*, p. 407.

explicit are thus modalities of a single experience of being-in-the-world. Similarly, the invisible activity of viewing and its visible productions are both modalities of the single experience of vision-in-the-world. Understood as a viewing subject that—by virtue of the particular nature of its embodied existence—can also be viewed, the film no longer merely contains sense, significance, meaning. Rather, it possesses sense by means of its senses, and it makes sense as a "living cohesion," as a *signifying subject*. It is as this signifying subject that it existentially *comes to matter* as a *significant object*, that is, can be understood in its *objective* status by others as sensible and intelligible.

The direct engagement, then, between spectator and film in the film experience cannot be considered a monologic one between a viewing subject and a viewed object. Rather, it is a dialogical and dialectical engagement of *two* viewing subjects who also exist as visible objects (if of different material and in different ways to be elaborated further). Both film and spectator are capable of viewing and of being viewed, both are embodied in the world as the subject of vision and object for vision. Zygmunt Bauman tells us, "All signification starts from the establishing of an affinity between its subject and object; or, rather, between two subjects, standing respectively at the beginning and the end of communication."[24] In the film experience, all signification and all communication start from the "affinity" that is the act of viewing, coterminously but uniquely performed by both film and spectator. This act of viewing, this *"address of the eye,"* implicates both *embodied, situated* existence and a *material* world; for to see and be seen, the viewing subject must be a body and be materially in the world, sharing a similar manner and matter of existence with other viewing subjects, but living this existence discretely and autonomously, as the singular embodied situation that makes this existence also a unique matter that matters uniquely.

Most theoretical reflection abstracts the act of viewing, the "address of the eye," from its *double* embodiment and *double* situation in—and as—the specific relations of vision that constitute the film experience. The existential, embodied nature of vision and its signifying power are elided. So, too, is the lived sense that cinematic vision in the film experience is articulated by *both* the film *and* the spectator simultaneously engaged in *two* quite distinctly located visual acts that meet on shared ground but never identically occupy it. The

[24] Zygmunt Bauman, *Hermeneutics and Social Science* (New York: Columbia Univ. Press, 1978), pp. 27–28.

theorist, abstracted from his own embodied experience in the movie theater, describes cinematic vision as the essential entailment of a *viewing subject* and a *viewed object* in what is thought of, rather than lived through, as a *single* and *disembodied* act of vision and signification.

Yet everything about my experience at the movies denies such description. The film for me is never merely a viewed "thing," that is, visible images that my vision sees, appropriates, and incorporates as "my own." No matter how I give myself up to the play of images I see and sounds I hear in the theater, those images and sounds are always to some degree resistant to my incorporation of—or by— them. Indeed, there would be no "play" were there not this mutual resilience and resistance I feel, this back-and-forth exchange I experience, in the encounter between myself and a film. Materially embodied, particularly situated, and informed by an intending consciousness that has its own "projects" in the world, I am never so vacuous as to be completely "in-formed" by even the most insinuating or overwhelming film. My experience at the movies is never lived as a monologic one, however easy and even often lazy my participation (or the film's) seems to be. There are always two embodied acts of vision at work in the theater, two embodied views constituting the intelligibility and significance of the film experience. The film's vision and my own do not conflate, but meet in the sharing of a world and constitute an experience that is not only intrasubjectively dialectical, but also intersubjectively dialogical. Although there are moments in which our views may become congruent in the convergence of our interest (never of our situation), there are also moments in which our views conflict; our values, interests, prospects, and projects differ; something is not understood or is denied even as it is visible and seen. Cinematic vision, then, is never monocular, is always doubled, is always the vision of *two viewing subjects* materially and consciously inhabiting, signifying, and sharing a world in a manner at once universal and particular, a world that is mutually visible but hermeneutically negotiable.

It is the embodied and enworlded "address of the eye" that structures and gives significance to the film experience for filmmaker, film, and spectator alike. The embodied eye materially presents and represents intending consciousness: the "I" affirmed as a subject of (and for) vision not abstractly, but concretely, in lived-space, *at* an address, *as* an address. Vision is an *act* that occurs from somewhere in particular; its requisites are both a *body* and a *world*. Thus, *address*, as noun and verb, both denotes a location where one resides and the activity of transcending the body's location, originating from it to exceed beyond it as a projection bent on spanning the worldly space between one body-subject and another. The address of the eye also forces us to consider the *embodied* nature of vision, the body's radical contribution to the constitution of the film experience. If vision is not regarded as transcendental (even if its address toward objects in the world transcends its originating and permanent if mobile residence in a "home body"), then two bodies and two addresses must be acknowledged as the necessary condition of the film experience.

Resonant with the body's other senses (particularly those of touch and sound), the "address of the eye" in the film experience expresses both the *origin* and *destination* of viewing as an existential and transcendent activity. It names a *transitive relationship* between two or more objective body-subjects, each materially embodied and distinctly situated, yet each mutually enworlded. Constituted from this transitive relation is a third, *transcendent space*, that is, a space exceeding the individual body and its unique situation yet concretely inhabited and *intersubjective*.

When the object of the eye's address is not only visible but also capable of vision, visual activity and its intentional projects are doubled and describe a semiotic/hermeneutic field. The visual activity of this doubled "address of the eye" (objectively invisible) calls to mind those strip comics and cartoons in which the characters' gazes literally "dash" themselves across space as hyphenated lines of force, crisscrossing each other in a complex circumscription of the space they both share. Such a circumscription of mutually lived space, such an intersection and connection of visual activity (neither fully convergent nor fully separate) creates a shared address whose semiotic ambiguity and existential richness cannot be reduced to geometry.

We are thus called to a radical reflection upon those presuppositions that inform classical and contemporary film theory. Instead of going forward in an ungrounded investigation of cinematic signification as it secondarily emerges fragmented into a syntactics, semantics, or pragmatics, we must now turn back to the origins of cinematic signification as it originally emerges in the systemic act of viewing, the address of the eye. Merleau-Ponty suggests the concerns of such a journey: "It is at the same time true that the world is *what we see* and that, nevertheless, we must learn to see it—first in the sense that

25

we must watch this vision with knowledge, take possession of it, say what *we* and what *seeing* are, act therefore as if we knew nothing about it, as if here we still had everything to learn."[25]

Beginning again and radically reflecting on the origin of cinematic signification in the embodied act of viewing, in the "address of the eye," we ground this investigation, appropriately, in the philosophical context and method of existential—and semiotic—phenomenology.

PHENOMENOLOGY AND FILM THEORY

Given contemporary film theory's general neglect and particular ignorance of phenomenology, it is necessary to explicate briefly the philosophy and phenomenological method that shape this study as a series of increasingly radical reflections on the semiotic/hermeneutic entailments of seeing, being seen, and visual/visible embodiment in the film experience. First, it is appropriate to provide a brief overview of existential phenomenology as both a philosophy of science and a research procedure and its few entailments with film theory. Then a discussion of Edmund Husserl's *transcendental phenomenology* will be distinguished from *existential phenomenology*, the latter most fully developed in its exploration of the semiosis of being by Maurice Merleau-Ponty.

It is existential phenomenology that grounds this present study. Existential phenomenology realizes transcendental phenomenology's unfulfilled aim of not only deriving its data from, but also relocating those data, in their meaningfulness, in the *Lebenswelt*, "the world of our lived experience."[26] It locates the origin of theory in practice, and essence in existence. It attempts to empirically describe, thematize, and interpret the being of language in the language of being. That is, its aim is to make explicit the dynamic structures of the "living bias" that condemns us to the experience of meaning and yet allows us to alter our meanings, reflect upon our experience, change our position and our perspective in relation to the horizons that the world limit-

[25] Merleau-Ponty, *The Visible and the Invisible*, p. 4.
[26] Herbert Spiegelberg, "Husserl's Phenomenology and Existentialism," *The Journal of Philosophy* 57 (January 1960), p. 64.

lessly provides us.[27] Meaning, for existential phenomenology, arises "in any given case" as "the synthesis of the subjective and objective experience" of phenomena.[28] Thus, the radical reflections of existential phenomenology do not retreat from the world of action and responsibility into the abstractions of bounded static essences or boundless dynamic relativities. Rather, reflection turns toward the world as it is lived, and toward a clear and insightful acceptance of the responsibility we have (whether we wish it or not) for the meanings that we choose, accept, and live. In this regard, it is important to emphasize that "phenomenological description is never an absolute process in the sense of arriving at a final definition of phenomena since our source of knowledge is still the perceiving subject whose experience itself is never a final attainment, but an ongoing process of synthesis."[29]

Existential phenomenology would suggest that we are as responsible for our epistemologies as we are for our methods and our ends. The practice of a semiotics and hermeneutics of the cinema cannot be abstracted from the theory of knowledge that grounds and justifies it. Thus, as Jean Mitry rightly recognized, "To wonder what is the cinema, that is to pose a question to philosophy, and to pose a question to philosophy is to begin to define the latter, that is to say a system."[30] As a *philosophy* of conscious experience, phenomenology systemically grounds the attempt of this study to make explicit the phenomenon of signification in the cinema as it is lived through and embodied in an enworlded subject of vision, that is, as it occurs ex-

[27] John Wild, "Existentialism as a Philosophy," *The Journal of Philosophy* 57 (January 1960), p. 50. This article also makes clear the distinction between the scientific world of facts and the *Lebenswelt*, the lived world of human facts.

[28] Richard L. Lanigan, *Speaking and Semiology*, p. 30.

[29] Ibid., p. 31.

[30] Mitry, *Esthétique et psychologie du cinéma*, Vol. 2, p. 457. My translation from the following: "Se demander ce qui est le cinéma, c'est poser une question à la philosophie, et poser une question à la philosophie, c'est commencer par définer celle-ci, c'est-à-dire un système." It is interesting to note Christian Metz's impatience with Mitry's "philosophizing" in "Current Problems of Film Theory: Christian Metz on Jean Mitry's *L'Esthétique et psychologie du cinéma*, Volume II," trans. Diana Matias, *Screen* 14 (Spring/Summer 1973), pp. 40–87. However, Metz also rightly criticizes a certain lack of effectiveness in Mitry's philosophical considerations because of their placement in the text and their lack of integration into his overall discussion of film form and structures. Nonetheless, Mitry is one of the very few film theorists who philosophically ground their theoretical discourse.

istentially and directly *for us* and *before us*, rather than abstracted from us or posited against us.³¹ The *data* for phenomenology are not the preconceived constructs we accept as "given" and objective facts, but the *capta* of human and lived existence that are "taken up" and structured as objective fact in the *acta*, or practices, of human experience.³²

As a *research procedure*, phenomenology calls us to a series of systematic reflections within which we question and clarify that which we intimately live, but which has been lost to our reflective knowledge through habituation and/or institutionalization. That is, the phenomena of existence are usually either lived as simply given and taken for granted, or they have been abstracted and reified objectively as the predicated constructs of what has come to be thought of as scientific inquiry. Through a process in which "one proceeds from phenomenological intuition, to analysis, and to description,"³³ the radical reflection of phenomenology attempts to *reanimate* the taken-for-granted and the institutionally sedimented. And, because it turns us toward the origins of our experience of phenomena and acknowledges both the objective enworldedness of phenomena and the subjective embodied experiencing of them, such radical reflection opens up not only fresh possibilities for reflective knowledge, but also fresh possibilities for living knowledge and experiencing phenomena, for seeing the world and ourselves in a critically aware way.³⁴

³¹ This central aim of investigating phenomena as they are engaged by consciousness and in the world so as to constitute the meaning that is experience can be found in the following texts, all of which have crucially informed the present study. See Don Ihde, *Listening and Voice: A Phenomenology of Sound* (Athens: Ohio Univ. Press, 1976), *Experimental Phenomenology: An Introduction* (New York: Paragon Books, 1979), *Existential Technics* (Albany: State Univ. of New York Press, 1983), and *Technology and the Lifeworld: From Garden to Earth* (Bloomington: Indiana Univ. Press, 1990); Maurice Merleau-Ponty, preface to *Phenomenology of Perception*, pp. vii–xxi; Maurice Roche, *Phenomenology, Language, and the Social Sciences* (London: Routledge and Kegan Paul, 1973); Calvin O. Schrag, *Experience and Being: Prolegomena to a Future Ontology* (Evanston, IL: Northwestern Univ. Press, 1969) and *Radical Reflection and the Origin of the Human Sciences* (West Lafayette, IN: Purdue Univ. Press, 1980); and Herbert Spiegelberg, *The Phenomenological Movement: A Historical Introduction*, 2d ed., 2 vols. (The Hague: Martinus Nijhoff, 1965).

³² For a succinct distinction of *data, capta,* and *acta,* see Richard L. Lanigan, "The Phenomenology of Human Communication," *Philosophy Today* 23 (1979), p. 8.

³³ Lanigan, *Speaking and Semiology*, p. 30. Note that "phenomenological intuition" is meant as a "strict adherence to knowledge as it is immediately given in experience."

³⁴ Practical experience of phenomenological method is given to the reader in Ihde, *Experimental Phenomenology: An Introduction*. For a general consideration of radical re-

The distinction between the existential phenomenology that informs this present work and the more well-known transcendental phenomenology associated with Edmund Husserl is of great importance in establishing the relevance of phenomenology to the study of cinematic communication. Of the small number of theoretical works that attempt to ground their investigation of film phenomenologically, the majority tend to do so within the context of transcendental phenomenology. Thus, they have faced the same problems and been subjected to the same charges of idealism and essentialism as has that philosophical project.[35] As well, most of these studies lack the systematic rigor emphasized by both transcendental and existential phenomenology and so appear—for want of an articulated method—at best metaphysically arcane, at worst metaphorically vague and mystically poetic.[36]

---

flection as a method, see Schrag, *Radical Reflection and the Origin of the Human Sciences*, pp. 97–130. For a lengthier explication of method, see Spiegelberg, *The Phenomenological Movement: A Historical Introduction*, 2d ed. Vol. 2, pp. 653–701.

[35] Works on cinema that derive from transcendental phenomenology are Henri Agel, *Le Cinéma et le sacré* (Paris: Editions du Cerf, 1961) and *Poétique du cinéma* (Paris: Edition du Signe, 1973); André Bazin, *What Is Cinema?* trans. Hugh Gray (Berkeley: Univ. of California Press, 1967); and Roger Munier, *Contre l'image* (Paris: Gallimard, 1963). Critiques of transcendental phenomenology in its application to cinema can be found throughout Mitry, *Esthéthique et psychologie du cinéma*, and in Andrew, *The Major Film Theories*, pp. 242–253. It should be mentioned here that Mitry's own quarrel with phenomenology is its transcendental turn—one that leads to a naive belief in the transcendent vision and revelation of the camera. (He is, himself, otherwise engaged in a phenomenology of cinema and is quite close to Merleau-Ponty in attitude and the development of his thought.) The reader is also directed to a brief article in English that calls for the application of Husserlian phenomenology to film: N. Patrick Peritore, "Descriptive Phenomenology and Film: An Introduction," *Journal of the Univ. Film Association* 29 (Winter 1977), pp. 3–6, and to a forthcoming article by Alan Casebier in *Quarterly Review of Film and Video*.

[36] While Agel's works concern themselves with the mystical aspects of cinema, the books that seem most vague and lack a coherent method are several works that have been associated (even if, in Cavell's case, wrongly) with existential phenomenology: Linden, *Reflections on the Screen*; Stanley Cavell, *The World Viewed: Reflections on the Ontology of Film*, enl. ed. (Cambridge: Harvard Univ. Press, 1979); and Yvette Biró, *Profane Mythology: The Savage Mind of the Cinema*, trans. Imre Goldstein (Bloomington: Indiana Univ. Press, 1982). A similar kind of enthusiastic but methodless "feel" for existential phenomenology can be found in Mark Slade, *Language of Change: Moving Images of Man* (Toronto: Holt, Rinehart and Winston of Canada, 1970) and in the remarkable but neglected work by Parker Tyler, *The Shadow of an Airplane Climbs the Empire State Building: A World Theory of Film* (Garden City, NY: Anchor Books, 1973).

There do exist a small number of works that counter both the essentialism and poetic mysticism found in most transcendental phenomenologies of the cinema, but they are relatively unknown (or unread) within the context of contemporary film theory.[37] Of them, Jean-Pierre Meunier's neglected *Les Structures de l'expérience filmique* should be singled out as a significant study of systematic clarity that explores the phenomenon of cinematic "identification" using the explicit framework of existential phenomenology and offering another (and more open) way to conceive of spectatorial engagement with cinematic images than the structure of "identification" defined by psychoanalysis.[38]

More recent has been the appearance of Gilles Deleuze's *Cinema 1: The Movement-Image* and *Cinema 2: The Time-Image*.[39] Drawing primarily upon Henri Bergson's philosophy and C. S. Pierce's semiology, Deleuze's work bears some relation to this present study and stands, in many respects, as parallel to it. Nonetheless, although it has been generally identified as a phenomenology of cinema, Deleuze rejects

[37] Andrew discusses at some length the existentially oriented phenomenology of Amédée Ayfre, particularly his *Le Cinéma et sa vérité* (Paris: Editions du Cerf, 1969), in *The Major Film Theories*, pp. 249–253. Other works that are relatively unknown or isolated within the "mainstream" of contemporary film theory and that promote and/or practice existential phenomenology are Andrew, "The Neglected Tradition of Phenomenology in Film Theory," pp. 44–49; Alan B. Brinkley, "Toward a Phenomenological Aesthetic of Cinema," in *Aesthetics II*, Tulane Studies in Philosophy, Vol. 20 (New Orleans: Tulane Univ. Press, 1971), pp. 1–17; Bryan K. Crow, "Talking About Film: A Phenomenological Study of Film Signification," in *Phenomenological Research in Rhetoric, Language, and Communication*, ed. Stanley Deetz, Doctoral Honors Seminar Proceedings sponsored by the Speech Communication Association and the Department of Speech Communication, Southern Illinois Univ. at Carbondale, 1979, pp. 4–15; Bruce Jenkins, "Structures of Perceptual Engagement in Film: Toward a Technology of Embodiment," in *Film Reader 2* (Evanston, IL: Northwestern Univ. Press, 1977), pp. 141–146; Brian Lewis, "The Question of Cinematic 'Essence': A Phenomenological Model of Representational Film Experiences," *Wide Angle*, 4, no. 4 (1981), pp. 50–54; and, of course, Maurice Merleau-Ponty, "The Film and the New Psychology," in *Sense and Non-Sense*, trans. Hubert L. Dreyfus and Patricia Allen Dreyfus (Evanston, IL: Northwestern Univ. Press, 1964), pp. 48–59.

[38] Jean-Pierre Meunier, *Les Structures de l'experience filmique: l'identification filmique* (Louvain: Librairie Universitaire, 1969). This work is mentioned briefly in Andrew, *The Major Film Theories*, p. 183.

[39] Gilles Deleuze, *Cinema 1: The Movement-Image*, trans. Hugh Tomlinson and Barbara Habberjam (Minneapolis: Univ. of Minnesota Press, 1986) and *Cinema 2: The Time-Image*, trans. Hugh Tomlinson and Barbara Habberjam (Minneapolis, Univ. of Minnesota Press, 1989).

this characterization because, according to his reading, existential phenomenology privileges a "natural perception" at odds with cinematic signification. He sees the cinema as a problem for phenomenology because it "can, with impunity, bring us close to things or take us away from them and revolve around them, and it *suppresses* both the anchoring of the subject and the horizon of the world. Hence it *substitutes* an implicit knowledge and a second intentionality for the conditions of natural perception."[40] Thus, within the context of existential phenomenology, as Deleuze interprets it, "cinematographic movement is both condemned as unfaithful to the conditions of perception and also exalted as the new story capable of 'drawing close to' the perceived and the perceiver, the world and perception."[41] Yet rigorous phenomenological description need never argue that the "implicit knowledge" and "second intentionality" of the cinema necessarily suppress the spectator's embodied situation or substitute for "natural perception." (That, in fact, sounds more like the psychoanalytic argument against cinema.) Citing only a few early works, Deleuze misses the dialectical and dialogic character of Merleau-Ponty's later semiotic phenomenology while he moves on to assert (phenomenologically) the *direct* and *preverbal* significance of cinematic movement and images. In many respects, the first volume's project is similar to the project here—less systematic, perhaps, in its grounding of cinematic signification as immanent and more elaborative in its discussions of specific films and the style of particular filmmakers. Deleuze, however, neglects the *embodied situation* of the spectator and of the film. In *Matter and Memory*, Deleuze's philosophical mentor Henri Bergson asserts, "Questions relating to subject and object, to their distinction and their union, should be put in terms of time rather than of space."[42] It is not time, but space—the significant space lived as and through the objective body-subject, the historical space of situation—that grounds the response to those questions and the question of cinematic signification in this present study. In this focus on embodiment and situation, existential, semiotic phenomenology is not out of step with the contemporary quest for an account of cinematic signification that grounds meaning as value-laden, committed, and socially active. Its aim is to locate the structure and

---

[40] Deleuze, *Cinema 1: The Movement-Image*, p. 57. (Emphasis mine)

[41] Ibid.

[42] Henri Bergson, *Matter and Memory*, trans. Nancy Margaret Paul and W. Scott Palmer (London: George Allen and Unwin, 1911), p. 57.

meanings of phenomena in the contingency and openness of human existence.

Husserl and Transcendental Phenomenology

Both transcendental and existential phenomenology are philosophies that reflexively and reflectively turn on the objective "truisms" of science and its various epistemologies not so much to reject them *in toto*, as to seek their subjective grounding in the ontology of conscious experience from which all epistemes and science are generated. Responsive to conscious experience, phenomenology is also a research procedure that is rigorous without being rigid. That is, it adapts itself to the phenomena under investigation as the latter are "given" by the world and "taken up" in human consciousness through the human activity of experiencing. As both systemic philosophy and systematic procedure, phenomenological inquiry is less a set of steps to be applied programmatically to phenomena than it is a series of *critical commitments* made by the researcher to respond openly to the phenomena of consciousness and to her own consciousness of phenomena. This was as much the goal of Husserl's transcendental phenomenology as it was of Merleau-Ponty's existential and semiotic phenomenology. However, some specific articulation of the major differences between the two should indicate the latter's pragmatic, qualified nature and its intersubjective, always already social, grounding not in the Husserlian "transcendental ego," but in enworlded and embodied persons.

For the sake of brevity, but with a reluctance that is shared here, Herbert Spiegelberg has offered elsewhere the "important constants" of Edmund Husserl's initially descriptive and eventually transcendental phenomenology. These "constants" are presented as a "minimum list of propositions" that define transcendental phenomenology as a science and then thematize it in regard to the matter and horizons of its inquiry, its method, and its project:

1) Phenomenology is a rigorous science in the sense of a coherent system of propositions; it goes even beyond positive science by aiming at *absolute certainty for its foundations* and at *freedom from presuppositions* that have not passed phenomenological scrutiny.

2) Its subject matter is the *general essences of the phenomena of consciousness*; among these phenomena, the phenomenologist distinguishes be-

tween the *intending acts* and the *intended objects* in strict parallel; he pays special attention to the modes of appearance in which the intended referents present themselves; he does not impose any limitations as to the content of these phenomena.

3) Phenomenology is based on the *intuitive exploration* and *faithful description* of the phenomena *within the context of the world of our lived experience* (*Lebenswelt*), anxious to avoid reductionist oversimplifications and overcomplications by preconceived theoretical patterns.

4) In order to secure the fullest possible range of phenomena and at the same time doubt-proof foundations it uses a special *method of reductions which suspends the beliefs associated with our naive or natural attitude* and shared even by science; it also *traces back the phenomena to the constituting acts in a pure subject*, which itself proves to be irreducible.

5) Its ultimate objective is the *examination and justification of all our beliefs, both ordinary and scientific, by the test of intuitive perception.*[43]

For Husserl, all knowledge of the world arises in experience and emerges as a *mediated* relation between consciousness and phenomena. European, or "traditional science," he charged, fragmented the absolute certainty of this mediated relation and thus was unable to satisfactorily explicate either the *phenomena of experience* or the *experience of phenomena*. Instead, our relations with the world were bifurcated into the Cartesian dualism represented in the sciences by *phenomenalism* on the one hand and by *psychologism* on the other. That is, the claims and procedures of phenomenalism or positivist science isolate phenomena from their appearance to consciousness, describing them as objects directly known only through physical perception (hence, phenomenalism's primary concern with "sensible" and material objects). In a similar manner, the claims and procedures of introspective psychologism isolate consciousness from its relation to sensible and material phenomena, describing the latter as constituted by and in consciousness and thus directly known only as mental perception (hence, psychologism's primary concern with states of "sensibility" or subjectivity).[44] Husserl's rigorous science of phenomenol-

[43] Spiegelberg, "Husserl's Phenomenology and Existentialism," p. 64. (Emphasis mine) The reader should note in proposition 4 the use of the words *pure* and *irreducible*. Here, where the transcendental ego emerges, existential phenomenology parts ways with the idealism of transcendental phenomenology.

[44] Richard Schmitt, "Phenomenology," in *Encyclopedia of Philosophy*, ed. Paul Edwards (New York: Macmillan Publishing Co., 1967), Vol. 6, pp. 135–151.

ogy arose in opposition to this bifurcated reduction of experience that dominated European science and burdened it with a stock of presupposed knowledge that obscured rather than illuminated the world of phenomena and our conscious relations with it.[45]

To counter this reductionism and dualism, Husserl emphasized the "fullness" of consciousness as it is experienced and nominated through the key phenomenological concept: *intentionality*. The term was used to designate the nature of consciousness as a "stream between two poles: subject and object," as "a *vector* that effects an *organized* synthesis."[46] Consciousness is not empty as it is given in experience. Consciousness as we live it and reflect upon it in experience is always mediated and mediating, is always *consciousness of something* (even when it is reflexive: consciousness of itself and its activity). For Husserl, then, *intentionality* was a term that described the invariant directedness of consciousness, its always correlational character or structure.[47] That is, the phenomena of our experience (the *noema*, or intentional objects of consciousness) are always correlated with the mode of our experience (the *noesis*, or intentional acts of consciousness). Intentionality is this invariant correlation that structures and directs our experience and, from the first, infuses it with meaning. As Merleau-Ponty points out in an explication of Husserl's use of the term:

> It is a question of recognizing consciousness itself as a project of the world, meant for a world which it neither embraces nor possesses, but towards which it is perpetually directed—and the world as this pre-objective individual whose imperious unity decrees what knowledge shall take as its goal. This is why Husserl distinguishes between *intentionality of act*, which is that of our judgements and of those occasions when we voluntarily take up a position . . . and *operative intentionality* . . . , that which produces the natural and antepredicative unity of the

[45] Ibid., pp. 135–139.

[46] Peter Koestenbaum, introduction to Edmund Husserl, *The Paris Lectures*, trans. Peter Koestenbaum (The Hague: Martinus Nijhoff, 1975), p. xxvii.

[47] For various explications of *intentionality*, in addition to Peter Koestenbaum's introduction in Husserl's *The Paris Lectures*, see (in order of ascending complexity) David Stewart and Algis Mickunas, *Exploring Phenomenology: A Guide to the Field and its Literature* (Chicago, IL: The American Library Association, 1974), pp. 8–9; Roderick N. Chisholm, "Intentionality," in *Encyclopedia of Philosophy*, Vol. 4, pp. 201–204; Spiegelberg, *The Phenomenological Movement: A Historical Introduction*, Vol. 2, pp. 107ff.; and Schrag, *Experience and Being: Prolegomena to a Future Ontology*, pp. 82–121.

world and of our life, being apparent in our desires, our evaluations and in the language we see, more clearly than in objective knowledge, and furnishing the text which our knowledge tries to translate into precise language.[48]

For Husserl, as well as for all subsequent phenomenologists, the intentional structure of consciousness in no way denies the world an objective status—even as the world is always engaged by a subject of consciousness. Thus, while phenomenology is unlike positivism in its insistence that the world is not available to us except in its engagement through consciousness, phenomenology is also unlike psychologism in its insistence that the world is not constituted by consciousness. That is, the world is not *in* consciousness but rather is always already extant *for* consciousness that intends toward it. The world exists objectively, providing us the inexhaustible horizons of our conscious experience, whether we reflexively reflect upon that experience, or live it in what Husserl called the "natural attitude" (identified in his later works as the *Lebenswelt*, or lived-world). This natural attitude is the necessary store of habitual or sedimented presuppositions and beliefs that inform both our ordinary and scientific activity, that surround us as the "reality" seemingly "given" to us by the world. We forget in the natural attitude that what counts as "reality" was, at some point, both culturally and individually "taken up" by us, and then taken-for-granted.

Husserl's goal was to interrogate the conventional assumptions about the nature of phenomena taken-for-granted in the natural attitude informing not only everyday life, but also scientific inquiry. In order to describe and specify the invariant and essential features of phenomena possible in all the situations in which they might be experienced by consciousness (rather than merely an institutionalized or ordinarily lived few), Husserl engaged in a series of investigative *epoches* or *reductions* (that is, a controlled and rigorous bracketing of presuppositions). These constituted a method with three major phases: the phenomenological epoche, the eidetic reduction, and the transcendental reduction.[49] Husserl's system of reflection is particularly notable in that it works in what traditionally would be consid-

---

[48] Merleau-Ponty, *Phenomenology of Perception*, pp. xvii-xviii. (Emphasis mine)

[49] Koestenbaum in Husserl, *The Paris Lectures*, pp. xix–xxvii, lvi–lx. See also Richard L. Lanigan, "Communication Models in Philosophy," in *Communication Yearbook III*, ed. Dan Nimmo (New Brunswick, NJ: Transaction Books, 1979), pp. 29–49.

ered a "backward" or reflexive movement. To get "to the things themselves,"[50] Husserl starts with a description of phenomena as they appear to consciousness in the natural attitude. Then, in the reductions, he proceeds to strip away the preconceptions and conventions that surround phenomena until their invariant features are discovered and their possibilities for existence are made as explicit as their actual existence. This movement is both reflective and reflexive. Indeed, it parallels the structure of our own "ordinary" movement in relation to the world. That is, the movement from our lived and un-reflected-upon experience of phenomena (the *noema*) to our reflection on both the phenomena and our mode of experiencing it (the *noesis*) to the emergence in this process of the previously "absorbed" subject of the experience of the correlation of action and object (the *ego* or *I*).[51]

The first phase of the reduction is the *phenomenological epoche*, which involves the interrogation and "bracketing" of beliefs and pre-suppositions held in the natural attitude. It is thus the beginning of a process of critically distancing oneself not from the phenomena under investigation, but from the taken-for-granted judgments, beliefs, and presuppositions that ground our everyday existence as "reality" and limit the possibilities for understanding the phenomena. The aim of this first phase is to put the natural attitude "out of play." To achieve this goal, "bracketing" must occur at three levels of the epoche. First, epistemological prejudices are removed in a *philosophical reduction* that demands that the investigator's method of research respond to the phenomena as experienced, rather than to an imposed methodological bias. Second, logical presuppositions that contribute to the creation of particular scientific constructs and their constraints on the imaginative and playful variation of possible alternative logics are removed in a *scientific reduction*. Third, ontological presuppositions and beliefs about the nature of reality and existence (the most entrenched and transparent prejudices of all) are removed in a phenomenological reduction that makes us confront our natural attitude and leaves us open to the experience of the phenomena as they appear to consciousness in their original or open possibilities.[52]

---

[50] "To the things themselves" (*zu den Sachen selbst*) are the catchwords that characterize Husserl's transcendental phenomenology. See Edmund Husserl, *Cartesian Meditations*, trans. Dorion Cairns (The Hague: Martinus Nijhoff, 1960), pp. 12–13.

[51] Ihde, *Experimental Phenomenology: An Introduction*, pp. 43–46.

[52] Lanigan, "Communication Models in Philosophy," p. 37.

The second phase of the reduction is the *eidetic reduction*. Here, after the phenomenological epoche, those essential or invariant features of the phenomena "left" to consciousness are intuited, made explicit, and thematized (that is, individual phenomena are treated as an instance of the more general phenomena).[53] There are two stages to this analysis. The first calls for a focus on "the abstract and general properties of, ideas about, or forms of the phenomenon under investigation."[54] The second calls for restraint in the consideration and analysis of particular examples. That is, although the abstract and general aspects of phenomena are originally drawn from and located in *actual* experience, the investigator should be critically aware of the necessity to remain open and independent of the particularities of any actual experience so that the essential aspects of the phenomena can emerge in the fullness and potential of their *possibilities* for experience.

The third and final phase of Husserl's series of reductions is the *transcendental reduction*. It is in this phase that the essence or invariant "shape" of the phenomenon in conscious experience (both actual and virtual) is *universalized* through an attempted "total bracketing" of existence. First, the *Lebenswelt* or lived-world in which consciousness and experience are correlated "into a sense of reality in both a preconscious/prereflective and conscious/reflective modality" is examined and isolated.[55] Second, the constituents of that life-world (that is, the network of intentions and implications that are the self, the other, and the world) are described and bracketed. Third, what remains as the culmination of the reductions after the bracketing of existence is the correlation of intentionality: the structure of consciousness intending toward the specific phenomenon. Belonging to no particular existence, indeed bracketed *outside* particular existence, intentionality is thus located by Husserl in what is a *transcendental ego*, that is, in a subjectivity made universal and objectively available to *any* existence. In sum, for Husserl, the transcendental reduction attempts an essential description of the phenomena of consciousness in all their possibilities for any existence and thus, in its universal relevance to all possible experience, demonstrates that "subjectivity is intersubjectivity."[56]

Although this latter proposition becomes central to the phenome-

---

[53] Lanigan, *Speaking and Semiology*, p. 31.
[54] Lanigan, "Communication Models in Philosophy," p. 38.
[55] Ibid.
[56] Ibid. See also Husserl, *The Paris Lectures*, p. 35.

nologists who follow Husserl, his transformation of subjectivity into an objective modality comes at too high a price and is in basic contradiction with the original aim of phenomenology to ground itself in the lived-world. As pointed out earlier, the subject of consciousness is known by means of its existence in the world and its active implication with phenomena. Implicit in acts of consciousness, the subject of consciousness is known reflectively and reflexively from the direct and active existential experience of phenomena. That is, direct experience is the invariant correlation of enworlded phenomena and embodied consciousness in an intentional structure that implicates and thus implies an intentional subject. The intentional subject therefore cannot be known transcendentally "bracketed" outside of existence and the correlational activity of intentionality. As well, such an abstraction as the transcendental subject could not logically escape its own inclusion in an intentional structure—itself intending toward, conscious of, the structure of intentionality as its own intentional object.[57]

Husserl's transcendental ego presents us with an unnecessary paradox. It is an abstraction from the *Lebenswelt* which cannot escape the *Lebenswelt*, suggesting only infinite regress. As a philosophy of consciousness and experience and a research method, phenomenology cannot avoid locating the subject of consciousness and experience as existence in the world. And, as existence in the world, the subject of consciousness and experience is *embodied*, *situated*, and *finite*. While accepting both Husserl's description of the intentional structure of consciousness and the basic direction and rigor of his method, existential phenomenology rejects his idealism, his essentialism, and his notion of the transcendental ego. It relocates "essence" as it is qualified in existence, in the *Lebenswelt* from which phenomena emerge and in which they have their only significance.

Merleau-Ponty and Existential (Semiotic) Phenomenology

The insistent focus of Maurice Merleau-Ponty's existential phenomenology is on the correlation of the lived-body and the lived-world. This correlation he calls *être-au-monde*, a term that suggests both a being-present-to-the-world and a being-alive-in-the-world. Thus, Merleau-Ponty follows Husserl in emphasizing intentionality as the

---

[57] Ihde, *Experimental Phenomenology: An Introduction*, pp. 45–46.

invariant correlative structure of acts of consciousness and their objects whose entailment generates meaning. However, Merleau-Ponty rejects the earlier philosopher's attempt to locate or situate intentionality in a disembodied and transcendental subject. And he rejects those of Husserl's reductions that "took phenomenology away from the empirical experience embodied in the person."[58]

Merleau-Ponty not only maintains that we cannot "bracket" a belief in existence as we explore the phenomena of consciousness and the latter's intentional structure, but he also insists that existence is the lived, situated, always in motion, always unfinished character that *is* intentionality. That is, intentionality is not merely a static correlational structure between *noesis* and *noema*. It is a dynamic structure creating temporality and spatiality as meaningful for embodied beings always in essential and existential motility. Intentionality as the basic structure of *être-au-monde* is not just a directionally reversible *vector of implication* between consciousness and its objects. It is a biased *trajectory of implication*, actively performed by an embodied consciousness correlated with enworlded objects in the context of an existentially significant project. As Merleau-Ponty tells us, "Consciousness is in the first place not a matter of 'I think that' but of 'I can'."[59]

The "I can" of existential embodied consciousness is the primary *expression of perception* performed by the lived-body subject in the *Lebenswelt*, a performance radically entailed with a primary *perception of expression* that is not thought but is carnally lived as the prereflective experience of world, other, and self. Thus, the lived-body becomes central to Merleau-Ponty's philosophy and investigation. It is the lived-body that actualizes intentionality in the very gesture of being alive in and present to the world and others. The lived-body articulates intentionality as "flesh"; that is, as dynamic, concrete, situated, and both materially and historically finite. My body is "my point of view upon the world."[60] I cannot refuse its situated and finite existence and thus its necessary and diacritical motility and self-displacements, and so I am "condemned to meaning."[61] I am always implicated and interested in the world and with it, always of its flesh,

---

[58] Lanigan, "Communication Models in Philosophy," p. 38.

[59] Merleau-Ponty, *Phenomenology of Perception*, p. 137.

[60] Ibid., p. 70.

[61] Ibid., p. xix.

always in the process of completing and disclosing its meanings as my own. I cannot "be" otherwise.

Rejecting Husserl's transcendental ego and the transcendental reduction, Merleau-Ponty emphasizes that, no matter how rigorous our procedure, we cannot ever stand "behind" existential meaning for we are immersed in it even in the midst of our most reflective and abstractive endeavors. The correlation, then, of an intentional act of consciousness and an intentional object of consciousness implicates and indicates not a transcendental ego, but an existentially embodied and situated subject of consciousness. Indeed, our understanding of both intentional acts and intentional objects and their correlation as the essential structure of consciousness is only meaningful *as* it is existential.

For Merleau-Ponty, the lived-body is not merely an object in the world, the flesh of its flesh; the body is also a subject in the world. It is both agent and agency of an engagement with the world that is lived in its *subjective* modality as *perception* and in its *objective* modality as *expression*, both modes constituting the *unity* of meaningful experience. We are told: "Every perception is a communication or a communion, the taking up or completion by us of some extraneous intention or, on the other hand, the complete expression outside ourselves of our perceptual powers and a coition, so to speak, of our body with things."[62]

Perception, then, is more than a mere mosaic of sensations on the body-object, more than a mere psychological phenomenon. Advancing from the Gestalt psychology that he admired but found still too dependent upon behaviorism, Merleau-Ponty describes perception as a dynamic ensemble that far exceeds the sum of its parts and, as well, confounds attempts to explain its dynamism solely in terms of psychic structures. Perception is the bodily access or agency for being-in-the-world, for having both a world and being. Perception is the bodily perspective or situation from which the world is present to us and constituted in an always particular and biased meaning.[63] Throughout Merleau-Ponty's writings, the lived-body is both a subject in the world and an object for the world and others. The lived-body's individual perception of the world is always also available for

[62] Ibid., p. 320.

[63] David Carr, "Maurice Merleau-Ponty: Incarnate Consciousness," in *Existential Philosophers: Kierkegaard to Merleau-Ponty*, ed. George Alfred Schrader, Jr. (New York: McGraw-Hill, 1967), pp. 374–387.

the world and others as the lived-body's objective expression, that is, the material and active realization of intentionality. Thus, Merleau-Ponty's *primacy of perception* is always also a *primacy of expression*, the latter articulated as the visible gesture of the former.

The lived-body, then, does not merely provide a "place" for perception and expression but also performs the commutation of perception to expression and vice-versa. From its first breath, the lived-body constitutes both an *intrasubjective and intersubjective system* in which being is both understood and signified as significant—that is, as intentional. In that every lived-body is both the subject of perception and expression and an object for perception and expression, every lived-body lives the commutation of perception and expression in a *simultaneously subjective and objective modality.* And because intentionality (the invariant and universal correlation of consciousness and its objects) is articulated in existence through the agency and activity of the lived-body being-in-the-world, every conscious lived-body is semiotically and hermeneutically competent in its ability to commute perception to expression and back again. Thus, the primacy of perception *as* the primacy of expression, the commutability of one to the other, is synopsized in lived-body experience as the *primacy of communication.*

The lived-body being-in-the-world establishes the concrete ground (that is, the premises as well as the necessity) for all language. Through the diacritical movement of intentionality actualized and situated as being-in-the-world, being *gestures.* The lived-body projects and performs its perceptual perspective and situation and bears meaning into the world as the expression of that situation. The highest level of this performance is *speech* and its fixation as *writing.* But the genesis of speech and writing occurs at the radical level of the lived-body. Thus, in Merleau-Ponty's existential phenomenology, the lived-body "becomes an essential condition of language rather than the merely instrumental transmitter of pure thoughts."[64] Indeed, there are no such phenomena as "pure thoughts." There can be no consciousness of anything, no intentionality, if there is no body and no world. All perception and expression, all its structural modalities, emerge in embodied and enworlded existence and partake of it. As Richard Lanigan observes: "This correlation unites the felt experience of the body and the resulting structure of perception

---

[64] Ibid., p. 396.

with the possibility of expression in which 'what' one experiences is probably 'what' the Other experiences. There is a unity of process in perception and expression that is the sign as signification and the agency of that process is the body experience as lived."[65]

Merleau-Ponty's emphasis on the lived-body experience of perception and expression in the *Lebenswelt* thus emerges as a phenomenology that is not only existential but also semiotic. It describes and articulates "the rediscovery of the subject in the act of speaking" in contrast "to a science of language which inevitably treats this subject as a thing."[66] A semiotic phenomenology, therefore, is not engaged in fragmenting the process and activity of existential speech into a syntactics, semantics, and pragmatics of the spoken. It is neither a linguistics nor an investigation of language as a system of codified symbols.[67]

In his introduction to Merleau-Ponty's *Signs*, Richard McCleary distinguishes these radically different approaches to language:

> Like the carnal intersubjectivity that is its ever-present source, speaking language is a moving equilibrium governed by the present and incarnate logic of existence. . . . The objective science of language turns toward the past of already established language and already acquired meanings. The phenomenology of language seeks to unveil the field of presence of the speaking subject and the "differentiation" and convergence of linguistic gestures he effects in his unending efforts to bring the implicit meaning-structures of experience to explicit expression. In their autonomy, science and philosophy mutually envelop one another within the dialectic of the constituted and the constituting.[68]

This mutual envelopment of science and philosophy, of the constituted and the constituting, is disclosed in Merleau-Ponty's advance upon Husserl's phenomenological method. Consisting of three progressive reflections, it refuses the transcendental reduction in favor of a *qualified essence*, one found in the finitude of existence and in the horizonal multiplicity of the world.[69] These three reflections form the

---

[65] Lanigan, *Speaking and Semiology*, p. 125.

[66] Maurice Merleau-Ponty, *Signs*, trans. Richard C. McCleary (Evanston, IL: Northwestern Univ. Press, 1964), p. 104.

[67] Lanigan, *Speaking and Semiology*, pp. 26–27.

[68] Richard C. McCleary, "Translator's Preface," in Merleau-Ponty, *Signs*, p. xxi.

[69] Maurice Merleau-Ponty, "What Is Phenomenology?" trans. John F. Banner, *Cross*

process and method of phenomenological description, reduction, and interpretation.

The *phenomenological description* focuses attention on the conscious experience of phenomena as it is immediately given in the *Lebenswelt* and as it is accessible to us in a reflection that originates in immanent *prereflective perception*. Because it is our perception that sets the boundaries of what is immediately present to our consciousness and also in what manner it is present, perception—as it relates us to the world in the living expression of the prereflective "natural attitude"—becomes the focus of description. Thus, once identified, the natural attitude is bracketed. This is not meant to put it "out of play" so that it does not interfere with our investigation of phenomena, but rather to see its function in experience from a reflective distance, to "disrupt our familiarity with it" so that the habitual and sedimented presuppositions we hold about experience can be distinguished from experience as it is prereflectively lived.[70] What description of the natural attitude reveals to phenomenological reflection is that the world invariably exceeds our perceptive access to it and our prereflective and reflective expressions of it. The lesson of the phenomenological description is that description is never complete. Meaning as sense and significance can never be exhaustively articulated or signified. Thus, Merleau-Ponty rejects Husserl's transcendental reduction and tells us, "The greatest lesson of the reduction is the *impossibility* of a complete reduction."[71]

The phenomenological description of the natural attitude reveals that prereflective embodied existence in the world provides the primary ground for secondary reflection upon both existence and embodiment. The act of being-in-the-world (an act both perceptive and expressive) is not originally reflective and reflexive. "I can" precedes "I think that." Thus, in relation to language, phenomenological description reveals that "speech speaking" (Merleau-Ponty's *parole parlante*) prereflectively grounds "speech spoken" (*parole parlée*). Merleau-Ponty clarifies the meaning of these terms in a significant passage that locates the genesis of language in the prereflective *Lebenswelt*:

Currents 6 (Winter 1956), pp. 59–70; and Lanigan, *Speaking and Semiology*, pp. 97–151, and "Communication Models in Philosophy," pp. 38–40.

[70] Merleau-Ponty, "What Is Phenomenology?" p. 64.

[71] Ibid.

It might be said, restating a celebrated distinction, that languages or constituted systems of vocabulary and syntax, empirically existing "means of expression," are both the repository and residue of acts of *speech*, in which unformulated significance not only finds the means of being conveyed outwardly, but moreover acquires existence for itself, and is genuinely created as significance. Or again one might draw a distinction between the *word in the speaking* and the *spoken word*. The former is the one in which the significant intention is at the stage of coming into being. Here existence is polarized into a certain "significance" which cannot be defined in terms of any natural object. It is somewhere at the point beyond being that it aims to catch up with itself again, and that is why it creates speech as an empirical support for its own not-being. Speech is the surplus of our existence over natural being. But the act of expression constitutes a linguistic world and a cultural world, and allows that to fall back into being which was striving to outstrip it. Hence the spoken word, which enjoys available significances as one might enjoy an acquired fortune. From these gains other acts of authentic expression—the writer's, artist's or philosopher's—are made possible. This ever-recreated opening in the plenitude of being is what conditions the child's first use of speech and the language of the writer, as it does the construction of the word and that of concepts. Such is the function which we intuit through language, which reiterates itself, which is its own foundation, or which, like a wave, gathers and poises itself to hurtle beyond its own limits.[72]

The process of phenomenological description forces us to confront conscious experience as the "perceptual logic" of the embodied subject.[73] It demands that we consider the embodied and enworlded subject as always already immersed in meaning, both supported and constrained by the inherited "fortune" of language. Phenomenological description returns us to the speaking subject who, from the first, is engaged in expressive acts that literally and figuratively "lend interest" to that "acquired fortune" by drawing upon it and investing it in a particular, personal existence. The embodied speaking subject speaks not to *substitute* for being or for a loss or lack of being, but rather to *extend* being and its projects, to embody being's excess beyond the discrete situation of its body. The expression of perception in existence as the consciousness of embodied and enworlded expe-

[72] Merleau-Ponty, *Phenomenology of Perception*, pp. 196–197.
[73] Lanigan, *Speaking and Semiology*, p. 82.

rience and the experience of embodied and enworlded consciousness thus constitutes "an existential semiotic capable of having all of human reality 'translated' into it."[74]

The *phenomenological reduction* is the second phase of Merleau-Ponty's method of radical reflection.[75] As experience is reflected upon in the phenomenological description, so consciousness is reflected upon in the phenomenological reduction. Husserl's bracketing of epistemological and scientific constructs and constraints provides the first level of analysis. Second, a radical gestalt locates the "qualified" or *existential essence* of the phenomenon. The "qualified essence" of a phenomenon is qualified by the nature of its structural or essential existence in a particular embodied consciousness; the structure of the phenomenon is part of an existential ensemble and irreducible to any one of its correlates.

That structure is identified through a process known as *free imaginative variation*. Bracketing epistemological and scientific presuppositions and constraints, the researcher imagines as present or absent all features of the phenomenon as it is experienced. This rigorous imaginative play attempts to open up the possibilities of the phenomenon for experience, as well as allow the "qualified essence" of the phenomenon to emerge. Through this process, that which is invariant and essential for the existence of the phenomenon to consciousness is described. In this manner, the *theme* of the phenomenon is articulated. (To stress the qualified rather than transcendental nature of the phenomenological reduction, the latter is often referred to as a "thematization" of the phenomenon.)

A third phase of the phenomenological reduction leads to the location of the *prereflective source* of the "qualified essence" or invariant theme of the phenomenon in existence. That is, the location of essence here "is not the end but the means." It is "our effective engagement in the world which must be understood and conceptualized," an effective engagement that is prior to our reflective judgments and habitual expressions about it.[76] The lesson of the phenomenological reduction is that reflective judgments and their expression in sedimented, habitual, conventional language, in "speech

---

[74] Ibid.

[75] Spiegelberg, *The Phenomenological Movement*, Vol. 2, pp. 680–684.

[76] Merleau-Ponty, "What Is Phenomenology?" p. 65. See also Lanigan, "The Phenomenology of Human Communication," *Philosophy Today* 23 (1979), p. 7, and "Communication Models in Philosophy," p. 39.

spoken" (*parole parlée*), emerge from and in conscious experience that is prereflectively embodied in existential speaking, in "speech speaking" (*parole parlante*). Although in the natural attitude (and in the phenomenological attitude as well) we *borrow* upon the spoken word, the sign as a cultural inheritance we cannot exhaust, we also *produce* signs in and as the expression of our personal investment in prereflective experience. Thus, Merleau-Ponty says: "It is the function of language to make essences exist in a separation, which is actually only apparent since they still repose on the antepredicative life of consciousness. In the silence of the original consciousness there appear not only the meanings of words but also the meaning of things, that primary core of signification around which acts of denomination and expression are organized."[77]

The *phenomenological interpretation* is the third phase of Merleau-Ponty's radical reflection. It attempts to understand the "meaning" or intentional correlation that links the phenomenon under investigation with consciousness. It attempts to grasp the *value relationship* that constitutes the structural ensemble as conscious experience. The specification of such a value relationship unites understanding of the phenomenon and its meaning as an existential hermeneutic and semiotic.[78] The interpretation of sensible phenomena in perception is reversible with the signifying phenomena in expression, and that reversibility is constituted as both significance and signification, signified and signifier. To legitimate the phenomenological description and the phenomenological reduction (or thematization) of the first two phases of reflection, perception as experience and expression as consciousness are revealed by the phenomenological interpretation as the value of their connection and commutability. Thus, the phenomenological interpretation has four procedural "moments" in which the researcher attempts to "seize again the total intention" that forms and informs the unity of the conscious experience of the phenomenon and constitutes its original "wild meaning."[79]

The first interpretive moment finds in the ensemble of the radical gestalt of the phenomenological reduction a "reversibility" whereby self-other-world are revealed as a synergetic network of intentions that dynamically implicate each element of the ensemble as a mani-

---

[77] Merleau-Ponty, "What Is Phenomenology?" p. 65.

[78] Lanigan, "The Phenomenology of Human Communication," pp. 7–8.

[79] Merleau-Ponty, "What Is Phenomenology?" p. 67.

fest modality of the whole. Conscious experience is thus communicable. The commutation of perception and expression in the unity of the lived-body experience is both intrasubjective and intersubjective. It allows for both sense and signification, existential speaking and sedimented speech.

The second moment of the interpretation discovers a *radical cogito* from this reversibility, an "ego" that is not first a transcendental and disembodied "I think," but rather an existential and embodied "I can."[80] The *cogito* is thus discovered by virtue of its *performance* in an existential situation, rather than by its transcendental claim of *competence*. The reversibility with the ensemble of the radical gestalt produces and locates a body-subject able to act prereflectively and able to reflect upon its prereflective actions.

The third moment of the phenomenological interpretation results in the emergence of *preconscious phenomena*, that is, phenomena *for* conscious experience.[81] In the world and available to, but as yet not intended by, reflective consciousness, such preconscious phenomena are rather like the submerged figures in a child's puzzle—there, but invisible because unintended. Initially, the picture presents itself in the natural attitude as, for example, foregrounding a tree in a garden. However, cued by the intentional directions that suggest there are animals to be found in the garden, the tree suddenly opens to reflective consciousness the figures of a squirrel, a deer, a bird, and an elephant configured in what before were merely its branches. These figures were preconsciously present to experience prior to reflection, but were not taken up or intended because of a conventional predisposition to look at the picture in a certain way. The third moment of the interpretation seeks to allow such phenomena to emerge in their presence to experience.

The fourth and final moment in the phenomenological interpretation is an *interpretation of the interpretation*. That is, the previous moments are synthesized and synopsized into a "hermeneutic judgment or specification of existential meaning, i.e., the meaning of the phenomenon as the person lived it."[82] The interpretation of the interpretation thus emphasizes the meaning of phenomena as contingent

[80] Merleau-Ponty, *Phenomenology of Perception*, p. 137, and *Signs*, pp. 88–89.

[81] Lanigan, "Communication Models in Philosophy," p. 39; Merleau-Ponty, "What Is Phenomenology?" pp. 63–64.

[82] Lanigan, "Communication Models in Philosophy," p. 40.

upon their being ascribed value by embodied persons in concrete situations.

As laid out above, the process of phenomenological description, reduction, and interpretation may seem belabored or arcane—for, as Merleau-Ponty emphasizes, "Phenomenology is accessible only to a phenomenological method."[83] That is, phenomenology is understood in its *performance* of describing, thematizing, and interpreting the existential experience of a specific phenomenon. However, Don Ihde offers a useful series of "hermeneutic rules" that indicate the path followed in this present phenomenological study of the emergence of sense and signification in the film experience. By themselves, these rules seem commonplace and commonsensical. Nonetheless, within the context of the previous explication of phenomenology as philosophy and research procedure, they can be seen as a demand for critical rigor and for an interrogation of the very common places and common senses from which they emerge.

The rules that inform the act of *phenomenological description* are 1) Attend to the phenomena of experience as they appear and are immediately present and given to the experience; 2) Describe, don't explain; and 3) Horizontalize or equalize all immediate phenomena and do not assume an initial hierarchy of "realities." Thus, the phenomenological description opens the field of experience in its fullness and multiplicity in preparation for the *phenomenological reduction*. The rule that informs the reduction is 4) Seek out structural or invariant features of the phenomena. Through the use of free imaginative variation that contextualizes features of the phenomenon within the whole and that allows for comparison and contrast of the phenomenon with other phenomena like and unlike it, a pattern of experience emerges, and with it emerges also the shape of the phenomenon as it is intended in the experience. The meaning of the phenomenon as it is lived meaningfully, as it is intended, is specified in the *phenomenological interpretation*. The connection between experience as described and consciousness as experience reduced and thematized is made explicit by a focus on the intentional correlation between experience and consciousness in a body-subject as it is both particular in existence and universal in structure. The last hermeneutic rule emphasizes the relative distinctions that differentiate person and world within the unity of their correlation: 5) Every experiencing has its ref-

---

[83] Merleau-Ponty, "What Is Phenomenology?" p. 60.

erence or direction toward what is experienced, and contrarily, every experienced phenomenon refers to or reflects a mode of experience to which it is present.[84]

Semiotic Phenomenology and the Address of the Eye

Existential and semiotic phenomenology as a philosophy and research procedure offers us a way of seeing the film experience freshly. It offers us, in fact, a new mode of seeing and reflecting upon our sight as the entailment of an *object of vision*, an *act of viewing*, and a *subject of vision* in a dynamic and transitive correlation. It is this correlation of cinematic vision *as a whole* that structures and informs what we call the "film experience" and gives it meaning as such. Being and seeing and being seen are, from the first, hermeneutic and semiotic acts.

As previously stated, a semiotic phenomenology attempts to describe, thematize, and interpret the structures of communication as they radically emerge in the structures of being. The object of inquiry is the rich and primary entailment of embodied existence and its significations and representations. As Richard Lanigan observes of Merleau-Ponty's work in this area: "The force of the semiology is a dialectic [of] perception and expression creating a meaning in the lived-experience. The perception of the phenomena brings forth the meaning that they have and expression causes them to have meaning. Such a synoptic perception is perception *as* expression—this is the lesson of the semiotic phenomenology."[85]

The relevance of semiotic phenomenology to an investigation of the nature of the film experience is clear. To ask the question, "What is it to see a film?" is to *doubly* entail the questions: What is it to see? How does seeing exist and mean? Who is seeing being and what is being seen? These questions refer not only to the spectator *of* the film but also to the film *as* spectator. Both are correlated in the structure that is the film experience and both are implicated in its meanings.

Given this project, semiotic phenomenology would take as its point of departure the *immanent act of viewing* as it engages an object and is performed by an embodied and enworlded subject sharing a world with other subjects who are also engaged in acts of vision. It

---

[84] Ihde, *Experimental Phenomenology: An Introduction*, pp. 34–43.
[85] Lanigan, *Speaking and Semiology*, p. 125.

49

is this primary act of perception and its expression that enables cinematic intelligibility and communication and grounds secondary and conventional semiotic and hermeneutic "codes." Merleau-Ponty's "speech speaking" (*parole parlante*) and "speech spoken" (*parole parlée*) are thus equivalent in cinematic terms to the incarnate gestures of being that are a "viewing-view" and to its constituted images or "viewed-view."

A semiotic phenomenology, then, will not presuppose the nature of the "viewing-view" and "viewed-view" in the act(s) of vision that constitute the film experience as meaningful. It will also not presuppose the cinema's communicative competence, that is, the intrasubjective and intersubjective exchange of perception and expression that is located in both the spectator of the film and the film as spectator. Finally, it will not presuppose the film as merely an object of vision, a common theoretical presupposition that leads to an interpretation of the film experience as ultimately monologic. Indeed, all three of these presuppositions become, themselves, the focus of a phenomenological inquiry into the relations and meaning of "being seeing," "seeing being," and "being seen."

The Act of Being with One's Own Eyes

THE CONCERN of this chapter is with the constitution and location of the viewing subject in the act of viewing. Without an act of viewing and a subject who knows itself reflexively as the locus and origin of viewing *as* an act, there could be no film and no "film experience." Thus, a description of the film experience as an experience of signification and communication calls for a *reflexive turn* away from the film as "object" and toward the act of viewing and its existential implication of a body-subject: the viewer. This chapter, therefore, will attempt to explore and describe how the act of seeing is entwined intimately with the act of being, how seeing *incarnates* being and connects it with the visible world in a living engagement. The chapter will attempt also to describe the viewing subject who is borne into the world by the embodied act of seeing, but who must be born to itself as well, who must come to re-cognize the invisible presence and agency of its eyes as the "I" that the body is, and through which it possesses the visible world as conscious experience.

The existential act of seeing-in-the world grounds the existential act of seeing the world with one's own eyes. The former is an *anonymous* mode of being situated that discovers the world as the experience of consciousness, whereas the latter is a *situated* mode of being that discovers the *self* in the world and recognizes the activity of seeing as *mediated*, as the consciousness of experience. Seeing the world with eyes is a condition of incarnate being available to an animal or a newborn infant, but seeing the world with one's own eyes—as an I, a viewing subject—is a condition not only of incarnate being but also of reflexive and reflective consciousness, a consciousness aware of its embodiment and situation and its own activity of seeing. Neither the animal nor the newborn infant has consciously located the situation of its being in the world. Both see the world as visible but cannot situate themselves uniquely in it as the "Here, where I am," as the place and origin of access to the visible. They cannot see *that* they see. They merely see *what* they see.

As film viewers capable of recognizing and constituting the significance of one visible phenomenon among many *as* a film, we are quite unlike the young infant or the experienced animal who perceptually encounters that which we call a film. We are aware not only of an experience or of some "thing" seen. We are also aware of an act of seeing. We are competent visual performers, capable of seeing not only as *subjects* of consciousness but also of making our own acts of vision *objects* of consciousness. Such a reflective performance is also reflexive. To engage in an act of seeing that sees seeing as an act presupposes a knowledge of what seeing is and what it is like to be both a seeing subject and a visible object. Such self-consciousness does not show itself in either the infant's or the animal's behavior toward that which we "immediately" see as a film. Certainly, both the baby and the animal have respectively an experience of seeing, each full of its own differentiations, its own discriminations, its own punctuations, its own significance. However, their experience is unlike our own which, when we view a film, is grounded in our knowledge of ourselves and others as both seeing subjects and visible objects, and in our knowledge of vision as the dialectical structure of being seeing and seeing being (that is, being seen). Thus, the baby is better left home when I go out to the movies, and the cat (who seems momentarily interested in some "thing" it sees on my home movie screen) cannot be expected to stay for the entire feature.

Consider the perceiving infant who reaches toward the light on the screen, reacts with its body to the visible fluctuations before it as something to be sought or to retreat from in tears or disinterest. The baby has an experience through its act of seeing, but what the baby sees is not sufficiently yet a significant "thing," and it is certainly not yet the significant thing we determine a film. The baby eyes are not yet open to the perception of what it sees *as* a seeing, not yet open to the mediating activity and agency of vision, and thus not yet open to the possibility of representing perception. Blind to the consciousness of its own activity of seeing, the baby is transparent and "invisible" to itself and its visual mode of access to the visible world. And, until it knows or "sees" itself as capable of seeing, the baby will not be able to see what it sees as that significant phenomenon we call a film.

My cat presents a slightly different case. Unlike the baby, what it sees on the screen is apparently not what it gets, and its behavior indicates that it is aware of the difference. Reaching, for example, toward a small moving object *on* the screen, rather than toward an entire play of light and shadow that is not yet a determinate "thing," the cat's discriminations seem specific. That is, it is able to distinguish between the object it sees and toward which it reaches (the representation of a moving car taken by it, perhaps, to be the presence of a moving insect) and its own effective touch. The cat's actions reveal its dissatisfaction with what it touches in relation to what it sees and intends as significant. One can perceive in its behavior a reevaluation of the situation, its awareness of some *mediating barrier* between its vision and the object it would reach for—because the cat purposefully walks *behind* the screen to look for another mode of access to that object.

Unlike the baby, then, my cat is not blind to the experience of mediation. However, it is conscious of mediation only as it exists *external to* and *other than* its own being. Thus, the mediation *of* being that *is* vision will forever elude its consciousness of experience. The screen exists for my cat like a pane of glass. That is, it mediates my cat's direct and immediate access to what it sees, but it does not become for my cat a place of representation. Unlike the baby, my cat is aware of mediation. Like the baby, however, my cat is blind to the act of seeing as mediating. Thus, it ascribes such mediation to the screen-object itself and sees it as a barrier that might be circumvented. My cat is unable to see that it sees, and so it cannot recognize the vision of another as it presents and represents the world of "things" (things that, of course, it sees as things only as they might have significance for a cat). Thus, although it is discriminating, my cat is not self-conscious and so will seek the object it desires behind the screen and chase its own visible tail as it would chase a caterpillar.

In short, despite the old saying that suggests the democracy of vision, a cat cannot look at a king for the very same reasons it cannot see a film. Both king and film are visible objects perceived in an interpretive strategy that perceptually constitutes their particular meaning on a ground of prior reflexive knowledge. That knowledge is of the lived-body as both the *subject of seeing* and an *object for seeing*. It is this knowledge that enables the transparent and invisible subject who sees with its eyes to represent its viewing body to consciousness as an "I": a visible individual. Unlike the cat, then, the baby will learn to see both king and film not through an act of conscious will, cognitive judgment, or trained application, but because it is a human being and uniquely capable not only of the experience of vision but also of the consciousness of vision. Informed by this capacity to reflexively reverse its vision and reflect upon sight as an object of consciousness, eventually the baby will come to possess its own vision, with and in the sight of others. It will come to see sight not only in its visible and objective form as the other's gaze, but also in its own intentional activity of seeing.

Indeed, without such reflexive and reflective consciousness of vision and that latter's reversible structure, what we *mean* by the film experience would not be possible. If we are to understand the structure of the film experience as specifically meaningful (consciously perceived as signifying and therefore possessing diacritical value or significance for us as a particular kind of experience), we must begin by understanding the structure of the act of viewing and ourselves as viewers. We must know ourselves as body-subjects living a perceptual encounter with the world and others that is always already communicative, always already expressive and semiotic in nature. This perceptual encounter with world, self, and others occurs prior to and provides the *ground* upon which we can then live a perceptual semiotic encounter with that *figuration* we call a *film*—the latter itself a perceptual and semiotic encounter with a world, self, and others. To see a film, we must match our immediate and living view of the visible with a reflexive and reflective knowledge of our subjective acts of vision through which the visible appears to us in its particular significance as an objective form. We must reflexively and reflectively take possession of our vision and make it visible. We must "say what *we* and what *seeing* are" before we can understand the nature and function, the structure and genesis, of cinematic communication and its incarnation as *film*—as a visible figure of *both* a world *and* an act of seeing.[1]

The first steps toward this possession of our own vision involve a radical reflection on the act of viewing and its relation to our being-in-the-world. They also involve a radical reflection on ourselves as viewing subjects who are aware of our own immediate and mediate access to the world and to others whom we are able to know also as viewing subjects (even as they appear to us as viewed objects). These radical reflections form the core of any exploration of vision as it is humanly lived and consciously experienced, as it occurs in both private and shared modalities, as it is both intrapersonal and interper-

[1] Maurice Merleau-Ponty, *The Visible and the Invisible*, ed. Claude Lefort, trans. Alphonso Lingis (Evanston, IL: Northwestern Univ. Press, 1968), p. 4.

sonal, subjective and intersubjective. Thus, the problematic of the act of viewing and its visible productions can be posed as the search for an adequate description of the *existential structure of vision* and the *existential function of viewing* through which the body-subject becomes self-consciously aware of its own acts of vision and, in this same activity of individuation, gains access to others as viewing subjects. Such a description should trace a path "from a world of private perception to a world of shared experience."[2] It should commute us from the self's *visual* grasp of the world to the other's (and the film's) *visible* grasp of it.

The starting point for such a description of the structure and function of vision can be found in the homologous relationship that exists between the irreducible structure of consciousness as the correlation of intentional act and intentional object, and the similarly irreducible structure of vision as the correlation of a viewing view and a viewed view. It is this homology that lays the philosophical and existential grounds for further consideration of the figures of self and other, seer and seen, as co-emergent, co-operative, and co-perceptive. The homologous relationship between intentionality and existential vision marks the possibility of the conditions for the emergence of viewing as not just subjectively experienced but also made objectively visible through a necessary and reversible co-relation of self and other. Thus, a discussion of this relation between *intentionality* and the *structure of vision* initiates the following sections.

Second, *subjectivity* as the emergence and distinction of self from other (of subject from object) within the realm of the intrapersonal will be considered within the psychoanalytic framework provided by Jacques Lacan, the neo-Freudian who has most influenced contemporary film theory because his work irreducibly links the structure of the psyche and the structure of language. Third, *intersubjectivity* as the emergence and distinction of myself from other selves (of subject from subject in the shared realm of the interpersonal) will be addressed within the framework of the semiotic phenomenology advanced by Maurice Merleau-Ponty. This semiotic phenomenology irreducibly links the structure of language and the activity of embodied being, focusing on the lived-body speaking the *Lebenswelt* (the lived world) and even occasionally "singing" it. In this regard, Merleau-

[2] Richard L. Lanigan, *Speaking and Semiology: Maurice Merleau-Ponty's Phenomenological Theory of Existential Speech* (The Hague: Mouton, 1972), p. 119.

Ponty's semiotic phenomenology will be offered as both a corrective and complement to Lacan's determined and determining insistence on the *barrier* between self and other and on the gap or *lack* that language announces and so "falsely" fills. For Merleau-Ponty, the lived-body gestures language as a fullness and presence of being to the world, not as a substitute for being but as an extension of it. The lived-body's commutation of perception into expression is an *excess* of being that provides *access* to other perceptive and expressive beings. Thus, according to Merleau-Ponty, "a philosophy of the flesh is the condition without which psychoanalysis remains anthropology."[3]

Finally, although the aforementioned discussions will be related to the film experience when appropriate, a concluding section will emphasize the relevance of both psychoanalytic and phenomenological description to the way in which we see and understand a film not merely as a *visible object* (some "thing" already-seen, already-constituted), but also as a performative and communicative *act of vision* (a now-seeing, a now-constituting activity) that implicates a *viewing subject* (an always-perceptive and always-constitutive enworlded lived-body) engaged in the act of signifying. The radical importance of these entailments to the significance of the film experience should be already apparent. This "enabling structure" entails the act of viewing with the differentiated experience of consciousness as *lived through* the subjectively embodied self and *perceived as* the objectively embodied other self. Such a structure also constitutes the boundary conditions, the diacritical distinctions, that make communication in its various forms from gesture to verbal language to filmmaking both possible and necessary. Thus, as mentioned in the previous chapter, this "enabling structure" is the "s-code" that sets the boundary conditions to allow secondary codes to be established as relatively specific and particular.[4]

Seeing is an act performed by both the film (which sees a world as visible images) and the viewer (who sees the film's visible images both as a world and the seeing of a world). As mentioned before, the

---

[3] Merleau-Ponty, *The Visible and the Invisible*, p. 276. Again, it must be emphasized that *flesh* as the term is used by Merleau-Ponty and in the context of the present work is not merely a psychophysiological concept, but rather one that stresses the *shared material nature* of the lived-body and the objective world.

[4] Umberto Eco, *A Theory of Semiotics* (Bloomington: Indiana Univ. Press, 1979), pp. 38–44.

existential structure of seeing is *doubled* in the film experience. This entailment of *two* acts of viewing in relation to each other not only constitutes the particular significance of the film experience but also poses to the film theorist the same questions about seeing and being in the world that are posed to the psychoanalyst and the philosopher. The meaning, value, and ethical significance that constitute the sufficiency of "what" we see cannot be severed from the necessarily constitutive act of seeing as a mode of knowledge, and these cannot be severed from existential connection with the being who sees being. Axiology, epistemology, ontology—all are irreducibly correlated in human experience and the existential act of viewing. Thus, in its description of the film experience and in its reflexive concern with the seeing subject, film theory cannot responsibly disavow its radical grounding in philosophy.

Intentionality, Embodiment, and Movement

In previous discussion of Edmund Husserl's transcendental phenomenology, I have described briefly the structure of consciousness called *intentionality*. That is, Husserl characterized consciousness as never "empty" and "in-itself." Rather, consciousness is invariantly *correlational*. Consciousness is always consciousness *of* an object that is other than, but always for, consciousness. Previous discussion has also introduced Merleau-Ponty's existential and semiotic phenomenology as a rejection of Husserl's essentialization of the invariant correlational structure of consciousness in a transcendental ego. By locating the essential correlational structure of intentionality in, and as, existence (that is, in its discrete material embodiment and, therefore, finite situation), Merleau-Ponty animates Husserl's static correlational structure. Of necessity and by virtue of the limitations of embodied and situated existence, intentionality is dynamized as *diacritical action* and generates *signifying power*.

As Jacques Derrida has pointed out in an essay on Husserl, the problem of transcendental phenomenology is that it describes intentionality as the essential structure of consciousness in its "static originality."[5] Thus, such a description cannot accommodate the existen-

---

[5] Jacques Derrida, " 'Genesis and Structure' and Phenomenology," in *Writing and Difference*, trans. Alan Bass (Chicago, IL: The Univ. of Chicago Press, 1978), p. 159.

tial openness of such a structure or its essential generative capacity, that is, the genesis of consciousness that "effects abusive transitions from one region to another."[6] These "abusive transitions" can be seen as emergent necessary and first *inflections* of consciousness *in existence*, the first actions of the lived-body marking *diacritical value*. It is this genetic inflection that originates embodied consciousness as a *particular* body (if not yet a particular self), differentiating intentional consciousness from the world and from others. And thus embodied particularly, the necessary and finite inflection of consciousness originates movement as always already diacritical. This genetic and diacritical movement provides the primary ground upon which the secondary diacritical movements of formal language can figure as those sets of differences that make a difference.

The problem is that transcendental phenomenology describes only the irreducible ground, the essential structure, the static "sameness" of consciousness—much as a still photograph describes the irreducible field of its vision, its invariant relations, the immutable "sameness" of its gaze. Such a phenomenology is insufficient to account fully for the genesis of "difference" within and against the irreducible ground it describes—much as the still photograph is an empty gaze at the world insufficient to account fully for the emergence of photographic movement as the motion picture. Although the gaze and its structure of sameness may be necessary *as* the photograph *for* the genesis of movement that is the difference of the motion picture, nonetheless it is insufficient to account for that genesis from its "essential" structure. Thus, what Derrida identifies as the problematic of transcendental phenomenology can be seen to apply also to the problematic transition from the *essential structure of vision* to the *existential act of viewing*, and from the *photograph* to the *film*. As he says, "The necessity of this transition from the structural to the genetic is nothing less than the necessity of a break or a conversion."[7]

It is precisely a conversion (rather than a break) that Merleau-Ponty effects with his existential and semiotic phenomenology. Essence is converted—or, more aptly—*commuted* to existence through the agency of the lived-body: that intentional form and sensate material Husserl called "intentional *morphē*" and "sensile *hylē*."[8] Whereas in-

[6] Ibid.

[7] Ibid., p. 164.

[8] Edmund Husserl, *Ideas: General Introduction to Pure Phenomenology*, trans. W. R. Boyce Gibson (London: G. Allen and Unwin, 1931), p. 247.

tentional form shapes, or in-forms, the living of the body in its being-in-the-world, the body in its finite, situated, and sensate materiality objectively expresses intentionality in the world as a subjective *in-scription* of time and *description* of space. In this sense, the lived-body is both a *speaking* and *writing* of intentionality as being-in-the-world. The condition of being conscious *of* the world is being a consciousness *in* it and sharing the materiality that provides consciousness with its objects as well as the grounds for its own subjective being. Thus, the theoretical and static categories of *time* and *space* as they might be described for a transcendental consciousness become for the existential consciousness lived materially, dynamically, and meaningfully as *finitude* and *situation*. Lived finitely and perspectivally, the very temporal and spatial limitations of embodied consciousness inaugurate a *need for movement* in the world—fulfilled by the *power of movement* made possible through the agency of the material and enworlded lived-body. Thus, in existence, the body's finitude and situation and its power of movement transform the abstractions of time and space, informing them with the weight of choice and the thickness of movement, with *value* and *dimension*.

In the still photograph, time and space are abstractions. Although the image has a presence, it neither partakes of nor describes the present. Indeed, the photograph's fascination is that it is a figure of transcendental time made available against the ground of a lived and finite temporality. Although included in our experience of the present, the photograph transcends both our immediate present and our lived experience of temporality because it exists for us as never engaged in the activity of *becoming*. Although it announces the possibility of becoming, it never presents itself as the coming into being of being. It is a presence without past, present, future. Thus, when we experience the "timelessness" that a photograph confers on its subject matter, we are experiencing the photograph's compelling emptiness; it exists as the possibility of temporality but is a *vacancy* within it. This temporal vacancy, this lack of finitude, affects the space of the still photograph. It is peculiarly flattened. Even in the most artfully lighted photos, figures do not seem to *inhabit* space, to dwell in it, but seem rather to rest lightly on its surface. Space seems not to be spatialized, not to provide a *situation*, and so objects tend to seem insubstantial, thin, not firmly enworlded. (Thus, photography, like painting before it, has often thickened its representations by producing narrative and temporality in a succession of images that, none-theless, are perceived as static and discretely atemporal.)

The lack of depth and dimension in the still photograph seems less a function of the phenomenal thickness of the subjects and objects that it displays than of the temporal hole it opens within the world in which we gaze at it. Indeed, the most "dynamic" photojournalism derives its uncanny power from this temporal hole, this transcen-dence of both existence and finitude *within* existence and finitude. One only need see, for example, classic photos like the suicidal woman caught in midleap from a building or the Vietnamese pris-oner at the moment of his execution by a bullet to the head. Death, as it is represented in the photograph, provides the clearest example of the self-engendered paradox, the logical *aporia*, of the transcen-dence that escapes finitude and yet resides in it.[9] The stillness and atemporality of the photograph as a structure both points to death's meaning (is its index) and also makes death meaningless within a structure where stillness is all and therefore has no diacritical value. The photograph, then, offers us only the *possibility* of meaning. It provides a significant gap that can be filled with every meaning, any meaning, and is itself meaningless in that it does not act *within* itself to choose its meaning, to diacritically mark it off. Like a transcenden-tal consciousness, the photograph as a transcendental structure pos-its the abstraction of a *moment* but has no *momentum*—and only pro-vides the grounds or arena for its possibility.

On the other hand, although necessarily dependent upon the pos-sibility of temporality that the still photograph announces but does not fulfill, the motion picture is not a transcendental structure. If the photograph is a "hole" in temporality and announces a vacancy, then the motion picture in its *motion* sufficiently fills up that vacancy and inaugurates a fullness. The images of a film exist in the world as a temporal flow, within finitude and situation. Indeed, the fascina-tion of the film is that it does *not* transcend our lived-experience of temporality, but rather that it seems to partake of it, to share it. Un-like the still photograph, the film exists for us as always in the *act of becoming*.

Thus, although made almost entirely using still photographs rather than live action, a film such as Chris Marker's *La Jetée* (1962) nonethe-less projects temporality and an existential becoming, even as it fore-

[9] For the significance of *aporia* in contemporary theoretical inquiry, see Christopher Norris, *Deconstruction: Theory and Practice* (New York: Methuen, 1982), pp. 49–50.

grounds the transcendental and atemporal potentiality of the photograph and its non-becoming. It is this explicit *dialectic* between the
transcendental moment and *existence as momentum* that gives *La Jetée* its
power and particular significance, providing both its structure and
its theme and explicitly representing the dialectic implicit in the nature of *all* film.[10] That is, film is always presenting as well as representing the coming into being of being and representation. It is a
presence inserted in the world and our experience not as a series of
discrete, transcendental, and atemporal moments, but as a temporal
movement—as a presenting felt as presence and its passing, as a presence that can then be said to have a past, a present, and a future.

Along with its objective existence for us as its spectators, a film
possesses its own being. That is, it *has being* in the sense that it *behaves*. A still photograph, however, does not behave; rather, it
waits—as a vacancy—for us to possess it.[11] Because a film behaves
and acts, its present movement adds dimension to the flat space of
the photograph. Abstract space is dynamized as habitable, as "lived
in," as described in the depth that lived movement, not geometry,
confers upon the world.[12] Thus, space in the film becomes the *situa-*

[10] For readers unfamiliar with the film, Chris Marker's *La Jetée* is a narrative with a
recursive structure. A survivor of World War III has a recurrent memory of a woman's
face and a scene at Orly airport where, as a child, he has seen a man killed. Because
of his vivid memories, his apocalyptic culture—underground, with minimal power,
and without hope—attempts to send him back into the past in order to develop his
facility for time travel. He eventually meets the woman in his memory, falls in love,
and then is sent into the future to secure help for his present. Desiring only to return
to the past and the woman he loves, he is helped by those in the future and returned
to the scene of his original childhood memory, only to find that he (as an adult) is
being pursued by people sent from his own present, and that his original memory
was, in fact, the vision of his own death. A film about love, memory, and time, *La Jetée*
is presented completely through the use of still photographs except for one sequence
in the film where the woman, lying in bed, blinks her eyes. (The sound track is continuous, using narration, music, and sound effects. There is no dialogue.)

[11] This issue of the different ontological status of photograph and film is discussed
most interestingly in Arthur C. Danto, "Moving Pictures," *Quarterly Review of Film
Studies* 4 (Winter 1979), pp. 1–21. See also my own "The Scene of the Screen. Beitrag
zu einer Phänomenologie der)Gegenwärtigkeit(im Film und in den elektronischen
Medien," trans. H. U. Gumbrecht, in *Materialität der Kommunikation*, ed. Hans Ulrich
Gumbrecht and K. Ludwig Pfeiffer (Frankfurt am Main: Suhrkamp, 1988), pp. 416–
428, in English as "Toward a Phenomenology of Cinematic and Electronic Presence:
The Scene of the Screen," *Post-Script* 10 (Fall 1990), pp. 50–59.

[12] Distinctions between our notions of geometric space and anthropological or "inhabited" space are discussed in Joseph J. Kockelmans, "Merleau-Ponty on Space Perception and Space," in *Phenomenology and the Natural Sciences: Essays and Translations,*

tion of an existence, and objects and landscapes take on a thickness and substantiality, an always emerging meaning that is chosen in the diacritical marking of movement (whether cinematographic or editorial). The film, then, offers us the existential actualization of meaning, not just the structure and potential for its being. Its significance is constituted in its emergence and existence to a world that is encountered through an active and embodied gaze that shares the materiality of the world and inscribes temporality as the concrete spatiality of its situation. Thus, although it is a favored description, there is no such abstraction as *point of view* in the cinema; rather, there is a specific and mobile engagement of embodied and enworlded subjects/objects whose visual/visible activity prospects and articulates a *shifting field of vision* from a world that always exceeds it.

Arthur Danto tells us that "with the movies, we do not just see *that* they move, we see them *moving*: and this is because the pictures themselves move."[13] Thus, while still objectifying visual activity into the solidity of the visible as does the photograph, the cinematic qualitatively transforms and converts the photographic through a materiality that not only claims the world and others as objects for vision but also signifies its own bodily agency, intentionality, and subjectivity (phenomenologically discovered, as we shall see, in that order). Neither abstract nor static, the cinematic brings the *existential activity* of vision into visibility in what is experienced as a *stream* of moving images. A film's continual and autonomous visual production and meaningful organization of its visible images testifies not only to the material objectivity of the world but also to an anonymous, mobile, embodied, and ethically invested subject of worldly space, a subject able to inscribe visual and bodily changes of situation as both open-ended and vitally bound by the existential finitude and bodily limits of its particular vision and historical consciousness (that is, its autobiographical narrative). Unlike the photograph, a film is engaged semiotically not merely as a mechanical objectification, a *reproduction*, that is itself merely an object for vision. Rather, however mechanical its origin, the moving picture is experienced semiotically as also intentional and subjective, as *presenting a representation* of the objective world. Perceived not only as an *object for vision* but also as a *subject of*

---

ed. Joseph J. Kockelmans and Theodore J. Kisiel (Evanston, IL: Northwestern Univ. Press, 1970), pp. 274–311. This distinction is also the major focus of Patrick A. Heelan, *Space-Perception and the Philosophy of Science* (Berkeley: Univ. of California Press, 1983).

[13] Danto, "Moving Pictures," p. 17.

vision, a moving picture is not experienced precisely as a *thing* that, like the photograph, can be easily controlled, contained, or materially possessed. The spectator can share (and thereby, to a degree, interpretively alter) a film's presentation and representation of its embodied and always self-displacing experience and production of meaning. But, except by radically passing cinema through the "defiles" of the electronic, the spectator cannot control or contain a film's always emerging and ephemeral flow and rhythm or materially possess its animated experience (although now one can easily possess its inanimate "body").[14] In sum, like the existential and embodied consciousness of which Merleau-Ponty speaks, the film effects the "abusive transition" from one region to another, generating cinematic situation from photographic point of view, and cinematic momentum from photographic moment. This genesis, however, is necessarily dependent upon *movement*. Thus, for both ourselves and the cinema, intentionality (the correlational structure of consciousness) inflected in existence is also always a mobile structure, inscribing itself in the world as the agency and movement of the *lived-body*.

Turning from Husserl in his location of intentionality in existence, Merleau-Ponty stresses the significance (as well as the signifying power) of the lived-body. The lived-body not only incarnates consciousness but also animates its intentional structure as the movement of a material and finite being-to-the-world that cannot but generate and mark diacritical value in its every expressive act of perception. Even as the structure of existential consciousness remains invariant in its finitude, its being present to the world, and in its possession of that world in a particular and limited set of modalities, the lived-body's genesis of meaning in the world occurs as situated and contingent. Thus, the lived-body's incarnation of intentionality allows for both the "static originality" that is the sameness and invariance of *being*, and for those "abusive transitions" that are the differences that motion marks off in its temporalization and spatialization of the world as *becoming*.

---

[14] This ability to control the autonomy and flow of the cinematic (through freezing images, "fast forwarding," "replaying" portions of the film's experience) and to possess its "body" so as to willfully animate it at home (rather than have to go to the theater where its animation is beyond one's control), is all a function of the "materiality" of the electronic (specifically the videocassette and player/recorder)—a medium that has its own ontology and, in numerous and radical ways, has appropriated and transformed the cinematic.

63

No matter how it changes, my body is always and invariantly mine: as me and with me, my primary and necessary mode of access to the world. My body is always where I and the world meet in the experience of consciousness and the consciousness of experience. However, being mine in a limited and finite way, allowing me access to a world that exceeds the situated and finite opening I have upon it and am within it, my body in its stubborn materiality makes it both necessary and possible to move within and spatialize the world that my intentions inhabit. Movement is necessary because my consciousness as incarnate is not a transcendental structure, omniscient and omnipresent. And movement is possible because as my consciousness is incarnate and in touch with the world, it now has the means and the matter to actualize and accomplish its intentional projects. As Mary Rose Barral puts it: "Very briefly: consciousness is a way of being; to be conscious is to communicate with the world and with others, to be with and not merely alongside things or others as exterior objects. There is a relation which embraces both spatiality and time: our manner of sensing our body is always tied to a condition which situates the body-subject as well as the related exterior objects in a certain place and at a certain time. No one can avoid this situation."[15]

In his analysis of Husserl, Derrida rightly points out that "it is always something like an *opening* which will frustrate the structuralist project. What I can never understand, in a structure, is that by means of which it is not closed."[16] The "something like an opening," the "that by means of which" the structure of consciousness is not transcendentally closed, is the lived-body. The lived-body is the "opening" through which the invariant structure of consciousness gains access *to* the world, but it is also what Merleau-Ponty likes to describe as a "fold" *in* the world (a nice insistence that the body is part of the world's materiality). The fold in the world that is the lived-body situates the *access* of consciousness to the world in a world that *exceeds* the lived-body's situation and perspective and that surrounds it as an infinitely rich and variable *horizon* toward which intentionality is concretely directed.

By locating the intentional structure of consciousness in existence and in the finite and situated lived-body, Merleau-Ponty dynamizes

---

[15] Mary Rose Barral, *Merleau-Ponty: The Role of the Body-Subject in Interpersonal Relations* (Pittsburgh, PA: Duquesne Univ. Press, 1965), p. 135.

[16] Derrida, " 'Genesis and Structure' and Phenomenology," p. 160.

the static structure of intentionality in existential *action*. Intentionality is *expressed* by the body-subject living in the world; it becomes manifest, *signified*. Thus, "the human body is the vehicle of human communication by reason of its mere physical existence."[17] In conventional semiotic terms, the lived-body is the *signifier* of intentionality, but it is so only in its action as an existence that intends, only in its *activity of signifying*. (A dead body is a signifier that has lost its signified: the power to signify.) The existential dynamization of intentionality through the lived-body also manifests the essentially correlational nature of consciousness as invariantly *directed*. That is, finite and situated as the lived-body, intentionality is manifest in the always *diacritical value* we live through perception and expression as the experience of consciousness and the consciousness of experience—in other words, as prereflective and reflective *meaning*. The meaning of any given situation or context is invariably correlated with how that situation or context is taken, but that situation or context must be taken finitely and within the limits of a situated perspective and its correlated direction. Significance and signification co-emerge with the directional movements of the finite lived-body—for as the lived-body intends *toward* one object of consciousness, it necessarily turns *away* from another. Thus, a *choice* is made, a *value* ascribed and inscribed. Such choice occurs even when it is not explicitly willed and, indeed, remains latent as the background against which deliberate choices stand out as willed.

Thus, it is important to emphasize that the lived-body chooses as the very condition of its existence in the world, and that this choosing need not figure *in* consciousness for it to mark consciousness *as* an active presence selecting what counts and has value for it. As Merleau-Ponty explains: "This is why Husserl distinguishes between intentionality of act, which is that of our judgments and of those occasions when we voluntarily take up a position . . . and operative intentionality . . . , or that which produces the natural and antepredicative unity of the world and of our life, being apparent in our desires, our evaluations and in the landscape we see, more clearly than in objective knowledge, and furnishing the text which our knowledge tries to translate into precise language."[18] What is being spoken of here is the original intentionality of the body-subject. "Operative

---

[17] Lanigan, *Speaking and Semiology*, p. 46.

[18] Maurice Merleau-Ponty, *Phenomenology of Perception*, trans. Colin Smith (London: Routledge and Kegan Paul, 1962), p. xviii.

intentionality" is primordial and does not need to be predicated to consciousness as choice for it to be choice. Thus, whether explicitly represented to consciousness through reflection or latently and primordially present in the action of prereflective consciousness, each and every "dimension of experience has its directional and referential focus: It is *intentional*."[19]

As Husserl's transcendental and static structure, intentionality creates only the possibility and potentiality for the emergence of meaning and signification. However, as an existential and dynamically functional structure, intentionality shows itself through the lived-body as it perceives and gestures in the world and genetically constitutes the human phenomena of meaning and signification. The "origins of perception, motility and representation" are "vital," Merleau-Ponty tells us; their original source is the lived-body that takes up the world and expresses it in an "intentional arc" that "endows experience with its degree of vitality and fruitfulness."[20] Merleau-Ponty thus converts Husserl's transcendental phenomenology to an existential and semiotic phenomenology, converts intentionality as the static structure of consciousness to intentionality as it is incarnate and dynamically constitutive of the meaning we live as *conscious experience*.

Thus, in the first of a set of "communication theorems," Richard Lanigan tells us, "Conscious experience is the minimal unit of meaning in communication."[21] This Theorem of Intentionality predicates conscious experience as the irreducible, and minimal, unit necessary to the existence of meaning. The theorem also points to the always social, directed, referential, mobile, and diacritical nature of intentionality as it functions as *choice* in existence and in the world. Meaning is reducible to neither a location in consciousness (it is not purely or transcendentally subjective), nor a location in the objects of consciousness (it is not purely or transcendentally objective). Rather, it emerges *in situ*, as the *intersection* and *correlation* of consciousness and object whose location is in the inhabited and intentional space lived temporally as the body being-in-the-world. Stressing communication as well as meaning, the theorem also logically entails *persons*—body-subjects—as the necessary agency and agents of meaning as it is ar-

---

[19] Don Ihde, *Experimental Phenomenology: An Introduction*, p. 157.

[20] Merleau-Ponty, *Phenomenology of Perception*, p. 157.

[21] Richard L. Lanigan, "Communication Models in Philosophy," in *Communication Yearbook III*, ed. Dan Nimmo (New Brunswick, NJ: Transaction Books, 1979), p. 46.

ticulated in the consciousness of experience. And, if all this sounds obvious, we should remind ourselves that the phenomena scrutinized by most rational and scientific approaches to the human sciences and the arts (including film) are perceived as objects amputated from the persons for whom they exist, by whom they are perceived, and from whom they acquire their meaning as objects.

It is the lived-body, the person, finite in his or her actual situation in the world, inserted in the world and present to it always "on the bias," who sets the *limits* of intentionality as the latter in-forms material existence and is ex-pressed by it. The limits of the body provide the impetus and need for the *directional movements* of consciousness. The body's limitations provide the necessity for choice, for the ascription of value to the world, and for the predication and recognition of choice and value as the lived-body inaugurates for consciousness the sense of its own choice-making necessity and power. Thus, the lived-body serves to animate the static reversibility of the transcendental structure of consciousness into a *directed trajectory.* This trajectory and its movement as a directed choice of consciousness functions to diacritically mark and distinguish an origin and a destination as the boundary conditions of an *intentional act,* and to mark off the poles of that act in an *intentional object* and an *intending subject.* The lived-body also locates and localizes the body-subject as unique and as an invariant and permanent address for intentional acts that consciousness, by means of its "mobile home," has the power to temporalize and spatialize both as "centered" experience and "personal" experience. As well, the lived-body not only situates intentionality as and at a permanent existential address but it also has the capacity to send this address forth as expression and to call it back as perception. Indeed, it is from this capacity to *reverse* the directional trajectory between intentional correlates (intending subject and intentional object) that the correlates emerge as diacritical markers of a lived *system* of differences, as the actual situation of diacritical value within the *unity* of a particular situated existence.

These correlational movements and their reversibility are effected through and as the lived-body in the commutation and dialectic of perception and expression. By virtue of its material presence to and situation in the world, the lived-body's commutation of essence to existence, of structure to genesis, is also a commutation of intentionality to perception and its reversibility as expression. Thematizing the necessary structure of communication, Lanigan puts it aptly, "In short, a person's perceptions set the expressed boundaries of trans-actions."[22] Thus, perception and its correlative modality of expression enjoy attention as the privileged objects of existential and semiotic phenomenology. Indeed, Merleau-Ponty has not only devoted an entire work to the investigation of perception (his *Phenomenology of Perception*) but has spent all of his philosophical life returning again and again to perception as the "original text" of conscious experience, and thus of phenomenology itself.[23] As J. Quentin Lauer says of Merleau-Ponty: "Like Husserl, the experience he chooses to describe is primarily perception, but the mutual conditioning of world and perceptive consciousness is a far cry from Husserl's purely constitutive phenomenology. The advantage of this is that it enables Merleau-Ponty to describe *man's body not as an object but as a condition for* objectivity, as the point of contact between consciousness and the world. Meanings are contributed by consciousness, it is true, but these are based on a pregiven world, whose givenness is mediated by the body."[24]

Merleau-Ponty goes to great lengths to demonstrate that perception is more than a mosaic of discrete sensations and more than their sum. Perception is a *primordial structure* of encounter and engagement of the lived-body with and in the world. It is the mode of access, the opening upon the world, that allows consciousness its objects through the agency of the body. Thus, perception becomes the existential paradigm of intentionality, the "original text" or expression of the structure of consciousness which "carries its meaning within itself" as it shows itself, as it is manifest as *être-au-monde* (being present at and in the world).[25] Before perception can be predicated (that is, intended as an object of consciousness), it must itself provide the horizon and grounds that make predication possible.[26] And this perception does. As a prereflective organizational encounter with the world, perception does carry its meaning within itself, does provide access to itself, does emerge in the world as the structuring action of prereflective consciousness that precedes and makes possible perception's manifestation to itself as its own object. Indeed,

---

[22] Ibid, p. 39.

[23] Merleau-Ponty, *Phenomenology of Perception*, p. 21.

[24] J. Quentin Lauer, *The Triumph of Subjectivity: An Introduction to Transcendental Phenomenology* (New York: Fordham Univ. Press, 1958), p. 182. (Emphasis mine)

[25] Merleau-Ponty, *Phenomenology of Perception*, p. 21.

[26] Ibid., pp. 36–37.

the word *action* here must be related to the most primordial involuntary gestures of existence rather than to the willed and deliberate performance of reflective consciousness. Barral points out that for Merleau-Ponty, "the general habits of the body can be meaningfully related to the motor habits; and if we understand these, then we can elucidate the general synthesis of the body, for in a very general sense any activity of the body could be viewed as a motion—that is, *even perception is a sort of movement towards the object;* further, it is often followed by the spatial movement towards the object perceived."[27]

In its manifestation as operative intentionality (the primordial lived-through choice or action by which consciousness has access to the world and others), perception originates and limits the field of experience—the *ground* against which it may itself appear to consciousness as the *figure* of experience. As Merleau-Ponty says, "Perception is not a science of the world, it is not even an act, a deliberate taking up of a position; it is the background from which all acts stand out, and is presupposed by them."[28]

Perception as Gestalt

Perception both grounds and figures as the very action and performance of existence. That is, it predicates itself as an always reversible figure-ground correlation and makes itself, existence, consciousness, and the body-subject stand not only as the grounds of intentional activity but also as figures available to consciousness as intentional objects. Merleau-Ponty tells us, "Perception is just that act which creates at a stroke along with the cluster of data, the meaning which unites them—indeed which not only discovers the meaning *which they have*, but moreover sees to it *that they have meaning*."[29] Correlating consciousness and the world through the agency and action of the lived-body, perception is a living and *organizing organization* of the world, a *textualizing* of the sensing body in its contact with a sensible world.[30] Thus, perception is always already the *expression* of inten-

[27] Barral, *Merleau-Ponty: The Role of the Body-Subject in Interpersonal Relations,* p. 140. (Emphasis mine)

[28] Merleau-Ponty, *Phenomenology of Perception,* pp. x–xi.

[29] Ibid., p. 36. (Emphasis mine)

[30] In connection here between "text" and perception and the sensing and sensible lived-body, emphasis is on the derivation of "text" from its sensible forms as "texture" and "tissue."

tionality in the world and, as such, always already a judgment, an interpretation. As Merleau-Ponty puts it: "Once perception is understood as interpretation, sensation, which has provided a starting-point, is finally superseded, for all perceptual consciousness is already beyond it. The sensation is not experienced, and consciousness is always consciousness of an *object*."[31] In its existential function, then, perception is always semiotic and hermeneutic. It is sense as primordial Logos.[32] It is the intelligible utterance of intentionality in the world.

Although he rejects its more causal determinations, Merleau-Ponty draws heavily upon Gestalt psychology and its investigations into the phenomenon of perception. Perception emerges in existence quite literally as a *con-figuration*: as both that which is *against* figuration and serves as its ground, and that which is *with* figure and stands out against a ground. While not a deliberate act, perception is the very deliberating action that predicates itself in the irreducible and reversible structure of a *figure-ground correlation*. This existential structure clothes the irreducible and reversible structure of intentionality in a material woven from embodied consciousness and its encounter with the world.

For both the Gestalt psychologists and Merleau-Ponty, the figure-ground correlation is the fundamental basis of perception—whether it is prereflectively lived-through as existential engagement with the world or whether it is reflectively and reflexively turned back on itself and transformed from the action of consciousness to its object. Whether we perceive the world or we perceive perception, perception—as an irreducible correlation of figure and ground—forms and organizes a *perceptual field*. Emphasizing this correlation, Merleau-Ponty says: "It is the very definition of the phenomenon of perception, that without which a phenomenon cannot be said to be a perception at all. The perceptual 'something' is always in the middle of something else, it always forms part of a 'field.' A really homogeneous area offering *nothing to be* cannot be given to *any perception*. The structure of actual perception alone can teach us what perception is."[33]

[31] Merleau-Ponty, *Phenomenology of Perception*, p. 37. (Emphasis mine)

[32] For elaboration of these connections regarding perception and Logos, see Alphonso Lingis, "Translator's Preface," in Maurice Merleau-Ponty, *The Visible and the Invisible*, pp. l–liii.

[33] Merleau-Ponty, *Phenomenology of Perception*, p. 4.

It is clear that the correlational character of perception existentially embodies and is isomorphic with the correlational character of intentionality. Perception, like the structure of consciousness, is never empty but always the perception *of* something. Given its existential nature, its link with the body that is finite and always has a particularly directed and biased access to the world, perception *of* something is invariably the marking of a choice and the setting of boundaries that constitute a field or context and its primary significance. That is, although figure and ground are *reversible* correlates in perception (what was figure can become ground and vice versa), they are *never equivalent* in existence (the figure is always the object and choice of consciousness and perception, the value marked against the ground that is the field or context of perception).

Perception, therefore, is the diacritical emergence of judgment in existence. Perception is the radical and prereflective deliberation of the body-subject who, through perception and its expressive activity, is intentionally directed toward the world it lives in as an always interested and engaged existence. We do not decide in advance, prior to our perceptual engagement, the arrangement and organization of our perceptual field—what shall be figure and what shall be ground, and when a reversal of these correlates shall take place. Unless we are playing with ambiguous optical figures (like the previously mentioned tree puzzle or the Necker cube), unless we are deliberately straining our visual will in an attempt to reverse whatever immediate perception or configuration we took in relation to the figure we are attempting to bring to visibility, our perceptual choices emerge with the "operational" projects of our lives. These operational perceptual choices form the *perceptual field* or *horizon* that is the world-for-us, the world-already-significant. These operational perceptual choices also inform the particular *attention* we pay to that already-organized and meaningful world, a world immediately "given" to us in specific and grounded figures that we have actively "taken up" and signified without a conscious thought. As Merleau-Ponty says:

> To pay attention is not merely further to elucidate pre-existing data, it is to bring about a new articulation of them by taking them as *figures.* They are preformed only as *horizons,* they constitute in reality new regions in the total world. . . . Thus attention is neither an association of images, nor the return to itself of thought already in control of its objects, but the active constitution of a new object which makes ex-

plicit and articulate what was until then presented as no more than an indeterminate horizon. . . . This passage from the indeterminate to the determinate, this recasting at every moment of its own history in the unity of a new meaning, is thought itself.[34]

The gestalt of perception, its structured and structuring expression of intentionality in existence, its constitution of both the grounds for systematicity and a concrete system of engagement with the world, gives it a privileged status, a primacy in any empirical investigation of the radical origins of language. As the empirically *formal* link between embodied consciousness and any significance the world might have for it, perception—as lived expression—brings a latent, operative *thought* and *language* into existence. In the sense that Merleau-Ponty speaks of perception as "thought itself," he speaks of a logic of the lived-body—an organizing structure, a theory-in-use that has not yet posed itself as an object of consciousness but is consciousness's busy activity in the world. Because perception not only *engages* consciousness with the world in a gestalt structure but also *expresses* through that gestalt the structure and structuring activity of consciousness in existence, perception is that primary action of the lived-body and consciousness that originates language as action and gesture. As primordial Logos, perception is the logic and inflection of the lived-body—a latent expression that has not yet heeded itself but is busy acting out its logical system of differences and commutations as communication with the world and with others.

Perception, existentially embodied, functions in a threefold manner. First, perception *presents* itself to the world *as* the concrete manifestation of intentionality. It *is* intentionality commuted to existence through the body's presence in the world; it is the body's material presence that gives intentionality existential form as a concrete activity. Second, perception *connects* intentionality with the world; it *points to* and indicates the world's presentness to consciousness and its objective presence—a presence toward which intentionality is directed through the lived-body and its perceptive activity. That is, as intentionality is made a concrete presence in the material world in the existential and embodied activity of perception, the activity of perception is able to commute the material world into an expression that is concretely available and meaningful to intentionality. Third, perception *represents* itself to itself and to others in the world as the existen-

[34] Ibid., pp. 30–31.

tial condition and expressive convention of intentionality. As consciousness is aware of itself in existence, it is aware as a perceiving consciousness capable of perception; perception is not only intentionality prereflectively presenting itself to the world and others through its projects, but it is also intentionality reflectively representing itself to itself as consciousness and its significant experience of existence.

Given these three functions of perception in existence, perception as it is lived and made concrete through the body-subject can be said to originate the correlations of the *sign* in the most primordial and seemingly prelogical movements of its being-in-the-world. Language and communication, however, do not emerge merely because I *have* a body as an *instrument* of perception that brings them into being. Rather, I *am* my body. My body as lived perceptively, as engaged intentionally with the world, is already languaging and communicating by virtue of its systemic structure and material correlation with the world. Thus, Merleau-Ponty says: "By these words, the 'primacy of perception,' we mean that the experience of perception is our presence at the moment when things, truths, values are constituted for us; that perception is a nascent *logos*; that it teaches us, outside all dogmatism, the true conditions of objectivity itself; that it summons us to the tasks of knowledge and action. It is not a question of reducing human knowledge to sensation, but of assisting at the birth of this knowledge, to make it as sensible as the sensible, to recover the consciousness of rationality."[35] As the nondeliberative but articulating action of existence through which consciousness has access to the world and to itself as a unified system of differences, perception simultaneously originates significance and semiosis. It originates a field of experience as the world *for* consciousness against which it may itself figure as consciousness *of* the world, as the world *expressed by* consciousness *to* itself.

Put in Umberto Eco's specifically semiotic terms, perception as gestalt and as a structuring action can be considered the *sign-function* of intentionality. That is, perception makes *intentionality* manifest in the world and to others as the *content plane* of conscious existence. Correlatively, as the agency and agent of intentionality, the lived-body

[35] Maurice Merleau-Ponty, "The Primacy of Perception and Its Philosophical Consequences," trans. James M. Edie, in *The Primacy of Perception*, ed. James M. Edie (Evanston, IL: Northwestern Univ. Press, 1964), p. 25.

73

can be considered the *sign-vehicle* of intentionality. That is, the *lived-body* is that which commutes and carries intentionality into the material world as a concrete manifestation and is thus the *expression plane* of conscious existence.[36] Together, perception and the lived-body—irreducible as the manifestation of conscious existence in the world—constitute the *sign* of intentionality in existence and the world. They also constitute the activity of signification, of *sign-production*.

C. S. Pierce's semiotic phenomenalism is particularly helpful in explicating the complexity of the sign of intentionality in existence that is the correlation of perception/lived-body. The way in which the perceptive body stands in relation to that which it is a sign of (intentional consciousness) has been briefly indicated already, but it can be clarified further through Pierce's classification of those relations as *iconic*, *indexical*, and *symbolic*.[37] An *iconic* sign is in *monadic* relation with what it signifies. That is, it claims similarity, resemblance, physical identity to its signified. In this sense, the perceptive body is an iconic sign. Perception, as it is lived through the body, diagrammatically represents the internal relations, the irreducible correlations, of intentionality and thus is identical in structure—homeomorphic—to the structure of consciousness. Perception *is*, therefore, intentionality-in-existence; it *presents* itself to the world and in it as the concrete, existential manifestation of intentionality. My perceptive body *is* my intentionality in the world, is in existence and as representation identical to it. As Merleau-Ponty puts it, "I am not in front of my body, I am in it, or rather I am it."[38]

---

[36] Eco, *A Theory of Semiotics*, pp. 48ff. Also note the recasting of the Saussurean SR/SD in the more existential terminology *vehicle* and *function*.

[37] For a brief discussion of Pierce's semiotic trichotomy, see Lanigan, *Speaking and Semiology*, pp. 52–54; Umberto Eco, "Pierce and the Semiotic Foundations of Openness: Signs as Texts and Texts as Signs," in *The Role of the Reader: Explorations in the Semiotics of Texts* (Bloomington, IN: Indiana Univ. Press, 1979), pp. 175–199; and Eugene Freeman, *The Categories of Charles Pierce* (Chicago, IL: Open Court, 1934). For specific discussions of Pierce's semiology and its relation to film, see Peter Wollen, *Signs and Meaning in the Cinema* new and enlarged ed. (Bloomington: Indiana Univ. Press, 1972), pp. 116–154; Gorham A. Kindem, "Pierce's Semiotic Phenomenalism and Film," *Quarterly Review of Film Studies* 4 (Winter 1979), pp. 61–69; Teresa deLauretis, *Alice Doesn't: Feminism, Semiotics, Cinema* (Bloomington: Indiana Univ. Press, 1984), and *Technologies of Gender: Essays on Theory, Film, and Fiction* (Bloomington: Indiana Univ. Press, 1987); and Gaylyn Studlar, *In the Realm of Pleasure: Von Sternberg, Dietrich, and the Masochistic Aesthetic* (Urbana, IL: Univ. of Illinois Press, 1988).

[38] Merleau-Ponty, *Phenomenology of Perception*, p. 150.

An *indexical* sign is in *dyadic* relation with what it signifies. It does not claim resemblance or identity, but rather contiguity with what it signifies; that is, an indexical sign has some existential bond or connection with what it represents. In this sense, the perceptive body is always also not only an iconic sign but an indexical sign. Perception as it is lived through the body is that which places intentionality in contiguity with the world and constitutes an existential bond between consciousness and the world. As mentioned previously, the perceptive body *points to* the world's presentness to and for consciousness, and to consciousness's presence to and in the world. It is the means of connection whereby I can say and know that I *have* a world.

Finally, a *symbolic* sign is in *triadic* relation with what it signifies. It does not depend upon resemblance or contiguity, but rather upon its formal connection with the signified and upon its conventional use. In other words, the symbolic sign's power to signify is ruled by *convention*: perceptive and expressive persons coming together in cultural agreement whereby the relation between the signifier and its signified is arbitrarily made to *stand as* a sign. This relation is triadic because it introduces the social "other" (or the conscious and reflective "self") as a term of the sign and as a necessary condition of its being taken as such. In this sense, the perceptive body can be understood not only as an iconic and indexical sign but also as a symbolic sign. Perception as it is lived through the body is that which is agreed upon in existence with others to stand for others as conscious existence. As mentioned previously, the perceptive body thus *represents* intentionality in the world to others and to the reflective consciousness that lives the perceptive body as "mine."

These relations in which, semiotically, the perceptive body stands iconically *as*, indexically *connected to*, and symbolically *for*, intentionality operate simultaneously and synoptically in existence. Gorham Kindem points out: "Pierce is unable to instance pure icons, indices, and symbols from his experience, finding mixtures of iconic, indexical, and symbolic *aspects* in every semiotic phenomenon he examines. Thus, Pierce's categories of signs are not mutually exclusive (except as theoretical entities), since they invariably overlap and are copresent in every experiential example."[39] The primary and most radical "experiential example" of this copresence of semiotic relations in a

---

[39] Kindem, "Pierce's Semiotic Phenomenalism and Film," p. 62.

single semiotic phenomenon is the perceptive and expressive body. Intentionality (the structure of consciousness) is *commuted* in existence to perception (its sign-function) through the agency of the sensible and material body (its sign-vehicle) and *communicates* (or represents) existence as the action and expression of consciousness in the world and to others. Thus, significance and signifying originate with the perceptive body and from its structure and modality of being-expression-in-the-world. As David Carr summarizes: "Through the gesture, the body becomes expression, the bearer of meaning into the world. The upper limit of this expression is speech, and the body becomes an essential condition of language rather than the merely instrumental transmitter of pure thoughts."[40] The material body (the body that matters) enacts the irreducible gestalt of perception and radically *incorporates* and *lives* the irreducible structure of the sign and the genetic process of sign production. Empirically as well as semiotically speaking, we *are* the signifying system of differences that expresses the person being-in-the-world to others and to ourselves.

Perception as Synaesthetic and Synoptic

Perception, we have seen, is a gestalt, the organizing activity of an embodied intentionality that engages the world in an always structured and structuring encounter. However, as the irreducible existential structure of consciousness animated by and as a sensible body, perception is also always *synaesthetic* and *synoptic*. That is, perception is not constituted as a sum of discrete senses (sight, touch, etc.), nor is it experienced as fragmented and decentered. *All* our senses are modalities of perception and, as such, are co-operative and commutable. Such cooperation among and commutation of our senses occurs in existence because our senses all figure on the finite and situated field that is our body. Each lived discretely as "mine" yet objectively available to others, our bodies provide the place upon and within which conscious experience is both inscribed and circumscribed.

The importance of the body as the agency and location of perception cannot be overemphasized. As Lanigan says: "The body is the vehicle for perception and expression and it is the agency that allows

---

[40] David Carr, "Maurice Merleau-Ponty: Incarnate Consciousness," in *Existential Philosophers: Kierkegaard to Merleau-Ponty*, ed. George Alfred Schrader, Jr. (New York: McGraw Hall, 1967), pp. 395–396.

one to engage in the reversible process of being in public and private existence. The body allows sensation and intellection to emerge as perception, and later on, the body will be seen as the medium in which language becomes speaking."[41] Perception, therefore, as it is lived by the body, is not reducible to either intellection or sensation. Rather, both in-form the body as the pervasiveness of *perception*. In existence, it is as impossible to experience or describe a "pure sensation" as it is to experience or describe a "pure thought." Sensation as it is experienced by the lived-body is brought to consciousness in thought and language—and thought and language as they are experienced by consciousness are brought to being through the sensibility of the lived-body.

David Carr points out, "The most isolated excitation of one sense takes place within a total field of perception and is in a certain relation—spatial, temporal, etc.—to other aspects of this field."[42] Or, as Merleau-Ponty puts it, "My body is the field within which my perceptive powers are localized."[43] Thus, it becomes literally nonsensical to talk of the senses as if they were isolated from their entailment in an intentional structure or from each other, to speak of them as if they were discrete modes of access to the world rather than *differentiated* modalities of perceptual access to the world. The senses are different openings to the world that cooperate as a *unified system* of access. The lived-body does not have senses. It is, rather, sensible. It is, from the first, a perceptive body.

The co-operative modalities and commutative system of the bodily senses that structure existential perception are called *synaesthesia*. As a perceptive body, I am able to see texture. My sense of sight is pervaded by my sense of touch. Smell is cooperative with taste and taste with sight. Even when my perception seems most focused and localized in a single of its modalities, when it seems dominated and directed by a single "sense," all of its other modalities form the ground of that focus and are usually (although not always) in sympathy with it. Merleau-Ponty deserves quoting at length in this regard:

The sight of sounds or the hearing of colours come about in the same way as the unity of the gaze through the two eyes: in so far as my

---

[41] Lanigan, *Speaking and Semiology*, p. 126.

[42] Carr, "Maurice Merleau-Ponty: Incarnate Consciousness," pp. 388–389.

[43] Maurice Merleau-Ponty, "The Philosopher and His Shadow," in *Signs*, trans. Richard C. McCleary (Evanston, IL: Northwestern Univ. Press, 1964), p. 166.

body is, not a collection of adjacent organs, but a synergic system, all the functions of which are exercised and linked together in the general action of being in the world. . . . There is a sense in saying that I see sounds or hear colours so long as sight and hearing is not the mere possession of an opaque *quale*, but the experience of a modality of existence, the synchronisation of my body with it, and the problem of forms of synaesthetic experience begins to look like being solved if the experience of a quality is that of a certain mode of movement or of a form of conduct. When I say that I see a sound, I mean that I echo the vibration of the sound with my whole sensory being. . . . my body is a ready-made system of equivalents and transpositions from one sense to another. The senses translate each other without any need of an interpreter, and are mutually comprehensible without the intervention of any idea.[44]

My sense of sight, then, is a modality of perception that is commutable to my other senses, and vice-versa. My sight is never only sight—it sees what my ear can hear, my hand can touch, my nose can smell, and my tongue can taste. My entire bodily existence is implicated in my vision.

This translation or commutability of the senses, their co-operation and co-presence as modalities of a perception that is localized in a lived-body, can be particularly appreciated if we look at research that explores the world of perceptually handicapped people. Here a focus on the "unusual" experience tells us something radical about the "ordinary" experience we take for granted as "given" in our everyday perceptual praxis. We can learn much about the fundamental synaesthesia we experience as perception but tend to consciously "fix" in its discrete modalities, by looking at investigations into embodied perception as diverse as Werner Herzog's *Land of Silence and Darkness* (a documentary film on blind and deaf people) and Oliver Sacks's *The Man Who Mistook His Wife for a Hat and Other Clinical Tales* (a set of narrative accounts about the perceptive worlds of neurologically impaired people).[45] Speaking to Merleau-Ponty's similar use of the unusual case of perceptual experience to put our "usual" perceptual experience in relief, Thomas Langan points out:

---

[44] Merleau-Ponty, *Phenomenology of Perception*, pp. 234–235.

[45] Werner Herzog, *Land of Silence and Darkness* [*Land des Schweigens und der Dunkelheit*] (1971); Oliver Sacks, *The Man Who Mistook His Wife for a Hat and Other Clinical Tales* (New York: Summit Books, 1985).

While both the voluntary ego and objective thing implicitly depend on the actual body's living in the world and making an experience possible in the first place, the bodily synthesis nevertheless goes about its task so silently, so fundamentally, that its . . . contribution is no more noticed than the light which illumines and thus makes possible every visible spectacle. Only unusual experiences revealing a fissure in the otherwise unrelieved atmosphere of an already constructed world—the hallucination, the illusion, anything which causes the smooth unfolding of the world suddenly not to be taken so much for granted—can provide the epoché—needed to suspend the practical experience's attention-absorbing hold on us.[46]

Thus, in our present quest to see vision as a radical act, to know what "we" and "seeing" are, blind people provide us perception's "unusual experience" and cause us not to take for granted the "smooth unfolding of the world" in which it seems our sight is absolutely distinct from our other senses.

If, for example, a person is congenitally blind, those of us in the "natural attitude" might expect that person's ability to understand or to perform an act of *depiction* would be nonexistent. That is, we would not expect the congenitally blind person to be able to *visibly* represent through a conventional system of inscription a referent experienced *visually*. This would seem to necessitate not only visual experience but also the consciousness of a system of commutation whereby the subjective visual act of taking up the world in images is transformed into the production of objectively visible imagery. The expectations of our "natural attitude," however, are subverted in actual existence.

A provocative article by John M. Kennedy recording the results of his research with blind people indicates that blind people can both understand and draw braille pictures in outline.[47] These depictions not only indicate an understanding of the commutative system whereby perception of an object is transformed as its expression but also indicate the presence of a clear sense of the qualities of "perspective" and motion and a system for their representation. Given various tasks to perform involving the explication of a set of braille

[46] Thomas Langan, *Merleau-Ponty's Critique of Reason* (New Haven, CT: Yale Univ. Press, 1966), pp. 22–23.

[47] John M. Kennedy, "Pictures and the Blind," *Journal of the University Film Association* 32 (Winter-Spring 1980), pp. 11–22.

drawings and their own spontaneous depiction of assigned subjects (a hand, a drinking glass, a table, a man, a man running, a wheel, and a wheel spinning), the choice of signifiers and the depictions of visually impaired people were surprisingly similar to those of their sighted peers. Naively, we might respond that such depiction is possible for blind people to achieve because they were depicting in braille; braille is, after all, a mode of representation that is commuted into objective intelligibility not through sight, but through the discrete sense of touch and its discriminations. If anything, this braille depiction seems to prove rather than disprove the discretion of the senses. However, the evidence of Kennedy's research goes beyond dramatizing the merely substitutive perceptive value of touch in relation to sight. Through their understanding of the concept of picture and their ability to translate their *sense of touch* into visible drawings that are intelligible to those with the *sense of sight*, the blind people of Kennedy's study are dramatizing not perceptual substitution but perceptual commutation. They are demonstrating the essential nature and function of perception as irreducible to any single of its modalities.

Kennedy considers some of the "general lessons" his research teaches us (lessons, phenomenology would suggest, we learn at the moment of our birth and live every moment of our lives but forget in the narrow figures and attention of our abstract thought). First, despite specific difficulties in depiction in specific instances, *blind people are capable of understanding depiction.* Kennedy reports: "They can draw. They can recognize. They can use elements like lines and dots. They can understand whole shapes, or parts. They can select what is important and capture that. They can recognize ambiguities. They can appreciate how two drawings will be more specific about an object than one."[48] Second, the blind are able to recognize and draw pictures that look pretty much the same as those drawn by sighted people. This evidence suggests that *picturing is more than a visual/visible expression of vision; it is the visual/visible expression of perception.* Describing the competence and performance of his blind subjects, Kennedy tells us:

> They have little or no previous pictorial experience. They have not been taught how to solve the mysteries of pictorial depiction. They figure out solutions on their own. Time and again, they come to iden-

[48] Ibid., p. 15.

tical realizations—individually, separately, each one facing the problems of *two-dimensional portrayal* on his own, they arrive at the same solutions. The inevitable conclusion is that the principles that underlie line representation belong to a *perceptual system that is not restricted to vision.* It is a system of principles that is *in common* to *haptics* and to *vision.* Presumably what is relevant is the apprehension of layout— shape, location, edge and surface. Also there is the principle that key relations can be extracted from a given object. . . . that boundaries can be shown by lines. . . . that the distribution of parts can be portrayed by the same distribution on paper, . . . that a *point of view* can be chosen, and the distribution of parts can be arranged to fit with a point of view. . . . none of the principles mention vision at all.[49]

Kennedy further describes two kinds of options that determine the manner of pictorial depiction and the application of its principles: Depiction can be literal, schematic, or metaphoric; and depiction can be organized under a single principle or several. And he goes on to stress the fact that these options do not inherently depend upon vision.

In this regard, the mathematical term *point of view* must be broadened and grounded—literally and empirically *incorporated* and *lived* as a "situation of being" available to both the sighted and the blind who are enworlded and embodied, perceptive and expressive. Thus, the third lesson of Kennedy's research is that *haptics includes perspective.* As might seem obvious—except for those who still consider pictorial depiction as totally dependent upon the capacity for visual activity— the blind not only experience perspective but can visibly depict it. Kennedy says of the blind: "The keys to perspective are already present in their familiar activities—a point of view, convergence, and shape transformation, and with good reason. Perspective is the mathematics of direction from a point. It makes no difference to perspective whether the directions are incoming like optics, or outgoing like pointing."[50] While one might quarrel with Kennedy's assumption that vision and pointing are unidirectional (one "incoming" and the other "outgoing") rather than reversible (both "incoming" and "outgoing"), it is clear that his research demonstrates that perspective is a *theoretical system* (and not the only system) derived and ab-

49 Ibid., p. 16. (Emphasis mine)
50 Ibid.

stracted from a *bodily system*.[51] Perception is a primary and lived systemic encounter with the world that is secondarily theorized as discretely dependent upon vision. Kennedy's work provides us with a dramatic reminder that perception is *synaesthetic* and that vision is only part of a co-operative production of sensible meaning and its representation.

Perception is also *synoptic*. That is, it is lived as the entirety and entity that is the lived-body as access to the world and to conscious experience. The various modalities of perception inform the body that is the field of perception and give perception form as conscious experience, as signification and significance. Thus, the body concretely and literally provides the *(bio)logical premises* for perception to be located as experience, as the meaningful encounter with a world. As Merleau-Ponty puts it:

> My body is the seat or rather the very actuality of the phenomenon of expression . . . , and there the visual and auditory experiences, for example, are pregnant one with the other, and their expressive value is the ground of the antepredicative unity of the perceived world, and, through it, of verbal expression . . . and intellectual significance. . . . My body is the fabric into which all objects are woven, and it is, at least in relation to the perceived world, the general instrument of my "comprehension."[52]

All the modalities of perception not only co-operate by virtue of their common field—my body, but also because of their common cause—my being-in-the-world, my body's intentional projection through existential projects. Thus, even before I have *represented* my being as a self to myself, I am living the sense and sensing the living of the organizing systemicity that is my *presentation* to the world as a presence in it. Although, in this primordial presentness, I may be "anonymous" to myself as the subject of my presentation, I am yet and always oriented to the world from the "here and now" that is the unified field of a body—not "any" body, but "some" body, a body that matters like no other because it is lived as "mine." It is my body that synopsizes the various modalities of perception so that the

[51] For a theoretical system of spatial relationships congruent with, rather than abstracted from, the bodily system of spatial coordination, the reader is directed to Heelan, *Space-Perception and the Philosophy of Science*.

[52] Merleau-Ponty, *Phenomenology of Perception*, p. 235.

perceived world makes its sense someplace, so that it has premises for its significance.

Even in the earliest stages of human development, long before there is self-consciousness, self-representation, and the constitution of the body-subject as an "I," there is a sense of *orientation* and a sense of *center*. As Richard Zaner says, "My animate organism has the sense of being the bearer of an orientational point, 'O', from which spatio-temporal coordinates organize and structure the milieu."[53] This is a description of the body as constituting the "zero-degree" of experience. A good deal of psychological research has demonstrated that the very young infant has no sense of differentiation from its world and from its mother in regard to its physical limits, its *boundaries* for being a synoptic organism. Nonetheless, research also has demonstrated that the "boundary-less" infant senses a *center*. The *circumscription* of self may not yet be accomplished; what is inside and what is outside the organism is not yet differentiated. However, the boundless *radius* of encounter with the world flows from and back to an *orientational center*, even if that center functions as an "invisible" and "anonymous" zero-point. "My organism, then," Zaner says, "is constituted for my experience as that 'on' and 'in' which fields of sensation are spread out, as the bearer of localized fields of sensation. As such it is a corporeal system or *context* of localized fields."[54]

Perception, then, is synoptic, however localized or global its particular modalities (vision, for example, more specifically localized than touch). It is lived as the body's total activity of accession to the world, its correlation of perceptive modalities to their function as enabling an intention toward and in the world. As Zaner says: "Just because of this functional correlation, the organism is itself *co-experienced* (co-intended) simultaneously with the sensuous perception of a content: every sensuous perception, to speak at a higher level, necessarily involves a co-perception of the organism itself as that with which I perceive and that by means of which what is perceived is perceived."[55] Unified spatially and temporally by its intentions toward the world and by its *sensed* as well as *sensible* encounter with that world's material substantiality, perception *co-heres* as the Here where intentions

---

[53] Richard M. Zaner, *The Problem of Embodiment: Some Contributions to a Phenomenology of the Body*, 2d ed. (The Hague: Martinus Nijhoff, 1971), p. 253.

[54] Ibid., p. 256.

[55] Ibid., p. 257.

emerge as existential action and where the world touches the lived-body and begins to have substance. That Here will be eventually constituted as the "self" to consciousness—as the reflective and reflexive body-subject, the "I" who perceives its own being. However, even in its primary and prereflective existence, the perceptive body has knowledge of its own existence. It may not yet be a Here where *I* am, but it is most surely a Here where material existence is sensibly experienced. Thus, the perceptive body is never just, or first, an anatomical *instrument* or physiological *object* of perception. It is always also uniquely the *subject* of perception; that is, it is always perceptive of its action of perceiving.

In *The Problem of Embodiment*, Zaner describes the four fundamental ways in which the body perceptively engages us in the world and articulates itself as perceptive at progressively higher, or more explicit, levels of consciousness. First, as has been mentioned previously, the perceptive body is the "bearer of the orientational point, O, with respect to which other objects are organized in the spatio-temporal surrounding world." Second, the perceptive body serves as an "organ of perception," that is, as a single technology with several sensory fields that provides us "that by means of which" we have access to the world and it exists for us. Third, the perceptive body is an organ of perception that, by virtue of its corporeal unity, synthesizes the several sensory fields as the place "on and in which my fields of sensation are spread out." Fourth, and last, the perceptive body is that which actualizes the spontaneous and operative "strivings of consciousness" and which, on a higher level, actualizes volition and signifies through gesture and language the intentionality of consciousness.[56]

The Here that is both a perceptive/sensing subject and a perceptible/sensible object, the Here that is the perceptive/expressive body, coheres. That is, it synoptically experiences the world and itself prior to self-articulation, self-representation. Zaner summarizes:

From the lowest levels of inner-time consciousness, consciousness is embodied: first of all, by its kinaesthetic flow-patterns, then, by the syntheses of identification, differentiation, and transfer of sense and unification, which constitute the various sensory fields as self-identical

---

[56] Ibid., pp. 249–251. See also Thomas Clark Knee, "A Dialogical Investigation of the Phenomenon of the Human Body," unpublished dissertation (Duquesne Univ., 1972), pp. 36–44.

and different from one another, and then constitute this organism as one single orientational point, . . . and so on. The phenomenology of the animate organism is, accordingly, the descriptive-explicative analysis of the continuously on-going automatic embodiment of consciousness by one organism singled out as peculiarly "its" own, and, at higher levels, graspable by me as "my own."[57]

Born(e) into the world with and as the action of a sensible *body*, perception has an existential and permanent address; it is situated, centered. Thus, even as perception extends beyond the body, transcends its permanent residence to reside in the world and with others, even as perception does not merely have an address but addresses the world and so continually decenters itself from its center, perception is always synaesthetic and synoptic by virtue of its finite and circumscribed embodiment of intentional consciousness.

Seeing and the Seen

Vision is a modality of perception. Thus, although it may be differentiated from our other "senses" (perceptive modes that give us access to the world as sensible), vision echoes in its particularity the intentional and gestalt structure of perception. It is also informed by the synaesthetic and synoptic articulations of perception as the text and texture that mark the perceptive body's ongoing engagement with a world as experience.

Vision is intentional in structure because it is never empty. It is invariantly an *act* correlated with an *object*; it is always the *seeing-of-a-some-thing-that-is-seen*. Merleau-Ponty tells us that "to see is *to have at a distance*."[58] Seeing as a structure thus implicates the visible world as exceeding vision and available to it as the provenance of vision's objects. Although sight possesses the world in its activity of seeing, it does not own or circumscribe the world. The seen comes into vision as potentially seeable by all, as occupying its own worldly space and concretely marking a distance between my incarnation and its own. This space is traversed by my intending gaze, and its traversal both affirms the object of my gaze and myself as the subject of the gaze in our mutually enworlded, but individual and differentiated, situa-

---

[57] Zaner, *The Problem of Embodiment*, pp. 260–261.

[58] Maurice Merleau-Ponty, "Eye and Mind," trans. Carleton Dallery, in *The Primacy of Perception*, p. 166.

tions. As consciousness is always consciousness *of*, indicating a difference and distance between consciousness and its objects within the intentional structure that is consciousness, so seeing is always seeing *of*, indicating a difference and distance between the visual activity of seeing and visible objects within the intentional structure invariably correlated as *vision*.

Like intentionality, vision is *directional in structure*. However, like the existential manifestation of intentionality in perception, vision is also always *directed in function*. It informs embodied existence as a finite and yet reversible motility. Thus, the movement of existential vision acts to diacritically differentiate and mark the visible from the invisible, the figure from the ground, the seen from the seer; and yet it also acts to transform each to the other or inform each with the other. Incarnate, vision is from its inception the intentional and existential *choosing* of the visible and the invisible. That is, what is taken up as seen by the act of seeing is taken from what will remain unseen. The *invisible* thus provides the grounds for the *visible* and is not only a *condition* but also a *content* of the act of seeing. The invisible is as much an empirical term of vision as is the visible. Seeing, therefore, like consciousness and perception, is a structuring action that is structured. It is an *open system* of engagement with the world that yields the specificity and forms of an intentional choice but also implicates the indeterminate and yet finite possibilities and context for that choice. Merleau-Ponty elaborates:

> That sort of diaphragm of the vision, which through a compromise with the whole to be seen yields my point of view upon the world, is to be sure not fixed: nothing prevents us from crossing the limits with the movements of the look, but this freedom remains secretly bound; we can only displace our look, that is transfer its limits elsewhere. But it is necessary that there be always a limit; what is won on one side must be lost from the other. An indirect and muted necessity weighs upon my vision. It is not the necessity of an objective frontier forever impassable, for the contours of my field are not lines. It is not cut out against an expanse of blackness; rather when I approach them, the things dissociate, my look loses its differentiation, and the vision ceases for lack of seer and of articulated things. Even without speaking of my motor power, I am therefore not shut up in one sector of the visible world. But I am curbed all the same, like those animals in zoological gardens without cages or bars, whose freedom gently comes to

an end by some trench a little too broad for them to clear at one bound. The openness upon the world implies that the world be and remain a horizon, not because my vision would push the world back beyond itself, but because somehow he who sees is of it and is in it.[59]

Vision is a system whose finite encounter with and in the world meets in the act of seeing at the axes of the visible and the invisible. Seeing can be described, therefore, as an activity of existential and semiotic choice in which the visible is inscribed in that *syntagmatic combination* called the "visual field" as a process of *selection* from the invisible, those *paradigmatic possibilities* offered by the world as "horizon." One's intentional projects are always inscribed in the selective combinations of vision—in the act of making visible, of choosing the limits of the seen and the situation of the seer. But this choice is never completed or completely discrete. What is seen and visible is infused with its partial invisibility and the alternative situations it presents as possible but not chosen by the seer. Similarly, what is not seen, what is invisible, is shaped and made present as much by its potential visibility as by its actual absence from the visual field. Thus, though absent from the visual field, the invisible is not *excluded* from that system of access to the world that is vision. Rather, "it is visible by right, it falls under a vision that is both ineluctable and deferred."[60] It seems no accident, then, that the word *seer* in our language situates its meaning problematically (yet aptly) on the border between the visible and invisible. *Seer* denominates one who *sees* that which is there to be seen in the present visual field, but it also names one who is able to *foresee*, to see temporally ahead beyond the limits of the visual field and its immediate presence to other visual fields, other visual situations with which the present one is always charged and connected.

The act of seeing echoes the irreducible but reversible structure of intentionality as it emerges in existence as the finite directedness of consciousness. It also echoes the similarly irreducible but reversible gestalt structure of perception as the organized and organizing relations of figure/ground. As an intentional activity that is finite in its incarnation and actualized as choice in existence, seeing manifests the diacritical directedness of intentionality—not merely its formal or theoretical *directionality*. The intentional trajectory of the act of seeing

---

[59] Merleau-Ponty, *The Visible and the Invisible*, pp. 99–100.
[60] Ibid., p. 137.

seeks its destination in *either* the intended objects of the world (or imagination) *or* in the intentional activity (and subject) of seeing, even as the trajectory of seeing binds the seen world and the seeing subject in the irreducible structure of its action. Thus, I cannot see the objects of the world insofar as I make my very act of seeing the object of my consciousness, and vice-versa. This is not to say that my visual field is nonexistent or empty when the object of my consciousness is my act of vision rather than visible objects. Rather, it is to indicate that when my visual field is unintended by me, it fades to a certain indeterminacy in which its visible contents are all equivalent. Merleau-Ponty provides a clear example of the intentional directedness of vision and its choices:

> I perceive this table on which I am writing. This means, among other things, that my act of perception *occupies me*, and occupies me sufficiently for me to be unable, while I am actually perceiving the table, to perceive myself perceiving it. When I want to do this, I cease, so to speak, to use my gaze in order to plunge into the table, I turn my back towards myself who am perceiving, and then realize that my perception must have gone through certain subjective appearances, and interpreted certain of my own "sensations"; in short it takes its place in the perspective of my individual history.[61]

In so far as I am plunged into the contents of my visual field by the agency of my gaze, I am occupied by the world and its intended meaning for me. But when I turn my consciousness intentionally toward my own conscious gaze, the world as the content of my visual field merely serves as the ground for the figure of my gaze. My visual field becomes an idle and equivocal presence to me that is not seen as meaningful. A mundane case in point would be the occasions when, "sightlessly," I "run" a red traffic light while driving. We've all done it: thinking about something not visibly present in our visual field, intending toward some other project than the act of seeing and the act of driving that have become automatic in their correlation, we're suddenly caught up short, after the fact, and realize we've driven through a red light. Perhaps an angry motorist honks, or perhaps our attention and intention is suddenly reflective on the previous content of our visual field and our lack of response to it. That visual field was seen, but it was not seen as intentionally meaningful

---

[61] Merleau-Ponty, *Phenomenology of Perception*, p. 238.

or determinate. Everything before our eyes was given equivalent and little value at the time we were disengaged from our vision, intending elsewhere. That is, our visual field still has visible content when we run a red light, but it does not "occupy" us, nor we it. Reflecting on what was seen (but unintended and thus unattended), we can now "see" the light as an intentional object. Its diacritical marking as an important figure to which we must respond is apparent to us in reflection as it was not in its actual visible presence.

Thus, the intentional structure of consciousness and its directedness in existence lays the foundation for the gestalt of perception and its particular modality as vision. The reversible but never-equivalent correlates *of* embodied consciousness (intentional act and intentional object) are expressed *as* the reversible but never-equivalent correlates of the visual field (ground and figure). The directedness of consciousness in existence chooses whether or not we will see our visual field as determining and determinate, and the directedness of perception as vision chooses what we shall see *in* that visual field, constituting in its intention and attention the visible figures of vision against its latently visible ground. The relation between the structure of consciousness and the structure of vision, then, can be described as one in which the *paradigmatic selection of consciousness* (its directed choice *either* toward its own intentional activity *or* toward its intentional objects) is in concert with the *syntagmatic combination in the visual field* (the field's correlative emergence as *both* figure *and* ground).

As intentional consciousness directs itself toward its intentional objects in the visible world, so *attention* brings that object into being with its focus. Attention determines the object as a figure against the unintended indeterminacy of its visible but "unseen" ground. Again, using the table as his example, Merleau-Ponty's description of the attending act is apt:

> I open my eyes on to my table, and my consciousness is flooded with colours and confused reflections; it is hardly distinguishable from what is offered to it; it spreads out through its accompanying body, into the spectacle which so far is not a spectacle of anything. Suddenly, I start to focus my eyes on the table which is not yet there, I begin to look into the distance while there is as yet no depth, my body centres itself on an object which is still only potential, and so disposes its sensitive surfaces as to make it a present reality. . . . The act of looking is indivisibly prospective, since the object is the final stage of my process of

focusing, and retrospective, since it will present itself as preceding its own appearance, as the "stimulus," the motive or the prime mover of every process since its beginning. . . . But every act of focusing must be renewed, otherwise it falls into unconsciousness. The object remains clearly before me provided that I run my eyes over it, free-ranging scope being an essential property of my gaze.[62]

There is, then, a certain latency in my visual field. There is something visible that is not yet a "thing," not yet a figure, that is merely an indeterminate ground from which my intention carves a figure in an active and ongoing attention and determination. Our visual field is filled, for example, with a visible light we do not precisely see that nonetheless enables us to see that which we consider visible. As Merleau-Ponty says: "Everyone with eyes has at some time or other witnessed this play of shadows, or something like it, and has been made by it to see a space and the things included therein. But it works in us without us; it hides itself in making the object visible. To see the object, it is necessary *not* to see the play of shadows and light around it. The visible in the profane sense forgets its premises; it rests upon a total visibility which is to be re-created and which liberates the phantoms captive in it."[63]

The painter, for Merleau-Ponty, is one for whom "profane" visibility and vision are not enough. (For us, such a one is the filmmaker.) To paint the profanely visible, the painter must be intimate with its premises, the ground of the visible within vision. Thus, the painter "interrogates with his gaze."[64] This painterly gaze is active and searching, resting not on the familiar forms or figures that vision has time and again constituted, but rather on the latent visibility from which such figures emerge and against which they stand in relation to its latency. Filmmaker Stan Brakhage captures this interrogation of the visible at the beginning of his *Metaphors on Vision:*

Imagine an eye unruled by man-made laws of perspective, an eye unprejudiced by compositional logic, an eye which does not respond in the name of everything but which must know each object encountered in life through an adventure of perception. How many colors are there

[62] Ibid, pp. 239–240. For further discussion of the particular structure of attention and its relation to cinematic vision, see also Vivian Sobchack, "The Active Eye: A Phenomenology of Cinematic Vision," *Quarterly Review of Film and Video* 12 (1990), pp. 21–36.
[63] Merleau-Ponty, "Eye and Mind," p. 167.
[64] Ibid., p. 166.

in a field of grass to the crawling baby unaware of "Green?" How many rainbows can light create for the untutored eye? How aware of variations in heat waves can that eye be? Imagine a world alive with incomprehensible objects and shimmering with an endless variety of movement and innumerable gradations of color. Imagine a world before the "beginning was the word."[65]

The painter's medium, the filmmaker's medium, is less paint or film than it is *sight*. Indeed, at their most rigorous, both painter and filmmaker practice a phenomenology of vision.

However (except, perhaps, when I am looking at paintings or watching films), I am not often so rigorous as the painter or filmmaker. My "act of perception, in its unsophisticated form . . . takes advantage of *work already done*, of a general synthesis constituted once and for all" as that visible object there in my vision.[66] The object is easy for my vision to locate. It is familiar to me, culturally and personally sedimented and reified as a constancy I re-cognize, rather than one I bring into being in the activity of my attentive and interrogative gaze. Living its everyday life, in its "natural attitude," the eye, Brakhage says, is "an eye which soon learns to classify sights, an eye which mirrors the movement of the individual toward death by its increasing inability to see."[67] Occasionally, my gaze does become interrogative and constituting when, for instance, I am not sure what I see in the distance. I cannot "make it out." (How clearly vernacular language connects us with our phenomenological experience of things if only we heed it and listen to what we say.) The vague figure is thus "taken up" and "made out" by me. It *emerges* under and in my scrutiny first as an indeterminate animal, and then as a cat and not a dog, as a specific "thing" for which I have a name.

The painter or the filmmaker, however, as a condition of painting and filmmaking, regularly interrogates the coming into being of figures from the indeterminate and latent ground of the visible. In "Eye and Mind," Merleau-Ponty describes this interrogation: "Light, lighting, shadows, reflections, color, all the objects of his quest are not altogether real objects; like ghosts, they have only visual existence. In fact they exist only at the threshold of profane vision; they are not

---

[65] Stan Brakhage, *Metaphors on Vision*, ed. P. Adams Sitney (New York: Film Culture, 1963), p. 1.

[66] Merleau-Ponty, *Phenomenology of Perception*, p. 238. (Emphasis mine)

[67] Brakhage, *Metaphors on Vision*, p. 1.

seen by everyone. The painter's gaze asks them what they do to suddenly cause something to be and to be *this* thing, what they do to compose this worldly talisman and to make us see the visible."[68] The painter's or the filmmaker's activity of seeing turns back on itself and looks not to *what appears* as visible, but to the visible's *mode of appearing*. Akin to the reflection of consciousness upon itself and its intentional activity, echoing its reflexive turn and its reversal of direction so that intentional activity becomes the object of intentional activity, this *active* seeing interrogates itself and thereby the nature of the way things become visible in vision. Again, Brakhage describes, without ever identifying it as such, this phenomenology of vision: "I suggest that there is a pursuit of knowledge foreign to language and founded upon visual communication, demanding a development of the optical mind, and dependent upon perception in the original and deepest sense of the word."[69]

Phenomenological reflection has revealed that there are two forms of vision in the same way that there are two forms of intentionality. One form of vision is passive, spontaneous, seemingly pre-given. It is "operative," to use Husserl's term to describe that intentionality "which produces the natural and *antepredicative* unity of the world and of our life."[70] This is the vision we take for granted and do not seem to actively work at. This is the vision we draw upon. Operative vision is lived antepredicatively as corporeal perception in its cultural familiarity with the world. That is, it is lived as that general and universal possession of the visible that is visible to all of us with eyes, and as that particular and concrete possession of the visible that is visible to all of us who share a culture and a history. As Richard McCleary says in his preface to Merleau-Ponty's *Signs*: "Corporeal perception is originally and fundamentally our presence to a world in which the active and the passive and the visible and the invisible are so little distinguishable that all our traditional categories become indefinite. Far from being able to demarcate a perceiving subject and the object he perceives, we can no longer tell precisely who is seen and who is seeing. . . . consciousness is basically the anonymous, pre-personal life of the flesh."[71]

[68] Merleau-Ponty, "Eye and Mind," p. 166.

[69] Brakhage, *Metaphors on Vision*, p. l.

[70] Merleau-Ponty, *Phenomenology of Perception*, p. xviii. (Emphasis mine)

[71] Richard C. McCleary, "Translator's Preface," in Merleau-Ponty, *Signs*, pp. xvi–xvii.

Vision also has a second form that is enacted as volitional: the visual taking up of the visible deliberately as an act of judgment, of conscious and intentional choice. Until it forgets itself, becomes habituated to itself, and loses sight of itself in its own predications and figurations, this vision is active, reflective, reflexive, and constitutive. Merleau-Ponty summarizes this differentiation of operative and deliberate vision: "Thus vision divides itself. There is the vision upon which I reflect; I cannot think it except *as* thought, the mind's inspection, judgment, a reading of signs. And then there is the vision that really takes place, an honorary or instituted thought, squeezed into a body—its own body, of which we can have no idea except in the exercise of it and which introduces, between space and thought, the autonomous order of the compound of soul and body."[72] (For a less theological flavor, one can responsibly read *intentionality* for *soul* in the above passage.)

Both forms of vision, however, whether operative or deliberate, are the expression of intentional and embodied consciousness in the world—one inflective and the other reflective, but both lived through the perceptive body as its signification of the world's and its own significance. Thus, it must be emphasized that reflective deliberate vision is grounded in exercised operative vision rather than abstracted and amputated from it. Again, the living and perceptive body stands as the primary ground of reflective acts. It is the flesh through which vision is accomplished in both of its forms and directional trajectories. This flesh is of the world as well as in it, sharing in the world's materiality and thickness. It is a flesh that occupies space and is occupied by it as time—a flesh that is finite and thus experiences finitude, that is durable and thus experiences duration, that is malleable and thus experiences form and change and motion. This is *vision embodied*—a material activity that not only sees but can be seen, that makes vision itself visible.

In the collected notes that comprise his last work, *The Visible and the Invisible*, Merleau-Ponty reminds us: "My body as a visible thing is contained within the full spectacle. But my seeing body subtends this visible body, and all the visibles with it. There is a reciprocal insertion and intertwining of one in the other. Or rather, if, as once again we must, we eschew the thinking by planes and perspectives, there are two circles, or two vortexes, or two spheres, concentric

[72] Merleau-Ponty, "Eye and Mind," p. 176.

when I live naively, and as soon as I question myself, the other slightly decentered with respect to the other. . . ."[73] In its expression of intentionality in existence and the world as a modality of perception, in its activity, its directedness, and its reversibility, vision echoes the intentional structure of consciousness. Or, rather, we could say more accurately that the intentional structure of consciousness echoes *within* our vision.

As mentioned previously, vision is not a discrete "sense" although it possesses a particular manner of access to and possession of the world. A modality of perception, vision partakes of perception's *synaesthetic* and *synoptic* character. That is, although sight is differentiated from our other modes of perception, it is not isolated from them. Rather, it is co-operative with them by virtue of the perceptive body all the senses constitute and share. As well, the activity and objects of vision have meaning only in relation to the *whole* that is the perceptive body and its intentional projection in the world. The activity of seeing is full of meaning, and sight is a sense in that vision gives the perceptive body access to the world in a manner that uniquely satisfies the body's desire to possess the world precisely in such a manner, that is, its desire to accomplish a living task visually. There is, then, no such sense as "pure" sight and no such activity as "just" seeing. Rather, seeing is informed by perception in all of its modalities. What is visible is shaped from within by the intentional projects of the lived-body that does not merely see the world but also wholly inhabits it.

If we think back to Kennedy's research with the blind and their ability to understand and draw pictures, we find that the meaning of *seeing* and of the *visible* world can exist without sight. Seeing and the meaning of visibility and the visible draw not only from the eyes' capacity to "have the world at a distance." Such meaning is drawn also from the perceptive capacity of the body to touch and feel, to hear, to smell, to taste, to move, to *inhabit* the world intentionally as a total being, a lived-body on whom, *as* whom, the senses describe a field and inscribe their meaning as conscious experience. Thus:

> The senses intercommunicate by opening on to the structure of the thing. One sees the hardness and brittleness of glass, and when, with a tinkling sound, it breaks, this sound is conveyed by the visible glass.

[73] Merleau-Ponty, *The Visible and the Invisible*, p. 138.

One sees the springiness of steel, the ductility of red-hot steel, the hardness of a plane blade, the softness of shavings. The form of objects is not their geometrical shape: It stands in a certain relation to their specific nature and appeals to all our other senses as well as sight. The form of a fold in linen or cotton shows us the resilience or dryness of the fibre, the coldness or warmth of the material. . . . If, then, taken as incomparable qualities, the "data of the different senses" belong to so many separate worlds, each one in its particular essence being a manner of modulating the thing, they all communicate through their significant core.[74]

The "significant core" of which Merleau-Ponty speaks is, of course, the perceptive body as a synoptically lived whole, as the field upon which the senses are spread out but contained, the field within which they communicate and significance is constituted as experience.

A provocative case in point (particularly for cinema studies) is that aspect of vision we call *perspective*. The visual phenomenon we conceive of as perspective is understood by blind people and can be depicted by them because their bodies *live* it in the world as the distance between the "Here, where I am, and where I have material thickness in the world" and the "There, where I am not yet, but could materially be," or the "There, where some other material thickness inhabits the world and offers resistance to my displacement of it." Perspective, as Kennedy has shown us, is not merely a geometric construction of sight, a purely visual thinking of spatial relationships that are held suspended before my eyes as the in-formation of the solely visible. Rather, perspective is a *theoretical representation* of a dimension and depth that are antepredicatively *lived through* by my body. Thus, as Merleau-Ponty says of perspective, "I see it [the third dimension] and it is not visible, since it goes toward things from, as starting point, this body to which I myself am fastened."[75] Perspective is not, through the sense of sight, empirically *visible*. Rather, it is the implication of vision with the body in its material relation to a world. It is the positing of an experience of possible motion that the body might undertake in the *depth* of the world among the *thickness* and *material-*

---

[74] Merleau-Ponty, *Phenomenology of Perception*, pp. 229–230.

[75] Merleau-Ponty, "Eye and Mind," pp. 172–173. On this issue, see also Maurice Merleau-Ponty, "Indirect Language and the Voices of Silence," in *Signs*, pp. 49–50.

ity of objects that share the world in the manner of the body and with it. This is not to claim that the body cannot feel itself occupying the world in another manner that de-emphasizes its thickness or that does not have motion as its operative or deliberate intentional focus. That is, because perspective is a *theoretical construct*, a *represented* way of seeing and being in the world, it is not the only possibility for signifying the significance of either existence or representation. The point to be made here is that what we take naively, in the "natural attitude," to be purely an aspect of vision is empirically also an aspect of haptics. The latter relations of the materially lived, perceptive body and the world inform vision and are represented in it as communicated by the body in its actual and possible motor projects.

Upon reflection, then, those attributes or qualities I ascribe to vision or the particular physiological function of my eyes as discrete and localized organs of perception are revealed as attributes and qualities of the perceptive body as synoptic totality. Although "seeing" as a perceptive and expressive activity may be located as originating from some invisible premises slightly "behind" my eyes, and although it may be differentiated from "hearing" by the kind of opening on the world it provides me, it still engages my *entire* perceptive body in its activity. Indeed, seeing gains its specific meaning as an activity lived through and for that body in a multiplicity of intentional and *cooperative* projects that mark the ongoing act of becoming that is being. Brakhage captures the synoptic nature and synaesthetic function of the embodied activity of the act of being with one's own eyes in the following burst of Joycean prose:

My eye, then, inspiralling, frictioning style-wise, being instrument for striking sparks, is bequeathed visions at every illumination it's stuck to create—Similar vistas being available to any viewer willing to release his eye for comparable movement. My eye so lost in space that fall feels ascenscional, so style-beguiled as to know no "reality," sea running down-up hill willy-nilly, waves not known by their phosphorescence but thru aesthetic reflection only—similar illuminations possible for any viewer capable of understanding his vision as a metaphoric creation either directly inspired by nature or watered down by the cliché sight of others.[76]

[76] Brakhage, *Metaphors on Vision*, p. 6.

THE VIEWING SUBJECT

Brakhage tells us, "I am not when I see."[77] Thus, the following question emerges: Through what agency does a viewer become "capable of understanding his vision as a metaphoric creation?" How does, in Merleau-Ponty's terms, vision "divide itself" so that there is the seeing "that really takes place . . . squeezed into a body—its own body, of which we can have no idea except in the *exercise* of it," and there is the seeing "upon which I reflect, which I cannot think except as *thought*"?[78] How is it that seeing is and does become visible to sight as a representation of itself and ultimately leads to sight's recognition of its origins in a seer, a body-subject? For, as we have seen, existential vision need not so divide itself, reflect upon itself. The cat, the newborn infant, all of us in the "natural attitude" of our everyday lives do not watch our vision even as we possess and posit its contents as the experience of consciousness.

Indeed, the *visual activity* of seeing is first experienced in consciousness as it is directed toward the *visible world*. That is, the intentional trajectory of consciousness is directed through vision toward that which can be *seen* in the act of seeing, and not toward the *unseen* originator of the act—the *seer* who is not the content sufficient to the visible but is its necessary and *invisible condition*. The cat's or the very young infant's vision has not divided itself. Theirs is the vision that is experienced from within as the body's exercise. It is a vision that is unreflected upon and unrepresented to itself. Clearly, then, the act of being in the world with eyes is the foundation for, but not the same as, the act of being in the world with one's *own* eyes.

However, just as the structure of human consciousness allows consciousness to become aware of itself by reflexively transposing and representing its intentional activity as an intentional object for consciousness, so human vision can reflexively turn in on itself. It can reverse its dominant and "natural" directedness toward the visible world back toward its own directed and invisible activity of making the world visible. This reflexive intentional movement is the act of *reflection*. And, at its most radical, the act of reflection discovers its origins in the *subjective body that sees* and rescues the latter from ano-

[77] Ibid., p. 48.
[78] Merleau-Ponty, "Eye and Mind," p. 176. (Emphasis mine)

97

nymity and invisibility by re-cognizing and re-presenting it to consciousness—that is, thinking it as the *body-subject who sees*.

Previous sections have elaborated upon the intentional structure and existential activity of vision—its irreducible correlation of the seeing with the seen, and its directed activity that marks existential choice as a diacritical hermeneutic and semiotic operation of the body even before it thinks itself as a subject. As well, two forms of vision have been described, both parallel in existence and through the body to the two forms of intentionality distinguished by Husserl as operative and deliberative, the former serving as the foundation and ground of the latter. Thus, Brakhage's statement "I am not when I see" and Merleau-Ponty's identification of a vision that is "exercised" by the body both describe that form of seeing that manifests itself in perceptual existence as *operative intentionality* at *visual* work in the world. This is a vision that is *anonymous* and *pre-personal*. It is the vision of the cat and the newborn and, indeed, informs all our adult human vision as the foundation upon and the ground against which a more deliberative vision can emerge as an act of judgment and thought aware of itself as such.

It is this latter kind of vision to which Brakhage refers when he describes sight as a "metaphoric creation" and to which Merleau-Ponty refers when he speaks of "vision as thought." Seeing, in this reflective and reflexive turn, expresses itself in perceptual existence as the *deliberative intentionality* that emerges from a body lived as a *visible* subject. This vision, therefore, is *predicative* and *personal*. It is a vision that represents and names itself as an expressive "utterance" of the perceptive body and that connects that body's eyes (first lived invisibly in the exercise of seeing) to an intending "I" who is visible to him or herself, who possesses visual experience consciously.

Therefore, as a modality of embodied perception, vision not only provides us fundamental access to the seen and visible world, but it also provides us fundamental access to ourselves—both as seen and visible subjects and as seeing and visual subjects. It is not surprising, then, that as a modality of perception vision has become radically entailed by those disciplines whose primary inquiry concerns human being and its objectivation and/or objectification as self-consciousness. (Objectivation, unlike objectification, is a primary form of self-representation not characterized as alienation.[79])

[79] For clear and pertinent distinction between the terms *objectivation, objectification*,

Both psychology and philosophy allow vision a central role in the constitution of the Self and the Other. More specifically, psychoanalysis has explored the act of seeing in its relation to the constitution of the Self "from the outside in"—thus positing, through the influential work of Jacques Lacan, the visibly *seen* as that Other who originates the visual seer. In the currency of contemporary critical terminology (much borrowed upon by film theory), the subject is posited rather than positing, is positioned rather than positioning. The Self, therefore, is less a subject of vision than the *direct object* of the visible, the seen Other: "That woman visible there sees *me* as visible." Alternatively and complimentarily, existential phenomenology has explored the act of seeing in its relation to the constitution of Self-consciousness "from the inside out." That is, as Merleau-Ponty elaborates in his work, the act of *seeing* originates the visual seer and the visible Other as co-emergent subjects of vision, as both see-able and seen, visual and visible. Thus, the subject is positing as well as posited, positioning as well as positioned. The Self, therefore, is the subject of vision as well as the visible Other's direct object of vision. Indeed, the Other who is visibly *seen seeing* is experienced by the visual *seeing subject* as both its *direct object* and as an *indirect subject*: "I see that visible woman there visually seeing me as visible."

Psychoanalysis and existential, semiotic phenomenology seem oppositional, particularly in the way each describes the constitution of the Self in consciousness through the act of seeing. Yet the dialectical tension between them and the opposing directions they take converge in the actual dialectical experience of the seeing subject. As well, both meet in their concern with language and its radical origins and relations to conscious and self-conscious experience and expression. Seeing, for both disciplines, leads to speaking, although each discipline relates seeing and speaking differently, making of Lacanian psychoanalysis (grounded in language) a *phenomenological semiotics* and of Merleau-Ponty's existential philosophy (grounded in embodiment) a *semiotic phenomenology*.

Thus, Lacan and Merleau-Ponty have dealt with the existential fact of vision and its relation to the self-recognition of the viewing subject in different ways. And yet their descriptions overlap in many areas, obscuring some of the radical differences between them. Because the

---

alienation, and *reification,* see Peter Berger and Stanley Pullberg, "Reification and the Sociological Critique of Consciousness," *History and Theory* 4 (1965), pp. 196–211.

discussion here of how the subject comes to self-articulation through an act of seeing must, of necessity, be relatively brief, it seems useful to preface the particular synopses of Lacan's and Merleau-Ponty's work in this area with a general and summary comparison and contrast of psychoanalysis and existential phenomenology. The purpose is to emphasize both their similarities of interest and their opposed and/or complementary directional thrust, which is to say, their dialectical relationship.

Psychoanalysis and Semiotic Phenomenology

Psychoanalysis, particularly in its Lacanian articulation, can be described as a phenomenological semiotics because it proceeds on the premise that the *structures of language determine the structures of being*. An existential and semiotic phenomenology, conversely, proceeds on the premise that the *structures of being determine the structures of language*. Both approaches, therefore, correlate language and being. However, where psychoanalysis judges individual performance (and its deviations) against the ground of a prefigured competence (and norm), semiotic phenomenology describes a competence that emerges in and with individual performance. This is to say, both psychoanalysis and semiotic phenomenology agree that conscious human existence entails a universal structure (the competence that defines one as human and conscious) and an always contingent performance (a style of being human and conscious in a specific context). Psychoanalysis, however, begins with the structure and judges individual performance against its "grammar," while semiotic phenomenology begins with an individual performance that describes and inscribes a structure whose "grammar" is always emerging.

Put another way, within the realm of psychoanalytic reflection, the individual's *context* of choice is seen as *determining* his or her *choice* in context. Within the realm of phenomenological reflection, the individual's *choice* in context is seen as *constituting* her or his *context* of choice.[80] Thus, while both psychoanalysis and existential phenomenology posit a *dialectical relation between choice and context*, the primacy

[80] Lanigan, "Communication Models in Philosophy," p. 35. See also Richard L. Lanigan, "A Semiotic Metatheory of Human Communication," *Semiotica* 27, no. 4 (1979), pp. 293–305.

afforded the terms that constitute the synthesis of the Self points to their radical difference.

Both psychoanalysis and semiotic phenomenology also seem to share a hermeneutic function. They both seek to disclose interpretive structures and activities in human behavior that give conscious experience its implicit and explicit meaning. Psychoanalysis, however, is therapeutic in thrust while semiotic phenomenology is descriptive. The former focuses on exposing the distortions of interpretive structures and activity and seeks to demystify those structures and activity as they reify and sediment encounters with the world and others. That is, psychoanalysis moves from an already-constituted *interpretation* of significant experience to a *reduction* of that experience as the effect of a distorting structure to an explicit *description* of that original engagement with the world in the actual experience that gave rise to the distortion. Semiotic phenomenology, on the other hand, focuses on describing the expressions of interpretive structures and activity. It seeks to demythify those structures and activity we take for granted or assume are in some way magical—the first resulting from our "natural attitude" and the second resulting from a romantic and/ or theological exaltation of expression without understanding. Unlike psychoanalysis, however, semiotic phenomenology moves from the *description* of an actual experience of engagement with the world and others to a *reduction* of that experience to its systemic structuring by and within an interpretive activity to an *interpretation* of the significance of that experience as it is lived.

One could say that psychoanalysis, as the "talking cure" and in its remedial and therapeutic focus, is a hermeneutic of the "abnormal" and the "unconscious" that presupposes the "normal" and "consciousness" without fully explicating them. Conversely, semiotic phenomenology as descriptive of expression and communication rather than of a predetermined "distortion" is a hermeneutic of the "normal" and of consciousness against which distortion can be seen as meaningful. Thus, psychoanalysis rests upon a foundation of communication and expression whose structure it does not disclose. It does not include a phenomenology of systemic communication and expression but emerges from it. Semiotic phenomenology, however, does include psychoanalysis as a "phenomenology of illness." As Alden Fisher suggests, "Phenomenology permits psychoanalysis to recognize 'psychic reality' without equivocation, the 'intra-subjective' essence of morbid formations, the fantastic operation that *reconstructs* a world on the margin of, and counter to, the true world, a lived history beneath the effective history—a world called illness."[81]

Perhaps the most radical differences between psychoanalysis and semiotic phenomenology occur in their assessment of the relation of language to human experience. They are both in agreement that language provides a means by which the individual consciousness is able to relate itself to itself and to others, and that in so doing language de-centers the individual. That is, language allows individuals to transcend the immanent finitude and situation of their discrete and permanent bodily address in the world. However, for the psychoanalyst, *signification is incommensurable with existence*. In semiotic terms, the signifier (SR) and the signified (SD), as well as the sign and the referent, are separate and different entities comprising a dual system in being. For the phenomenologist, on the other hand, *signification is synonymous with existence*. The SR and SD, the sign and the referent, are linked and differentiated rather than regarded as different entities. As modalities of perceptive existence expressed by the same lived-body, they comprise a single system of being.

For psychoanalysis, language functions as a substitute for being, as merely a representation of presence. The sign thus designates the absence of the referent and its existential presence. Speech becomes a substitute for a loss, a vacancy, in experience. Again, phenomenology approaches language more sanguinely. Language functions as an extension of being, as the presentation of more than is present. The sign thus designates the presence of the referent by means of representation. Speech becomes an extension of the experience of being-in-the-world, a transcendence that is very much present in existence. The substitutive function of language for psychoanalysis leads to Lacan's description of the formation not only of ego-consciousness but of the unconscious. Thus, *language is held to be the essential condition of the unconscious*. Language is the wedge that splits the self, that allows for two different realms of signification and for intrasubjectivity (the person's system of representing primal experience to him- or herself). The extensional function of language for semiotic phenomenology leads to Merleau-Ponty's description of the movement from the preconsciousness of the subjective-body to the consciousness of the body-subject—that is, from the unreflective and unreflexive ex-

[81] Alden L. Fisher, introduction to *The Essential Writings of Merleau-Ponty* (New York: Harcourt, Brace and World, 1969), p. 81.

perience of consciousness to the reflective and reflexive consciousness of experience. Thus, *the lived-body is held to be the essential condition of consciousness and language.* Language is the link that connects the self not only with its own primordial experience but also with other selves, allowing for a communality of signification or intersubjectivity.

Lacanian psychoanalysis assumes a subject inserted into language and constituted by it. Language includes the subject and positions it. The Other (as holding the always-already present power and authority of language) authorizes and positions the subject and constitutes it as object. Thus, language is the given for psychoanalysis. It is the lived-Logos that produces both body-subject and world as its reified predications. Alternatively, semiotic phenomenology describes a subject inserted into language and constituting speech. The subject, therefore, while included in language, also includes it—positions it through speech in and as personal be-ing. The subject (in always-already holding the power of authorship, in existentially speaking a *parole* that constitutes and reconstitutes *langue)* includes the Other and authorizes its authority as also a subject. It is lived-experience as perceptive and expressive that is a given for phenomenology. In its intentional engagement with a world that exceeds it, the lived-body extends its being beyond its own premises, predicating and reifying it as Logos.

These differences in the relation of language to being distinguish the directions from which psychoanalysis and semiotic phenomenology approach the issue of self-consciousness (the representation of self to self). They should be kept in mind in the following sections that concentrate on the function of vision in the formation of self-consciousness, the ego, the subject, the Self. From the phenomenological perspective this present study takes, vision and the act of viewing as a modality of perception have already been described as also expressive, as a "wild signification" exercised anonymously and prepersonally. Such a description does not discount or reject psychoanalytic accounts of the function of vision. However, it does find them incomplete and insufficiently explicative of their own grounds. In the "natural attitude," we may, indeed, live our vision and produce ourselves from the "outside in," and so lose sight of ourselves in the visible images we produce and reify. But we also, and most directly, live those produced images, as Merleau-Ponty suggests, from the "inside out." It is this dialectic of lived-experience that semiotic phenomenology describes, a dialectic that, with its tension and reversible movements, produces the *viewing and visible subject*, the viewer who can view a film and understand it as both a *viewing-view* and its production, the *viewed-view*.[82]

Jacques Lacan: Being Seen and Seeing

The act of viewing, for Lacan, both figuratively and literally gives the infant access to itself as a seeing subject, as a subject whose perception consciously expresses its being. However, as previously summarized, Lacan describes this access from the "outside in." That is, within the anonymous and prepersonal activity of seeing that the sighted infant performs from birth, the discretely lived body-subject that the infant *is* emerges as self-consciousness in its confrontation with the *seen*, with what is *visible* in vision. Thus, self-consciousness and its representation begin with that intentional correlate of vision that is not the intentional *act* of seeing but rather the intentional *object* of seeing. There, in the visible object, begins the reflective and reflexive trajectory of vision to Here, to its origin in the visual address of the eye, to the body-subject that is invisible to itself as it sees. Given the direction of this trajectory of vision and its starting point, it is clear why the *mirror* enjoys such a privileged status as both literal and metaphorical object in Lacan's account of the structuration of the Self, the ego-subject. (It is also apparent why film theorists find this particular aspect of Lacan's schema so attractive.)

[82] For further discussion of the differences between and similar concerns of psychoanalysis and existential phenomenology, see Maurice Merleau-Ponty, "Phenomenology and Psychoanalysis: Preface to Hesnard's *L'Oeuvre de Freud*," trans. Alden L. Fisher, *Review of Existential Psychology and Psychiatry* 18, nos. 1–3 (1982–1983), pp. 67–72; Jacques Lacan, "Merleau-Ponty: In Memoriam," trans. Wilfried Ver Eecke and Dirk De Schutter, *Review of Existential Psychology and Psychiatry* 18, nos. 1–3 (1982–1983), pp. 73–81; J. B. Pontalis, "The Problem of the Unconscious in Merleau-Ponty's Thought," trans. Wilfried Ver Eecke and Michael Greer, *Review of Existential Psychology and Psychiatry* 18, nos. 1–3 (1982–1983), pp. 83–96; Dorothea Olkowski, "Merleau-Ponty's Freudianism: From the Body of Consciousness to the Body of Flesh," *Review of Existential Psychology and Psychiatry* 18, nos. 1–3 (1982–1983), pp. 97–116; Michael Hyde, "Jacques Lacan's Psychoanalytic Theory of Speech and Language," *Quarterly Journal of Speech* 66 (1980), pp. 96–118. For lengthier consideration of the subject, see also Rosalind Coward and John Ellis, *Language and Materialism: Developments in Semiology and the Theory of the Subject* (Boston: Routledge and Kegan Paul, 1977), pp. 129–152; and Paul Ricoeur, *Freud and Philosophy: An Essay on Interpretation*, trans. Denis Savage (New Haven: Yale Univ. Press, 1970).

It is through the objective agency of the *visible* mirror image (and not the subjective agency of its own situated and embodied visual activity) that the infant comes to see itself seeing and eventually recognizes the actual locus of vision as the *effect* of an externally induced rather than reflexively produced *reflection*. This recognition inaugurates the child's entry into the symbolic world, where it assumes the power and constraints of language in both the conscious and unconscious realms of its being and experience. Although our primary concern here is with the act of seeing and its implications of a body-subject who sees itself and its own activity of seeing, Lacan's mirror stage should not be isolated from his total schema that includes descriptions of other moments or "orders" of the ego's development. (Indeed, this isolation has been a major problem with certain cinematic applications of Lacan to both the film experience and the film viewer.)

Lacan describes three psychoanalytic orders whose relations within and among each other comprise a schema or *system* in which the ego develops. These orders are called the Imaginary, the Symbolic, and the Real. The Imaginary order, associated with the mirror stage, is "characterized by the prevalence of the relation to the image of the counterpart," the counterpart being "another who is me."[83] Within the Imaginary, the image is con-fused with the real. It is *not* perceived *as* an image (that is, as an expression, a mediation, an SR of some kind). The child sees itself There in the mirror, not Here from where it casts the reflection that is There. Thus, in the Imaginary order, there is no *sign function* as such. (In this regard, it is interesting to note that Eco's semiotic theory identifies specular reflections as *pseudo-signs*. They are not true signs because they are *virtual* images and so do not stand *as* or *for* something else. That is, they exist in equality with other things, rather than in similitude.[84]) The Imaginary order, then, is a set of relations based on the play of non-signs, on perception functioning as illusion rather than expression. Presymbolic and pro-symbolic, the Imaginary order is not yet symbolic, and it initiates the first "rough-cast" of the ego in an "irremediably deceptive" experience.[85]

The Symbolic order is bound up with the Oedipal phase of ego

---

[83] J. Laplanche and J.-B. Pontalis, *The Language of Psycho-Analysis*, trans. Donald Nicholson-Smith (New York: W.W. Norton, 1973), p. 210.

[84] Eco, *A Theory of Semiotics*, pp. 201–202.

[85] Laplanche and Pontalis, *The Language of Psycho-Analysis*, p. 210.

development and the acquisition of language and all such acquisition implies: That is, the discovery of both personal autonomy and dependence upon others, and the power of the word one speaks and the prohibitions of the word as spoken. Most immediately, the entrance into the Symbolic entails the "de-coalescence" of the SR and the SD, and the release of the infant from a false identification with its specular self as it re-cognizes the latter as merely a *sign* of itself. Such a release into the freedom and constraints of language and the language community, into a recognition of representation, results in the infant's self-objectification. The infant ego divides itself. It becomes not only distinguishable from others but also becomes both a "me" and an "I" (a self that is *as* it speaks and that also speaks *of* itself through a medium of objectification, language).

In the acquisition of language, the self also simultaneously divides its conscious significations from its more fearsome and primally predicated impulses and experience. Thus, primary signifiers are repressed to constitute the self's *unconscious*. Entrance into the Symbolic order, then, is repressive as well as liberating, although it is the latter aspect that is appreciated in self-consciousness (even as the infant encounters the linguistic prohibition "No"). As Lacan puts it, aptly using a metaphor appropriate to cinema, "Language permits him [the infant] to consider himself as the engineer, or the *metteur en scène* of the entire Imaginary capture of which he could not be otherwise than the living marionette."[86] Although not quite qualifying yet as a full-fledged *auteur*, at least the infant has assumed directorial responsibility for his images.[87]

Brief mention must also be made of the order of the Real, although

[86] Jacques Lacan, "La Direction de la cure," cited in *The Language of the Self: The Function of Language in Psychoanalysis*, trans. with notes and commentary by Anthony Wilden (New York: Delta Books, 1968), p. 176.

[87] I have used the masculine pronoun here quite consciously given the debate feminist film theory has with psychoanalytic theories of subject formation and, specifically, the processes of identification (even as Lacanian psychoanalytic theory has provided the foundation for feminist film theory). Whether a female can be a subject in language (and assume "directorial responsibility" for her images) is at issue within this discursive field, one of the reasons this present study has refused the limited descriptions of subject formation and identification offered by psychoanalytic theory. Although an enormous amount of material has now been written on this issue (without much resolution), the uninitiated reader can find a clear and cogent summary in the first chapter of Mary Ann Doane, *The Desire to Desire: The Woman's Film of the 1940s* (Bloomington: Indiana Univ. Press, 1987), pp. 1–22.

it does not occupy a major place in Lacan's analyses. This set of relations is not to be seen as describing some "objective" reality external to human experience and perception. The Real is not "for-itself." Rather, the Real is that inaugural experience and perception of the world that occurs prior to the constitution of the subject as such. It is the foundation upon which relations of all subsequent orders rest, upon which engagement with the world is based. (As we shall see, generally neglected by Lacan, it is this order that is commensurate with the primary area of Merleau-Ponty's concern.) For Lacan, the order of the Real founds the *need* that is later transformed into *demand* and *desire*, into the will to power that eventually becomes constituted as the ego and evidences itself in language. And, as the foundation upon which all the other orders are based, the relations of the Real transcend both the image and the sign, are their excess, and cannot be contained by them. Thus, according to Freud, and Lacan after him, the relations of the Real are "the domain outside symbolization."[88] They are, however, not outside the domain of the subject, for "the Real is not synonymous with external reality but rather with what is real for the subject."[89]

What is crucial to keep in mind about the relationship among the three Lacanian psychoanalytic orders is their simultaneous existence and their imbrication in the mature ego. Thus, the Imaginary order, with its mirror phase, is not a set of relations somehow passed "beyond" or "gotten over." Neither is the most fundamental and unarticulated order of the Real, nor the "primary" order of the Symbolic—with its Oedipal phase. (Lacan considers the Symbolic order "primary" because it is the order that "represents and structures" the other orders so they can be reflectively known to consciousness).[90] This co-existence and intersection of the Imaginary, Real, and Symbolic as functions of the mature subject should contextualize the emphasis here on the visual relations of the mirror stage in the Imaginary order. It is the mirror stage and the Imaginary order that have enjoyed the close attention of film theorists.

Despite the term *stage* or *phase*, and despite its correlation with a particular chronological development of the human infant, for Lacan the mirror stage is as much a structural concept as it is a literal expe-

---

[88] Wilden in Lacan, *The Language of the Self*, p. 281; see also p. 295.
[89] Ibid., p. 161.
[90] Ibid.

rience. Thus, Wilden comments: "The Imaginary components of the mirror play of the child (as a perceptual relationship) absolutely require the *stade du miroir* to be read in three ways at once: backwards—as a symptom of or a substitute for a much more primordial identification; forwards—as a phase in development; and timelessly—as a relationship best formulated in algorithmic terms."[91] The concept of the mirror stage describes the *presymbolic* phase of ego development in which primary identification occurs. It is a stage that precedes and forever contextualizes the later Oedipal phase that Freud saw as the nexus of ego constitution. However, the infant's primary moment of identification need not come about literally as the result of contemplating a mirror. It occurs through the child's perceptual identification with a powerful and significant Other—at this early point in its life with its mother (or someone who serves the maternal nurturing function). This Other presents a unified and powerful body upon which the helpless infant gazes and upon which the infant depends. The Other is that visible presence whom the infant has come to realize has the autonomous power to remove herself from or make herself available to both vision and the infant's needs.

Prior to the onset of the mirror stage (said to occur between six and eighteen months), the infant has no concept of self as such. Therefore it does not perceive its being as powerless and fragmented (that is, as partially invisible to itself and therefore visible only in parts—an arm here, toes there). Indeed, the infant makes no distinction between self and other. Inaugurally, all is a mass of undifferentiated experience in which inside and outside, self and other, are con-fused and merge. As Lacan puts it playfully, the infant is born into the world an "hommelette"—"a little man and also like a broken egg spreading without hindrance in all directions."[92] It is in concert with the visual perception of an Other and its own image in the mirror that the infant comes to see and recognize its own coherence and unity. Wilden summarizes the crucial importance of the child's encounter with the mirror or its equivalent:

> The significance of children's attempts to appropriate or control their own image in a mirror is that their actions are symptomatic of . . . deeper relationships. Through his perception of the image of another human being, the child discovers a form *(Gestalt)*, a corporeal unity,

[91] Ibid., p. 174.
[92] Coward and Ellis, *Language and Materialism*, p. 101.

which is lacking to him at this particular stage of his development. . . . Lacan interprets the child's fascination with the other's image as an anticipation of his maturing to a future point of corporeal unity by identifying with this image. Although there are certain difficulties in Lacan's expression of his views on this extremely significant phase of childhood, the central concept is clear: this primordial experience is symptomatic of what makes the *moi* an Imaginary construct. The ego is an *Idealich*, another self, and the *stade du miroir* is the source of all later identification.[93]

The paradigm of the Imaginary order, the mirror stage, involves the child's conscious perception of self as self, but because this self is *alienated* as a specular image, the child does not yet perceive this *perception* as its own *self-expression*. (This description stresses objectification rather than objectivation.) Thus, "Lacan's view of the *moi* as an alienated self . . . corresponds to the internalization of the other through identification: we are conscious of this self, but unconscious of its origins."[94] That is, the actually mediated perception of Self There as *visible object* seen in the mirror (the self *at* which the infant looks) is granted a power of origin belonging to the perception of Self Here as *invisible subject* who sees (the self *from* which the image of self is perceived and from which the expression and reflection of existence and movement originate).

Constituting the ego in its initial casting as a coherence that is visible as a unified corporeal body, the mirror image functions usefully but *deceptively*. The Self There as an image in the mirror is the "*moi*" or "me" that is predicated by my vision as its *direct object*. Thus, the Self There is alienated, seen as Other than the Self Here, the *subject* of my vision (who is not visible but is lived through the eye, the primordial "I"). Further, as it is visible, this direct object (the Self There) becomes identified with the visible Other (the Mother) who also appears in the mirror. Through this process of identification and re-cognition, the self comes to visibility in consciousness in what Lacan calls *méconnaissance*, a deceptive knowledge. It is only in the acquisition of language and the entrance into the Symbolic order through "the defiles of the signifier" and the relations of the Oedipal phase that the child can redress its original mis-taken notion of itself as Other. It is only through acquiring language that the child can pro-

---

[93] Wilden in Lacan, *The Language of the Self*, p. 160.
[94] Ibid.

claim and claim itself as the autonomous and invisible subject who constitutes itself in action, speech, and an ongoing recognition—or *reconnaissance*—of its true locus, its own situation.[95]

In their discussion of Lacan's work, Rosalind Coward and John Ellis emphasize that the mirror phase has a double aspect: "There are two simultaneous moments implicit in the narcissistic identification of the mirror-phase, and these correspond to the distinction between the ideal ego and the ego-ideal. The first, the ideal ego, is the *imaginary identification* of the real, corporeal image as a *unified* image. The second, the ego-ideal, involves the fact that in order to see its *fragmentary* being *in the place of* the image that confronts it, the child sees its being in relation to *otherness*."[96] The Other and "otherness" are crucial to the productive and yet mis-taken process of self-differentiation. It is the Other—as a third term—who positions the infant in relation to its image. The Other provides the means by which the infant can jubilantly acknowledge its corporeal unity and relate that unified image to its fragmented visible being in a process of narcissistic identification.

What gives the Other this power over the constitution of the infant's self is its presence in the infant's vision as *doubly seen*. A unified body and a source of power, the Other is doubly seen as both a visible object There-in-front-of-the-mirror and a visible object There-in-the-mirror. Thus, the objective Other constitutes a visible system of *resemblance* and *homeomorphism* based on a lived-body that is visible in *both* its terms—quite unlike the infant's body, visible only as a single term, as its image in the mirror. Through this system, and in concert with the sight of its own unified body image seen as an object There in the mirror, the infant is able to differentiate its self-image as *different* from the image of the Other, but to see its self-image as a *visible* body-object *like* the Other.

The Other thus provides the grounds for the infant's recognition of difference at the same time that it *bears witness to* and *authorizes* that difference as making a difference. That is, the Other is crucial as a logical third term of relation that not only introduces difference as a sufficient condition of identity but also provides similitude as the necessary condition for the recognition of existence. The *double visi-*

[95] For additional discussion of the concepts of *méconnaissance* and *reconnaissance*, see Wilden in Lacan, *The Language of the Self*, pp. 96–97, 166.

[96] Coward and Ellis, *Language and Materialism*, p. 110. (Emphasis mine)

bility of the *same* unified body-subject that is the Other allows the infant to relate the visible mirror image of itself to the "missing term" that is its coherent and visible self not seen before except in fragments—to that other self *in front* of the mirror who sees invisibly yet is *expressed* by its own *reflection*. Thus, through the agency of the Other, the infant enters into a narcissistic engagement with an image that is recognized as its own and different from the image of the Other, but that also is identified with the visibility of the Other and objectified as (is) the image of the Other.

Initially, this narcissism springs from the infant's "jubilant assumption of the specular image . . . in which the 'I' is precipitated in a primordial form, before it is objectified in the dialectic of identification with the other."[97] However, this jubilant narcissism is dependent upon a "retroactive fantasy" experienced by the infant as it assumes its specular image and precipitates the primordial "I." As mentioned previously, prior to this stage of psychic development, the infant has no sense of self. Therefore, it has no sense of its own visibility as fragmented. It has no sense that it lacks both a corporeal center and conceptual adhesive that would bond all of its separate visible bodily parts together and make of them a coherent unified entity. However, once the mirror-phase has constituted the first casting of the ego as a *corporeal unity*, once the infant sees and knows itself as a self (however "false" the basis for this primary identification), the infant fantasizes *retroactively* about its "body-in-pieces." (Lacan calls this the fantasy of *le corps morcelé*, and it well might be compared here to the film spectator and theorist's "retroactive fantasy" of the "film-in-pieces.")[98]

This fantasy can emerge only within the infant who knows what corporeal unity looks like (much as its complementary fantasy for the film spectator and theorist can occur only from knowledge of the film as a "whole"). Thus, the fantasy is not primordial but retroactive. It is a reflection on the time when the infant visually lived its visible "body-in-pieces," but—having no reflective knowledge of vision or corporeal unity—did not know its body as other than this visible experience. That is, neither unity nor fragmentation had significant presence or meaning for the infant. (Here, in relation to the fantasy

---

[97] Jacques Lacan, "The Mirror-Phase as Formative of the Function of the I," trans. Jean Roussel, *New Left Review* 51 (September-October 1968), p. 72.

[98] For discussion of *le corps morcelé*, see Wilden in Lacan, *The Language of the Self*, p. 174, and Laplanche and Pontalis, *The Language of Psycho-Analysis*, pp. 251–252.

of the "film-in-pieces," it is worth recalling Béla Balàzs's anecdote about the Siberian girl who, not yet understanding the "corporeal unity" of a film, merely saw its edited close-up images of human heads, torsos, etc., as literal "bodies-in-pieces."[99]) It is the visible self as the unified body reflected in the mirror that happily contradicts the retroactive fantasy of the "body-in-pieces" in the normal child, who seeks again and again the mirror image's verification that the fantasy is not true. Thus, the self-image as *visible object* becomes a *visible Other* who bears witness to, verifies, and authorizes the infant from a necessary but alienated and external situation There in the mirror. So begins the lifelong fascination with one's mirror image: the basic narcissistic relationship between the child and its visible image that will later mature into an interest in and relationship with others.

Wilden usefully summarizes the alienated emergence of the infant's *ego* at this primary stage as *alter ego*. Discussing Lacan's "Schema L" (the schematic of ego formation), Wilden says:

Lacan shows the dual relationship between *moi* and other as a dual relationship of objectification (and, inevitably, of aggressivity) along the lines of Sartre's analysis of our sadomasochistic relationship to the other who is an object for us, or for whom we make ourselves an object. Aggressivity is intimately linked to identification. . . . the other we fear is often the other we love. The *moi* is thus another, an *alter ego*. In Lacan's interpretation, perception is certainly primary in human experience, but *it is the notion of self, rather than that of subjectivity,* which perception generates.[100]

That is, perception in the presence of the mirror and an Other constitutes the infant's ego from *outside*. This is the *objective self*, the *visible self*, the self that is the direct object of vision as *"me."* According to Lacan, then, perception generates the seen self rather than the seeing self—the self in its visible objectivity rather than its visual subjectivity.

Thus, in this encounter with the mirror and the Other, the infant is *subjected to* the visible Other who is seen to have the power to bear witness to and authorize the infant's existence. As Wilden continues: "The child's release from this alienating image, if indeed he is re-

---

[99] Béla Balázs, *Theory of the Film: Character and Growth of a New Art*, trans. Edith Bone. (New York: Dover Publications, 1970), pp. 34–35.

[100] Wilden in Lacan, *The Language of the Self*, pp. 160–161.

leased from it, will occur through his discovery of subjectivity by his appropriation of language from the Other, which is his means of entry into the Symbolic order in the capacity of subject. . . . He begins that crucial moment of entry through the phonemic organization of reality evident in the *Fort! Da!*, which Lacan has never ceased to stress."[101] *Fort! Da!* is the infant's vocalization of absence and presence in a crib game noted by Freud. These phonemic oppositions in relation to the game were seen as an articulation of a system of differences necessary to the later entrance into language. As well, they stand as a major symbolization of the absence and presence of the M/ Other, an absence or presence that the infant could control in the game as it could not in its real experience.

The movement, then, from *self* to *subjectivity* is accomplished through the power of control and function available to the infant as and through language. The infant cannot generalize and "use" its mirror image; it can, however, generalize and use its sight—as it can generalize and use language.[102] The parallels between this subjective possession of vision (located in the act of seeing rather than as the seen) and the possession of language as subjectivity are apparent as Wilden goes on: "Later the child will appropriate personal pronouns for himself and others, along with the whole category of what linguists call 'shifters.' It is well known that personal pronouns present important difficulties for the child, who usually tends to prefer the apparent *solidity* of a proper name (a case of valid *ostensive* definition) to an 'alienable' word like *I*, which seems to be the property of others and not something designating the child himself."[103] The "me" in Lacan's schema precedes the "I," as the *seen object* in the mirror-phase takes precedence over the *seeing subject*. The knowledge of the eye finds its self-articulation in the infant's shift of identification in its use of the "I." Vision, in its intentional function, becomes not merely operative but also deliberative.

For Lacan, these transformations occur in the Oedipal phase of the Symbolic order. Unlike my exemplary cat, in its accession to language, the child does acquire consciousness of its own subjectivity. Thus, it can learn to see a film as a vision that is intentional in both

[101] Ibid., p. 161.

[102] For a brief elaboration of this distinction between the possession of one's own image and the ability to generalize and use it, see Richard Wollheim, "The Cabinet of Dr. Lacan," *New York Review of Books*, 25 January 1979, p. 37.

[103] Wilden in Lacan, *The Language of the Self*, p. 161. (Emphasis mine)

operative and *deliberative* modes, as a phenomenon that presents both a *seeing act* and its *seen objects* correlated in the irreducible lived-experience of an invisible but implicit and embodied *seeing subject*. While forever entwined with it, the pre-Oedipal mirror phase accedes to the Oedipal phase at that developmental and structural moment when, according to Lacan, the mirror "I" (the infant's image) is deflected in identification to the social "I" (the Other who is seen in the mirror seeing). As Lacan says: "This moment in which the mirror-phase comes to an end inaugurates, by the identification with the *imago* of the fellow and the drama of primordial jealousy (so well high-lighted . . . in the phenomenon of infantile *transitivism*, the dialectic which will henceforth link the "I" to socially elaborated situations."[104] The infant who cries when it *sees* an Other fall down points to this "infantile transitivism" and identification—as does the infant's desire to possess the Other's visible source of pleasure. *The objectified "I" belongs to the same class of visible objects as do those Others who are seen.* Thus, the moment of identification with and objectification of the mirror image is a *social* moment, as well as a moment in which *intrasubjective* dialogue emerges as a dialectic between the image in the mirror that *is* "me" and the image in the mirror that *sees* "me," between the image of the infant that is at once "me" and validating, authorizing, Other.

Entering into this dyadic social relation and passing through it into the triadic relations of the family and its legislation of culture, entering into the sociality of language, the infant simultaneously alienates itself from its instinctual drives. It identifies these drives from without as the Other who sees them, who names them, and represses them to form the unconscious. As Lacan suggests, this moment that ends the mirror-phase is momentous: "It is this moment that decisively shakes the whole of human knowledge in the mediatization by the desire of the other, constitutes its objects in an abstract equivalence by virtue of the competition of the other, and makes the *I* into that system for which every instinctual thrust constitutes a danger, even though it should correspond to a natural maturation—the very normalization of this maturation being henceforth dependent, in man, on a cultural go-between. . . ."[105]

The infant, according to this schema, can now *see seeing* as well as

---

[104] Lacan, "The Mirror-Phase as Formative of the Function of the I," p. 75.
[105] Ibid., pp. 75–76.

the seen. That is, it can see the act of seeing not merely as externalized and objectivated, but also as alienated—objectified and objectifying. Seeing transfixes the subject from *outside in;* it is the Other who is seen seeing me. Lacan is hostile, therefore, to what he regards as existential philosophy's claims relative to the "self-sufficiency of consciousness." He writes: "These [existentialist] propositions are denied by all our experience, inasmuch as it teaches us not to regard the *ego* as centred on the *perception-consciousness system,* or as organized by the "reality principle"—a principle which is the expression of a scientistic prejudice most hostile to the dialectic of knowledge. Our experience shows that we should start instead from the *function of mis-recognition* which characterizes the *ego* in all its structures. . . ."[106] Consciousness, Lacan argues, is not self-sufficient. For the acquisition of self-knowledge, it is dependent upon the Other (who serves a variety of Lacanian functions). *Being seen*—that is, the being of the Other as *visible,* and the being of the Other as validating the ego's existence by *seeing* it—is thus privileged in Lacan's "Schema L" over the perceptive act of seeing. As Wilden aptly points out, "An analyst would obviously be less than sympathetic to philosophies taking their departure or their certitude, directly from the *cogito,* or centered on it."[107]

Maurice Merleau-Ponty: Seeing and Being Seen

A psychologist as well as philosopher, Maurice Merleau-Ponty certainly recognized the importance of the infant's perceptual encounter with its own image and the Other to the formation of the ego-subject as an "I," a self-consciousness *visible* to consciousness. He, too, discusses the child's engagement with its specular image and specifically mentions Lacan in his published lecture "The Child's Relation with Others."[108] However, in that essay, Merleau-Ponty suggests that

---

[106] Ibid., p. 76.

[107] Wilden in Lacan, *The Language of the Self,* p. 93.

[108] Maurice Merleau-Ponty, "The Child's Relation with Others," trans. William Cobb, in *The Primacy of Perception,* pp. 135–136. On the major issues covered by this section, see also Hugh J. Silverman, "Merleau-Ponty's New Beginning: Preface to *The Experience of Others,*" *Review of Existential Psychology and Psychiatry* 18, nos. 1–3 (1982–1983), pp. 25–31; and Maurice Merleau-Ponty, "The Experience of Others (1951–1952)," trans. Fred Evans and Hugh J. Silverman, *Review of Existential Psychology and Psychiatry* 18, nos. 1–3, (1982–1983), pp. 33–63.

Lacan's description of the first casting of the child's ego in the mirror phase is only a *partial* description of that encounter, and that it neglects its foundation in the more fundamental perceptive experience that informs it.

Merleau-Ponty's work indicates that he agrees with Lacan that you can't make an "hommelette" without breaking eggs and that the very young infant is indeed "like a broken egg spreading without hindrance in all directions," possessing no immediate limits or boundaries to its being and becoming that could be considered the self-containment that marks the *ego*.[109] However, Merleau-Ponty's work suggests an emendation of Lacan's description. Phenomenological reflection reveals that, unless unnaturally or pathologically "scrambled," the "hommelette" does have a *center*, a nucleus, a living and lived-in situation from which it spreads out its existence in all directions—not as ego, but as an embodied subjectivity. (Indeed, we could refine Lacan's metaphor and suggest that an "hommelette" exists from the beginning as both albumen and yolk contained within a shell—the former comparable to the "id" in its spreading claim upon the world, the latter comparable to the "ego" in its nuclear form, and the shell comparable not only to the marker between different fields of existence but also to the "superego" in its clear marking of existence's limits.) Thus, although the "hommelette" is not *self-contained*, it is *subjectively centered*. Merleau-Ponty does not reject Lacan's description of the relations of the mirror stage but rather radically *incorporates* it—reaffirming the primacy of perception that is lived prereflectively as the subjective body.

Wilden's analysis of Lacan's approach to the mirror stage bears repeating in this context: "In Lacan's interpretation, perception is certainly primary in human experience, but it is the *notion* of *self*, rather than that of *subjectivity*, which perception generates."[110] For Merleau-Ponty, however, *self* is a "notion" or thought founded on an *incarnate subjectivity* that is precisely *not* a Kantian "notion" or reflection generated by perception. Rather, it is lived through the flesh prior to the "notion" of Self and is the ground of that "notion." If incarnate subjectivity is in any way reflective and reflexive, it is so as an *inherent* reflection and reflexivity of the body upon itself in its *adherence* to the world. Merleau-Ponty elaborates this lived reflection of the body that

---

[109] Coward and Ellis, *Language and Materialism*, p. 101.

[110] Wilden in Lacan, *The Language of the Self*, pp. 160–161. (Emphasis mine)

is not perception as thought *of* Self but is rather perception *as* the expression of subjectivity:

> My body must itself be meshed into the visible world; its power depends precisely on the fact that it has a place *from which* it sees. Thus it is a thing, but a thing I dwell in. . . . There is a relation of my body to itself which makes it the *vinculum* of the self and things. When my right hand touches my left, I am aware of it as a "physical thing." But at the same moment, if I wish, an extraordinary event takes place: here is my left hand as well starting to perceive my right. . . . The physical thing becomes animate. Or, more precisely, it remains what it was (the event does not enrich it), but an exploratory power comes to rest upon or dwell in it. Thus I touch myself touching; my body accomplishes "a sort of reflection." In it, through it, there is not just the unidirectional relationship of the one who perceives to what he perceives. The relationship is reversed, the touched hand becomes the touching hand, and I am obliged to say that the sense of touch here is diffused into the body—that the body is a "perceiving thing," a "subject-object."[111]

Counter to and contextualizing Lacan, Merleau-Ponty describes perception in existence as an original subjectivity. The "thought" of Self is a secondary and reflexive reflection on that original subjectivity. To state it more strongly (and in terms parallel to Wilden's analysis of Lacan's position), for Merleau-Ponty perception is indeed primary in human experience. It is the body's expression of subjectivity as *sense lived through* rather than the "notion" of Self that perception generates.

The empirical incorporation of Lacan's psychoanalytic description by Merleau-Ponty's existential, semiotic phenomenology is a radical transformation of the former. What Richard Lanigan says of the relations of perception to speaking can be seen also as a precise description of the relations between Merleau-Ponty's phenomenology of the lived-body and Lacan's psychoanalysis of ego-formation: "Merleau-Ponty posits the existence of man as the sense of perception—a semiology of meaning from within—as the ground on which is manifest the figure of speaking—a semiology of meaning from without—which is 'the external existence of the sense' or its essence."[112] Lacan's psychoanalytic interpretation of the relations of the

---

[111] Merleau-Ponty, "The Philosopher and His Shadow, p. 166.
[112] Lanigan, *Speaking and Semiology*, p. 96. For full elaboration, see Maurice Merleau-

mirror stage emerges, therefore, not as the ground for the formation of the ego and the advent of language, but as their figuration. Described by existential and semiotic phenomenology, the *specular image* is always related to and founded upon the existence of a *subjective body*, a *primordial subjectivity*. The literal and figurative reflections of the mirror phase that give rise to the Self in the Imaginary order are always in-formed by the body's perceptive and expressive *accomplishment* in the order of the Real. Perhaps "outside of symbolization," the domain of the Real nonetheless *signifies* the body's intentionality and produces its meaning in the world and in its lived-reflection. Therefore, the relationship of the infant to its specular image is not "just the unidirectional relationship of the one who perceives to what he perceives." The relationship is also reversible. To paraphrase Merleau-Ponty, the seen body becomes the seeing body, and we are obliged to say that the sense of sight is diffused as much into the body as it is into the image of the body, that in front of the mirror the body is both perceiving and a thing, a "subject-object."

Self and Other emerge as discrete but related figures against the common ground of the primordial subjectivity of a body that also has status as an object in touch with the world and materially part of it. As Merleau-Ponty writes:

> Thus since the seer is caught up in what he sees, it is still himself he sees: *there is a fundamental narcissism of all vision.* And thus, for the same reason, the vision he exercises, he also undergoes from the things, such that, as many painters have said, I feel myself looked at by the things, *my activity is equally passivity*—which is the second and more profound sense of the narcissism: not to see *in* the outside, as the others see it, the contour of a body one inhabits, but especially to be seen *by* the outside, to exist within it, to emigrate into it, to be seduced, captivated, alienated by the phantom, so that *the seer and the visible reciprocate one another and we no longer know who sees and which is seen.* It is this Visibility, this generality of the Sensible in itself, this anonymity innate to Myself that we have previously called *flesh,* and one knows there is no name in traditional philosophy to designate it.[113]

There is, for Merleau-Ponty, a reciprocity, a reversibility, a dialectic at work in vision between the seer and the seen, the infant and the

---

Ponty, *Consciousness and the Acquisition of Language,* trans. Hugh J. Silverman (Evanston, IL: Northwestern Univ. Press, 1973).

[113] Merleau-Ponty, *The Visible and the Invisible,* p. 139. (Emphasis mine)

image, the Self and the Other Self. However, unlike Lacan's vision, this vision is not regarded as "deceptive" in its emergence as visibility.

As we have seen, it is the deception of the visible that structures Lacan's analysis. For Lacan, the infant's ego emerges in and according to the deceptive, alienating, objectifying character of the relations the infant as seer has to its specular image. It is through a perceptual "mistake," an act of *méconnaissance*, that the little "hommelette" originates the sense of its corporeal limits, meets the resistance of the image that is the Other, and constitutes in this resistance the boundary conditions of its own existence. Without rejecting this description or the differentiation it marks between the Self and the Other, Merleau-Ponty does transform its negativity and literally fleshes out its dialectical and diacritical possibilities. He does this by contextualizing the specular alienation of the mirror encounter within a primordial and immanent knowledge the infant always already possesses—a knowledge of the subjective body lived perceptively from within as "mine." It is this a-deceptive, lived knowledge (a knowledge that might be called *connaissance* in its immanence and immediacy) that in-forms the mirror relations described by Lacan. This primordial in-formation of the mirror encounter by the subjective body grounds the *objectification* of the subject in the *objectivation* of subjectivity. (Objectivation is ontological in character: the way in which subjectivity *produces* itself in the world. Objectification is epistemological in character: the way in which the produced subjectivity and the world are *apprehended* as Self and Other.[114]) That is, the mirror encounter is less an originating act of *méconnaissance* (mis-taken knowledge) than of *reconnaissance* (knowledge re-taken in a different modality). This *reconnaissance* or reflective knowledge is the infant's awareness that the subjective body can be perceived from without as well as lived perceptively from within.

Thus, where Lacan originates the Self in the "being seen" in the mirror (that is, with the visible), Merleau-Ponty originates subjectivity in the "seeing being" in the mirror (that is, with the visual), in the infant's lived knowledge of the invisible and prepersonal intentional activity of the subjective body, centered and situated in the world. It is this primordial knowledge of the body that contextualizes the vis-

---

[114] Given the unfamiliarity of this distinction, again the reader is directed to Berger and Pullberg, "Reification and the Sociological Critique of Consciousness," pp. 196–211.

ible Other seen in the mirror and informs the visible Other with subjective as well as objective status. As Merleau-Ponty elaborates:

> The reason why I am able to understand the other person's body and existence "beginning with" the body proper, the reason why the compresence of my "consciousness" and my "body" is prolonged into the compresence of my self and the other person, is that the *"I am able to"* and *"the other person exists"* belong here and now to the same world, that the body proper is a premonition of the other person, the *Einfühlung* [spatial and temporal projection], an echo of my incarnation, and that a flash of meaning makes them *substitutable* in the absolute presence of origins.[115]

The mirror image is understood by the infant, not misunderstood. That is, prereflectively, the body lives a knowledge of its *seeing being as being seen*, a knowledge reflected in the mirror as the *reversibility*, the extensional and substitutable nature, of the specular image. The act of seeing ("I am able to") that is invisible as it is lived from within, and the seen activity ("the other person exists") that is visible as it is lived from without, are both irreducible correlates of vision that—with the body—constitute a *system* of *connection* and *commutation* between subjectivity and self-consciousness, and between self and consciousness of the Other as self. Embodied, the Other in the mirror is both seeing and visible, both subject and object in the world, both subjectivity and self for itself, and Other who can see and who can be seen by me. As visible object, the subjective body in its expression of perception initiates, at the most primordial level, a dialectic of human existence that is both intrapersonal and intersubjective, at once privileged and individual in its *self-possession*, and common and social in its *dispossession of itself as other self.*

Focusing on the mirror image, Lacan tends to overlook the bodily presence before it. At best, he emphasizes that body's incapacities and impotence—further reason that the infant is held in such thrall to its specular image and the Other. For Merleau-Ponty, however, no matter how uncoordinated and dependent, that infant body is also a capable and potent body. It is *present* to and at and in the world and *acting* before the mirror and others, as well as *perceiving* the presence and action of others. The infant's thralldom or subject-ion to the Other is but part of a *system* in which the Self and Other are not nec-

---

[115] Merleau-Ponty, "The Philosopher and His Shadow," p. 175. (Emphasis mine)

essary rivals in subjectivity. Rather, they are co-operative figures constituted against the ground of the primordial experience of the body-being-in-the-world—always given to the "hommelette" as *mine*. Centered, but without limits to contain and isolate it from the world it encounters and whose materiality it shares, the infant *incorporates* others and "takes up" their bodily conduct or style of being in the world as part of a primordial *me*. Merleau-Ponty elaborates:

> We must neither treat the origin of consciousness as though it were conscious, in an explicit way, of itself nor treat it as though it were completely closed in on itself. The first *me* is . . . virtual or latent, i.e., unaware of itself in its absolute difference. Consciousness of oneself as a unique individual, whose place can be taken by no one else, comes later and is not primitive. Since the primordial *me* is virtual or latent, egocentrism is not at all the attitude of a *me* that expressly grasps itself (as the term "egocentrism" might lead us to believe). Rather, it is the attitude of a *me* which is unaware of itself and lives as easily in others as it does in itself—but which, being unaware of others in their own separateness as well, in truth is no more conscious of them than of itself.[116]

The issue that needs explication, then, is not simply how, in Lacan's schematic, the child is able to *reclaim* its subjectivity from its initial subjection to the Other it sees in the mirror. The issue is not, in other words, how the Self (mis-taken as Other) can re-take itself as a subject. Rather, the issue that precedes and contextualizes this problematic is how the infant—born into the world as a subjective body lived always through the modality of a primordial *me*—can recognize the objective body of the Other it incorporates in its perception as also a subjective body. For existential phenomenology, the question is, How can the Other be differentiated as a *subject-for-itself* within my subjectivity that perceives and incorporates the Other as a *subject-for-me*, as my intentional *object*. Merleau-Ponty poses this original and asymmetrical perception of the Other thus: "In so far as the other person resides in the world, is visible there, and forms a part of my field, he is never an Ego in the sense in which I am one for myself. In order to think of him as a genuine *I*, I ought to think of myself as a mere object for him, which I am prevented from doing

---

[116] Merleau-Ponty, "The Child's Relation with Others," p. 119.

by the knowledge which I have of myself."[117] This asymmetry is balanced, however, by the presence of my body in a world shared by other bodies, by the fact of our mutual and material incarnation. There is a "correlation between consciousness of one's own body and perception of the other" as a subject.[118]

Obviously, incarnation has special meaning for Merleau-Ponty. It is seen as radically transforming classical psychology's notion of the "psyche" as privately experienced and only inferred from without. The psyche is not *inside* the incarnate person, just as the meaning is not *in* a word. Rather, the psyche is incarnate action; it is a "conduct" of the body that describes (and makes visible in the world) a *style* of being, an *intentional* and *postural schema*. This is not behaviorism. Rather, the body's animated display is acknowledged as *making sense* of the world through its *sensible presence* in the world. This sense is sensible both subjectively and objectively, from "within" and "without." As Lanigan puts it: "The point that Merleau-Ponty is making is quite succinct: 'The mental . . . is reducible to the structure of behavior.' The assumption in this theory is that *the behavior that is visible from the outside by another person is at the same time visible from the inside by the actor*, hence 'another person is in principle accessible to me as I am to myself; and we are both objects laid out before an impersonal consciousness.' "[119] This "impersonal consciousness" is in no way a transcendental consciousness in the Husserlian sense. Rather, it is a recognition of the transcendence of perspectives, the potential alterity of one's bodily situation in the world which exceeds one's immediate and immanent view and grasp. This recognition brings to awareness both the invisible aspects of a vision usually reduced to the visible and vision's transcendently intersubjective—that is, social—nature.

Incarnate and situated in the world as a sensing and sensible body, the infant lives its primordial *me*—its "psyche"—as a behavior in a world of other bodies and other behaviors. These the infant's body perceives and appropriates as motor possibilities of its own. What occurs when the very young infant smiles in response to a smile (any smile, for we are not talking of personal recognition here) is not an

---

[117] Merleau-Ponty, *Phenomenology of Perception*, p. 352.

[118] Merleau-Ponty, "The Child's Relation with Others," p. 120.

[119] Lanigan, *Speaking and Semiology*, p. 101. (Emphasis mine) Internal reference is to Maurice Merleau-Ponty, *The Structure of Behavior*, trans. Alden L. Fisher (Boston: Beacon Press, 1963), pp. 221–222.

imitation of gesture based on thought, but rather a bodily sympathy with other bodies. As Merleau-Ponty suggests, even prior to the mirror encounter the child incorporates the Other into its own body "unaware of himself and the other as different beings."[120] This psychogenesis is precommunicative, but procommunicative—for "the other's intentions somehow play *across* my body while my intentions play across his."[121] Outside the domain of symbolization, we, nonetheless, are never outside the act of signifying intentionality with that situated but "floating" signifier that is our incarnate being. Thus, Merleau-Ponty says, "Between my consciousness and my body as I experience it, between this phenomenal body of mine and that of another as I see it from the outside, there exists an *internal relation* which causes the other to appear as the *completion of the system*."[122]

It is precisely such a system that Merleau-Ponty elaborates in "The Child's Relation with Others." This system accounts not for the Self as subjectivity (this, as we have seen, is immanent to prereflective and embodied consciousness), but rather for the Other as subject (as an other "myself," however incorporated within the compass and circumscription of my perception). In its attempt to schematize the positive nature of self-identity in terms of the Other, this "system of four terms" contrasts with Lacan's "schema L," which describes the negative nature of self-identity and a dysfunctional experience of the Other founded in *méconnaissance*. Thus, Merleau-Ponty's system accounts for *subjectivity as intersubjectivity*, whereas Lacan's schema accounts for *subjectivity as objectified*.

Merleau-Ponty describes his "system of four terms":

The problem of the experience of others poses itself, as it were, in a system of four terms: (1) myself, my "psyche"; (2) the image I have of my body by means of the sense of touch or of cenesthesia, which, to be brief, we shall call the "introceptive image" of my own body; (3) the body of the other as seen by me, which we shall call the "visual body"; and (4) a fourth (hypothetical) term which I must reconstitute and guess at—the "psyche" of the other, the other's feeling of his own existence—to the extent that I can imagine or suppose it across the appearances of the other through his visual body.[123]

[120] Merleau-Ponty, "The Child's Relation with Others," p. 119.
[121] Ibid.
[122] Merleau-Ponty, *Phenomenology of Perception*, p. 352. (Emphasis mine)
[123] Merleau-Ponty, "The Child's Relation with Others," p. 115.

Merleau-Ponty's recasting of the classical notion of "psyche" posits in his first term a subjectivity that is not inaccessible from "without" even as it is not publicly lived. Rather, this "psyche" is a subjectivity revealed and expressed through and across the body as the inscription of primal intentional behavior—as a mode of having being. This "my psyche" is primordial self-awareness, experienced by the infant as an undifferentiated and yet centered "me exists" and "me wants." While observations of infant behavior affirm the infant's lack of awareness of its limits and discretion as an entity, they also affirm this primordial sense of "myself." (Infants have long been known to begin crying when they hear *other* infants cry—demonstrating transitivism and incorporation of the Other. But it has also been demonstrated that infants only twenty hours old stop crying when a tape recording of their *own* crying is played to them—evidence of a primordial self-recognition at work.) Thus, as Lanigan points out, Merleau-Ponty's first term ("myself, my 'psyche' ") refers to the self as it is known "prior to the experience of self-as-other or prior to knowing the other"; "myself, my 'psyche' " is "the *cogito* as radical *cogito*."[124]

Merleau-Ponty's second term is the "introceptive image." This term nominates the infant's image of its own body as it is *sensibly lived through*, that is, as it is sensed from *within* by the psyche as also possessing an *exterior* modality of being-in-the-world. It is with regard to this term that Lacan and Merleau-Ponty can be seen to differ radically in their approach to the specular image and the infant's relation to it. As Lanigan describes it, that relation is not the one of duality and rivalry posed by Lacan: "The power of the realization that there is another myself exterior to me and a public figure on display for others is seen most accurately in the experience of seeing oneself in a mirror. In the mirror experience there is *the literal perception of psyche looking at body, yet the understanding that the image and the psyche are one*."[125]

The relation between "myself, my psyche" and my "introceptive image" is one that is lived through *prereflectively*. Nonetheless, it is the relation that presents and initiates sign production in its first casting. "Myself, my psyche" and my "introceptive image" exist in a *reversible* relation of signifier to signified. That is, lived subjectively from within, "myself, my psyche" is the SR of my "introceptive im-

[124] Lanigan, *Speaking and Semiology*, p. 210.
[125] Ibid., p. 109. (Emphasis mine)

age" (the SD), but lived objectively from without, as in Lacan's schema, my "introceptive image" is the SR of "myself, my psyche" (the SD).

The relation Merleau-Ponty describes between "myself, my psyche" and my "introceptive image" is not, as Lacanian psychoanalysis would have it, a "coalescence of the signifier with the signified" in the Imaginary order.[126] Rather, these relations are seen as a dialectic that emerges in the mirror phase as the "synthesis of coexistence," as *two* modalities of being *one-self*.[127] It is through this lived and pre-reflective synthesis that the infant is able to come to a state of *reflection*, to understand the lived logic whereby "unless I have an exterior others have no interior."[128] It is the relation between the first two of Merleau-Ponty's four terms which provides the infant two modalities of being and two "views" of its subjective body. Thus, this relation of "myself, my psyche" and "introceptive image" provides the infant with an *intrasubjective system* whereby the other can be systemically understood not only as an *object-in-itself-for-my-perception* but also as a *subject-for-itself-and-as-me*.

The "visual body," the third term in Merleau-Ponty's system, designates the body of the other as it is visible and seen by me. With respect to that initial relation that holds between "myself, my psyche" and my "introceptive image," the "visual body" of the other is the *visible* presence that allows me access to the other as a being such as myself and who, by virtue of my own experience of myself, is hypothetically in possession of its own being introceptively. As Lanigan puts it: "My sense of body and that of another's body come to constitute a *common* form or structure that is knowable by contrast and comparison. In this analysis of likeness and dissimilarity of corporeal perception there are two ways in which to view the other."[129] The body thus provides a *commutative function* between my *introceptivity* and the other's *exteriority*—that is, between seeing and being seen, between perception and its expression. The other's body can be understood as simultaneously both perceptive and expressive because I have a body that I live as capable of these two modalities, a body that reversibly functions as both SR and SD. "In short," Lanigan says, "the visual body is the medium through which the individ-

[126] Laplanche and Pontalis, *The Language of Psycho-Analysis*, p. 210.

[127] Merleau-Ponty, "The Child's Relation with Others," p. 140.

[128] Merleau-Ponty, *Phenomenology of Perception*, p. 373.

[129] Lanigan, *Speaking and Semiology*, p. 110. (Emphasis mine)

ual body-subject comes to an awareness of others whose bodily existence bears analogy to his own."[130]

Through this "visual body" and its mode of being that parallels my "introceptive image" as the body's "other side" (its visible expression), a fourth term emerges. This is the other's "psyche," the "other's feeling of his own existence" in the world and with others (one of whom is I, perceived by the other as a "visual body"). Unlike my own "psyche," however, the other's "psyche" is hypothetical in that I do not live it. It is thus intuited logically within a co-operative system as an "invisible" term not immanent as my perception. That is, the other's "psyche" is the SD of its "visual body" for me—and the other's "visual body" is the SR of another "psyche's" existence as a "myself." Because of my own lived knowledge of myself as constituted in the relation "myself, my psyche" and "introceptive image," I am able to also comprehend the other's "visual body" in its function as an SD for the relation between the other's "introceptive image" and "myself, my psyche," a relation that transcends my immanent experience but is systemically like my immanent experience. This "system of four terms" inaugurates the person as both individual and social, as both privately and publicly available, as both a self and an other whose lived-body constitutes a language with which I am—and you are.

Evoking the relations of the sign as ontological and the person as textual, Merleau-Ponty wrote in his notes for *The Visible and the Invisible:*

> The other, not as a "consciousness," but as an inhabitant of a body, and consequently of the world. Where is the other in this body that I see? He is (like the meaning of the sentence) immanent in this body (one cannot detach him from it and pose him apart) and yet, more than the sum of the signs or the significations conveyed by them. He is that of which they are always the partial and nonexhaustive image—and who nonetheless is attested wholly in each of them. Always in the process of an unfinished incarnation—Beyond the objective body as the sense of the painting is beyond the canvas.[131]

In Merleau-Ponty's logical system of four terms, I can recognize reflectively the presence of another subjectivity that transcends my perception even as it is present to my perception and is grasped by it.

---

[130] Ibid., p. 111.
[131] Merleau-Ponty, *The Visible and the Invisible*, pp. 209–210.

The other and I mirror each other. We acknowledge a reciprocity of being—as "seeing being" and "being seen," as transcendent and immanent, as invisible and visible.

Certainly, as Lacan's schematic suggests, there can be a competitive rivalry between Self and Other, a relation in which one is subjected to the other and becomes an object rather than a subject. However, such rivalry rests upon an implicit and lived knowledge of the reversibility of its terms. The dualism it announces is false. There could be no rivalry were we not vulnerable *to* each other *as* each other. Lanigan points out, "What one must be aware of is the separation of myself and the other, not as subject and object, but as corporality and corporality with the possibility of psychic reflection that is a claim to immediacy (i.e., the lived-body experience)."[132] It is this corporality that the infant lives from birth and that is reflected in the mirror and appears beside it. It is this corporality that serves as the commutation between the self and others, between perception and expression, between immanence and transcendence, between *flesh* and *language*. Whether seen as a specular image or as a substantial body, "the other and I are the possibility of one another and can know each other as the like body of myself. And, the presence of the other moves from a possibility, from the potential X, to the constituted other through the action that is gesture, facial movement, bodily position, and *speech* to an experienced actuality."[133]

It is as the acting body that the other becomes constituted for me as another subjectivity. Through its intentional activity, Merleau-Ponty tells us, "the other body has ceased to be a mere fragment of the world, and becomes the theater of a certain process of elaboration, and, as it were, a certain 'view' of the world." And, he continues:

> I say that it is another person, a second self, and this I know in the first place because this living body has the same structure as mine. I experience my own body as the power of adopting certain forms of behaviour and a certain world, and I am given to myself merely as a certain hold upon the world: now, it is precisely my body which perceives the body of another person, and discovers in that other's body a miraculous prolongation of my own intentions, a familiar way of dealing with the world. *Henceforth, as the parts of my body together comprise a system, so my body and the other person's are one whole, two sides of*

[132] Lanigan, *Speaking and Semiology*, p. 115.
[133] Ibid., p. 113.

127

one and the same phenomenon, and the anonymous existence of which my body is the ever-renewed trace henceforth inhabits both bodies simultaneously.[134]

By virtue of our common *form* and our common *wor(l)d,* we live both intrapersonally and intersubjectively from the moment of our birth. However, we share neither our *bodily situation* in the world nor our immanent experience of its intentional spatialization lived in the world as a *uniquely inscribed temporalization.* Self and Other emerge from these differences as the diacritical markers of particular modes of existence, but they do so against the common ground of our anonymous similarity as beings-in-the-world. Seeing and being seen, the viewing subject is visible to other subjects because she is incarnate and shares a world, because she has a point of view that can transcend, displace, and negate itself in intentional action. Seeing and being seen is an open system that signifies flesh and materiality as meaningful and allows for the possibility of communication in all its modalities. This is semiotics as it begins with the subjectively lived objective body, always already thrown into the world as both privately and publicly experienced. Thus, counter to Lacan, Merleau-Ponty says, "Even if each of us has his own archetype of the other, the very fact that he is open to participation, that he is a sort of cipher or symbol of the other, obliges us to pose the problem of the other, not as a problem of access to another nihilation, but as a problem of initiation into a symbolics and a typicality of the others of which the *being for itself* and the *being for the other* are reflective variants and not the essential forms."[135]

It is this symbolics, this system of four terms, that the infant learns in the mirror or its analogues. And it is this symbolics that initiates us into the bodily reflection that gives us the visibility of our own vision. We become viewing subjects in possession of our own eyes, our own sight. We know "what *we* and what *seeing* are."

FILM AND/AS VIEWING SUBJECT

There is no one who would argue the claim that the act of viewing is essential to the film experience and to cinematic communication.[136]

---

[134] Merleau-Ponty, *Phenomenology of Perception,* pp. 353–354. (Emphasis mine)

[135] Merleau-Ponty, *The Visible and the Invisible,* p. 82n.

[136] The fact that a film can be experienced by blind people does not counter this

Indeed, it is precisely because such a claim is so obviously and summarily descriptive of what we already know to be true to experience that it seems complete and in need of no further explication. The aim here, however, has been to interrogate the act of viewing as it provides the foundation for the intelligibility and signification that constitute cinematic experience, to describe rigorously both the existential act of viewing as an essential structure and its genetic function as the ground for any further figures of theoretical elaboration. Thus, the act of viewing has not been presupposed, nor has it been fragmented into discrete and isolated parts or terms.

These initial descriptions have deferred extended discussion of the film in relation to the spectator. They have revealed, however, that the film is not merely the viewed object that it has been considered in the conventional reifications of the "natural attitude." Reflection also has revealed that the spectator is not to be presumed isolated and detached from her own processes of visual production, even in the "normal" viewing situation. The spectator as viewer is not abstracted from the act of viewing—in current terms, "objectified" and "alienated." If anything has been presupposed by phenomenological reflection, it is that if we desire to understand the cinema as an object of vision for a human viewer, the act in which the film is seen and through which it appears as the phenomenon it is provides us with the initial field of our inquiry. For it is only in the act of viewing that the film is given to our experience as meaningful, and it is only in the act of viewing that the film possesses existence for itself as well as for us. A film can't *be seen* outside of *our* act of viewing it, and a film can't *be* outside of *its own* act of viewing. We must see a film for it to be seen, and a film must constitute an act of seeing for us to be able to see it. Therefore, it is the act of viewing that links the spectator *of* a film and the film *as* spectator.

Taken for granted in the "natural attitude," reflection has shown us that vision is irreducibly complex in its existential structure and function. First, we have seen that vision has an *intentional structure* that is irreducible in its correlation of a *seeing act* and a *seen object*. This correlation is as irreducible in cinematic vision as it is in the film

---

claim. Insofar as a film has music and dialogue, it can be engaged by visually impaired people. Nonetheless, that engagement is not a full one and is not, properly, a cinematic one (even if, in the interests of convention, it is nominated as such). Even given some of the astonishing advances in prosthetics (e.g., electronic devices that "translate" visual images into tactile inscriptions on the body in a way that is not symbolic as is braille, but is diagrammatic), the experience would be a "translation."

spectator's vision. Even in the most "abstract" films, even in films where actual technique has not used the camera's ability "to see" referentially (such as those in which paint is applied to the celluloid), the resultant projection of the film evidences the relation of a "seeing act" to a "seen object" (in these cases, a referentially indeterminate but nonetheless visible visual field).

Intentional in structure, the act of viewing is also *existential*. It manifests perception as intentionality lived through a body-subject. Thus, in its irreducible correlational structure, the act of viewing is always directed and diacritical. Embodied vision is not only an intentional correlation of the seeing and the seen, the viewing-view and the viewed-view. Made in the context of existence, the act of viewing is also an act of choice that marks off the visible from the invisible as it finitely inscribes its field of intention and attention and gives it systemic value. Although existential vision maintains a structural reversibility of direction (what is seeing can be seen, what is invisible can become visible, what is an intentional act can be transposed to an intentional object), the act of viewing always diacritically chooses a direction and chooses its figures—thereby ascribing value to its objects.

Thus, embodied vision exists in an essential form of nonequivalence. There is always the invisible horizon that grounds the visible visual field. And there is always a latency in the visible visual field that provides the ground for the actively constituted visible figure. As a modality of existential perception, the act of viewing manifests itself in a figure/ground correlational structure or gestalt in which figure and ground are reversible. Nonetheless, what counts as figure always will be the dominant correlate of the relation. Here, we might recall Merleau-Ponty's remarks about the simultaneous openness and finitude of vision. As we are, so vision is condemned to meaning and signification, condemned to the bounded freedom of existential choice. Merleau-Ponty tells us: "Nothing prevents us from crossing the limits with the movements of the look, but this freedom remains secretly bound; we can only displace our look, that is transfer its limits elsewhere. But it is necessary that there be always a limit; what is won on one side must be lost from the other."[137]

What has been said here of the act of viewing is as descriptive of the visual performance of a film as it is of the visual performance of

---

[137] Merleau-Ponty, *The Visible and the Invisible*, p. 100.

the person watching it. Suggested in this same passage, however, is what might be regarded as a radical difference between the seeing that a film performs before us and the seeing we perform before it. Merleau-Ponty points out that the "necessity" that limits human vision is hardly abrupt. It is neither an "objective frontier" nor made of impassable lines "cut out against an expanse of blackness." Our vision ends gently rather than geometrically. And, as we get very close to them, "things dissociate," and "our look loses its differentiation, and the vision ceases for lack of seer and of articulated things."[138]

At first glance, "cut out against an expanse of blackness," the film's *frame* seems to mark the conditions of its vision as radically different from our own. And yet, as the film's vision approaches the figure of its concern, as it intends and attends toward things, other things visible in its field do "dissociate." Approached too closely (although how closely relative to human vision is another matter), they become vague and undifferentiated as figures. As well, as the film's vision moves toward its intentional objects, others gently peel away out of frame—and much less abruptly than we *think*. Rather, *experience* reveals a sort of loss of differentiation (no matter how clear the technical focus), a relegation to visible latency by which things become gradually invisible before they vanish from the frame and the visual field and the particular "vision ceases for lack of seer and of articulated things." This is not to deny the geometric rectangularity of the frame nor its function for us as objective spectators, but it is to assert that the frame's function in the subjective visual activity of the film is not to halt vision abruptly.

The frame is *invisible* to the seeing that is the film. It is a limit, but like that of our own vision it is inexhaustibly mobile and free to displace itself. Although the frame is visible to *us*, it functions as the "secret" boundary of the film's act of vision. *We* may see the film's seeing as "cut out against an expanse of blackness," but the *film's* seeing does not "cut out" its vision as a geometric act committed upon the world it engages visually. Rather, its visual freedom in the activity of seeing gently comes to an end (unless, as I might test the contours of my visual field by trying to "outlook" them, the film is bent on exploring the limits of its own vision). For the film as for us, then, the openness upon the world that is the act of viewing "implies

[138] Ibid.

that the world be and remain a horizon" that extends beyond any immediate view seen by an existential presence that "is of it and is in it."[139]

The perceptive act of viewing has been revealed as a gestalt that is always already expressive in its systemic organization of both the visible and the invisible (the selection of the visual field from the world as horizon of visual possibility), and the latent ground and the active figure in the visible. Because vision is both selective and combinatory for both spectator and film, the act of viewing is not only the *passive perception of the visible* but also their *active visual expression*. Seeing is a lived-logic. As a modality of perception, vision is both a *reflection* of existence in its conventionally organized structure and an *inflection* of existence as an inventive organizing activity. What is visible to us as spectators and what is visible to the film's vision as "images" are both already organized and structured as syntagmatic combinations of figure/ground relations selected from the paradigmatic possibilities of the unseen and invisible horizon of vision—and selected within the context of a culture and a history. In this system of vision, the visible is thus a reflection of existence. However, what is usually invisible to us as spectators and to the film's own vision (both usually intent on constituting the visible image), is the *coming into being* of visual organization, the *structuring activity* of our vision engaged with a world. This is vision as an inflection of existence, as a personal description of our contingent intentions toward that world.

Seeing, therefore, is a primordial "thought" and a *primary* "language" enacted by the body-subject being-in-the-world. In its structure and activity, embodied vision initiates the logic and signifying power found in all *secondary* semiotic codes and systems. Whether in the act of seeing that is performed by us or by a film, vision is hermeneutically and semiotically systemic. And it communicates in a manner that does not require passage through the defiles of "natural" language, because it is lived both naturally and conventionally through incarnate engagement with the world whose fleshy material it shares. The structure of embodied vision functions semiotically as an iconic, indexical, and symbolic sign of intentionality, world, and seeing subject engaged in a trichotomy of always social intersubjective relations. Seeing presents itself as the seen, it points to the seen, and it represents the seen to and for an other who sees.

[139] Ibid.

Previous description has clarified that, as one of many modalities of perception and access to the world, seeing is not only a visual activity. Seeing is both *synaesthetic* and *synoptic*. Whether human or cinematic, vision is informed and charged by other modes of perception, and thus it always implicates a *sighted body* rather than merely transcendental eyes. What is seen on the screen by the seeing that is the film has a texture and solidity. This is a vision that knows what it is to touch things in the world, that understands materiality. The film's vision thus perceives and expresses the "sense" of fabrics like velvet or the roughness of tree bark or the yielding softness of human flesh. It not only understands the world haptically but also proxemically, that is, in terms of a spatiality that is lived as intimacy or distance in relation to the objects of its intentions.

The film, therefore, is more than "pure" vision. Its existence as a "viewing-view/viewed-view" implicates a "body." Realized by the physical presence of the camera at the scene of the cinematography yet not the same as the camera, the film's "body" need not be visible in its vision—just as we are not visible in our vision as it accomplishes its visual grasp of things other than itself. Still, the film's "body" is always implicated in its vision, just as our whole being as embodied informs what we see and makes us present to the visible even as the visible appears as present to us. This incarnation of vision inhabits a world—a world that exceeds its bodily limits, and to which it relates finitely and from an embodied situation. (In the next chapter, I will return to the film's "body"—where the quotation marks indicating an irregular, questionable, or metaphoric usage of the term *body* will be removed through phenomenological description of what is, in experience, an empirical and functional subject-object.)

My insistence here on vision as an embodied activity is not an argument for or description of the conventions of what is called "realist" cinema. Rather, given the act of viewing and its implication of an incarnate "seer," I am suggesting the *materialism* of cinema. (And, as we have seen and shall further elaborate, that materialism is ontologically dialectical.) The act of seeing is an incarnate activity. It presents a world (any possible world imaged or imagined) whose horizons exceed its immediate visibility. The act of seeing also suggests that the source of its activity shares a material equivalence with that which appears to it in the world it presents. Whether the much-maligned "classical" or "bourgeois" Hollywood cinema, a Bugs Bunny cartoon with its explicit and "impossible" transformations, a computer-generated short, a cinéma vérité documentary, or a structural-materialist film, *all* film presents not only the seen but also the seeing. In so doing, it posits a lived, inhabitable, and intentional *distance* that structures and is structured by the act of vision, a distance that begins at and ends in a seer who is capable of seeing, who is embodied. Thus, in its structure as an existential activity and its implication of an embodied viewer, the act of vision (whether human or "mechanical") is always *dimensional*, always has thickness as it possesses possible or actual *movement* in the world as intentional and diacritical activity.

Previously, the frame was mentioned as a limit upon the film's vision, but not the kind of limit that its seemingly hard-edged geometry might suggest to those of us looking at the film's vision *from without*. (Again, the skeptical here might look to how our own vision is not hard-edged or geometric in its limits, and yet how it appears so in others if we regard the form and limits of their eyes.) The frame, however, serves another function that is both invisible to the film's seeing of its world and yet visible to us. The frame provides the *synoptic center* of the film's experience of the world it sees; it functions for the film as the field of our bodies does for us. That is, as does every lived-body, the frame literally provides the *premises* for perception as expressed experience. It provides seeing a place where sight can "co-Here," where it can signify and take on significance. Indeed, here it is useful to recall Zaner's description of the four fundamental ways in which the body perceptively engages us in the world and articulates itself as perceptive at progressively higher levels. His elaboration of the body's functions suggests how the frame serves a similar function *for* the film and also represents that function *to* those of us who look at the film's vision from outside its vision and its material embodiment.

However mobile, the frame (like the human body) is invariantly the bearer of the film's "orientational point, O, with respect to which other objects are organized in the spatio-temporal surrounding world." Like the human body, the frame also functions as an "organ of perception" (although not the only one); however, it provides a single instrumentality that accommodates several sensory fields (not only sight, but touch as noted, and also, significantly, sound), and it functions as "that by means of which" the film has access to its world and the world exists for it (and for us). As well, by virtue of its unity (the frame is always the same frame even as it decenters itself and moves and its visible contents are displaced), the frame synthesizes these several sensory fields as the premises "on and in which" the film's "fields of sensation are spread out." Finally, the frame—that "invisible" trace of the activity of the film's seeing—actualizes both the film's operational and deliberative desire to see and to show, to perceive and express—at its "highest level," actualizing the reflective vision or deliberative intentionality that transforms the operative and signifying experience of consciousness into the signification of conscious experience.[140]

A phenomenological description of the act of viewing inevitably leads to an *embodied viewer*—not visible *in* the act or its productions but generative *of* the act and its existentially directed and diacritical structure. This viewer is not transcendentally located, however invisible it is in vision. It is only through *reflection* that the viewer can be "seen," that is, intended as an object of vision. As Lacan and Merleau-Ponty have suggested, in human body-subjects this reflection is most concretely accomplished through an engagement with a mirror and, later, more generally accomplished through use of the linguistic shifter, "I." While often making use of the concrete mirror encounter, the film's activity of reflection on its own existence has also tended to take more general and mature forms of *reflexivity*. In both instances, however, reflection and reflexivity are merely ways of making *explicit* what exists *prior to* reflection and reflexivity and, indeed, provides their grounds. Just as there is a primordial human subjectivity that anonymously provides the ground upon which Self can figure in a relation that is reflective and intrapersonal, so also is there a primordial and anonymously lived cinematic subjectivity that provides the ground upon which a self-conscious cinema can figure as a reflection upon and interrogation of the nature and function of its own being.

The lack of explicit reflection and reflexivity in no way means that this primordial subjectivity is not humanly or cinematically present and lived-through. Whether or not the film uses the visual equivalent of the verbal shifter "I," its very existence is predicated on the "me"—the "myself, my psyche" that is the first of Merleau-Ponty's four terms. Indeed, what I am suggesting here is that the power of the medium and its ability to communicate the experience of embodied and enworlded vision resides in the experience *common* to both

---

[140] Zaner, *The Problem of Embodiment*, pp. 249–251.

film and spectator: the *act of viewing as experienced from within*. Both film and spectator are engaged in the act of seeing a world as visible, and both inhabit their vision from within it—as the intrapersonal relation between "myself, my psyche" and my "introceptive image." (It should be noted, however, that insofar as this intrapersonal relation exists in a lived-body and in the world, it is always also an extrapersonal relation—that is, its intrapersonal terms are informed by culture and history.) At the very least, then, the film *duplicates* the structure and activity (although not necessarily the particular content and significance) of its spectator's vision.

Although the intrapersonal structure and activity of vision is common to both film and spectator, the film's vision is *not* the spectator's vision—although as Lacan suggests and Christian Metz elaborates in regard to cinema, this homology can lead to a confusion of the spectator's vision and the film's vision.[141] We are not dealing here with a *single* act of viewing or with solely *intrapersonal* relations (that is, the self as both subject and object of its own consciousness, the Self as its own Other). Again, Merleau-Ponty's system of four terms helps us recognize how we can see the film's seeing as the seeing of another who is *like* myself, but *not* myself.

In the ordinary experience of our encounter with another person, our *intersubjective* recognition of an other *as* a subject ("another myself") is marked by the initial relations given to me as immanent experience. Those relations that obtain between "myself, my psyche" and my "introceptive image" as the "inside" (or, more accurately, the "other side") of the "visual body" reflect how (or so the mirror tells me) "myself, my psyche" and my "introceptive image" appear lived from "outside" that initial and intrapersonal relation. The "visual body" of another acting in my vision is thus understood as having an "inside" or "other side," of being-for-itself an "introceptive image" lived from within by another "myself, my psyche."

In our ordinary human experience of each other, one term in this system of four terms is not immanent to either of us. The "invisible" term in the system, the "hypothetical" term for each of us, is the "psyche" of the other. (*See Figure 1.*) The "psyche" of the other is revealed only as a visibly "absent" presence, as "transcendent" rather than immanent in my experience. Yet it is a presence nonethe-

[141] See Christian Metz, "The Imaginary Signifier," trans. Ben Brewster, *Screen* 16 (Summer 1975), pp. 14–76; and *The Imaginary Signifier: Psychoanalysis and the Cinema*, trans. Celia Britton, Annwyl Williams, Ben Brewster, and Alfred Guzzetti (Bloomington: Indiana Univ. Press, 1982).

INTERSUBJECTIVE RELATIONS

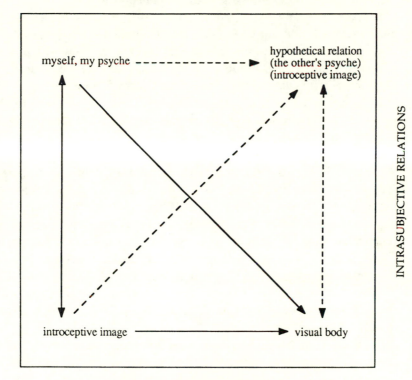

FIGURE 1. Person/Person Relations (Merleau-Ponty's System of Four Terms)

less, for although I can't see it, I can see its activity. The other's "psyche" is inscribed in the visible conduct and behavior, in the postural schema or style, of the other's "visual body." As it intentionally inhabits and relates to a world, this body's visible behavior is understood as a possible (if not necessarily probable) intentional motor project that could be taken up by my own body, and it signifies the presence of the other as a subject-for-itself as well as an intentional object for me.

The spectator's encounter with a film, however, is somewhat different. Unlike other viewing persons I encounter, the film *visibly* duplicates the act of viewing from "within"—that is, the *introceptive* and *intrasubjective* side of vision. Whereas the other seeing person's "visual body" is visible to me in our encounter with the world and each other, the film's "visual body" is usually invisible to me. Indeed, it is as generally invisible as my own "visual body"—which, nonetheless, I introceptively live and perceive in my ordinary experience (including that of watching a film). In my usual visual encounter with another who is engaged in an act of vision, the "invisible" or "transcendent" relational term is the other's "myself, my psyche." The other's "psyche" is known only by virtue of its immanent activity, its inscription of intentional behavior as it is lived through the other's "visual body." My encounter with the film, however, does not present me with the other's activity of seeing as it is inscribed through and translated into the activity of a visible "visual body." Rather, the film's activity of seeing is immanent and visible—given to my own vision as my own vision is given to me. The film's vision does not visibly appear as the "other" side of vision (the other's "visual body") but as vision lived through intentionally, introceptively, visually as "mine."

Despite its status as an other viewing subject who is not me and does not live my body nor occupy my situation, yet unlike other seeing persons, the film's interpersonal and intersubjective visibility is given to me uniquely from the "inside out," inscribed and made *visible* as the *intrapersonal* and *subjective* modality of vision. Instead of seeing the visual conduct and postural schema of the other's visible "visual body," I see the other's visual conduct and intentional postural schema as a uniquely visible "introceptive image." The film's vision is given to me as it is lived in the relation "myself, my psyche" and "introceptive image." Thus, the "hypothetical" or "invisible" term in my encounter with the film as an other's activity of viewing and its visible images is the film's "visual body." (*See Figure 2.*) I see no "visual body," but I do see a *visible conduct.* I see the film's seeing as it exists in relation to a world and others. I see the film's *visual behavior* as it inscribes as visible a *postural schema* and an *intentional style.*

In its intrasubjective structure, the film's visual conduct is thus given to me as homologous to my own visual conduct in watching it. Yet, it is clear, by virtue of this intrasubjective conduct's *intersubjective visibility* to me, that it is not *my* visual conduct. Even as I perceive it

INTERSUBJECTIVE RELATIONS

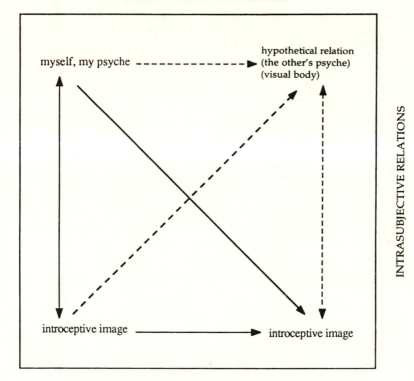

INTERSUBJECTIVE RELATIONS

———————————— = immanent relations

- - - - - - - - - - - - - - - = inferred relations

FIGURE 2. Spectator/Film Relations

as lived from within vision, it does not emerge as my own lived vision because I am seeing it as visible from without. Thus, the film's visual conduct and postural schema are experienced as *different* from my own, even as they are included in my vision. I see the autonomous, introceptive, and mobile visual behavior of an other subject in the world, and this visual conduct is contained *in* my own vision, but it is not contained *by* my vision (as might be the other's "visual body"). This is a seeing from "my side" of vision that is not performed by me, even as it is visible to me. Here, it is useful to recall Merleau-Ponty's summary of this transformation of the other as an intentional "object-for-me" to an intending "subject-for-itself-for-me" (although critically amended by interior bracketing to indicate the fact that the film's "visual body" is not immanent—"given" to me—in this encounter): "the other [body] has ceased to be a mere fragment of the world and becomes the theater of a certain process of elaboration, and as it were, a certain 'view' of the world."[142] How better to pose the experience of visually engaging the nature of the film's visible visual behavior?

Thus, the film presents itself within our vision not as an other's "visual body" from whose conduct we understand the living logic of an "invisible" and "hypothetical" intentionality that is enacted in the intrasubjective relation of "myself, my psyche" and "introceptive image." Rather, the film is engaged by our vision directly, as the intrasubjective and intentional experience lived by an other. Thus, the film is never contained in our vision as merely the intentional *object of our sight* but is always also significant and signifying as the intentional *subject of its own sight*. In visual possession of the world, this subject significantly enacts it as a *personal history*. If, as Merleau-Ponty says, "I am given to myself merely as a certain hold upon the world," then the film makes visible its "certain hold" and predicates its subjectivity (its "myself, my psyche" and "introceptive image") for itself and for me.[143] Speaking of the human other who is given to our acts of viewing in the conduct of his "visual body," Merleau-Ponty says: "I know unquestionably that that man over there *sees*, that my sensible world is also his, because *I am present at his seeing*, it is visible in his eyes' grasp of the scene. And when I say *that* he sees, there is no longer . . . the interlocking of two propositions, but the mutual unfocusing of a 'main' and a 'subordinate' viewing."[144] We know the film sees because we are present at its seeing. But its seeing—unlike the access we have to the vision of human others—is visible *through,* not in, its eyes' grasp of the scene. Given that its eyes are invisible to us, our mutual "unfocusing" occurs in the film "scene," in the film's "seen," and the conscious experience of a "main" and "subordinate"

---

[142] Merleau-Ponty, *Phenomenology of Perception*, p. 353.

[143] Ibid., p. 354.

[144] Merleau-Ponty, "The Philosopher and His Shadow," p. 169.

viewing is overtaken by a co-operative visual exploration of the visible world.

What is often regarded too quickly as a rivalry of vision is really a yielding to the mutual and intersubjective seeing and sharing of a visible world. This con-cession does not inherently entail a subjection to the vision of an other. It is also not a mis-taking of the other's vision as my own in a false and alienating but necessary identification. Through acts of vision experienced as present to each other, communion or conflict may occur in the world, but one viewer does not, and finally cannot, "usurp" the other viewer's situation, intentional and postural schema, and personal history. The purpose of visual communication is to share sight—to see as another sees, or to get another to see as I do. Yet, however small, there is always a distance between the self and the other self that necessitates communication in the first place and subsequently inaugurates and institutes a dialogue and dialectic of visions. Again, what Merleau-Ponty says of such dialogue in its human situation can be said also of the visual dialogue that occurs (however silently) in the dialectic of perception and expression that exists between film and spectator—both viewers engaged in acts of viewing that engage each other:

> In the experience of dialogue, there is constituted between the other person and myself a common ground; my thought and his are woven into a single fabric, my words and those of my interlocuter are called forth by the state of the discussion, and they are inserted into a shared operation of which neither of us is the creator. We have here a dual being . . . ; we are collaborators for each other in consummate reciprocity. Our perspectives merge into each other, and we co-exist through a common world. In the present dialogue, I am freed from myself. . . . It is only retrospectively, when I have withdrawn from the dialogue and am recalling it that I am able to reintegrate it into my life and make of it an episode in my private history, and that the other recedes into his absence, or, in so far as he remains present for me, is felt as a threat.[145]

If this sounds like an idealistic version of the film experience, it is so not by virtue of an inaccurate description of the engagement be-

---

[145] Merleau-Ponty, *Phenomenology of Perception*, pp. 354–355. For a parallel discussion of dialogue as it is experienced in relation to the aesthetic text, see Hans-Georg Gadamer, *Truth and Method* (New York: The Seabury Press, 1975), pp. 325–341.

tween film and spectator, but rather because it suggests a condition of mutual freedom bound in sociality and language that we do not often acknowledge in the current climate of theoretical pessimism. Such a description in no way denies the tyranny that *can* and *does* occur in such transactions, but it also affirms that tyranny is not a necessary or absolute *condition* of our encounter with others, be they humans or films. At the level of our lived-experience of consciousness (rather than at the level of our thought), the film, in its visual and visible intentional activity, exists within our vision but not as our vision. It presents and represents an other who is with us and for us and in itself as an "object-subject." Or, as Mikel Dufrenne says of the aesthetic object, it is a "quasi-subject."[146] Thus the film is encountered not merely as a visible object but also as a viewing subject, and our engagement with it is necessarily—if often invisibly—dialogic and dialectical (the experience of which we shall return to in subsequent chapters).

The strategy of this chapter and its descriptions has been phenomenological—not only in its taking up and investigation of vision as a phenomenon of consciousness but also in its method. That is, the chapter's process of description has moved reflectively "backward" from the *film "object"* (from what in the "natural attitude" first appears to vision as a visible thing), to the *act of viewing* (in which that "object" is seen as constituted in its very mode of appearing to vision). This thematization of vision as an activity has led us even further "backward" to reflexive reflection; that is, to the location of a *viewing subject* invisible in the act of vision but presently enabling it. This backward movement, however, has also been a movement forward. In describing the act of viewing necessary to the viewing of a film as an object of conscious experience, there also has been a description of the act of viewing necessary to the being of a film as a subject of experience. Phenomenological description has revealed that the film both perceives and expresses perception, that it sees and expresses its seeing so that its vision is sensible and significant. In this process of description, the existence of that "other seeing being" that is the film has been posited as constituting embodied subjectivity: "the sense of perception—a semiology of meaning from within." This "sense of perception" has also been revealed as expressive, ca-

[146] Mikel Dufrenne, *The Phenomenology of Aesthetic Experience*, trans. E. S. Casey et al. (Evanston, IL: Northwestern Univ. Press, 1973), pp. 146, 190, 196, 227, 382.

pable of signifying in the world and to others its own and the world's significance. Thus, this "sense of perception" is experienced within my own sense of perception as the expression of perception, "a semiology of meaning from without—which is 'the external existence of the sense' or its essence."[147]

The film presents an analogue of my own existence as embodied and significant. It is perceptive, expressive, and always in the process of becoming that being which is the conscious and reflected experience of its own expressed history. Like ourselves, the film's vision is an irreducible viewing-view and viewed-view, a lived vision that grasps a world and a reflective vision that reflexively grasps itself and its own signification. It is also a vision that is situated, finite, and necessarily diacritical in its direction and movement. Like our own vision, the film's vision is an embodied vision—even though, unlike our encounter with the visual experience of others, we do not usually see its "visual body." It is to the nature and function of the film's "body" that we turn in the next chapter. However, in closing this chapter, we must consider certain aspects of the human body that have particularly occupied contemporary film theory.

Whose Body?
A Brief Meditation on Sexual Difference and Other Bodily Discriminations

Except for comments in the Preface, a few parenthetical remarks, and a note or two, thus far I have avoided particularizing the body in terms of gender (or, for that matter, of race). This neglect has been purposeful. First, insofar as the present project is a response to the constraints of a binary thinking that would limit description of the terrain and terms of embodied vision as it relates to cinematic experience, I have resisted introducing the accepted terminology of "sexual difference" or starting my description relying on the ground staked out by dominant theoretical discourse. Second, insofar as any discussion of the body's specificity "outside" of the terms provided by dominant discourse calls for a new mode of articulation, it seemed important to introduce and work through the process and language of phenomenological description by first focusing on the body's ac-

[147] Lanigan, *Speaking and Semiology*, p. 96.

tivity of visual perception and visible expression. Third, insofar as existential and semiotic phenomenology suggests that "coding" and containing the body's excessive, mobile, and "wild" signification is a cultural and historical activity that stakes out upon the body's broader meaning-producing field a limited and mutable circumscription of significance, it has seemed important to introduce the lived-body in terms of its essential ontological functions—that is, those functions that do not precede, but do provide the ground for, the marking of and discrimination against the lived-body and its excessive, ambiguous, and over-running semiosis. The ground of discrete, strategic, and contested areas of value, differentiation, and discrimination, the lived-body is never merely or wholly male or female, white or black. (To initially take it up in such terms is an essentializing act that confuses epistemological qualifications with ontological conditions.) Rather, the lived-body is excessive and ambiguous in its materiality, its polymorphism, and its production of existential meaning. It manifests "the fleshy consciousness which inhabits a multi-dimensional field where the senses intermingle, a field open to a multiplicity of possible foci and interpretations. In Merleau-Ponty's understanding of the ambiguity and overflowing of perceptual experience we find the portent of the *différance* on which later French writers dwell."[148]

This section can suggest only briefly a direction and method for the further investigation of human embodiment as it is, first, always an essential set of ontological functions that enable "being-in-the-world" at all, and, second, always a qualified and specific set of epistemological functions that determine "being-in-a-particular-world" in a particular modality. The primary focus of this current work is on the ontological conditions of embodiment—specifically, insofar as they inform the existential activity of vision and suggest a system of commutation that provides the grounds for cinematic intelligibility. However, in no way does this focus preclude, deny, or contradict the simultaneous epistemological conditions by which embodiment is culturally and historically known in its materiality and nominated as a limited set of discriminations. The essential body is always also a qualified body.

[148] Jeffner Allen and Iris Marion Young, introduction to *The Thinking Muse: Feminism and Modern French Philosophy*, ed. Jeffner Allen and Iris Marion Young (Bloomington: Indiana Univ. Press, 1989), p. 5.

Cultural and historical practices always both generalize and discriminate in relation to the lived-body—on the one hand, recognizing its capacity as a vehicle of signification and its wide variety of signifying functions, and, on the other, reconstituting and containing its semiotic freedom by selecting from its excessive and particular features a limited number of binarily related, marked and unmarked elements.[149] Those features of bodily existence marked as most significant by and within our global culture and historical time are, of course, the body's "sex" and the body's "race." However, there are also other features of the body that have been marked as culturally and historically significant, that have been "given" meanings "taken up" by those living their bodies in the binary—and unequivalent—terms of the "marked" and "unmarked." Thus, focusing on the marked term (the "figure" selected against the invisible and "natural" ground that is the unmarked term and the cultural dominant), we can add to the "female" body and the "colored" body further significant discriminations: the "diseased" body, the "impaired" body, the "fat" body, the "old" body, and even the "deprived" body. (Along with "gender" and "race," "class" also makes its mark upon the body and the body its mark—and thus is open to phenomenological description.) These are the lived-bodies significantly marked and "disfigured" in our current culture. The term *disfigured* here is not used poetically but literally. That is, I am using the term with emphasis on its Latin roots: "*dis*-(in sense of 'spoiling') + *figurare*, to fashion, form."[150] Although to re-mark a bodily aspect or quality is to take it as a figure, it is also to spoil, mar, harm the lived-body *as a whole*. Marked elements thus *de-face* the lived-body in a synecdoche that refuses the body-*subject*: its existence as intentional and its activity of becoming.

I have introduced this variety of marked or "disfigured" bodies here so that the section's primary and limited focus on issues surrounding the discrimination of (and against) the "female" body can contextualize and be contextualized within a broader range of culturally significant bodily discriminations. By introducing such discrimi-

---

[149] For elaboration of the logic informing "marked" and "unmarked" terms in communication and language theory, see Elmar Holenstein, *Roman Jakobson's Approach to Language: Phenomenological Structuralism*, trans. Catherine Schelbert and Tarcisius Schelbert (Bloomington: Indiana Univ. Press, 1976), p. 131.

[150] *Webster's New World Dictionary of the American Language*, College ed. (Cleveland and New York: The World Publishing Company, 1966), p. 419.

nations now, I also hope that the models of phenomenological inquiry used by certain feminist philosophers to describe the lived-body experience of "women" in a culture that marks or "disfigures" lived-bodies as "female" might be suggestive for film theory and its descriptions of other discriminate lived-body experience in its engagement of cinema.

Insofar as it has focused on the human body at all, film theory has emphasized the body's "sexual difference" and the social construction of its gender, particularly as both relate to the processes of spectatorial identification and visual pleasure.[151] More recently, attention has also focused on the body's ethnicity and "racial difference"—or (only a bit less abstractly, and more specifically) on the spectatorial experience of "people of color."[152] In the first instance, theories of sexuality, sexual difference, and spectatorial engagement have

[151] The literature here is vast. For a sampling of book-length studies and anthologies focused on these issues, the reader is directed not only to the previously cited de Lauretis, *Alice Doesn't*; Doane, *The Desire to Desire*; and Studlar, *In the Realm of Pleasure*; but also to Teresa de Lauretis, *Technologies of Gender: Essays on Theory, Film, and Fiction* (Bloomington: Indiana Univ. Press, 1987); Lucy Fischer, *Shot/Countershot: A Dialogue on Women and Film* (Princeton, NJ: Princeton Univ. Press, 1989); Stephen Heath, *Questions of Cinema* (Bloomington: Indiana Univ. Press, 1981); E. Ann Kaplan, *Women and Film: Both Sides of the Camera* (New York: Methuen, 1983); Annette Kuhn, *Women's Pictures: Feminism and Cinema* (London: Routledge and Kegan Paul, 1982), and *The Power of the Image: Essays on Representation and Sexuality* (London: Routledge and Kegan Paul, 1985); Tania Modleski, *Loving with a Vengeance: Mass-Produced Fantasies for Women* (New York: Methuen, 1984), and *The Women Who Knew Too Much: Hitchcock and Feminist Theory* (New York: Methuen, 1988); Constance Penley, *The Future of an Illusion: Film, Feminism, and Psychoanalysis* (Minneapolis, Univ. of Minnesota Press, 1989); Kaja Silverman, *The Subject of Semiotics* (New York: Oxford Univ. Press, 1983), and *The Acoustic Mirror: The Female Voice in Psychoanalysis and Cinema* (Bloomington: Indiana Univ. Press, 1988); Mary Ann Doane, Patricia Mellencamp, and Linda Williams, eds., *Re-Vision: Essays in Feminist Film Criticism*, The American Film Institute Monograph Series, Vol. 3 (Frederick, MD: Univ. Publications of America, 1984); and Constance Penley, ed., *Feminism and Film Theory* (New York: Routledge, 1988).

[152] In comparison to the work available on sexual difference and cinematic identification, the theoretical literature here is scant and has tended to focus on "black" representation and spectatorship. For a sampling (as well as further bibliographic material), see Kobena Mercer, ed., *Black Film/British Cinema*, ICA Document 7 (London: British Film Institute Production Special, 1988); Mbye Cham and Claire Andrade-Watkins, eds., *BlackFrames: Critical Perspectives on Black Independent Cinema* (Boston: MIT Press, 1988); "Racism, Colonialism, and the Cinema," Special Issue, *Screen* 24, no. 2 (March-April 1983); "Other Cinemas, Other Criticisms," Special Issue, *Screen* 26, nos. 3-4 (May-August 1985); and "The Last 'Special Issue' on Race?" *Screen* 19, no. 4 (Autumn 1988).

emerged primarily within the context of psychoanalytic discourse (even when this libidinal theory of the subject is characterized by feminist film theorists as universalizing, patriarchally biased, and heterosexist). In the second instance, the issue of "race" and its information of spectatorship has emerged primarily within the context of colonial discourse analysis and its concern with structures of power, domination and subordination, centrality and marginality.

It is hardly surprising that, in the first instance, the problem of "sexual difference" has been focused on the marked term of "female" spectatorship (and, more recently, on sexual orientation focused on the marked terms of "gay/lesbian/bisexual" spectatorship). In the second instance, the problem of "race" has devolved around the marked term of "colored" spectatorship.[153] In both instances, a common sense of exclusion is articulated—exclusion both from the domain of cinematic expression and from the domain of theory. Both the expression of cinematic perception and the language of theory are regarded as suspect and limited but are all that is available to describe a range of human experience that neither cinema nor theory apparently can—or cares to—nominate and describe. Thus, for those whose experience has been elided or marginalized within the homogenizing rhetoric of culturally dominant discourses, a major task has been to locate a "place" from which women, people of diverse sexual orientations, and "people of color" can speak, and to find a "language" that can express not only the perception of their differences, but also their different perceptions.

Existential and semiotic phenomenology maintains that "place" and "language" can be found in the unique situation of each lived-body, even as it inhabits and moves in a social world of other lived-bodies that would deny its rightful residence and constrain its movements. What is often forgotten both in the homogenizing practices of dominant cinema and in abstract and "objective" theories of spectatorship is that the *particular* human lived-body (specifically lived as "my body") is *in excess* of the historical and analytic systems available to codify, contain, and even negate it. However, although perfectly consonant with the expressed aims of existential phenomenology and its insistence on meaning as always contingent and contextual as

---

[153] Of particular interest here is an attempt to deconstruct the unmarked and grounding term of racial difference; *white*. See Richard Dyer, "White," *Screen* 19, no. 4 (Autumn 1988), pp. 44–64.

it is individually, but also socially, lived by embodied subjects, this assertion in some ways radically challenges existential phenomenology's actual practice of "radical" description. Even Merleau-Ponty, whose contribution to phenomenology has been an insistence upon and elaborate description of human embodiment as the ground of all meaning and semiosis, has neglected any consideration of bodily existence as it is culturally and historically lived in certain forms of critical differentiation and discrimination. This is to say that the "lived-body" of existential and semiotic phenomenology has been explicitly articulated as "every body" and "any body" (even as it has implicitly assumed a male, heterosexual, and white body).[154] Sexual difference (and orientation) and "racial" difference have been ignored, although each human lived-body is, to at least some degree, a sexed and sexual body, and each has a skin, one of its qualities being color. This oversight and its implications have not gone unnoticed or uncriticized by feminist philosophers—even as many of them find in existential phenomenology a positive mode of reflection on particular forms of lived experience and a language that accommodates the latter's description.

On the one hand, certain feminist philosophers are drawn to existential phenomenology as "a philosophy of liberation that recognizes the potential for change exercised by individual and collective action."[155] Insofar as existential phenomenology emphasizes the lived-body in its situated freedom and its continual activity of self-displacement or "becoming" and understands even "the most apparently immutable human attributes . . . to be the product of human definition and thus subject to change," existential phenomenology offers feminists a positive context for reflection.[156] That is, as both a philosophy and reflective procedure, existential phenomenology interrogates the "given" and the "natural" determinants of existence and suggests that they might be and indeed could be otherwise. As Jeffner Allen puts it: "The excitement of existentialism, for a feminist philosopher such as myself, is its unwavering affirmation of change. Existential

[154] For examples and elaboration of this critique, see Jeffner Allen, "Through the Wild Region: An Essay in Phenomenological Feminism," *Review of Existential Psychology and Psychiatry* 18, nos. 1–3 (1982–1983), pp. 241–256; and Judith Butler, "Sexual Ideology and Phenomenological Description: A Feminist Critique of Merleau-Ponty's *Phenomenology of Perception*," in *The Thinking Muse*, pp. 85–100.

[155] Allen and Young, introduction to *The Thinking Muse*, p. 2.

[156] Ibid., p. 3.

emphasis on the primacy of existence over essence shows that I have no "nature": I am not destined to enact the dictates of biology, social custom, or political institutions. I am what I become through my choices to resist fixity and to create a new freedom. . . . change is effected through an intense focus on the possibilities which lie, albeit ambiguously, in my worlds of experience."[157] In this sense, although emphasizing its central task as radical description, existential phenomenology challenges normative experience and opens the way to revolutionary action. "The fact that one is a slave today determines nothing about one's being tomorrow." "One is not born a woman. Femininity and masculinity are socially defined forms of identity that need not . . . exist at all."[158]

On the other hand, existential phenomenology has been subject to critique from feminist philosophers. Indeed, whatever possibilities it offers for the radical description of existence and experience and however much it has challenged categorical and binary thinking, existential phenomenology is also rightfully seen as itself historically patriarchal. That is, in its project of describing and interpreting *human* being-in-the-world and the experience and significance lived and constituted by the *body-subject*, existential phenomenology has encountered the same kind of feminist critique that has been leveled at other "humanisms." Apart from Simone de Beauvoir's *The Second Sex* (its own feminist existentialism limited by patriarchal and binary ascriptions of activity and passivity linked to sexual difference), the insights that one is not born a woman and that femininity and masculinity are social forms that need not exist at all are not articulated in the philosophical canon.[159] Thus, despite her enthusiasm for existential phenomenology, Jeffner Allen also writes, "To the extent that existential description and the concepts which animate that description equate the masculine with the human, existentialism renders a reductive and misleading account of experience, specifically, of women's experience."[160]

Existential phenomenology in general (as well as Merleau-Ponty's work in particular) assumes "the neutrality and universality of the

---

[157] Jeffner Allen, "An Introduction to Patriarchal Existentialism: A Proposal for a Way Out of Existential Patriarchy," in *The Thinking Muse*, p. 71.

[158] Allen and Young, introduction to *The Thinking Muse*, p. 3.

[159] Simone de Beauvoir, *The Second Sex*, trans. H.M. Parshley (New York: Alfred A. Knopf, 1952).

[160] Allen, "An Introduction to Patriarchal Existentialism," *The Thinking Muse*, p. 72.

subject" and "devalues gender."[161] (For similar reasons, it also devalues "race" and "ethnicity.") In a powerful deconstruction of Merleau-Ponty's "The Body in Its Sexual Being" (an unusually brief and disturbingly vague chapter in the *Phenomenology of Perception*), Judith Butler summarizes the philosopher's implicit patriarchal and heterosexist orientation, what she calls his "sexual Cartesianism":

> Merleau-Ponty's conception of the "subject" is . . . problematic in virtue of its abstract and anonymous status, as if the subject described were a universal subject or structured existing subjects universally. Devoid of a gender, this subject is presumed to characterize all genders. On the one hand, this pre-sumption devalues gender as a relevant category in the description of lived bodily experience. On the other hand, inasmuch as the subject described resembles a culturally constructed male subject, it consecrates masculine identity as the model for the human subject, thereby devaluing, not gender, but women.
>
> Merleau-Ponty's explicit avoidance of gender as a relevant concern in the description of lived experience, and his implicit universalization of the male subject, are aided by a methodology that fails to acknowledge the historicity of sexuality and of bodies. For a concrete description of lived experience, it seems crucial to ask *whose* sexuality and *whose* bodies are being described, for "sexuality" and "bodies" remain abstractions without first being situated in concrete social and cultural contexts.[162]

Arguing that critical deconstruction of existential phenomenology and Merleau-Ponty's devaluation of gender and of women is a major task of feminist philosophy, Butler nonetheless calls for a "feminist appropriation of Merleau-Ponty." Appreciating the philosopher's emphasis on the body as expressing and dramatizing existential themes, Butler suggests that insofar as these themes are "gender-specific and fully historicized," phenomenological reflection allows access to and description of "a scene of cultural struggle, improvisation, and innovation, a domain in which the intimate and the political converge . . . a dramatic opportunity for expression, analysis, and change. The terms of this inquiry, however, will not be found in the

---

[161] Allen and Young, introduction to *The Thinking Muse*, p. 16.

[162] Butler, "Sexual Ideology and Phenomenological Description," *The Thinking Muse*, p. 98.

texts of Merleau-Ponty, but in the works of philosophical feminism. . . ."[163]

Thus, it is not to Merleau-Ponty, but to a feminist philosopher that I will turn for phenomenological descriptions of lived-body experience that is gender-specific and historicized. The work of Iris M. Young is exemplary in providing a model that, on the one hand, is based on certain ontological assumptions about embodiment shared with Merleau-Ponty and, on the other hand, qualifies the character of a specific body as it is marked, constrained, and lived as "female" in our present culture.[164] Young's phenomenological descriptions of women's experience are positive as well as critical; they focus on the particular and quite distinctive pleasures of being a female body as well as on the ways in which, in certain cultures such as our own, the female body-subject has, in the performance of certain intentional projects, often lived her body tentatively and in heightened consciousness of it as an object.

Of particular relevance here is Young's "Throwing Like a Girl: A Phenomenology of Feminine Body Comportment, Motility, and Spatiality." On the one hand, the essay criticizes phenomenological description that has not lived up to its radical aspirations and has failed to describe adequately "the modalities, meaning, and implications of the difference between 'masculine' and 'feminine' body comportment and movement."[165] On the other hand, Young uses phenomenological description to trace "some of the basic modalities of feminine body comportment, manner of moving, and relation in space" in "women situated in contemporary, advanced industrial, urban, and commercial society" and to thematize the "intelligibility and significance" of "certain observable and rather ordinary ways in which women in our society typically comport themselves and move differently from the ways that men do."[166] (Young is very careful to indi-

---

[163] Ibid., p. 99.

[164] See, particularly, Iris M. Young, "Pregnant Subjectivity and the Limits of Existential Phenomenology," in *Descriptions*, ed. Don Ihde and Hugh J. Silverman (Albany: State Univ. of New York Press, 1985), pp. 25–34; "Throwing Like a Girl: A Phenomenology of Feminine Body Comportment, Motility, and Spatiality," in *The Thinking Muse*, pp. 51–70; and "Breasted Experience: The Look and the Feeling," in *Throwing Like a Girl and Other Essays in Feminist Philosophy and Social Theory* (Bloomington: Indiana Univ. Press, 1990), pp. 189–209.

[165] Young, "Throwing Like a Girl," in *The Thinking Muse*, p. 52.

[166] Ibid., p. 53.

cate on what cultural and historical bases and within what limits she presumes to thematize comportment and movement as "feminine" and therefore "typical" of "women.") At first glance, Young's essay might seem irrelevant to our concerns here with sexual difference and spectatorship. Her major focus is on "activities which relate to the comportment or orientation of the body as a whole, which entail gross movement, or which require the enlistment of strength and the confrontation of the body's capacities and possibilities with the resistance and malleability of things," activities that aim "at the accomplishment of a definite purpose or task."[167] Nonetheless, insofar as vision is an existential activity that emerges within an entire bodily schema and "orientation of the body as a whole toward things and its environment,"[168] Young's phenomenology of purposive action may reveal the bodily in-formation of women's experience of spectatorship (whether as film-goer or filmmaker).

Young begins with a phenomenological description of ordinary activities, noting empirically observable and specific features of women's bodily comportment, motility, and use of space—particularly as they are differentiated from male behavior in the performance of similar tasks. These features include "a failure to make full use of the body's spatial and lateral potentialities"; a relative lack of bodily "openness" in "gait and stride" and a tendency to close the body in on itself whether sitting, walking, or carrying objects; not putting the whole body into engagement with "tasks that require force, strength, and muscular coordination"; the tendency to concentrate motion in "one body part"; tentative rather than "fluid and directed motion"; and limited reaching, extending, leaning, stretching, or following through "in the direction of her intention."[169] In relation to space, Young also describes how, even in sports activities, women tend to "remain in one place more often than men" and "react" within that constricted space to objects that approach them rather than appropriating space in an active movement toward objects.[170]

These observable differences between men and women are in no way attributed to biological difference or some inherent feminine or masculine "nature." Rather, and as might be expected, Young lays out a number of historical and cultural factors that might "explain"

[167] Ibid.
[168] Ibid., p. 54.
[169] Ibid., pp. 55–56.
[170] Ibid., p. 57.

the difference—and again indicates that her descriptions and generalizations are limited in their claims. As a phenomenologist, however, Young is less interested in sociological explanation than in the explication of the lived meaning of these bodily differences. Thus, she proceeds to a phenomenological reduction or "thematization" of the features mentioned above. She tells us: "The three modalities of feminine motility are that feminine movement exhibits an *ambiguous transcendence*, an *inhibited intentionality*, and a *discontinuous unity* with its surroundings. A source of these contradictory modalities is the bodily self-reference of feminine comportment, which derives from the woman's experience of her body as a *thing* at the same time that she experiences it as a capacity."[171] As has been indicated previously, the lived-body has been described by phenomenology as both immanent and transcendent. An object in the world and immanent in its materiality and situation, the body is transcendent nonetheless; it is lived as a subject, as intentional, as "pure fluid action, the continuous calling forth of capacities, which are applied to the world."[172] Young, however, points out that relative to masculine bodily existence "feminine bodily existence . . . is *overlaid* with immanence, even as it moves out toward the world."[173] Only part of a woman's body moves toward the accomplishment of a given task, "while the rest remains rooted in immanence."[174] Unsure of her physical capacity, often finding it unwieldy or expecting it to be inadequate, attempting tasks the woman "often lives her body as a burden, which must be dragged and prodded along, and at the same time protected."[175] Hence, the lived-body's transcendence is ambiguous when it is lived as a woman.

Similarly, in the culture and historical moment of which Young speaks, living one's body as a woman in certain gross motor activities inhibits its expression of intentionality, constitutes a contradiction (or dialectic) between the lived-body's inherent "I can" and the feminine body's acculturated "I cannot." (One can also see this contradiction or dialectic in men when they are engaged in "purposeless" or "aesthetic" motion such as social dancing.) Although any lived-body has to deal with the contradiction between its own intentional aims and

[171] Ibid., p. 58.
[172] Ibid., p. 59.
[173] Ibid.
[174] Ibid.
[175] Ibid.

the world's "opacities and resistances," the woman's lived-body often experiences this contradiction as the very structure of her intentional aims. Young points out: "To the extent that feminine bodily existence is an inhibited intentionality . . . the same set of possibilities which appears correlative to its intentions also appears as a system of frustrations correlative to its hesitancies. By repressing or withholding its own motile energy, feminine bodily existence frequently projects an 'I can' and an 'I cannot' with respect to the very same end."[176]

Previous discussion has also emphasized the lived-body's synoptic and synthesizing functions, its existence as a unified field and an organizing agency through which engagement in the world sensibly coheres as significant experience. Thematizing the various features of feminine comportment and motility, Young, however, suggests that feminine bodily existence "stands in *discontinuous unity* with both itself and its surroundings."[177] Performing their bodies only in part(s) rather than as a whole relative to certain motor tasks, women's motion is discontinuous with itself, that is, "that part of the body which is transcending toward an aim is in relative disunity from those which remain immobile. The undirectedness and wasted motion which is often an aspect of feminine engagement in a task also manifests this lack of body unity."[178] All three of the modalities of feminine bodily existence thematized by Young are structured in contradiction. And all have their source in the fact that, for women, "the body frequently is both subject and object for itself at the same time and in reference to the same act," an experience heightened in a culture in which a woman's body is regarded as "a *thing* which exists as looked at and acted upon."[179]

This observation, of course, says nothing new, particularly to feminist film theorists who have spent most of their efforts in laying out the "split subjectivity" that marks the female spectator who exists as both subject and object of what has been argued is essentially the cinema's male gaze. What is new, however, is that Young has reached this observation not through psychoanalysis but through phenomenological description and thematization of empirically observable phenomena—and she has described not essential structures

176 Ibid., p. 60.
177 Ibid.
178 Ibid., pp. 60–61.
179 Ibid., p. 61.

from which there is no escape but existential structures shaped by culture and history that could be otherwise. As well, of particular usefulness is her further elaboration from these data of a particular *feminine spatiality*. As has been discussed previously, space is not an abstract, objective category for phenomenology. Rather, it is lived and significantly constituted as the *relation* between the intentional body-subject prospecting and acting and the objective world that provides the context and horizons for projects and action. Thus, Young says: "If there are particular modalities of feminine bodily comportment and motility, then it must follow that there are also particular modalities of feminine spatiality. Feminine existence lives space as *enclosed* or confining, as having a *dual* structure and the feminine existent finds herself as *positioned* in space."[180]

Young notes that women appear to have a more clear sense of the boundaries of their bodies than do men and that they do not fully use or inhabit the phenomenal space that is physically available to them. Specifically, "Feminine existence appears to posit an existential enclosure between herself and the space surrounding her, in such a way that the space which belongs to her and is available to her grasp and manipulation is constricted, and the space beyond is not available to her movement."[181] Feminine existence also often experiences space as dually structured—the noematic complement to the inhibited intentionality informing certain feminine noetic activity as both an "I can" and "I cannot." Young describes this double and discontiguous spatiality as a

> space which is "yonder" and not linked with my own body possibilities, and the enclosed space which is "here," which I inhabit with my bodily possibilities.
>
> The space of the "yonder" is a space in which feminine existence projects possibilities in the sense of understanding that "someone" could move within it, but not I. Thus the space of the "yonder" exists for feminine existence, but only as that which she is looking into, rather than moving in.[182]

How particularly poignant and new this description is in relation to, for example, the final image of a film like *Stella Dallas* (King Vidor,

[180] Ibid., p. 62.
[181] Ibid., p. 63.
[182] Ibid.

155

1937). For women whose lived experience of space is so separated, how much more moving and significant cinematic images of exclusion and longing become when they are articulated as the looking from a constricted "here" into an other "yonder" space which they can intend but cannot inhabit.

Young also points out that feminine existence generally experiences itself not as constituting or *positing* space through its activity as a *body-subject*, but rather as *positioned in* space as a *body-object*. As a body-subject, one does not exist *in* space the determinate way a book or automobile does; rather, one constitutes and lives space as a *situation*. However, Young tells us: "[To] the extent that feminine motility is laden with immanence and inhibited, the body's space is lived as constituted. To the extent, that is, that feminine bodily existence is self-referred and thus lives itself as an *object*, the feminine body does exist *in* space."[183] And insofar as feminine existence feels itself as an object "rooted in *place*" rather than a subject positing space, its spatial perception of and relations with other objects in the world have their own modality. Young points to studies that show females as generally "field dependent"—that is, as having a "tendency to regard figures as embedded within and fixed by their surroundings."[184]

Of particular significance to film theorists is Young's implication of *visual perception* in these particular modalities of feminine comportment, motility, and spatialization. Acknowledging the synthetic and synaesthetic function of the lived-body's sensorium, she refers to Merleau-Ponty's description of the reversibility of visual perception and motility (or bodily expression) to conclude that "an impairment in the functioning of one . . . leads to an impairment in the functioning of the other."[185] Thus, although sharing in certain ontological features and functions common to all lived-bodies, insofar as history and culture qualify it as a particular and delimited lived-body, the female lived-body will experience visual perception and visual space in a modality complementary to its bodily qualification. Therefore, as Young says: "If feminine body spatiality is such that the woman experiences herself as rooted and enclosed, then on the reversibility assumption it would follow that visual space for feminine existence also has its closures of immobility and fixity. The objects in visual

---

[183] Ibid., p. 64.
[184] Ibid.
[185] Ibid.

space do not stand in a fluid system of potentially alterable and interchangeable relations correlative to the body's various intentions and projected capacities. Rather, they too have their own places and are anchored in their immanence."[186]

Young concludes her essay with a phenomenological interpretation. That is, having described empirical features of feminine comportment, motility, and spatiality as they are lived in the accomplishment of certain specific tasks, and having then thematized both the noetic and noematic correlates of feminine intentional acts and intentional objects, she goes on to correlate them as they are lived, as they signify and are significant in the life-world of those who live them. Finding the source of these themes or modalities of feminine existence not in anatomy or physiology or some female "essence," but in "the particular *situation* of women as conditioned by their sexist oppression in contemporary society," Young points out that, insofar as it is lived "in accordance with the definition that patriarchal culture assigns" and in cultural practices that are obvious to all of us, the female lived-body is constituted as physically handicapped: "inhibited, confined, positioned."[187] Nonetheless, the definition and circumscription of the lived-body as "female" cannot be seen as only "privative." It also informs feminine modalities or styles of bodily existence "positively." That is, the female lived-body is not simply "lacking" in certain of its engagements with the world; over time, it also acquires and assumes certain forms or styles of comportment and motility that increasingly mark it as "feminine." Empirical study reveals that "it is in the process of growing up as a girl that the modalities of feminine bodily comportment, motility, and spatiality make their appearance."[188] In closing, Young emphasizes the profound *source* of this process of feminine bodily modalization and locates it in patriarchal society's definition of woman as a body-object rather than a lived-body. She says, "An essential part of the situation of being a woman is that of living the ever present possibility that one will be gazed upon as a mere body, as shape and flesh that presents itself as the potential object of another subject's intentions and manipulations, rather than as a living manifestation of action and intention."[189] And, as we know, this objectification is not merely im-

[186] Ibid., pp. 64–65.
[187] Ibid., p. 65.
[188] Ibid., p. 66.
[189] Ibid.

posed from without and through the gaze of a normative—and currently male—Other. Within the context of the patriarchal social relations in which women exist, it is also self-imposed. The feminine body is introceptively lived out less as "myself, my psyche" than as "me, my thing." Thus, as a "thing," it can be appropriated and possessed by others or it can be self-possessed. It has a "place" in which it is kept, positioned by others or protected and preserved for itself.

Limited to studying the feminine lived-body of a particular segment of contemporary industrial culture in relation to its performance of certain definite gross motor tasks as compared to masculine performance of similar tasks, "Throwing Like a Girl" does not elaborate on what kind of "thing" the feminine body is for patriarchy. However, insofar as we understand from its discourses and activities the kind of subject that acts as the culture's normative lived-body (latently marked as "unmarked" and masculine), we could speculate that the constraints and inhibitions placed on feminine bodily comportment, motility, and spatiality have to do with 1) Cartesian, patriarchal, industrial society's separation of the lived-body's reproductive capacity into discrete and chronological functions and responsibilities at the same time this society has separated the lived-body's productive capacities in similar ways, and 2) its exclusion of the invisible from the existential activity of vision at the same time it has excluded the lived-body's introceptive and subjective experience from its extroverted and objective appearance. In this cultural context, one of the two bodies necessary to reproduction has been marked because it is the body that *visibly* demonstrates its capacity to *extend, exceed,* and *re-produce* itself. (As Linda Williams points out in *Hard Core: Power, Pleasure, and the "Frenzy of the Visible,"* it is no accident that certain forms of cinema attempt to redress the other "unmarked" reproductive body's normally *invisible* excess of its own being by devolving around the visible representations of extended and engorged penises, ejaculation as the lived-body's privileged act of exceeding itself, and the latter's repetitious re-production in what, aptly, has been called both the "come shot" and the "money shot."[190] What is of interest is that these films struggle to constitute the male body not as unmarked and normative, but as marked and singular.) Given these particular bifurcations, patriarchal society's inhibition

[190] Linda Williams, *Hard Core: Power, Pleasure, and the "Frenzy of the Visible"* (Berkeley: Univ. of California Press, 1989).

and enclosure of feminine comportment, motility, and spatiality is a direct and threatened response to the unmarked (male) body's own perceived bodily "lack" of visible proof of the lived-body's capacity to exceed, outrun, and regenerate itself.

I have spent most of this section focusing on the ways in which "feminine" lived-bodies are historically and culturally marked and constituted as particular and limited modalities of the "lived-body" in its polymorphous possibilities for signifying its own and the world's significance. Given the brevity of this discussion in relation to the issues involved, I have been less exhaustive than suggestive. However, in closing this chapter, I want to draw attention to what a phenomenological investigation like Young's can provide film theory—not only as it attempts to explicate the structure and activity of spectatorship in relation to the "feminine" lived-body, but also to the "colored" body, the "diseased" body, the "impaired" body, the "fat" body, the "old" body, and even the "deprived" body.

These are all lived-bodies that, at the ontological level, share existence and the world under similar conditions and in similar ways to all other lived-bodies not so nominated. That is, as discussed previously, all lived-bodies are material, intentional, motile, and finitely and perspectivally situated. Correlated with intentional consciousness, all lived-bodies constitute an "orientational point, 'O', from which spatio-temporal coordinates organize and structure the milieu." All lived-bodies are "organs of perception" or "that by means of which" there is access to a world that can be said to exist; as perceptive organs, all lived-bodies also synthesize several sensory fields and are the material "that on and in which . . . fields of sensation are spread out" and synoptically experienced in their modality as "mine." And, to varying degrees, all lived-bodies actualize both the operative and deliberative "strivings of consciousness."[191] However, although grounded in a common ontology and intentional capacity, these "female," "colored," "diseased," "impaired," "fat," "old," and "deprived" bodies are also synecdochically marked, disfigured, defaced, and incapacitated—made particularly, rather than individually, significant and generalized as a category. And, as Young has demonstrated, the delimitation of the whole lived-body-subject into a part-icular and de-signated body-object leads to correspondent modalities of bodily comportment, motility, and spatialization and cor-

[191] Zaner, *The Problem of Embodiment*, pp. 249–251.

respondent modalities of perception (including vision for those who are sighted). Insofar as these bodies are presently intentionally inhibited within the cultures that have so marked them, and insofar as they are marked negatively, it is likely that some of the features Young has laid out in relation to feminine comportment, motility, and spatialization might be shared among them. Yet bearing different marks than "female" (or in addition to being marked "female"), other of these lived-bodies will have their own existential character and praxis—both privative and positive, and differentiated in relation to specific kinds of intentional activities.

In this regard, phenomenological inquiry suggests beginning with concrete and empirical description of these historically and socially "significant" bodies as they are "disfigured" and perceived as pleasing or threatening to me in the "natural" attitude of my institutionalized culture. Marked as "female," "colored," "diseased," "impaired," "fat," "old," and "deprived," these bodies can only be described, thematized, and interpreted by me as they are immanent in the pleasure or threat they hold for me, and as I live them subjectively and/or objectively. Here, for example, I might have been able to describe the subjective modalities of my bodily comportment, motility, and spatiality as I've lived them not only as female, but also (because I've had cancer) as significantly "diseased." As a female in our particular cultural milieu, for most of my life (until I refused to "take up" such designation as my own), I have almost always lived my introceptive bodily image negatively as "fat" (whatever my physical size or whether I was regarded so by those engaging my visual body), and I could rigorously describe the indelible sense of material immanence that dragged on my upright posture, made my movements clumsy and "gross," and made me feel as if I had to squeeze into worldly space as if it were a too-tight dress. I am beginning also to become aware of the immanence of significantly living my body as "old"—experiencing, for example, a certain kind of devitalization and a consequent shrinking of my intentional being (soon my body) when certain younger persons look at me with a glance that, by virtue of its disinterest and dismissal, "withers" my embodied presence. However, my access to being marked as "colored," "impaired," or "deprived" is, for the moment, limited to my objective engagement with other lived-bodies so marked. This objective access is also lived by me and no less valuable or significant, but here I approach and describe the other marked body not introceptively, but (to use

Merleau-Ponty's term) visually. The introceptive description and thematization of being a "colored," "impaired," or "deprived" body must be performed by those so marked. The phenomenological interpretation of these disfigurements will be *verified*, however, only in the *correlation* of their subjective and objective forms.

In its focus on the lived-body's postural schema, its subjective activity, and its objective forms of "taking up" and engaging space, phenomenological inquiry locates the "subject," "consciousness," and "meaning" in actual and embodied existential praxis. However, because of its attention both to the lived-body as a commutative system of perceptive and expressive functions and to a horizon of existential possibilities broader than any specific praxis, phenomenological inquiry also indicates how the forms of specific existence are not an essential "given" and, however "natural" they may seem, could be otherwise. This has several implications for film theory. First, less programmatically than does psychoanalysis, phenomenology allows a critical reading of actual cinematic practice that could engage consideration of both specific films and their specific spectators in terms not of determinate psychic structures of identification but of postural, motor, and spatial practices as they are lived both introceptively and objectively. Such phenomenological description might, for example, take another kind of look at those films that (perhaps quite aptly) have been called "women's pictures" (but now are "objectified" as "family melodramas"). As has been suggested, what might be described are the correlated postural schemas, motility, and spatiality of both the spectators watching the film and the film itself as spectator—e.g., the film's composition or stance as it engages the world of objects and others, the scope and style of its motility in actualizing its intentional projects of perception and expression, and its appropriations or inhibitions in relation to "taking up" and living space as significant experience. Insofar as the film's bodily schema and motor projects are correlated and interpreted as compatible (or incompatible) with the spectator's, another more concrete and less deterministic way of describing cinematic "identification" becomes possible. Second, phenomenological description of these actual bodily practices (both by the spectator and the film) should provide the concrete grounds for practicing them consciously (that is, purposively)—or changing them. Here I am suggesting something much more subjectively grounded and less programmatic than what has emerged as the objective and too general category of "alternative" film practice.

That is, insofar as phenomenological scrutiny reveals both the introceptive and visible modalities of embodied intentionality as they are perceived introceptively, these modalities can be expressed objectively, articulating a visual style (as well as a visible content) of being that has not been allowed to fully become, that has to contest and overcome its delimitation.

The next chapter will focus on an elaboration of what I have been calling the film's "body." The nonmetaphorical way in which I am using the term has already been remarked upon. Phenomenological description has revealed the lived-body as a commutative system that reverses perception and expression. It also has pointed to the lived-body as serving certain ontological (as well as epistemological) functions. Insofar as a film is revealed as a similar commutative system and performs similar ontological functions in constituting the experience of consciousness and the consciousness of experience, it can be said to be "embodied." However, whatever the specificity of its material nature, the film's "body" is not disfigured in the same way as is the human lived-body. That is, historically and culturally, we do not speak of the *concrete materiality* of the cinematic apparatus in the same terms we use when discussing human bodies (although often we do speak of the film's style and perspective in such terms).

The film's "body" is not sexed, although it is sensible and sensual. It is not "colored," although today its vision usually takes up the world as such. It is not "impaired," "fat," "old," or "deprived"— although, as a whole, certain films have been described as "physically handicapped" by, for example, their silence or lack of color, as "excessive" or "padded" in their expressive behavior, as "old" in their outmoded interest or ways of engaging the world, and as "deprived" in their "low-budget" lack of resources to actualize the intentionality informing their perceptive and expressive projects. Obviously, films are only films insofar as they are made through human artifice and intention and engaged by human spectators. Obviously, their significance as the kind of phenomena they are is dependent upon and qualified by the kind of phenomena we are. Nonetheless, insofar as the film's material conditions for providing access to the world, accomplishing the commutation of perception and expression, and constituting or signifying a significant coherence are *different* from our own, they provide us actual and possible modes of becoming other than we are. Thus, even as human bodies engage the film's body in an always correlated activity (whether of filmmaking or spectating), the film's material body also always engages us in its possibilities as a nonhuman lived-body. In this sense, and in the context of this section, the embodied film exists not as a prosthetic device but rather, to use Donna Haraway's characterization, as a "cyborg"— an other body that signifies possibilities and liberation from the disfigured bodies some of us presently live.[192]

[192] Donna Haraway, "A Manifesto for Cyborgs," *Socialist Review* 80 (1985), pp. 65–107.

Film's Body

ALTHOUGH HE OFTEN MENTIONS the cinema in his major works, Merleau-Ponty has devoted only a single essay to its particular consideration. In "The Film and the New Psychology," the cinema becomes a paradigm of gestalt phenomena, visibly demonstrating the complex organization and structure of the perceptual field. The cinema is privileged also as constituting a philosophical model of phenomenological description. Concluding the essay, Merleau-Ponty questions the relationship of Gestalt psychology and existential philosophy to cinema, particularly as both have developed coincidentally with the medium and its technology:

> This psychology [*gestalt*] shares with contemporary philosophies the common feature of presenting consciousness thrown into the world, subject to the gaze of others and learning from them what it is: it does not, in the manner of the classical philosophies, present mind *and* world, each particular consciousness *and* the others. Phenomenological or existential philosophy is largely an expression of surprise at this inherence of the self in the world and in others, a description of this paradox and permeation, and an attempt to make us *see* the bond between subject and world, between subject and others, rather than to *explain* it as the classical philosophies did by resorting to absolute spirit. Well, the movies are peculiarly suited to make manifest the union of mind and body, mind and world, and the expression of one in the other. That is why it is not surprising that a critic should evoke philosophy in connection with a film. . . .
>
> Finally, if we ask ourselves why it is precisely in the film era that this philosophy has developed, we obviously should not say that the movies grew out of philosophy. Motion pictures are first and foremost a technical invention in which philosophy counts for nothing. . . . Therefore, if philosophy is in harmony with the cinema, if thought and technical effort are heading in the same direction, it is because the philosopher and the movie-maker share a certain way of being, a certain view of the world which belongs to a generation. It offers us yet another chance to confirm that modes of thought correspond to technical

methods and that, to use Goethe's phrase, "What is inside is also outside."[1]

A great deal is invested in these lines, particularly as they relate to the rest of Merleau-Ponty's work. Not only is the cinema a visible paradigm of our inherence in the world and others, but its technology is joined to intentional consciousness and is predicated as an instrumentality of the latter. Indeed, technology is considered here as the means of a certain way of being-in-the-world. Thus, to Goethe's phrase, we can add Martin Heidegger's: "The essence of technology is by no means anything technological."[2]

Drawing parallels between *modes of consciousness* and *technical methods* in relation to the cinema, Merleau-Ponty is also speaking of his thematization of the *lived-body* as a system enabling access to and engagement with the world when he quotes Goethe: "What is inside is also outside." As described previously, the body lived from "inside" or "introceptively" is also visible from "outside" as the "visual body," and "modes of thought" or the intentional activities of consciousness find their correspondence in the body's "technical methods"—that is, the behavior and conduct that realizes and signifies consciousness in the active accomplishment of existence. Stressing this perceptive and expressive accomplishment of existence, Merleau-Ponty's work consistently reminds us of the privileged nature and function of the lived-body in its *incarnate instrumentality*.

Thus, what is suggested by Merleau-Ponty in his brief discussion of the cinema is a correspondent view of the cinematic apparatus as an *intentional technology*. This way of considering technology animates human artifacts that extend and alter human existence with human function and significance, while refraining from either a mystical anthropomorphism or a correct but superficial conception of technology as merely "a means and a human activity" (what Heideg-

[1] Maurice Merleau-Ponty, "The Film and the New Psychology," trans. Hubert L. Dreyfus and Patricia Allen Dreyfus, in his *Sense and Non-Sense* (Evanston, IL: Northwestern Univ. Press, 1964), pp. 58–59. The correspondence between "technical methods" and "modes of thought" can also be found in Martin Heidegger, "The Question Concerning Technology," trans. William Lovitt, in *Martin Heidegger: Basic Writings*, ed. David Farrell Krell (New York: Harper and Row, 1977), pp. 287–317; Donald M. Lowe, *History of Bourgeois Perception* (Chicago, IL: Univ. of Chicago Press, 1982); Don Ihde, *Existential Technics* (Albany: State Univ. of New York Press, 1983); and Stephen Kern, *The Culture of Time and Space 1880–1918* (Cambridge: Harvard Univ. Press, 1983).

[2] Heidegger, "The Question Concerning Technology," p. 287.

ger calls "the instrumental and anthropological definition of technology."[3]) This consideration of technology or "instrumentality" as intentional in function and significance cannot be reduced to a discussion of mere mechanisms, of discrete apparatus designed to fulfill single functions. Rather, the focus is on the common and cooperative function of technology, its historical activity and teleological accomplishment of human intentional projects and productions—and its simultaneous, literal, and historically particular alteration of human consciousness and the latter's possible existential projects of "being-in-the-world." New modes of production constitute not only a "new age" but also new modalities of consciousness and, most significantly, self-consciousness. (Here, we might think not only of the cinema, which makes the introceptive and subjective features of vision objectively visible for the first time, but also [and more recently] of the computer, a "mechanism" that nonetheless can catch viruses and makes us regard consciousness and intelligence as "artificial.")[4] The passage from Merleau-Ponty cited above, therefore, suggests the following: If modes of intentional consciousness correlate and correspond to technical methods, then the film is to cinematic technology as human perception and its expression is to human physiology. In both instances, the irreducible structure of perception (perceiving act/perceived object) is dependent upon and enabled by the conduct and behavior of an instrumentality that synoptically accomplishes and expresses in the world a perceptive and perceptible intention, that is, a lived-body.

As previously described, however, it would seem that the human lived-body is privileged as an enabling technology, for it enables intending consciousness itself. The lived-body, we have seen, is not

[3] Ibid., p. 288. For brief but relevant discussion of Heidegger's thought on this issue, see Ihde, *Existential Technics*, pp. 32–33. For an extended phenomenological study of technology, see also Don Ihde, *Technology and the Lifeworld: From Garden to Earth* (Bloomington: Indiana Univ. Press, 1990).

[4] For a discussion on this issue of the historical correlation of "technical methods" and "modes of consciousness" as they relate to the photographic, the cinematic, and the electronic, see my own "The Scene of the Screen: Beitrag zu einer Phänomenologie der)Gegenwärtigkeit(im Film und in den elektronischen Medien," trans. H. U. Gumbrecht, in *Materialität der Kommunikation*, ed. H. U. Gumbrecht and K. Ludwig Pfeiffer (Frankfurt am Main: Suhrkamp, 1988), pp. 416–428, in English as "Toward a Phenomenology of Cinematic and Electronic Presence: The Scene of the Screen," *Post-Script* 10 (Fall 1990), pp. 50–59.

merely the *objective instrument* of intentional consciousness but also the *instrumental subject* of intentional consciousness. Whether the same can be said of cinematic technology, of what here shall be called the film's "body," poses the major concern of this chapter. Radical reflection about the film as a "viewing-view/viewed-view" has disclosed the intentional structure of vision as situated in a body-subject that is always also an objective body in relation to the vision of others. Thus, from a phenomenological perspective, we are bound to explore just what might be implicated in the term *body* as it relates to the particular materiality and enabling functions of cinematic technology.

The preceding chapter initiated this exploration of the film's body. It described the fundamental and irreducible structure of the viewing-view and its visible production, the viewed-view, or visible image. This structure was seen as visibly expressing both human and cinematic existence as the expression of intentional and perceptive behavior realizing significance in its perceptive objects and the world. Not only was the film seen to implicate an objective (if generally invisible) body—an instrumentality through which the *visible behavior* of an intending consciousness is expressed; it was seen also to implicate a visual body-subject, an agent who autonomously, introceptively, and visibly perceives the *visual behavior* of others.

The film lives its perception without the volition—if within the vision—of the spectator. It visibly acts visually and, therefore, expresses and embodies intentionality in existence and at work in a world. The film is not, therefore, merely an object for perception and expression; it is also the subject of perception and expression. Thus, a discussion of cinematic technology that focuses on the *machinery* of the film's vision seems not particularly relevant to our understanding of the film's material and functional significance as it is given to and in our experience. More to the point would be a discussion that focuses on cinematic technology's function of materially embodying perception and expression as a situated, finite, centered and decentering *lived-body* that, through its commutation of perception and expression, is able to accomplish the signification of vision as significant. To describe cinematic technology as it has to do with the film that we see as a process of seeing is to describe cinematic ontology: the emergence of the motion picture as a unique form of communicative existence both in its general and particular instances, that is, as the "history" of the medium as a mode of production and the "autobiography" of an age, and the "autobiography" or "discourse" of each individual film. Both are communicated in the visible predication of visible existential praxis enabled by the film's body.

Indeed, it could be said that cinematic ontogeny recapitulates phylogeny. That is, the technical or instrumental history of the cinema is the record of the cinema as a medium realizing itself and its perceptual projects, and adapting its technology, its "body," to accomplish those intentions—constituting, as it does so, a different world and a "new age." But such a history is always also freshly inscribed in the personal story, the autobiography, the "discourse" that is the emergence of the being of each individual film as it radically lives and rediscovers vision, movement, and hearing, and as it constantly tests the sophistication and conventionality of its current vision against the primordial openness and invention of its inaugural visual encounter with a world. Regarding cinematic technology as the instrumentality of an intending consciousness inscribing itself as such by its perceptive and expressive activity in a world, we are led to a consideration not only of the nature of that instrumentality but also to a consideration of the emergence of its performance and its increasing range of physical competence. The film's body matures in its perceptive grasp of the world, in its physical hold upon being, in much the same manner that the human body matures and successfully synopsizes its efforts as the ease of the lived-body, competently realizing its intentions in a world inexhaustibly available to its perception and expression.

The film's body, the subject of this chapter, will be approached in the following pages in two ways. First, it will be considered in its existence as enabling the filmmaker's and spectator's perception and expression, as the *instrumental mediation* necessary to *cinematic communication* between filmmaker and spectator. However, the film's body will be considered also as the film's means of perceptually engaging and expressing a world not only for us but also for itself. Thus, the film's body will be considered as a *direct means* of having and expressing a world—given to us as a technologically mediated consciousness of experience, but given to itself, through the praxis of its existentially functional body, as the immediate experience of consciousness.

TECHNOLOGY AND INSTRUMENTALITY

Throughout the preceding pages, I have made only tentative mention of cinematic technology. I have referred only briefly to the *camera*, *projector*, and *screen* and have placed minimal emphasis on what Jean-Louis Baudry terms the "cinematic apparatus."[5] On the one hand, my hesitation in initiating discussion of cinematic technology too early in the present study has come from a strong desire not to confuse the film with its enabling mechanisms. That is, while they enable the commutation of perception and expression that is the film, neither the camera nor projector (nor lenses, editorial equipment, optical printers, sound recording and transfer equipment, screen, et al.) are themselves the film we experience and see, which itself visually signifies vision as visible and significant experience. The film is a dynamic and synoptic gestalt that cannot be reduced to its mechanisms, much as a human perception and intentional conduct cannot be reduced to or explained in terms of its physiological and anatomical source, even as the latter enable or allow that perception and intentional conduct to come into being. The discrete mechanisms of the cinema are necessary but insufficient to account for the film as it appears as a particular and significant phenomenon in our experience.

This philosophical distinction between necessary and sufficient conditions is extremely relevant to the point being made here. As Lanigan summarizes: "Simply put, a necessary condition announces the minimal characteristics required for a fact. . . . With the use of *necessary condition*, we assert *that* something is, thereby making a metaphysical claim. By contrast, a *sufficient condition* . . . indicates the minimal characteristics which a fact can have. . . . A sufficient condition tells the observer *what* something is, thereby making an epistemological claim."[6] It is, or at least has been, too easy for film theo-

---

[5] Jean-Louis Baudry, "Ideological Effects of the Basic Cinematographic Apparatus," trans. Alan Williams, *Film Quarterly* 28 (Winter 1974–1975), pp. 39–47. See also Baudry's "The Apparatus," trans. Jean Andrews and Bertrand Augst, *camera obscura* 1 (Fall 1976), pp. 104–126; James Spellerberg, "Technology and Ideology in the Cinema," *Quarterly Review of Film Studies* 2 (August 1977), pp. 288–301; and Theresa Hak Kyung Cha, ed., *Apparatus* (an anthology) (New York: Tanam Press, 1980).

[6] Richard L. Lanigan, "Communication Models in Philosophy," in *Communication Yearbook III*, ed. Dan Nimmo (New Brunswick, NJ: Transaction Books, 1979), pp. 30–31.

rists to mistake necessity for sufficiency, to describe and explain *what* a film is by describing the discrete but cooperative mechanisms that merely allow it to be what it is. Thus, as descriptions of the physiology of human perception never really account for *what* is seen but only for the fact *that* it is seen, so descriptions of the "physiology" of the camera's perception and the projector's expression and the screen as an organizing and organized field have not adequately accounted for *what* the film is as a particular form of existence and meaning. This is an appearance with a significance that such "physiology" indeed enables, but in which it does not figure—except, on occasion, *secondarily*. For example, structural/materialist films that attempt to "deconstruct" the cinema to its materials and mechanisms must rely on the construction that *is* the film as *what* it is for such a deconstruction to be visible and intelligible *in* the film as a reduction to the necessity *that* the film is.

On the other hand, my hesitation at addressing cinematic technology too hastily comes also from the sure knowledge that technology must be considered in a phenomenological description of the film as existentially situated, finite, *embodied*. Such a consideration of technology, however, must be always related concretely to the film it enables, to the film that is visible in a way that the technology itself can never be—no matter how reflexive or concerned the film is with its own mechanical origins and materiality. The relation of technology to the film is a radical one. This relation begs for a description that has some congruence with the film existence *as* perceptual experience *in* perceptual experience. Thus, it seemed preferable to defer such a phenomenological description of cinematic technology until the complex and dynamic intentional nature and function of vision was explored, and the body that lives this vision as a being in and at the world was recognized as something more than the sum of its anatomical parts.

This tendency to reduce the cinema to its "anatomy" and "physiology," to the material operations of the cinematic "apparatus," has been criticized eloquently by Parker Tyler:

So far as the technical baggage of the film goes—all the craft books about films, how they are made or how to make them—what seems important is that all such lines of thought are concerned with post-mortem material, insofar as they compose the generic anatomy of a particular film or of the generic thing known as filmmaking. . . . Such books are much like anatomy lectures over human corpses that explain how a living man, in general "works," how this or that of his organs functions, how the constellation of the body's vital energies—the blood stream, the muscle and nerve systems, the brain itself—operate in concert to make possible all the physical and mental movements of which a living man is capable. However, with unbeating heart and the total blank of unconsciousness, only man's diagram is left.[7]

The following discussion, therefore, will not attend to the physiology or anatomy of cinematic technology—just as the last chapter did not find it necessary to attend to human physiology or anatomy to describe what it is to see and be seen simultaneously as both a subject of vision and an object for vision. Rather, the interest here is with the function of cinematic technology as, in Heidegger's sense, "nothing technological."[8] As a systemic "apparatus," cinematic technology functions to afford the film a material *instrumentality* for its perceptive and expressive *intention*, and to exist invisibly "behind" the film's perceptive and expressive activity as the film's ground, as its incarnate and substantial being, as the film's *body*. In sum, the film's material existence may be *necessarily* in its immanent celluloid, chemical emulsions, and mechanisms of cinematography and projection, but its material existence is *sufficiently* in its transcendence of its technological origins and dependencies. A film is experienced and understood not as some objective mechanism like a water heater. It is also not experienced and understood as an enabling and extensional prosthetic device like the telephone or microscope. Rather, the film is experienced and understood for what it is: a visible and centered visual activity coming into being in significant relation to the objects, the world, and the others it intentionally takes up and expresses in embodied vision.

Instrument-Mediated Perception

In his *Experimental Phenomenology*, Don Ihde points out that "the question of how a given phenomenon is or may be made present,

[7] Parker Tyler, *The Shadow of an Airplane Climbs the Empire State Building: A World Theory of Film* (Garden City, NY: Anchor Books, 1973), pp. 104–105.
[8] Heidegger, "The Question Concerning Technology," p. 317.

necessarily, leads in a philosophical direction."[9] This is true because the mode of a phenomenon's appearance or presence in experience is always a correlate of human intentionality, that dynamic and reversible structure linking objects of consciousness (the *noema*) with acts of consciousness (the *noesis*). The description of a phenomenon's appearance is made more complex, however, when technology and instrumentation are introduced into and are a condition of the phenomenon's presence, as is the case with cinema. Although interested in the relevance and application of phenomenological inquiry across a range of disciplines, Ihde raises questions pertinent to "instrument-mediated perception" primarily within the context of technology as it functions in the natural sciences—looking, for example, at the microscope and reflecting upon the intentional connection that exists between an act of perception and its object when an *instrument* effects (and affects) the accomplishment of that perception in an intentional structure.[10]

While his observations are certainly pertinent to the cinema, they are only partially descriptive, for Ihde addresses only a *single* act of perception that cannot be merely *doubled* to account for the instrument-mediated nature of the film experience. Ihde's description gives us an account of either a single scientist peering at a cell through a single microscope, or of many scientists peering through many microscopes. It also gives us an account of the intervention or mediation of other forms of instrumentation that relate the scientist to the cell in one or many single acts of perception. In each instance he describes, a single act of instrument-mediated perception is intentionally fulfilled when it accomplishes the perception of the cell. The cell as an intentional object founds the *limit* of the intention, which is to say that the cell does not serve as a conduit from one perception to another.

The double acts of instrument-mediated perception and expression

---

[9] Don Ihde, *Experimental Phenomenology: An Introduction* (New York: Paragon Books, 1979), p. 137.

[10] In his *Existential Technics*, Ihde does consider briefly some more complex forms of instrument-mediated perception such as the telephone. (It might be mentioned here that the telephone and its embodiment in "apparatus" does commute perception and expression; however, it does not—as does the cinema—constitute itself as intentional in this commutation. That is, the telephone does not function as a *subject* of perception and expression, nor is it experienced as such. Rather, it is understood and experienced only as an *object* for enabling the perception and expression of other intentional subjects.

that occur in the film experience are quite different. Respectively mediated by instruments that are not the same instruments although their intentional object is the same object, two intentional acts engage and address each other in a complex and *reversible* structure. That is, through the respective mediation of camera and projector (mechanisms that intervene in acts of perception and expression, both duplicating and reversing them), the filmmaker and spectator are brought into indirect perceptual engagement with each other, and into direct engagement with a world that is their *mutual intentional object*. They are brought also into perceptual engagement with each other's perceptive and expressive acts. Two embodied acts of perception and expression—each enabled by instruments—meet in a coterminous perception of a world that is also the coterminous expression of that world by the perceptive consciousnesses that engage it. Unlike the scientist's slide that exists as the intentional object of his perception mediated by the microscope, the world that is visible in the film and as the film (that is, as the perception of a world and its expression) does not found the *limit* of the intentional structure of perception in the film experience. As a coterminous perception and expression of a mutually lived world, the film serves as a conduit for perception—its enabling technology also the technology able to bridge the spatial and temporal separation of filmmaker and spectator so that their perception and expression might still encounter each other's activity, dialectically addressing each other's vision (or "world view") in visual *dialogue*.

Ihde's reflections give us two variants of a model that describes a single and unidirectional act of instrument-mediated perception. As the fulfillment of two perceptive acts, however, the film experience calls for a *communication model* of instrument-mediation—a model that can describe the double perception and the reversible structure of cinematic instrumentality which enable *instrument-mediated perception* to be commuted to and exist as *instrument-mediated expression*. This is a technological mediation that is able to reverse itself so that "what is inside is also outside." Ihde's discussion of instrument-mediated perception as it is relevant to cinematic technology and communication reminds us of the first of Lanigan's Communication Theorems: "Conscious experience is the minimal unit of meaning in communication."[11] That is, Ihde echoes this Theorem of Intentionality in that he considers the machine in its relation to a singular *conscious experi-*

[11] Lanigan, "Communication Models in Philosophy," p. 46.

ence as the *minimal unit* in the structure of possible communication. This illuminates the relations that obtain respectively between the filmmaker, camera, and world in one mediated perceptive act, and between the spectator, projector, and world in another. However, in looking at the function of cinematic technology as it connects filmmaker, film, and spectator and conjoins their singular perceptive acts into a much more complex perceptive experience, Ihde's model and descriptions are incomplete. This is to say that each single instance of instrument-mediated perception provides us with the "minimal unit" of meaning in cinematic communication, but it does not inscribe a *system* for that communication. The conditions for such a system are stated in the second of Lanigan's Communication Theorems, the Theorem of Punctuation: "The reversibility of expression and perception is the minimal system-code for communication."[12] Such reversibility is found in the double instrument-mediated perception that occurs in the film experience and, in its doubling, commutes perception to expression.

Despite the limited focus of Ihde's descriptions of instrument-mediated perception, his work is particularly useful to our understanding of cinematic communication. First, it explicates the structure of the *minimal units* of each such perception necessary to cinematic communication. Second, and even more importantly, it emphasizes the *intentional correlations* of that structure—correlations that do not change in the communicative act but are multiplied and enriched by their increased possibilities of existential relation. Here, Merleau-Ponty is suggestive: "The probable is everywhere and nowhere, a reified fiction. . . . Generality and probability are not fictions, but phenomena; we must therefore find a phenomenological basis for statistical thought. It belongs necessarily to a being which is fixed, situated and surrounded by things in the world."[13] Film is just such a basis. And its technological "body"—fixed, situated, and surrounded by things in the world—provides us with the phenomenon from which the minimal system-code for cinematic communication emerges not as a transcendental or "statistical" structure or as a system governed by technical rules and operations, but as an existential system actualizing its intentional projects in perceptive and expres-

[12] Ibid.

[13] Maurice Merleau-Ponty, *Phenomenology of Perception*, trans. Colin Smith (London: Routledge and Kegan Paul, 1962), p. 442.

sive commerce with the world and others. In criticizing prevalent attitudes about the cinematic apparatus and its function, Parker Tyler speaks to what is at stake here when he tells us that "one cannot think a set of rules, a repertory of camera manipulations, is anything but a shell, and a shell without pre-determined shape or extent,"[14] and that "technique is sufficient to the motives thereof, but technique is never a substitute for motivation."[15]

Instrument Mediation as Embodied

Ihde attempts to consider "what occurs when experience is directed through, with, and among technological artifacts (machines) of which scientific instruments are a sub-class."[16] He begins, however, with a piece of blackboard chalk, exemplary precisely because its simplicity as an instrument allows the character of instrumentality to be described more readily. Using the chalk, Ihde examines his experience and discovers one type or modality of instrument-mediated perception. (There will be another type described as well.) He says: "I experience the blackboard . . . *through* the chalk—I *feel* the smoothness or the roughness of the board *at the end of the chalk.* This is, of course, also Merleau-Ponty's blind man who experiences the 'world' at the end of his cane. If I begin to be descriptively rigorous, I find I must say that what I feel is felt locally at the end of the chalk or, better, at the chalk-blackboard junction. The 'terminus' of my intentional extension into the world is on the blackboard, and I have discovered (contrary to empiricism) that touch is also a distance sense."[17]

If we substitute the motion picture camera for the chalk, Ihde's initial description will seem familiar to anyone who has ever confidently engaged the world with that mechanism (confidence here invoked because it implies an already appropriated knowledge of, and experience with, a machine more complex in its operations than a piece of chalk). For the filmmaker, the world (whether "real," drawn, or constructed in any other fashion) is experienced *through* the camera. It is seen and *felt* at the *end of the lens.* Or, more precisely, it is seen and felt at the *lens-world "junction,"* the "terminus" of the filmmaker's

[14] Tyler, *The Shadow of an Airplane Climbs the Empire State Building*, p. 104.
[15] Ibid., p. 106.
[16] Ihde, *Experimental Phenomenology: An Introduction*, p. 139.
[17] Don Ihde, "The Experience of Technology," *Cultural Hermeneutics* 2 (1974), p. 271.

intentional extension into the world. (It is appropriate to recall the earlier discussion of vision as also a "distance sense" that, contrary to empiricism, can "feel" the world and entails the proximal sense of touch.) The meaning of *terminus* as Ihde uses it here needs some clarification, lest it be interpreted in the positivist sense of an "end point." In its use by phenomenologists, *terminus* refers not to a theoretical location of static essence, but rather the lived location of a realized and realizing noesis-noema relation, an intentional correlation that is not *static* but dynamic and existentially *ecstatic* (in the Greek sense of *ek-stasis* borrowed upon by both Heidegger and Merleau-Ponty, and here by Ihde).

In a more ambiguous manner, Ihde's description of this first modality of instrument-mediated perception is descriptive also of the spectator's relation to the world as it is engaged and made visible by means of an instrument, the projector. Ambiguity arises from the very issues I consider in this section—namely, the *inclusive* relations of perception as it entails technology in both the *instrument-mediated perception* of human beings in the film experience and the *instrument-enabled perception* that is also the *instrument-enabled expression* constituting the film within that experience as *mediating* perception and expression. In the relation Ihde describes, the spectator can be said to experience the world of the film *through* the projector. The world is visibly expressed as perceptible for the spectator only *at the end of the projector's throw of light*—or, more precisely, at the *light-screen "junction."* Here the light is stopped, providing the spectator's "terminus" as the signifying and significant *image* of a *visible world*. In this regard, it should be emphasized that we are not in Plato's cave. Nor is the screen the terminus of the spectator's perception in the way that Ihde's blackboard is the terminus of his chalk-mediated perception. This intentional correlation is more complex. That is, the "light-screen" terminus is itself a mediation through which a visibly significant world is realized as the terminus in which the correlation of both the filmmaker's and the spectator's noetic activity produce a visible and significant image.

Ihde goes on to note other features of his experience with the chalk. Reflection reveals that in this particular use of the chalk, the chalk as instrument is not given to his experience as "thematic" or as that experience's intentional object. It is toward the blackboard that he intends his present action of perception. The chalk—*through* which the blackboard is perceived—has been *incorporated* into the intentional act, into Ihde's "self-experiencing" of the blackboard. As he describes it, the instrument that is the chalk is not felt as *separate* from his activity but has become a physical and instrumental *extension* of his incarnate being as well as of his ability to name things and, by writing, to make them mean. As he says: "The chalk is only secondarily an 'object,' while more primarily it is absorbed into my experiencing as an extension of myself. It is true, that the chalk is not totally absorbed in that I have what might be called an 'echo focus' in which I feel simultaneously a certain pressure at the juncture fingers/chalk with what I feel at the end of the chalk. Nevertheless, in the primary focus it is the board which I feel."[18]

Again, for the filmmaker perceiving the world through a camera, the mechanism is only secondarily the object of his or her intentional activity. Rather, it is primarily absorbed into the human and intentional experiencing of the world that is engaged and visible through it. However this mediation is not totally absorbed, for there is what Ihde calls an "echo focus" at the juncture of *eye/viewfinder* and/or *fingers/focusing ring*, etc. There is a slight pressure existent between the flesh of the body lived introceptively and the exterior and opaque material of the camera that slightly resists the filmmaker's introceptive appropriation of the instrument. Nevertheless, as Ihde suggests, in this modality of instrument-mediated perception, the primary focus and intention of the experience is located in the world and is felt there by the filmmaker as the world's visibility rather than the camera's.

Similarly (although again ambiguously), for the spectator perceiving a world through the instrumentality of the projector, it is primarily the world in its visibility upon which his or her perception focuses. The mechanism barely exists as an intentional "object" but is secondary and latent in the spectator's experience of perception, enabling it rather than providing its terminus. The projector thus functions in this modality of instrument-mediated perception as an extension of the spectator's being. It is no accident that the normal mode of perceiving a film is by sitting in front of rather than behind the projector. In either position, the film can be perceived in its significance as the imaging and images of a world, but it is in the former position that the instrument loses most of its force as a mediating

[18] Ibid.

instrument and is best "absorbed" into the perceptive act as an extension of the spectator's existence.

Again, the absorption of the projector and the instrument-mediation is not total. Instrument-mediated perception is never experienced as exactly identical to direct perception, that is, perception experienced introceptively through the lived-body as "mine." This is a point too often neglected in those theories of cinematic identification that suggest the spectator's total subjection to an Other's vision and speak of the "illusionism" and "imaginary" of the cinema. Absorption is never complete; the mechanism is never wholly incorporated into the spectator's lived-body. There is always an "echo-focus" in the spectator's perception of the world that marks the perception as mediated by an instrument. (Here we might note that although literally embodied, prosthetic devices, too, are never completely "naturalized." For example, however one incorporates eyeglasses into one's being, there is still the objective feel of them there on the bridge of one's nose.) Obviously, the "echo focus" of the film spectator is not likely to be as localized as the "pressure" felt when the filmmaker's introceptively lived flesh meets a slight resistance in the cool and opaque substance of the camera. Rather, for the spectator, the "echo focus" is experienced as more diffuse—but equivalent, nonetheless, to the pressure and resistance experienced by the filmmaker. For the spectator, this pressure and resistance seem to occur at two different junctures.

The first juncture occurs where the spectator's introceptively lived vision meets the external constraints of the framing screen rectangle within which the world appears in its visibility but does not completely fill the spectator's visual field with its appearance. (In this regard, the "Exit" signs we often see as we watch the film are thus an ironic but literal marking of the vision's limits, both the film's and our own.) For the spectator in the theater, the resistance met by the filmmaker in the cool and opaque material of the camera is matched by the dark and opaque ground that visibly surrounds the figured projection of world for the spectator. This is the junction of *perception/frame* (or limit) that echoes the projector's instrumentality in effecting (and affecting) the shape of a visual field that is included *within*—and is therefore visible as *unlike*—the elliptical and unsharp limits of the spectator's visual field.[19] Certainly, this kind of "echo focus" can be

[19] Ihde, *Experimental Phenomenology: An Introduction*, pp. 55–56.

muted to a great degree. In the case of Cinerama and other dimensional modifications of projection that attempt to soften this resistance and pressure by filling the spectator's entire visual field and making the screen perception isomorphic with the spectator's, the sense of instrumentality is lessened.

Nonetheless, pressure and resistance are still present in the spectator's perceptual experience, at the second juncture of person and machine. This second echo of the machine is both as necessary and as invisible to the film experience as the air we breathe. However, its invisibility and seeming insubstantiality have encouraged theoretical discussion that treats it as an abstract phenomenon rather than one intimately grounded in the real materiality of the human body as it inhabits a world. This purely theoretical phenomenon is called *point of view*. More aptly and concretely, this second juncture of spectator and machine is that of the *spectator's bodily space/projected visual space*, a juncture that echoes the different situations of the spectator's body and the film's body and creates in the spectator a resistance to the projected perception, an inability to absorb it totally. In other words, from all that phenomenology has revealed about the perceptive modality of vision and its information of and by all other modalities of bodily perception, we cannot meaningfully abstract vision from the spectator's lived-body.

If my vision were merely a discrete sense, then perhaps Cinerama or some future holography might wear away the last of my abstract knowledge that my perception of the world was instrument-mediated. Indeed, my point of view and the film's would be the same, isomorphic, identical. However, I do not have a *point* of view. As a lived-body engaged in intentional acts of perception in an intended world, I have a *place* of viewing, a *situation*. My vision is informed by and filled with my other modes of access to the world, including the tactile contact of my posterior with the theater seat. In so far as the *visual space I see before me* is not completely isomorphic with the *bodily space from which I see*, there will be a pressure from, an echo of, the machine that mediates my perception. Again, however, in this first type of person-machine-world relation described by Ihde, the machine's presence or "echo" in the perceptual experience is secondary and latent. It is the world and its image as terminus that is primary and active.

Diagramming this type of person-machine-world relation in phenomenological terms (that is, as they constitute the intentional correlates of perceptual consciousness: the *noesis* or intending act and the *noema* or intentional object of perception), Ihde draws the relation between person and machine as a *symbiotic* one. That is, the machine is given in this kind of experience as part of the *noetic act:*

(Human-machine) → World

The inclusive parenthesis in the diagram stands for this symbiotic relation whereby the machine enables the perceptive act and the person appropriates or incorporates the machine as an extension of his or her own body. Ihde elaborates the effect and affect of such a relation:

> With this we have one type of human-machine relation, an experience *through* a machine. The correlational structure of intentionality remains, in that I do experience something other than the machine being used, and at the same time, my experiencing is extended through the machine for that intentional fulfillment. I may thus describe the chalk as having a partial *transparency relation* between myself and what is other. And in fact, the better the machine, the more "transparency" there is. Likewise, I can use a language now, which speaks of the machine as part of myself or taken into myself, so far as the experience is concerned.[20]

As it relates to the goal of the natural sciences (which generally is to see and observe "World" rather than its own instrumentation), Ihde's discussion obviously diverges in its valuation from the economy of an instrument-mediated aesthetics. That is, it could be argued that the "better" machine in this latter realm of experience need not be necessarily the "more" transparent. Rather, necessity calls for only a *minimum* degree of transparency. Without at least a minimal transparency, the instrument could not be considered to have accomplished or "fulfilled" the intentionality of perception as an act, aesthetic and/or communicative. In the cinema, to the degree that the filmmaker incorporates the machine in the transparency relation that Ihde's diagram describes, the filmmaker can accomplish the perception that will result finally in the film. (This transparency relation is necessary for the accomplishment of even the most reflexive, materialist, or minimalist film.) Similarly, to the degree that the spectator incorporates the machinery of projection into her perceptive act, that

[20] Ihde, "The Experience of Technology," p. 272.

spectator will fulfill her intention of seeing a perceived world. Even the most theoretical or bored of spectators must necessarily be in a partial transparency relation with the projector and screen if a world appears as visible, if significant images are produced. That is, as images appear as such, they appear *through* the machine (even as the machine's "echo" appears quite prominent in the perception of the theoretical or bored spectator).

Ihde continues his phenomenological description of aspects of this transparency relation: "The machine- or instrument-mediated experience in which the instrument is taken into one's experience of bodily engaging the world, whether it be primarily kinesthetic-tactile or the extended embodiment of sight (telescope) or sound (telephone), I term an *embodiment relation*. These relations genuinely *extend intentionality* into the world, and when they operate properly, the sense of a *new realism* in the phenomenon can be retained."[21] Insofar as it concerns the technology of the cinema, this embodiment relation between perceiver and machine genuinely extends the intentionality of both filmmaker and spectator into the respective worlds that provide each with objects of perception. It is this extension of the incarnate intentionality of the person that results in a sense of *realism* in the cinema. However, this sense of realism is not—as theorists like Baudry would contend—an illusion. It is also not a predication of the world as "real" in some abstractly objective sense, some disembodied sense. That is, this sense of realism does not make a truth claim about *World*, but rather makes it about *perceptive experience* of the world. This is an experience that—although finite—is open in structure, even if it may be limited and conventional in exercise. It is subject to transformation and is itself transforming. In this mode of instrument-mediated perception, the machine as instrumental is incorporated into the structure of human intentionality as it is articulated existentially as perception and its expression. In this modality, the machine is incorporated as part of the *noetic correlate* (i.e., the act of viewing) in an embodiment relation with the intending perceiver. What is conventionally experienced as the sense of realism *in* the phenomenon (i.e., in the *noematic correlate*: the significant image of the world) is genuinely lived *as* the experience of a real or existential act of perception.

As Ihde also points out, however, the transparency or sense of re-

---

[21] Ihde, *Experimental Phenomenology: An Introduction*, p. 141. (Emphasis mine)

alism in this embodiment relation is "enigmatic." On the one hand, there is the sense of the genuine accomplishment of an intentional perceptive act, the sense of a "real" perception that does indeed extend the filmmaker's or the spectator's intentionality so that it engages the world of phenomena in an action similar to perception that does not involve instrument-mediation. On the other hand, "it is equally clear that what is experienced is in some ways *transformed*."[22] This transformation can both *reduce* and/or *amplify* perceptual engagement with the intended object.

For Ihde, the chalk-mediated experience of the blackboard is less rich and full than the experience of the blackboard perceived directly through his finger, the latter experience encompassing texture, temperature, spatiality, and so forth (although the finger's perception of the blackboard is not directly commutable to writing and communication). Compared to the experience of his "naked" touch, the experience of the blackboard *through* the chalk is a *reduced* experience. The instrument that is the chalk is less perceptive of the board than the unmediated engagement of his finger. However, Ihde also offers a counter example in which instrument-mediated experience is felt as enriched and *amplified*. A fine instrument like a dentist's probe allows Ihde a transformed experience of the blackboard—one that engages him with its texture more precisely than does his finger. A microscope would transform the experience of the board in still another way that would enrich and amplify his ordinary perception. As he says: "In each of these variations in the experienced use of machines, I continue to note that the embodiment relation is one in which I experience otherness through the machine, but that the experience through the machine transforms or stands in contrast to my ordinary experience in the 'flesh.' "[23]

In each of these instances, it is the "flesh," the lived-body as the original incarnation of my intentionality, that is normative in my evaluation of the paucity or richness of my perceptual experience of phenomena when mediated by machinery and instrumentation. That is, I have a sense of experiencing "more" or "less," but always in relative comparison to the bodily perception I was born with that inaugurated my access to the world. This says something Ihde doesn't (although it is implicit in his brief discussion): Although I can see

[22] Ihde, "The Experience of Technology," p. 272.
[23] Ibid., p. 273.

through or *according to* a machine or instrument, I cannot see *like* or *as* a machine; I cannot see except against the ground of my human lived-body and I cannot see unintentionally.

The transformations of perception are peculiarly compounded by the various but synoptic cinematic mechanisms. For the filmmaker, the camera is an instrument that simultaneously can reduce and amplify perceptual experience of a world in this embodiment relation it has with the filmmaker's "flesh." Reductive of "normal" experience, the camera is not able to discriminate among certain gradations of shadow and illumination so finely as can the human eye. As well, in that the camera is a visual instrument, it reduces the world to primarily visual experience (although, as I have emphasized, visual experience is always informed by other senses and is synaesthetic). The filmmaker's body can see the world and also reach out and touch it in order to experience the intended phenomenon in two or more perceptive modalities. Seeing the world through the camera realizes the filmmaker's touch *only* as it in-forms sight—for the camera, although it has substantiality and can move through and inhabit the world, does not have literal touch in the way it has a literal optic system of sight. In this sense, the camera offers the filmmaker a perceptual experience reduced from the one s/he might have without it, or with some other instrument.

The camera also simultaneously offers the filmmaker an *amplification* of perceptual experience, offers "more" as well as "less" in relation to direct lived-body engagement with phenomena. Thus, while the filmmaker is no longer able to directly touch the intended object, s/he may be able to see it much more closely and clearly than human vision allows. As a different kind of visual "organ" than the human eye, the camera is visually able to engage the filmmaker's perception with the world in ways unavailable to human vision, to "ordinary" flesh in its "normal" modes of access to the world. This is clearly why Siegfried Kracauer, that most dogmatic and literal of realist film theorists, saw nothing paradoxical in his valorization of such "unnatural" capacities of the camera as microcinematography and slow motion.[24]

The camera's talents allow for a genuine, if abetted, human perception of the world, for the extension of human intentionality that can

[24] Siegfried Kracauer, *Theory of the Film: The Redemption of Physical Reality* (New York: Oxford Univ. Press, 1960), pp. 46–59.

realize itself in its objects more richly through a "better" embodiment than the human eye. Extending our intentional relations with the world, such instrument-mediated perception has been celebrated in both theory and practice by Dziga Vertov who, sounding like a Soviet Walt Whitman, writes:

> I am eye. I am a mechanical eye.
>
> I, a machine, am showing you a world, the likes of which only I can see.
>
> I free myself today and forever from human immobility, I am in constant movement, I approach and draw away from objects, I crawl under them, I move alongside the mouth of a running horse, I cut into a crowd at full speed, I run in front of running soldiers, I turn on my back, I rise with an airplane, I fall and soar together with falling and rising bodies. . . .
>
> My road is towards the creation of a fresh perception of the world. Thus I decipher in a new way the world unknown to you.[25]

No matter how "artificial" the device, this embodiment relation of human and machine is transparent in that the mechanism is seen *through*: The world is the "terminus" of the instrument-mediated perception. Thus, the machine is incorporated into the human intentional act of perceiving the world, even as the machine enables a patently "impossible" human perception, that is, one otherwise unrealizable without the machine's incorporation.

Enigmatically, however, and duplicating the way in which intentional consciousness informs human perception as always directed both toward and away from perceptual possibilities offered by the world's horizon, the camera simultaneously reduces perceptual experience in one realm by amplifying it in another. Merleau-Ponty acknowledges what the enthusiastic Vertov does not. What Merleau-Ponty says of human vision and its existential limitations can be said also of the extensions and transformations of machine-mediated perception: "What is won on one side must be lost from the other."[26] For example, as the camera engages the filmmaker's intentions toward the world in a primarily visual modality, it reduces his or her tactile intentions to their realization primarily through sight. (Sound can also render the world substantial and realize touch in an alternative

---

[25] Dziga Vertov, " 'Kinoks-Revolution' Selections," in *Film Makers on Film Making*, ed. Harry M. Geduld (Bloomington: Indiana Univ. Press, 1967), pp. 86–87.

[26] Merleau-Ponty, *Phenomenology of Perception*, p. 99.

modality.) In such a reduction, however, the camera simultaneously amplifies the tactile capacity of the filmmaker's vision, his or her eyes through the camera informed by a capacity to touch the world, to intend *texture* through this machine-mediated vision. The perceptive function of the camera enigmatically and ambiguously fulfills and transforms the filmmaker's perceptive intention toward the world, even as s/he appropriates and embodies the camera as a transparent extension of his or her intentionality.

For the spectator, the projector and all its attendant mechanisms similarly reduce and amplify the bodily norm of directly experienced human perception. Experience is reduced in many ways. The spectator cannot smell the flowers at which s/he gazes, and so crude an attempt as Smell-O-Vision dramatically demonstrates this reduction. Like the other senses, smell is not an abstract or disembodied sense. Odor, therefore, also has depth and dimension and emerges from and adheres to its original substantial source and is perceived across a distance. Smell occupies space rather than a point in our experience and its diffusions and concentrations are extraordinarily subtle.

The spectator's perception of a world can also be amplified through an embodiment relation with the projection mechanisms. (These are, of course, constructed to complement the camera mechanisms so that the latter's perceptive capacity is reversed and commuted to an expressive capacity that can be perceived as the expression of perception by a spectator.) A human face, for example, can be seen with a clarity and dimension impossible in "ordinary" unmediated, lived-body vision. If I get too physically close to another, the other's face loses its precise visible presence as a figure in my visual field even as it increases in haptic presence. The visible face partially blurs as it fills my visual field, thus becoming, in part, its ground. Indeed, some of the face flows into *indeterminacy* and the final invisibility that marks the *horizon* of my perceptive act. An extreme close-up of a human face mediated for me by the projector (as it is for the filmmaker by the camera) is given to my experience transformed. It is *centered* in *my* visual field (even if not literally centered in the projection on the screen). Its *entirety* is the *figure* of my perception, not its ground, and thus does not flow into indeterminacy in my vision (even as it might in the camera's).[27] Such instrument-mediated perception allows me a focus I cannot achieve in the unmediated and direct perception I

[27] Discussion of the visual field and pertinent terms can be found in Ihde, *Experimental Phenomenology: An Introduction*, pp. 55–66.

have of another's face. Here, one can see clearly why Béla Balázs devotes an entire chapter in his *Theory of the Film* to the cinema's particular ability to perceive and express "The Face of Man."[28]

Again, however, as with the embodiment relation between filmmaker and camera, the embodiment relation between spectator and projector is enigmatic in its transparent extension of human intentionality. That is, there is often an inverse ratio between the reduction and amplification of direct perception in this instrumental extension of human embodiment in the world. Although the smell of the flower is lost to the spectator's perception (if not to the filmmaker's), s/he is able, for example, to perceive the flower in an otherwise perceptually inaccessible kinetic transformation—its expansive movement from bud to flower amplified into visibility. And, although the spectator's own kinesthetic activity is drastically reduced when watching a film, the perception of movement and its kinesthetic "sense" or significance seems immensely amplified because of the relative quietude of the spectator's movement. It is as if the spectator's body were kinetically "listening" to the movement of another.

What must be stressed here is that the instrument-mediated perception, however much reduced in one quarter or amplified in another, is a *genuine* perception of world as it exists in an *embodiment relation* with technology. Instrument-mediated perception is an extension and transformation of direct perception but is enigmatic in that extension and transformation. That is, the "transparency" of this embodiment relation is always only partial. The human body never entirely incorporates the technology that enables its perception and expression. There is always an "echo focus" of its presence as something other than the body I live and directly experience as "mine." Nonetheless, as the machine is incorporated as a primarily transparent extension of an embodied *perceptive act* (that is, as it is part of the *noetic correlate* of perceptive experience), a perceptive intention toward an intended object is genuinely accomplished—even as it is also translated, transformed, and literally transfigured.

Instrument Mediation as Hermeneutic

Ihde points out that "instrumentation that embodies perception is not the only instrumental possibility for perception."[29] He contrasts

---

[28] Béla Balázs, *Theory of the Film: Character and Growth of a New Art*, trans. Edith Bone (New York: Dover Press, 1970), pp. 60–88.

[29] Ihde, *Experimental Phenomenology: An Introduction*, p. 142.

the experience of one's perception as it is embodied *through* a machine with the experience of one's perception *of* a machine that is perceiving phenomena in the world. Again, he seeks a simple example and finds it in an engineer "reading" machines in a room full of dials and switches, gauges and rheostats. In this instance, although the technology is in *direct* relation with the world, the engineer's perceptual relation to the world is *indirect* and thus dependent upon what the gauges reveal to him of the phenomena beyond his immediate bodily experience. Ihde elaborates:

> Returning to our correlational model, this experience of a machine is curious. Through the machine something (presumably) still happens elsewhere, only in this case the engineer does not experience the terminus of the intention which traverses the machine. Thus we may model the relation as follows:
>
> Human → (machine-World)
>
> His primary experiential terminus is with the machine. I shall call this relation a *hermeneutic relation*. There is a partial opacity between the machine and the world and thus the machine is something like a text. I may read an author, but the author is only indirectly present in the text.[30]

This hermeneutic relation with technological "perception" raises some interesting questions about the nature of the single relations of instrument-mediation between filmmaker and camera and spectator and projector. It is also of the utmost importance in determining the deep structure of the communicative and dialectical encounter between filmmaker and spectator as it occurs through and across their respectively different relations to camera and projector.

In the first instance, a genuine hermeneutic relation exists between filmmaker and camera. In this relation, as Ihde says, checking on the final terminus of the perception of the world is an immediate, or direct, impossibility for the human eye. The camera in these cases (with its companion projector) is, as Ihde puts it, "the hermeneut who enters the cavern to hear the saying of the oracle and we are left to his interpretation."[31] The hermeneut, in this instance, functions perceptively in a different spatial and temporal relation to the world

---

[30] Ihde, "The Experience of Technology," p. 275. See also the "Watergate model" of elementary communication structure in Umberto Eco, *A Theory of Semiotics* (Bloomington: Indiana Univ. Press, 1979), pp. 32–40.

[31] Ihde, "The Experience of Technology," p. 276.

than does the filmmaker. Take, for example, slow or fast motion—the perception of a drop of water falling from a faucet or the perception of a plant turning toward the light. Although the filmmaker uses the camera to perceive these phenomena, s/he does not directly or immediately see them through the lens. It is the camera in concert with the projector which literally perceives and expresses the perception of these phenomena. Indeed, until the projection process that expresses the camera's—not the filmmaker's—direct perception, the filmmaker has no direct experience of the phenomena except as s/he imaginatively intends (or projects) them.

The hermeneutic relation between the spectator and the projector, however, is of another sort. In its most extreme instance, the mechanism may almost completely fail in its mediating function—such as when the projected film loses its loop or slips in both the gate and our gaze. Ingmar Bergman's *Persona* re-presents this slippage *within* its vision explicitly, but it does so *as* its vision is projected by a machine that transparently presents this slippage as visible, precisely because it exists in an *embodiment relation* with the film's spectators. However, usually there are only few occasions when the hermeneutic relation between projector and spectator is particularly strong and dominates its embodiment relation. (As we shall see, the spectator's relation with the camera is another matter.) These occasions occur in films that foreground the instrument-mediated nature of perception and its expression by *representing* the *rupture* of the smooth and synchronous reversibility of perception and expression that exists between camera and projector in relation to the spectator's incorporation of the latter. (This is not the same as the aforementioned case of slow and fast motion, for although the usual synchrony of camera and projector is disrupted to achieve the perception of slow or fast motion, the projector remains transparent to the spectator, and the intended object of perception is *not* the cinematic mechanism.)

The kind of film that foregrounds the spectator's relation with the projector may emphasize, for example, the projector's "flicker" and disrupt the *continuity* and *apparent motion* that camera and projector achieve through their mechanical synchrony and their allegiance to the structure of human perception—that is, to their appeal to those phenomena of perception Gestalt psychology refers to as *fusion* and the *phi phenomenon*.[32] These films break what might be called the

[32] For the best summary of these phenomena and their perceptual and ideological

"technical code" of the cinema. They thus represent and call attention to the way in which cinematic mechanisms meet the necessary and minimal perceptual demands of the human lived-body in order to yield perceptual phenomena that "count" or signify as coherent and moving objects of perception.

However, insofar as this *hermeneutic relation* to cinematic technology is realized (by both filmmaker and spectator) in an experience of instrument-mediated perception, the former is a *secondary representation* articulated against the ground of an original and originating *embodiment relation* with cinematic technology. A film must be successfully—that is, transparently—projected and perceived *through* the projector in an unruptured and embodied instrument-mediated perception for it to *represent* the rupture of the very mechanisms that make the perception of it possible. Thus, a perceptual paradox, although not a logical one, emerges in such films: The spectator must perceive *through* the projector to accomplish perception *of* the projector in its act of technologically mediating perception.

The represented hermeneutic relation between spectator and projector is never precisely parallel to the genuine hermeneutic relation that can exist between filmmaker and camera—that relation in which the camera is the "hermeneut" and has privileged access to what the filmmaker's lived-body does not and cannot approach, that relation in which the intentional object of perception is perceived directly only by the machine. The projector is the *expressive* mechanism of cinematic technology, not its *perceptive* mechanism, although its commutative function enables *perception as expression.* Conversely, the camera is a *perceptive* mechanism that, although not instrumentally *expressive*, commutes and enables *expression as perception.* The projector, therefore, expresses no more and no less than what the camera and the spectator perceive as visible. Expressing the camera's perception of slow motion (as previously noted, a perception based on a deliberate rupture of the synchrony between camera and projector speed, and realized by a filmmaker who is not able to perceive the motion directly), the projector expresses the camera's perception, and the spectator sees that motion as both visible and slow. That is, in this instance of instrument-mediated perception, the spectator

relation to cinematic technology, see Susan J. Lederman and Bill Nichols, "Appendix A: Flicker and Motion in Film," in Bill Nichols, *Ideology and the Image: Social Representation in the Cinema and Other Media* (Bloomington: Indiana Univ. Press, 1981), pp. 293–301.

sees *through* the projector in an *embodiment relation* that enables the spectator to see slow motion, as visible, in a way unavailable to the filmmaker for whom, at the time of filming, the camera is the sole hermeneut in regard to this particular kind of intended perception. Thus, the filmmaker must join the ranks of spectator and see *through* some projection mechanism in order to see what s/he perceptually intended but *never saw* at the time s/he used the camera that realized the perceptive intention.

What is being suggested here in the explication of these *single* instrument-mediated perceptions that occur between filmmaker/camera and spectator/projector is the *primacy* and *originality* of a transparent *embodiment relation* with cinematic technology. Although, as we have seen, such a relation is never completely transparent, it is nonetheless a radical and genetic necessity for the constitution of the film experience, for it enables and results in the *film* that is itself the agency through which two intending perceptions (and persons) can be said to share and communicate conscious experience. Simply, the filmmaker must see *through* the camera and the spectator must see *through* the projector for a film to emerge as "the perception of an expression which is perceived." This does not mean that there is no *hermeneutic relation* in force at this original level. Such a relation is revealed in the constant and pervasive "echo focus" that emerges at the juncture of the film's technological body and the human lived-body and informs the latter's sense of perception as mediated—experienced as an embodied perception not completely "my own."

This "echo focus" always informs the human incorporation of the machine *through* which perception is realized with the latent perception *of* the embodied machine as having a body that is other than one's own. If, however, the hermeneutic relation, the perception *of* the machine, were primary, and the embodiment relation reduced to a merely latent "echo focus," the film that might result (if, indeed, one did) would be "disabled" rather than "enabled." That is, it would come as close as possible to being an "empty" perception and expression, given that no perception or expression can be completely empty if it is said to exist at all. Uninformed by either the intentionality of the filmmaker or the spectator (both having fulfilled their intending acts respectively not at the terminus of the world but at the terminus of the machine as hermeneut), the film—to be a film at all—would still have to be minimally structured as a "perception of x" in an intentional noetic-noematic correlation, although x would be barely visible as a visual figure. As a necessary intentional object, x would exist sensibly only in the latency of an "echo focus" and would be, therefore, nearly nonsensical.

Instrument-Mediated Perception as Dialectic

The *single* technological relations of individual embodied persons to instruments that Ihde describes are necessary but not sufficient to the film experience. They are imbricated in, but cannot, in themselves or in their sum, account for the *doubled* and *inclusive* machine-mediation of the film experience, an experience that results in the constitution of a *reversibly perceptive and expressive text* and in *intersubjective* communication. In the film experience, instrument-mediated intentional acts not only intend the perception of objects but also intend, through instruments, the perception of other intentional acts, that is, the intentional acts of another intentional, perceptive and expressive subject. The single relations Ihde describes are compounded in the doubled instrumentation and doubled perceptive and expressive activities that constitute the film experience as such.

This commutation and doubling of perceptive and expressive activities as they engage filmmaker and spectator, camera and projector, are complex and dialectical. The film experience implicates what are two primary and "reversed" *embodiment relations* between human and machine in a secondary, higher-order, synthetic *hermeneutic relation* between humans and machines and between humans and humans. This latter hermeneutic relation emerges as the dialectical synthesis of two original and "reversed" embodiment relations. These embodiment relations (necessary and original to the film experience) are included and incorporated in the hermeneutic relation at a higher level of abstraction (or mediation), and it is this synthesis that provides the film experience its sufficient conditions.

Thus, while the filmmaker is engaged in a *single* instrument-mediated perception of an intended object through the enabling and transparent relation s/he has with the camera, the spectator is engaged in *two* instrument-mediated perceptions of the intended object—one inclusive of the other and yet also in dialectical tension with it. The first and primary instrument-mediation the spectator experiences entails the *projector*, with which the spectator has a transparent and enabling *embodiment relation*. The second and higher-order instrument-mediation the spectator experiences entails the filmmaker's enabling *camera*, with which the spectator has a more opaque *hermeneutic relation*. This hermeneutic relation synthetically includes *both* the spectator's embodiment relation with the projector *and* the filmmaker's embodiment relation with the camera, but the latter exists in a dialectical tension with the former because it is never experienced directly by the spectator as that embodiment relation which is "mine."

In other words, the filmmaker perceives an intended world *through* the camera. The spectator, however, perceives *through* the expressive instrumentality of the projector an intentional perception *of* the filmmaker/camera's embodiment relation *through* which the intended world is perceived. The spectator's perception through a machine (the projector) is of a machine (the camera) that, even though twice-removed, originally enables both the filmmaker's and the spectator's intentional fulfillment of the wish to see, to hear, to feel, to know, and to speak. Thus, the hermeneutic relation with the camera experienced by the spectator, who is also primarily in an embodiment relation with the projector, doubly distances the spectator from the "terminus" intended by two acts of perception. The hermeneutic relation that emerges from the spectator's experience of this *double mediation* is extraordinarily complex, if systemically coherent. It involves the respective and mutual human embodiment of mechanisms in which neither the humans nor the mechanisms are identical in their respective and discrete embodiments, but in which both are reversibly equivalent to each other in intentional structure and existential function.

The complexity of this hermeneutic relation that includes, incorporates, and dialectically exchanges embodiment relations can be schematized in Ihde's diagrammatic terms. At the primary level, in the *single relations* of instrument-mediated perception, Ihde diagrams the symbiotic and transparent incorporation of human and machine in an *embodiment relation* thus:

$$(\text{Human-machine}) \rightarrow \text{World}$$

Respectively and in an oppositional technological operation, the primary and single relations of embodiment between filmmaker and camera and spectator and projector can be mapped onto Ihde's diagram:

(Filmmaker-camera) → World
(Spectator-projector) → World

However, these single embodiment relations are complicated by the similar intentional projects of both filmmaker and spectator, that is, by their similar intentional directedness toward the perceptual expression of a world. Brought together in their mutual interest and intent (but not identical in their embodiment or situation), filmmaker and spectator thus *share* perception of a world in the following schematic:

(Filmmaker-camera) → World ← (Spectator-projector)

However, this diagram reveals a significant asymmetry. Although the embodiment relation still obtains in both acts of instrument-mediated perception, it becomes enigmatically charged in the above diagrammatic description. That is, one can see in the diagram the position of the projector "behind" the spectator (as it is in the concrete existential experience in the theater). It is as if in the embodiment relation between spectator and projector the machine incorporates the human to achieve the expression of a world, a reversal of the relation that exists between filmmaker and camera. However, this reversal is quite ambiguous in nature. The projector reifies perception as expression—but whose? The human spectator is *perceiving through* the projector, yet the projector has, in a sense, incorporated the spectator as the former is engaged in *expressing* the filmmaker's perception *through* the spectator's own perceptive and expressive activity.

This primary embodiment relation is further compounded by the nature and function of the double instrumentality involved. In their single relations, both camera and projector respectively function as mechanisms each of which, as they are humanly incorporated, enable the reversibility of perception and expression at an *intrasubjective* level. Perceiving through the camera, the filmmaker expresses perception to him or herself, and for itself (that is, on the undeveloped privacy of the film stock). This expression, of course, will later become *intersubjectively* visible through projection. Similarly, the spectator perceives through the projector and in so doing expresses his or her own perception intrasubjectively (in previous terms, introceptively), even as this same projector expresses the filmmaker's original perception so that it is intersubjectively visible for the spectator. That

193

is, as I watch a film, I see through the projector what another sees but also express my own process of seeing as uniquely mine. Thus I am able to engage the visible in a dialogue that results from the marked similarities and re-marked differences between *what I see* and *what is seen by another* even as I see it.

It is in this convergence and divergence of perception that the hermeneutic relation to cinematic technology arises in the spectator's experience. And, as we have seen, within this context the projector is a particularly ambiguous machine. It both expresses the mediation of the camera between the filmmaker and the intended world and enables the spectator to perceive that mediation. Simultaneously, it incorporates and expresses the embodiment relation between filmmaker and camera, and it is itself incorporated as the embodiment relation between spectator and projector that allows perception. Thus, the projector enables the spectator to perceive one instrument-mediated relation as hermeneutic while transparently living another as embodied.

It is in this *dialectic* of instrument-mediated perception as it is entailed in *embodiment relations* and *hermeneutic relations* that the film experience originates, and in which it duplicates the structural relations and dynamics that exist in and between perceptive and expressive human beings as communication. As is the case with language in human communicative exchanges, the commutative exchange between intrasubjective and intersubjective perception and expression in the film experience is as open a system as it is finitely and situationally bounded. The communicative texts we create for ourselves and with others are both effortlessly intelligible (and transparent) and effort-full and problematic (opaque). We are never completely intelligible and transparent even to ourselves, and others are also never completely unintelligible and opaque in their otherness. Through the instrumentality of camera and projector brought together in their perceptive and expressive functions and reversible operation, there arises a *partial opacity* between the filmmaker's perceptions of the world through the camera and the spectator's perceptions of that same world through the projector. But, there arises, as well, a *partial transparency* that enables both filmmaker and spectator—through instruments—to perceive, express, and communicatively share a common world.

As the filmmaker's perception through the machine is experienced through and included in the spectator's perception through the machine, the spectator experiences the filmmaker's embodiment relation with the camera *indirectly* and thus in a hermeneutic relation to him or herself. That is, the spectator experiences the filmmaker's original and enabling (Human-machine) → World relation as, to use Ihde's words, "something like a text."[33] That text, of course, is the *viewing-view/viewed-view*, the visual and visible vision whose synopsis signifies as the *film*. That text is produced as the expression of a *(Human-camera) embodiment relation* that the spectator perceives as a *(camera-World) hermeneutic relation*.

As previously indicated, Ihde's diagram of the single hermeneutic relation is:

$$\text{Human} \rightarrow (\text{machine-World})$$

What is described in this diagram is the human perception *of* a machine that mediates between the perceiver and the world, rather than a human perception *through* a machine that realizes its terminus *in* the intended object. In the film experience, the spectator's double engagement with reversible technology and dually mediated perception transforms the filmmaker/camera embodiment relation through which a world is perceived into a hermeneutic relation in which the spectator is aware (to whatever degree, but always to some degree) of the instrument-mediation that enables perception. That is, the spectator is *given* the filmmaker's perception of the intended world as a (Human-machine) relation—as the relation: (Filmmaker-camera). However, this relation is *taken* up in the enabling (Human-machine) relation necessary to the spectator's own primary perceptual engagement: the (Spectator-projector) relation.

Thus, the initially "given" (Human-machine) or (Filmmaker-camera) relation is *transformed* as it is "taken up" and incorporated by another at second remove from the object of perception. Altered through the concrete perceptual abstraction performed by the spectator, the (Human-machine) relation is experienced as a (machine-World) relation. That is, the (Filmmaker-camera) relation is experienced by the spectator as a (camera-World) relation. This transformation can be diagrammed in Ihde's schematic to indicate the *inclusive* nature of the spectator's engagement with the world as the terminus of the perception and thus that engagement's difference from the filmmaker's. Such a diagram also situates the "place" of the

[33] Ihde, "The Experience of Technology," p. 275.

transformation—that is, *where* the embodiment relation becomes a hermeneutic relation, where the perceived world becomes "text" and "film":

(Filmmaker-camera) → World

embodiment relation

(camera-World) ← (Spectator-projector)
embodiment relation

HERMENEUTIC RELATION

This diagram, however, is still incomplete as a description of the film experience. It does indicate the hermeneutic relation that emerges in the spectator's encounter with any and every film—no matter how much or how little the latter explicitly imitates the spectator's lived-body perception, and the sedimented and conventional intentions that historically constitute the spectator's "natural attitude" and reify the world as a "given." The diagram, however, does not yet indicate the enigmatic and dialectical structure of the spectator's access to the world as it is *expressed* in perception. It also does not indicate that, like the filmmaker, in its perceptual encounter with the world the *camera is invisible*—even as the spectator sees its *visible relation* to the world in its presented and represented activity. That is, rather than seeing the camera itself as not only the visual but also the visible organ of the film's "visual body," the camera's *visual activity* (its "introceptive image") and its *produced images* are what is visible to the spectator in and as the *film*.

This is an accurate description of even the most reflexive films, for even when a camera appears as visible *in* a film, that imaged camera is not the embodied camera *introceptively* and *invisibly enabling* the production of the *viewed view* or *image*. In those self-reflexive instances when the enabling camera appears as visible in a film by virtue of its mirrored reflection, what is visible is an image of a camera perceiving itself from a distance where it is present and invisibly situated "in front" of its reflection yet "behind" the perceptive activity that is visible as the viewing-view/viewed-view that yields its reflection.[34] As Susan Sontag suggests, "It's impossible ever to penetrate behind the final veil and experience cinema unmediated by cinema."[35] In this regard, one could say that the contemporary valorization of "reflexive" films that "critique" and "expose" cinematic mediation emerges as a contrary and barely latent desire to achieve transcendental vision.

Indeed, like any embodied human being, the filmmaker is only indirectly present *in* the direct perception s/he enables. Thus, the filmmaker's presence in the perception is even more indirect when s/he effects that perception through the mediation of the camera. Similarly, the camera that mediates and realizes the filmmaker's original perception is only indirectly present in the spectator's perception of the world as it visibly appears to his or her vision. Thus, the spectator perceives the world in a complex "invisible" and introceptive mode, that is, within his or her own perception lived bodily as "mine," and within the camera's and the filmmaker's perceptions, both also lived bodily as "mine."

The hermeneutic relation previously diagrammed is made enigmatic in experience because, like the filmmaker, the enabling and viewing camera is not visible as an other's "visual body." (Here, as it applies to the visible and invisible relations between embodied human beings and to the differently articulated relations between human being and film, Merleau-Ponty's "system of four terms" is particularly relevant.) The spectator is aware *of* a mediating instrumentality but not of the instrument itself. Thus, although still hermeneutic in its relation to a mediated perception sensed as *"not mine,"* the spectator's experience of a film also *includes* the filmmaker's embodiment relation with the camera as an *introceptive experience* of perception sensed and signified as *"mine."* That is, as it is visibly experienced as visual activity, the filmmaker's introceptively experienced embodiment relation with the camera is a relation *isomorphic* with the introceptive structure of the spectator's own embodiment relation with the projector (and, indeed, with the spectator's directly introceptive perceptual engagement with the world). As the camera

[34] For discussions of this "infinite regress" of reflexivity in relation to cinematic perception as always—and necessarily—situated invisibly outside what is visible, see Erving Goffman, *Frame Analysis: An Essay on the Organization of Experience* (New York: Harper Colophon Books, 1974), particularly pp. 378–438.

[35] Susan Sontag, "Godard," in her *Styles of Radical Will* (New York: Dell Publishing Co., Delta Books, 1970), p.170.

is not visible *in* the perception of the world but enables it, the spectator's hermeneutic awareness of instrument-mediation is constituted ambivalently and dialectically, as a *quasi-embodiment/hermeneutic relation* to what appears *visible* as the *viewing-view/viewed-view*: the visible visual act of perceiving the visibly perceived world. This complex intentional structure can be diagrammed as follows:

(Filmmaker-camera) → World

embodiment relation

camera's (perception of World) ← (Spectator-projector)
embodiment relation   *embodiment relation*

QUASI-EMBODIMENT/HERMENEUTIC RELATION

What the above diagram now describes are the dialectical possibilities of relating to the instrument-mediated perception that constitutes the film (expressed and perceived as perception of World, as viewing-view/viewed-view). That is, such instrument-mediated perception can be experienced as *either* hermeneutic *or* embodied within a structure of perception which is *both* embodied *and* hermeneutic in its relations with technology and with human others. Thus, the spectator can engage the world through the double instrumentality and enabling power of camera and projector *transparently*—with only an "echo focus" of the mechanisms providing the perceptual cues that prevent the spectator from experiencing his or her perception of the world as totally unmediated (that is, directly experienced as "mine"). Or the spectator can engage his or her perception of the world in an awareness that the latter's visibility is effected and affected by the enabling mechanism of the camera. In this mode, the spectator is aware of the perception's *opacity*—an opacity lightened only by the "echo focus" of the spectator's own embodiment relation with the projector which, indeed, enables the awareness that the camera's perception belongs to an "other."

These two extremes found the boundaries of the structure in which instrument-mediation and awareness of it occur in the film experience. They are the dialectical poles *of* a dynamic structure and are marked and chosen diacritically in the contingency of each existential moment of film viewing. However, they are also synthesized *as* the framed structure that *is* the film: the visible intentional activity of vision correlated to a visible intentional object of vision. Although the spectator is always partially aware *of* a mediating instrumentality, s/he is always also given partial perceptual access to a visible world *through* that mediating instrumentality—and thus "World" is always, at the very least, the object of a partially fulfilled and realized perceptual intention. That is, the world and the activity of mediation are encountered in the same visual and visible space. And both are correlated in an irreducible and dialectical structure that synthesizes instrumentality in both its embodiment relation and its hermeneutic relation to human perception. Thus, the partial opacity of the (machine-World) relation to the perceiver is transformed in and as the film as text to become also the partial transparency of the (Human-machine) relation that realizes itself not in the film as text but in the world as text (as happens in direct perception).

Thus, whether signified through conventional or unconventional "ways of seeing" and images in the film experience, "World" becomes visible to the spectator in and through the instrument-mediated viewing-view/viewed-view that is the film. "World" occupies a portion of the last diagram as that relation:

camera (perception of World)

Here, the camera is implicated in the perception but is not itself visible in the perception. What exists as the film, then, is a perceptual analogue of human intentionality. That is, the "eye/I" enables intentional acts correlated with intentional objects but is implicit rather than explicit in that correlation and is only discovered in a *reflective* and *reflexive* intentional action secondary to the primary experience of intending *toward* the world. In existence, the primary experience of perception is directed as follows:

camera → (perception of → World)

Reflective and reflexive perception, however, turns toward its origins in an embodied subject by moving from its initially intended object back to its activity of perception and, finally, to its embodied situation. It is directed thus:

camera ← (perception of ← World)

This backward, reflexive, and reflective turn is predicated always on the initial experience of prereflective perception directed toward the world and the accomplishment of being in the world.

Ihde discusses this original and primary structure of human intentionality as directed "outwards" by the intending subject.[36] And he diagrams it as follows, using phenomenological terminology:

(I) noesis → noema
(experiencer) experiencing-experienced

The "I" or ego is not given to experience *within* the correlation, just as the camera (and the filmmaker who incorporated the camera in an embodiment relation) is not given to the experiencing of the experienced within the perceptual structure that is the film. There is, of course, the danger here of mistaking the implicit "I" for the transcendental "I," of making a Husserlian move to describe the distanced and enabling "I" as further reduced and described by a *transcendental ego* that is somehow both implicated in the correlation and yet removed from it.

Ihde diagrams this Husserlian transcendental relation (as we shall see, to indicate its unnecessary descriptive redundancy). This diagram follows—except that I have added brackets to stress how final reduction of the correlation to include the *transcendent* ego/experiencer moves Husserl to posit a *transcendental* ego/experiencer for whom the implicit ego is immanent and explicit in the correlation:

Transcendental Ego (I'')

[Ego (I') noesis → noema]

The cinematic analogue of Ihde's diagram follows, with the filmmaker here serving the all-inclusive transcendental function located "behind" the transcendent and implicit camera:

Transcendental Filmmaker (I/Eye'')

[Camera (I/Eye') viewing-view → viewed-view]

As Merleau-Ponty reminds us, however, there is no transcendental ego *in existence*. Rejecting Husserl's final and transcendental reduction, he tells us, "The greatest lesson of the [phenomenological] reduction is the *impossibility* of a complete reduction."[37] Ihde also points

---

[36] Ihde, *Experimental Phenomenology: An Introduction*, p. 44.

[37] Maurice Merleau-Ponty, "What is Phenomenology?" trans. John F. Bannan, *Cross Currents* 6 (Winter 1956), p. 64.

to the problem inherent in positing such a transcendental "presence" reflecting upon existential experience from "outside" and yet also enabling that intentional experience and its essential structure. Not only is such a transcendental reduction impossible, he suggests, but it is also *unnecessary*. The transcendental ego is not a necessary condition for the reflective and reflexive moment and movement of consciousness that locates its radical origins in an enabling subject of experience. He says:

> On the one hand, the whole correlation is the noema for the transcendental ego (I"). Conversely, the transcendental ego (I") is interpreted as above and outside the correlation. But if *the correlation is itself the ultimate structural feature of human experience*, then this transcendental move is questionable. On the other hand, there remains a sense in which *the transformation of reflection upon experience still retains the correlation structure*, in that the transcendental ego is actually only a *modification* of the ordinary ego (I') and, as transcendental ego, must be correlated with the new noema. This feature might be diagrammed as:
>
> Transcendental Ego (I") noesis → noema
> (Ego-noesis-noema-theme)
>
> But this *reduces* the "outside" and "above" of the transcendental ego to the simple (I) noesis-noema correlation, and makes the transcendental interpretation *unnecessary*.[38]

Translated into cinematic terms, "outside" the visible correlation that is the film, and also "behind" the invisible but implicated camera, the "transcendental" Eye/I of the filmmaker is still "inside" the correlational structure of existential perception. S/he still engages the world in the intentional structure of the viewing-view/viewed-view. S/he "still retains the correlation structure," not only of the film experience, but also of all visual experience. Thus, the filmmaker as "transcendentally" reflective ego and eye, and the camera as "transcendent" and prereflective ego and eye, are merely two modalities or "modifications" of the existential and perceiving subject always engaged in a noetic act correlated with a noematic object. Following Ihde's characterization of the "distanced" and "removed" transcen-

---

[38] Ihde, *Experimental Phenomenology: An Introduction*, p. 46. (Emphasis mine)

dental ego as irreducibly "being in correlation," and thus not transcendental at all, a cinematic model might be diagrammed as follows:

(Filmmaker/I/Eye) perceiving → perceived

(Camera/I/Eye-perceiving-perceived-World)

As Ihde suggests, this diagram can be reduced further to the simpler irreducible correlation that describes the primary intentional structure of perception as it exists for filmmaker, camera, spectator (and film theorist) alike. The transcendental interpretation is unnecessary and impossible, for the following correlation cannot be escaped by any being-in-the-world:

(I/Eye) perceiving → perceived

Filmmaker and camera, therefore, exist in the *same* relation to the correlation that is the film as viewing-view/viewed-view, as "perceiving → perceived." Neither filmmaker nor camera are immanent or given to the spectator in the film experience. Nonetheless, both can be *located* as the existential and enabling source of cinematic perception. As well, given their primary embodiment relation, both filmmaker and camera can be reduced to the common enabling subject of the perception that is objectified as the film's viewing-view/viewed-view. Together, they constitute a common eye that, although *not inscribed in* the correlation, is always engaged *in the process of inscribing* the viewing-view/viewed-view. This enabling subject and eye can be located as such in a reflective and reflexive activity performed both by the film and/or the spectator, although the latter has the benefit of a broader horizon of reflective vision than the former has. (This occurs because the latter's reflection on perception includes the former's.) As well, this common eye and subjectivity is located and identified in reflection precisely as an *existential* eye. It cannot be abstracted "outside" its perception (the film) as the transcendental singularity of the filmmaker as human being with a particular anatomy and autobiography, or as the transcendental singularity of the camera as inanimate "thing" with a particular mechanical structure. Always implicated in and contingent to the visible perception that is the viewing-view/viewed-view of the film, the *author* of that perception is not the filmmaker or the camera distanced and abstracted from each other and from the perception they *together* enable and enact.

Rather, the author of the viewing view/viewed view that is the film is the *filmmaker-camera embodiment relation*. Similarly, always implicated in and contingent to the visible expression that is the viewing-view/viewed-view of the film, the *spectator-projector embodiment relation* is author of that expression of the film that they *together* enable and enact in the contingency of their particular conjunction. It is in the imbricated and existential conjunction of these *two* embodiment relations and *two* modalities of the viewing-view/viewed-view that a hermeneutic relation emerges, and that a dialectic of perception and expression comes into being as the dynamic complexity of the cinematic "text."

THE FILM EMBODIED

Thus far, this discussion of technology and its imbrication in the film experience has emphasized the perceptual engagement with cinematic mechanisms lived through by filmmaker and spectator in respectively different modalities of instrument-mediation. But what of the film, the correlated viewing-view/viewed-view perceptible as the expression of perception? What is the film's relation to the technology that enables it? In what manner—if any—can the film that exists for *our* perception as an instrument-mediated expression of perception be said to exist perceptually and expressively also for *itself*? How might it be legitimate to speak of something so "invisible" and seemingly metaphoric as the film's "body"? Or to describe in concrete terms that invisible presence of an other who perceives and expresses perception in the film experience along with, as well as opposed to, the spectator?

Following the perceptual engagement with technology experienced by the human participants of the film experience along the phenomenological trajectory traced by Ihde's diagrammatic thematization, we have seen the film emerge as an intentional and irreducibly correlated structure animated by its existential and motile visual activity. Enabled by an eye that belongs neither solely to the filmmaker, the camera, or the spectator, the film exists as the *visible visual relation* between an embodied eye and a sensible world. As *visible* and *significant*, the film exists as the correlation:

$$(\text{perceiving} \rightarrow \text{perceived})$$

We can put this correlation in terms more specific to both the existential activity of vision and the significance of cinema:

$$(\text{viewing-view} \rightarrow \text{viewed-view})$$

As we engage it, the film is visible solely as the intentional "terminus" of an embodied and seeing subject, as an intentional activity irreducibly correlated with an intentional object. That is, the mechanisms and humans who *enable* the correlation to visibly exist as vision are not themselves visible in the correlation—nor can they then be said to function as mediating instruments or agents *within* that correlation. In a very real sense, it can be said that the enabled film emerges and inscribes an existence of its own.

Neither the camera nor the projector mediate *between* the perceiving act and its intentional object, between the viewing-view and the viewed-view. Neither do the filmmaker nor the spectator. Certainly, there are films that *secondarily* and visibly indicate the mediation of instruments that either enable or partially block the perceiving act's accomplishment of its intentional fulfillment in and as the perceived object. That is, within the expressed perception, such films show instrument-mediation as embodied or hermeneutic. There are also films that visibly alter their perception of an intended object, visibly transforming their normative "bodily" perception by, for example, "looking through" a microscope. (The genre of science fiction film is perhaps the most explicit in this regard, exploring both the limits and extension of perception, bodies, and cinema itself.[39]) Nonetheless, it must be emphasized that these visible instrumental interventions and mediations are secondary interventions in and mediations of perception and its expression. The *radical* and *primary* perceptual correlation that is visible as the film is a correlation not *mediated* by instruments, but *enabled* by them. As an accomplishment of perception

---

[39] For elaboration on the generic explorations and transformations of the SF film, see Vivian Sobchack, *Screening Space: The American Science Fiction Film*, 2d enlarged ed. (New York: Ungar, 1988). I might also emphasize here how the *human* body in that historical and cultural domain staked out as "postmodern" has increasingly reconceived itself as a *technological* body. The genre of science fiction literalizes this existential re-cognition, but it is enacted all around us. For elaboration of this claim, see particularly Chapter 4, "Postfuturism," of *Screening Space*, pp. 223–305, and Sobchack, "Toward a Phenomenology of Cinematic and Electronic Presence: The Scene of the Screen."

and its expression, the film is enabled by its mechanisms much as our bodies provide us with the sensing and sensible means to accomplish our perceptual and expressive intentions in an intended and expressed object. Thus, in a sense quite different than relating cinematic technology to our own human bodies, the mechanisms and technological instrumentation of the cinema can be understood as the *film's body*, functioning as its sensing and sensible being at and in the world.

Our own perceptual and intentional correlations with the world are activities of engagement that have structure and presence but no physical substantiality. That is, they are not *things*. Indeed, they are *no-thing* but the dynamic and dialectical *relation between* "things." However, no matter how immaterial, these acts of correlation are dependent upon *embodiment* for their realization and presence in the world. That is, my perceptual encounter with the world is not a thing and has no material substance. Thus, it is completely dependent upon my body for its articulation and visibility—even as my body seems to have no visible presence *in* the encounter it enables, and even as my perception is so visibly present *to* me as to take on the quality of substantiality. Similarly, as the film is no-thing but the dynamic and dialectical relations visibly correlated as the perceiving act accomplishing a perceived object, the film is also completely dependent upon a substantial, if invisible, incarnation. This incarnation is responsible for the emergence and continuation of perception as visible and expressed. And it also originates the significance and bias of that perception as it engages a substantial world that has meaning—makes sense—only to a vision that is also sensible by virtue of having a substantial origin. In this sense, the camera and projector and accompanying mechanisms can be said to *substantially embody* the film and to function in a way that far exceeds their characterization as merely mechanical instruments and discrete pieces of apparatus. In this sense, the film can be said to genuinely have and live a body.

The Function of the Film's Body

The primary function of cinematic technology (what here shall also be called the film's body) is to enable *acts* of introceptive perception and their expression. From the first, the film's body functions to visibly *animate* perception and expression in existence. Thus, its primary function always already entails *movement*. This original movement *of* the film's body invisibly grounds those movements *in* the film which figure as visible (object movement in the viewed-view and subject movement of the viewing-view). Even before it visibly moves, the film's body visually moves—accomplishing vision in·a visible image that is meaningful. This ongoing accomplishment and articulation of the film's vision enables us, as Merleau-Ponty says, "to understand motility as basic intentionality."[40]

The film's body, then, is radically distinguished by its motility. Its viewing-view is always in motion, even if that motion is expressed introceptively and appears to the body-subject of an "other" as non-movement. The most "static" of films is not static at all. Thus, Arthur Danto rightly tells us: "Moving pictures are just that: *pictures* which move, *not* just (or necessarily at all) pictures *of* moving things. For we may have moving pictures of what are practically stolid objects, like the Himalayas and nonmoving pictures of such frenetically motile objects as Breugel's reeling peasants and Rosa Bonheur's rearing horses. Before the advent of moving pictures, it would not have been illuminating to characterize nonmoving pictures as nonmoving; there would have been no other sort."[41] Except, of course, for those "moving pictures" accomplished and projected without reel changes by our own lived-bodies.

The film's body originally perceives and expresses perception as the very process and progress of the viewing-view as it constitutes the viewed-view as visible both for itself and for us. This movement and process is the concerted and synoptic production of two primary "organs" of the film's body: the camera as its perceptive organ and the projector as its expressive organ. (The latter may enable the spectator's perception of the film's vision, but, for the film, it functions to express perception.) The co-operation of camera and projector existentially enables and realizes the film as a "moving picture." Thus, Danto reminds us, "With the movies, we do not just see *that* they move, we see them *moving*: and this is because the pictures themselves move."[42]

Here, critics of the "cinematic apparatus" will raise the objection that this movement is but an illusion, that each viewing-view/viewed-view that constitutes the film must be perceived both by the

[40] Merleau-Ponty, *Phenomenology of Perception*, p. 137.
[41] Arthur C. Danto, "Moving Pictures," *Quarterly Review of Film Studies* 4 (Winter 1979), p. 15.
[42] Ibid., p. 17.

camera and expressed by the projector *in arrest*, that is, fixed and immobile before lens and light source, and distinctly separated from preceding and subsequent perceptions by a shutter that punctuates and differentiates each single viewing-view/viewed-view by interrupting vision with its negation, nonvision (or blindness) and immobility. Thus, it is argued, cinematic movement is not movement at all, but only its representation, only something illusory taken as something real. This argument certainly explains how cinematic movement is *mechanically achieved*, but it does not address our experience of what cinematic movement *is* and what it *means*. Thus, it does little to further our understanding of what the moving picture is and from whence it gains its significance. As Hugo Münsterberg wrote in 1916, "The perception of movement is an *independent experience* which cannot be reduced to a simple seeing of a series of different positions."[43]

Thus, although the mechanics of constituting the film's visual and visible movement are *necessary* conditions for that movement, they are hardly *sufficient*. Film theorists would hardly suggest that human movement is a secondary construction rather than an ontological condition of human being. Nor would they suggest that human movement is inherently charged with deceit, that it is not "real" but instead an illusion. Past physiological and philosophical reductions of human movement to a set of "static" moments in serial combination have told us little about movement as a lived phenomenon. Thus, it is more useful to our understanding of the cinema's significance to consider cinematic movement as an *existential* function of the film's body, a function always enabling the accomplishment of perceptive and expressive projects in a world.

Indeed, we could liken the regular but intermittent passage of images into and out of the film's material body (through camera and projector) to human respiration or circulation, the primary bases upon which human animation and being are grounded. The lungs fill and collapse before they fill again. The valves of the heart open and shut and open again. Both respiration and the circulation of blood are not continuous but segmented and rhythmic activities. Yet, in regard to the "mechanics" of this radical and invisible animation of our bodies, we do not consider or understand ourselves as "re-

---

[43] Hugo Münsterberg, *The Film: A Psychological Study The Silent Photoplay in 1916*. (1916; reprint New York: Dover Press, 1970), p. 26.

ally" inanimate, as being only and always in "intermittent motion." Similarly, if more visibly (to others as well as to ourselves), we do not visually experience our attentive gaze as intermittently disrupted by the blinking of our eyelids.

The point to be made here is critical in relation to the "natural attitude" we hold toward the nature and function of our own bodies on the one hand, and toward the nature and function of the film's body, on the other. However, reflection on temporal existence as it is spatially embodied and enworlded in experience tells us that heartbeat, blink, and shutter do not *interrupt* movement. Nor do they *dissemble* or *disassemble* movement. Rather, they are a *constitutive part* of what movement is and what it means as a structural and temporally dynamic *whole*. What is analyzed by some as a series of discrete incremental photographic "moments" passing themselves off in expression as real movement *is* real movement. These "moments" achieve real movement through the film's existential activity. That is, they temporally come into being as they are introceptively perceived through the camera and visibly expressed through the projector. They are no longer "moments," set beside each other as a digital series of discrete points. Rather, they radically resolve themselves into the analog fluidity of intentional action, initiating and completing its tasks and constituting significance against the double horizon of a world and a lived-body. Never experienced as "moments," this commutation of the photographic into the cinematic inscribes a very real and intentionally directed "momentum." As breathing or seeing is for us, so this visual introception and its commutation to visible projection is to the cinema. The reversible and dynamic movement in which the active and intrasubjective "viewing view" constitutes itself simultaneously as intersubjective "viewed view" or "moving image" is the original and real movement that grounds every other movement and so becomes the zero-degree against which other visual/visible movement in the cinema is marked.[44]

As do our own bodily mechanisms, the film's bodily mechanisms co-operate and synopsize their functions into the co-Herence and comprehension of a significant lived-body experience. Nonetheless, given the preeminence of the visual and visible (and to a lesser de-

[44] For phenomenological elaboration of further modalities of cinematic movement, see Vivian Sobchack, "The Active Eye: A Phenomenology of Cinematic Vision," *Quarterly Review of Film and Video* 12 (1990), pp. 21–36.

gree, the audible) in the film's experience of making sense, the camera tends to be the cinema's most privileged mechanism, the most foregrounded part of the film's anatomical body (which is more than, and therefore not equivalent to, the camera). The camera is the enabling instrument that allows perceptual access to a world. The camera is itself substantial and thus can inhabit and move about in that world among other substantial and sensible phenomena with which it can relate existentially.

Thus, the camera enjoys special privilege because it marks its perceptive competence in the *existential performance of materially embodied perception*. Its perception is prominently *visible* in its activity of perceiving a world and constituting its viewing-view/viewed-view as the expression of perception. Although the camera's material substance is not seen in this correlation that is the film, it makes its presence to the world (and to us) *sensible* through its materialized activity of looking and moving in relation to what it perceives. Its activity inscribes, therefore, an occupation of substantial space by a substantial and embodied eye. In its material existence, this eye is always *situated* in the world at which it looks and in which it moves and is always *finite* in its lack of visual omniscience and omnipresence, in the necessity of its perspectival vision.

Thus, even the embodied film's imagination is lived in terms of its concrete bodily situation and finitude, no matter how it speculates, and objectively actualizes a "viewed view" that envisions omniscience and omnipresence. That is, the visually fractured images of a film such as Fernand Léger's *Ballet Mécanique* may present a visible but physically uninhabitable world as the simultaneous experience of multiple bodily situations. However, the viewing-view that constitutes and synopsizes that world as its viewed-view still looks at it with a situated and finite eye. Privileged because its perceptual activity is inscribed within its productions, the camera announces the invisible but substantial presence of an embodied and intending consciousness, one always marked in the very activity and movement that exists significantly as the expressed intentional perception we see as the film.

The projector and the screen function more latently, less visibly, than does the camera whose visual perception they commute to visible expression. The projector and screen do not insist upon their cooperative function in embodying and expressing the camera's perception, in giving it substantiality and presence as that which is not only visual but also is visible. Despite the latency of its presence, however, the projector is responsible for and allows the camera's perception its visible presence. It transforms that subjective perception to objective expression—in a process of reversal that is analogous to the way in which our subjective or "introceptive" knowledge of our bodies is commuted by the substantiality of our bodies in the world to the objective knowledge others have of us as our "visual bodies." The projector expresses the camera's perceptual encounter with the world and enables its visibility in the same way that our seemingly passive flesh provides the expressive material that makes visible the active, yet insubstantial, presence of our gestures.

The screen, too, functions in a similarly passive manner. It acts latently, but crucially, to express the co-operative nature and coherence of the film's body. That is, it articulates the film's "fleshly" boundaries; it marks a synoptic substantial being-to-the-world in its *comprehension of perception*. And, in its containment of the perception's spatializing traversal of the world's space, it constitutes also the expression of a personal and finite temporal existence. The screen rectangle functions, then, as the *singular situation* of a perception that is, itself, mobile. It functions to *center* the *discrete, discontinuous,* and *de-centered* experience of consciousness as it shifts its modalities and reverses its directions and alters or experiences contradiction in and among its intentional projects. In sum, the screen acts to contain the reversals and dialectic of perception and expression in the *unity* of a *spatial situation* that *includes* the dynamic, temporalized experience of *displacement* and *rupture*.

For us, the unity of spatial situation is achieved by our bodies. All the discrete, discontinuous, and incoherent experiences of consciousness are synopsized by our particular and consistent spatial embodiment. Indeed, it is this synopsizing function of the body that generates *temporality*, or the consciousness of experience. Here again, it is useful to recall Richard Zaner's discussion of the functional characteristics of the body. The body, we have seen, serves as the "zero point" for sensing and sensible encounters with the world; that is, all objects of perception are organized spatially and temporally in relation to it. The body is also a *single* instrumentality providing access to the world through a *variety* of means or "senses" that co-operate synaesthetically. The body, as well, *synopsizes* those various sensory fields and puts them all at the service of realizing the perceptions of an intending consciousness.

210

These functions of the body were first discussed to demonstrate that vision is not an abstract or discrete bodily activity but is intentional in its structure and irreducibly correlated to the concrete existence of a lived-body. These same functions were later discussed in relation to the film's *frame*. That is, the perceived geometry of the projected image was seen as setting the film's nongeometric *perceptive boundaries*, providing a circumscription of the premises of the camera's perception analogous to the way in which the lived-body provides the bounded premises for human perception. The frame is to the camera what the screen is to the projector. The frame functions to *center* discrete perceptions, to give them a spatial *co-Herence* that unifies and makes temporally meaningful the lived-experience of a constantly shifting and mobile vision. As that *techno-logical condition* of the cinema that announces and inscribes perception's emergence from a *finite* and *situated* source, the frame marks off the visible from the invisible and inscribes the necessary *limits* and *perspectivity* of embodied perception. Discussed in this way, the film frame is not a thing and has no materiality of its own, just as the bio-logical condition that situates and limits our visual field is no thing and immaterial. Both, however, are dependent upon the substantial and material. Just as our substantial flesh is necessary to both the existence and the limitation of our visual field, so are the *frame* and *screen* necessary to both the existence and the limitation of the film's visual field. The screen, then, is the substantial "flesh" that allows the perceptive activity of the film *situated* presence and *finite* articulation. The screen is the material substance that enables the frame its function. Passive as it seems (much as the "corners" of our eyes and the configuration of our eye sockets are passive and, themselves, not the source of visual activity), the screen provides the function of the frame its formal place, its concrete situation, and the spatial unity necessary for the synopsis of experience as conscious and temporal.

The mechanisms of cinematic technology, then, function cooperatively to enable the film as the realized and expressed perception it is. They are synoptically engaged in the intentional project of seeing, and of expressing sight. They provide perception the grounds of its being in the "flesh," the substantiality, necessary to the existential encounter between the *immaterial and subjective activity* of intending consciousness and the *material objectivity* of the world. Obviously, the film's body is made of a material quite different from the human flesh of our lived-bodies. That material difference is marked further by what, in the "natural attitude," we think of as the spatial and temporal fragmentation of the film's body into discrete mechanisms.

Indeed, this material difference tends to become problematic when the film's perception attempts to reflect on its own material presence, or when it pretends, at the level of its perceptual inscription of the world, to possess a material form and anatomy that is human. (These instances will be addressed at length in a later discussion of the nature of the film's body). Nonetheless, whatever its material difference from the human body, the film's body functions like our own, evolving through its perceptive activity an expressed bodily style of being in a world. Generally invisible in its perception, the film's material body—like our own—enables that perception and its expression, and it does so finitely in an always contingent and particular situation in which that body is invested and interested in an always biased and bounded way. These constraints, as well as the freedom to displace (but not escape) them, constitute the conditions for individual personality, for a particular and unique "style" of accomplishing existence.

In *The Prose of the World*, Merleau-Ponty discusses the emergence of personal style as the articulation of a *bodily* way of being-in-the-world. Much of what he says is as descriptive of a film as it is of a human being inscribing a presence in the world through the inherently expressive nature of embodied perception. In regard to the passage I quote below, it is particularly important to recall previous discussion of 1) the original embodiment relation that exists between the experienced filmmaker and the camera and 2) the transformation of that relation as it becomes visible through projection. That original embodiment relation is transformed, we remember, into a hermeneutic relation in which the contingent and autonomous action of an other's Eye/I inscribes an anonymous, yet subjective, intentional life before us—a life instrumentally achieved by cinematic *technology* but inescapably charged with its radical origin in *human* conscious experience.

Given to *our* experience as the visible inscription and gesture of its *own* experience, the film lives out before us a perceptual life expressed as kin to our own. It is a life actively engaged, enacted, and inscribed in the embodied and reversible processes of perception and expression. This perceptive life is expressed as having its own *integrity*, its own force and source of inscription as present and original *discours*—even as it secondarily represents the description and *histoire* of an absent filmmaker, even as it is secondarily circumscribed by the perceptive and expressive activity of a spectator who is engaged also in the inscriptive production of *discours* and the descriptive consumption of *histoire*.[45]

In the passage that follows, Merleau-Ponty also describes the film's body as he speaks of our human lived-bodies and their "miraculous" instrumentality; that is, their ability to effect an "infinite summation of spaces and instants" and their ability to give us the world grasped by our intentions. Cinematic technology transcends its mechanisms as the human lived-body transcends its physiology. It enables the intentional perception and its expression that is the film's very activity of summing up spaces and instants—not only for us as it is visible, but also for itself as it is visual, as it functions for itself "invisibly" and "introceptively." What our bodies instrumentally are for us, the mechanisms of the cinema are for the film—the camera and projector always (and usually effortlessly) engaging the world visually in the compass of a bodily and perceptive style of being. Thus, I would claim for the film's body Merleau-Ponty's description of ours. That description is worth quoting at length:

> We can at least recognize that this miracle is habitual and natural to us, that it begins with our incarnate life. . . . Here, the spirit of the world is ourselves as soon as we know how *to move ourselves* and *to look*. These simple acts already contain the secret of expressive action. As the artist makes his style radiate into the very fibers of the material on which he is working, so I move my body without even knowing which muscles and nerve paths should intervene or where I should look for the instruments of this action. I want to go over there, and here I am, without access to the inhuman secret of the bodily mechanism, without having adjusted it to the objective requirements of the task or to the position of the goal defined in relation to some system of coordinates. I look where the goal is, I am drawn by it, and the whole bodily machine does what must be done for me to get there. Everything happens in that human world of perception and gesture,

---

[45] The seminal distinction between *discours* and *histoire* as it is used here is made in Emile Benveniste, *Problems in General Linguistics* (Miami, FL: Univ. of Miami Press, 1971), pp. 205–215. However, of relevance to the secondary constructions of discourse and story that constitute the temporality of narrative, see also Seymour Chatman, *Story and Discourse: Narrative Structure in Fiction and Film* (Ithaca, NY: Cornell Univ. Press, 1978).

but my "geographical" or "physical" body obeys the requirements of this little drama which never ceases to produce a thousand natural miracles in my body.

My glance toward the goal already has its own miracles. It, too, installs itself in being with authority and conducts itself there as in a conquered country. It is not the object which draws movements of accommodation and convergence (from the eyes). On the contrary, it has been demonstrated that I would never see anything clearly and that there would be no object for me, unless I used my eyes in *such a way as* to make the view of a single object possible. To complete the paradox, one cannot say that the mind takes the place of the body and anticipates what we will see. No, it is our glances themselves, with their synergy, their exploration, and their prospecting which bring the immanent object into focus. The corrections would never be rapid and precise enough if they had to rely upon actual calculation of effects. We must therefore recognize that what we call a "glance," a "hand," and in general the "body" constitutes a system of systems devoted to the inspection of a world and capable of leaping over distances, piercing into the perceptual future, and outlining, in the inconceivable platitude of being, hollows and reliefs, distances and gaps, in short, a meaning. . . .[46]

Is this not an accurate description of the "devotion" of the film's body to intentional perception as much as it is a description of the "devotion" of our own bodies to "the inspection of a world"? Indeed, the discussion that follows (as well as the general project of this work) constitutes a dialogue with this passage.

What the passage suggests is that the mechanisms that constitute the film's body do not yield up merely mechanical perception. That is, they do not see the world nor express it *generally*. Embodied perception, whether cinematic or human, is not lived *theoretically*. In this regard, insofar as they both generalize in their empirical descriptions, both Merleau-Ponty's observations and this present work do so at the juncture of actual embodied praxis and its possibility. Thus, if such generalization is regarded as constituting a theory, it must be regarded paradoxically as a theory of the moment when there is no theory, when theory is both unthought and incomplete in its momentum as *praxis*.

[46] Maurice Merleau-Ponty, *The Prose of the World*, ed. Claude Lefort, trans. John O'Neill (Evanston, IL: Northwestern Univ. Press, 1973), pp. 77–78.

Thus, the active and synergetic relation between the viewing-view/
viewed-view that is visibly given to our experience as the film is a
relation that is visible and significant only in the accomplishment of
concrete *intentional tasks*—not in "objective" tasks projected geometrically in relation to "some system of coordinates." The perceiving
glance of the film's body goes where it must. Indeed, this perceiving
glance authorizes its objects in the very bodily stance of its Eye/I that
seeks out and "prospects" the world, bringing the "immanent object
into focus." The film, enabled by the camera and projector and emergent as the visible *action* and *gesture* of perception encountering a
world, hardly accomplishes its initial grasp of the world in "an actual
calculation of effects."

Such "calculation" does occur in the instrument-mediated perception of the filmmaker *prior to* the actual shooting. This is when the
mechanism must be considered as such, and when the filmmaker is
in a hermeneutic (rather than embodied) relation to the instrument-
mediation of cinematic technology. During shooting, however, the
filmmaker and technology are conjoined in the transparent symbiosis
of an embodiment relation, that is, until some problem in actualizing
the perception occurs and a recalculation must take place in order to
effect that perception or to amend it, at which time the filmmaker
again distances the technology from his or her own body, becomes
aware *of* it, rather than aware *through* it.[47]

Insofar as the film is visible as the successful realization of a perceptive act in an intended perceived object, the camera and projector
and all other enabling cinematic technology are synaesthetically synopsized as the film's body. Together, co-operatively, they are the
film's means of *directly* having and behaving in a world—no matter
how abstract or reflexive its intentional conduct or how imaginative

[47] In this regard, Parker Tyler is also worth quoting here. In *The Shadow of an Airplane
Climbs the Empire State Building*, he points to "learning" filmmakers and "film-buff critics" as treating

> whole films as if they were great machines constructed by a canny compilation of devices.
> Any film can be made to seem, as a result, a veritable garden of technical flowers. But all
> that, however beguiling and legitimate, is not in the least *what I have in mind here*. I would
> like to ignore "the film" as a sort of computerized fantasy of camera effects and concen-
> trate instead on its organic nature, viewing all such material means and classified effects
> as irrelevant, insofar as they are but mechanical details whether they pertain to "creating
> a film" or to a "created film." . . . Technique is sufficient to the motives thereof, but tech-
> nique is never a substitute for motivation. (pp. 105–106)

215

its intentional object. This synaesthesia, synopsis, and synthesis of the apparatus functions, as Merleau-Ponty describes it, to "constitute a system of systems devoted to the inspection of a world." Invisible to itself as we are to ourselves in the intentional action and direction of our glance in the world, the film's body is indeed "capable of leaping over distance, piercing into the perceptual future," and carving out with its vision the particularity of a lived-world and a unique discursive existence within it. The film, as it appears to us and for itself, is not the inscription of a mechanical, repetitive, generalized, or "platitudinous" being (no matter how hard it may intend platitudinous conduct and utterances), but rather inscribes the activity of a singular intentionality, outlining—in its presence to the world—"hollows and reliefs, distances and gaps, in short, a meaning."

Thus, although initiated by and informed with the intentional bodily style of the filmmaker (who has embodied cinematic technology but also dealt with the hermeneutic instances in which his or her perceptual intentions through the machine required focus on and adjustment of the machine), the film emerges as having an existential presence in its own right. As it comes into being through projection, the film becomes. As it has being on the screen, the film behaves. It *lives* its *own* perceptive and intentional life before us as well as for us, inscribing an invested and contingent response to the world it singularly (if still socially) inhabits, possesses, and signifies. Thus, the film is not merely a cartographic representation of the filmmaker's worldly explorations. Certainly, the film exists for us in the secondary move of reflection as just such an *inscribed topographic history*. It represents, for us and to us, the filmmaker's perceptual life mediated and enunciated through the camera and projector as a *past* engagement with the world in which the intervention of the filmmaker-camera relation is invisible and "events seem to narrate themselves."[48] However, the film is primarily present to our experience (and its own) as an *inscribing autobiography of exploration*. In our presence, the film's perception is lived as a visual, kinetic, and gestural discourse, as the immediate and direct enunciation of its own *present* engagment with a world enabled by a bodily presence in it.[49] In this sense, the

---

[48] Benveniste, *Problems in General Linguistics*, p. 208.

[49] A particularly relevant discussion of autobiographical textuality from a phenomenological perspective can be found in Hugh J. Silverman, "Autobiographical Textuality: The Case of Thoreau's *Walden*," *Semotica* 41, nos. 1–4 (1982), pp. 257–275.

cinema challenges the theoretical separation of being, speaking, and writing and forces us to see the lived-body as their concrete and common denominator. At the cinema, we see seeing writing itself. We hear speaking listening to and recording itself. We see action emplotting itself. We comprehend meaning gathering its significance. We see this not only *after* it occurs but also *as* it occurs. Thus, although Jacques Derrida has revealed the grammatology of writing as structured by *différance* (the experience of meaning as an algorithmic point between what has already become indifferently meaningful and what is always deferred to the future in the ongoing becoming of meaning), *différance* is nowhere sensed so explicitly as in cinema.[50] Neither reifying temporality as "past" or "present" (except in theory), the cinema's own meaning originates not in time, but in space and movement—in its being as an always emergent, dynamic, evanescent, embodied, and (Derrida notwithstanding) ungraspable *presence*.

There is a certain equivalence of *presence* and *perceptual activity* between the film and the spectator as they convene in the privileged space of the theater. Both the film's body and the spectator's body are implicated in their respective perceptive activity, enable it, and allow it expression in the world. Both the film's body and the spectator's body intend their perception *coterminously*, and both also express their perception as lived *introceptively*. As the embodied source of the perceptive activity, their respective material presence is invisible in the perception not because of their absence or separation from the perception and its expression, but because the perception is lived from within and directed outward toward a world. Unlike the filmmaker, neither the film's body nor the spectator's body is absent from the perceptive activity they originate and the perceptual dialogue initiated by their encounter. Although the filmmaker's perceptive activity is *represented* in his or her *absence* as *histoire*, the film's perceptive and expressive activity is *presented* by its body's *presence* as *discours*, as an embodied and intentional consciousness inscribing its prereflective and reflective bodily conduct for itself before us. Thus, as a phenomenon of experience (both given to our perception as ours and yet also as its own), the film emerges as an autonomous presence in its intrasubjective perceptive and expressive activity. That intrasub-

---

[50] See Jacques Derrida, "Différance," in his *Speech Phenomena and Other Essays on Husserl's Theory of Signs*, trans. David B. Allison (Evanston, IL: Northwestern Univ. Press, 1973), pp. 129–160; also David Wood and Robert Bernasconi, eds., *Derrida and "Différance"* (Evanston, IL: Northwestern Univ. Press, 1988).

jective activity, however, is also intersubjectively visible in our presence. The film shares the theater with us as we share the existential structure of perception and a world with it.

It is an intentional and visual bodily presence (not an objectively present and intended visible body) that becomes inscribed in and as the viewing-view/viewed-view, the perceiving → perceived relation visible as the film. This fluid, centered and decentering intentional encounter with a sensible and significant world implicates a bodily being in and of it and indicates a consciousness able to sense and make sense through movement and sight and reflection upon movement and sight. Thus, as Merleau-Ponty says in a passage quoted at the beginning of this chapter, "The movies are peculiarly suited to make manifest the union of mind and body, mind and world, and the expression of one in the other."

Unlike the filmmaker in his or her relation to the film's body, the film need not necessarily have "access to the inhuman secret of the bodily mechanism" to manifest and live this union of mind and body and mind and world. It also need not (although it can) reflect upon and reflect the technology that enables its activity of perception and expression. At the primary level of cinematic existence, the film's *noetic* correlate need only relate to the *noematic* object of its intentions. It need not turn to reflexively locate its *own* origin and address in an enabling lived-body whose material substantiality becomes problematic as it becomes visible, much as does our own.

Reflexively reflecting on our own lived-bodies as they enable our experience, we tend to a disabling and dysfunctional relation with the world and with our bodies. We make them visibly present but we lose the nature of their perceptive and expressive presence. If we live our own bodies primarily from without, we become both alienated from the world and absorbed in a hermeneutic relation with our own flesh. Such absorption is generally diagnosed as "hypochondria" or, if warranted by the body's breakdown, as "illness" or a behavior that signals and signifies "old age." Why, then, should we especially valorize those films that are preoccupied with their own bodies or that constantly point self-consciously inward to their own perceptive activity—unless, as was discussed in the last chapter, we should want to present and represent the bodily comportment, motility, and style of someone (in our present culture) who is neurotic, ill, or elderly to some specific purpose. In all films, the film's body is primordially expressed as an intentional, if anonymous and unpresent, presence.

It inscribes itself significantly in action and gesture and makes its presence known as what poet Wallace Stevens has called "the life that is lived in the scene it composes."

The Nature of the Film's Body

What Merleau-Ponty refers to as "the inhuman secret of the bodily mechanism" are the clockwork relations of our anatomy and physiology. These relations not only remain hidden and secret from us in the immediate, responsive, and intentional humanity of our actions and tasks; unless our bodies are forestalled in their tasks and don't "work," these relations also seem "inhuman" insofar as we apprehend them objectively, taking up our own body as a mechanism.[51] Applied descriptively to the film, however, this "inhuman secret of the bodily mechanism" takes on an ironic and yet poignant literalness. Emerging from the symbiotic cooperation of humans and technology, the film's enabling body is partially mechanical and inhuman—and, as well, partially intentional and human. Inhuman, its concrete, material body seems scattered about space and time and is constituted in its substantiality by metal, plastic, glass, celluloid, emulsion, and electronic and mechanical circuitry. And yet, like the human body, the film's body is animated and lived with existential prospects and purpose. Indeed, the film's body is intentional, centered, and self-displacing in its dynamic reversals of perception and expression and in its movement in a world, both of which provide the bases for signifying and significant experience.

Thus, we can say that the film's body is a *lived-body*, discovered through the functions that make its existence in the world analogous to our own. The "inhuman secret" of the partial inhumanity of the film's body in its material substantiality and clockwork physiology is not a secret that is necessarily revealed by the film (the perceptual

[51] Here, of course, this alienation of the body that *is* the subject from the body *as* object is compounded by contemporary biological and medical discourses—and, most recently, by the discourses of electronic technology. See, for example, Michel Foucault, *The Birth of the Clinic: An Archaeology of Medical Perception*, trans. A. M. Sheridan Smith (New York: Vintage Books, 1973). Also of interest here (and suggestive material for a phenomenological description within the context of a specific historical moment and mode of cinematic production) is Mary Ann Doane, "Clinical Eyes: The Medical Discourse," a chapter in her *The Desire to Desire: The Woman's Film of the 1940s* (Bloomington: Indiana Univ. Press, 1987), pp. 38–69.

correlation of the viewing-view/viewed-view). In an intentional expression of perception, the film *lives* its body as that body enables the perception as intentional. Camera, projector, screen, film stock, chemicals—all are as crucial to the existence of the film and as "inhuman" in such anatomical dissection as would be a similar dissection of our human bodies into organs, bone, skin, tissue, blood. Such anatomical and physiological categorization calls up the *essential material nature of the body*—whether the film's or our own. However, such categorization does not evoke or describe the *existentially transcendent function of the body*, the body as *lived-body*.

Whether human or cinematic, the lived-body is more than the "sum" of its essential materials. It synoptically, synaesthetically, and intentionally moves with more than knee-jerk reaction to more than random stimulation from a more than merely materially significant world. In other words, we discover the film's body as "inhuman" much as we discover our own: when it troubles us or when we look at its parts upon a dissecting table. Otherwise, the film's body exists for us as do our own bodies: as animate and intentional, as actually engaged in existential functions, as living in a sensible world taken up in the intentional activity of consciousness and constituted as meaningful experience.

Thus, not only is the "inhuman secret of the bodily mechanism" generally hidden from the film in its own perception, but it is also generally hidden from the spectator. That "secret" emerges as a secret only on those occasions when the exact *material nature* of the film's body is either *interrogated* or *disguised* in some fashion that finds *explicit* expression *in* the film's perception. Primarily because the material nature of the film's body differs in substance and spatial organization from the human body and yet performs similar functions to the human body in its commutation of perception and expression, such explicit interrogation or disguise is problematic for both the film and the spectator. A peculiar and sensed disparity arises when the film attempts to reflect on its own material embodiment, or when it pretends for the sake of the filmmaker's *histoire* or the narrative to represent its own bodily *discours* as human in substance and conduct.

In the first instance, material reflexivity in the cinema has been valorized precisely because it seems to "rupture" the perceptual correlation of the viewing-view/viewed-view and to acknowledge the different body "behind" the cinematic vision before us. To visibly show the camera and the various mechanisms that constitute the film's body *within* the correlation as the *source* of that correlation has been regarded by contemporary theorists as disrupting and deconstructing the *illusionism* of the cinema, as making explicit those mechanisms that originate the perception and are, themselves, in their mechanical nature, non-intentional. Such reflexivity as a film's revelation of its material body visibly expressed in the act of seeing (as, for example, reflected in a mirror image) makes visible not only the fact that the film's perception is not transcendentally accomplished, but also makes visible the difference between the spectator's body and the film's body.

This kind of bodily revelation raises the question of the *authority* with which the film as an activity of perception and expression has been unreflectively invested by the spectator, who otherwise accepts the perception and expression and understands them, we are told, as his or her own. As well, such reflexivity questions the *reality* that the perception posits through its very activity of looking at and inhabiting a world in an intentional structure that imitates our own. And, finally, such reflexivity promotes the spectator's recognition of mechanism qua mechanism and foregrounds the cinematic apparatus and the fact that it can be manipulated to produce perception and its expression in ways other than those dominant and sedimented, unquestioned and invisible modes of vision associated with "classical" cinematic practice and the historically constructed conventions of "bourgeois perception."[52]

Certainly, the socially constructive project of cinematic deconstruction that foregrounds and valorizes mechanical reflexivity is admirable in its aim of restoring discursive consciousness and power to the spectator. The assumptions that ground this project, however, are questionable. Not only does the project assume, in relation to discursive power and freedom, that the spectator has, like Pauline Kael, "lost it at the movies." It also assumes that cinematic perception and expression can be *reduced* to their anatomical and physiological material and ignores the transcendent function of that anatomy and physiology to engage with, produce, and realize that which it is not. The reflection of a camera within the film's expressed perception (and, admittedly, this is the simplest kind of reflexive recognition of

---

[52] For elaboration see Donald M. Lowe, *History of Bourgeois Perception*; and Jean-Luc Comolli, "Machines of the Visible," in Teresa deLauretis and Stephen Heath, eds., *The Cinematic Apparatus* (New York: St. Martin's Press, 1980), pp. 121–142.

the film's body) neither duplicates nor explicates the intentionality with which that mechanism is presently charged and by which it is animated: that is, the desire to see itself, the reflexive urge itself.

As well, in such instances, the camera seeing itself and visible in the perception remains only a *partial* revelation of the film's body. It is partial not merely because the originating and enabling camera must always be "behind" its own perception as it is "in front of" its own mirror image, but also because the camera is always only visible as a *dissected part* of the film's body. That is, although the film's body is functionally similar to the spectator's body, it is spatialized and temporalized differently from the spectator's body. Its synoptic and synaesthetic "organization" of the sensible world occurs in such a way as to incorporate not only a variety of mechanisms but also human beings in its coherence. This is another way of saying that while, as spectators, we spatially and temporally include the film's expressed perception within our own, the film's body spatially and temporally includes us or others like us. The film's body materially surrounds us as other human bodies never can after we leave the womb.

The camera is thus visible in its own perception only as a discrete and objectified sense *organ* of the film's lived-body. It deserves its privilege, perhaps—for of all the film's sense organs, it is the one that sees and hears and is able to move in the world in the act of seeing and hearing. It is, nonetheless, only an organ of the film's body. Discretely visible in the perception it realizes as the object of that perception, the camera is thus *abstracted* from both its *intentional function* (which is, after all, to see rather than to be seen) and from its *total incorporation* into a "system of systems devoted to the inspection of a world." Indeed, the camera as visibly present *in* the perception is present only as a *representation* of the film's "visual body" as a whole, and it is only a partial representation at that. In sum, the camera functions in its visibility as merely *synecdochic*—pointing not only to the film's inhuman material embodiment but also to its own incompleteness as the representation or reflection of the film's lived-body, a totality that is both material and intentional.

What is suggested here is that the totality of the film's material body cannot be represented as visible *in* the perception that such a body is itself generating and expressing in the moment of perception *as* it is visible. It cannot be shown to us or seen by itself as the film's "visual body"—that form of embodied presence to the world that

Merleau-Ponty attributes to human beings as they appear visibly and materially to each other *as the other in the act of being*. The impossibility of such representation is grounded not merely in the fact that the film's bodily organs are totalized across too much space and synopsized over too broad a period of time and so confound their visibility as the object of the film's situated and finite visual organ, the camera; the representation is impossible also precisely because the film's organs, as they become visible, manifest themselves as *objects* of perception. Thus, they bear no immediate relation to the entire synaesthetic and synoptic bodily act of *subjective* and *introceptive* perception presently objectifying some of the enabling body's parts. Those cinematic mechanisms visible in the very perception they enable are not objectively visible as *intentional* in being materially *present* to perception. Rather, those mechanisms take up intentional significance and gain material *presence* only in their visible *function* of perception. That function is to introceptively engage the world visually and aurally, and to objectively express that introceptive perception *as such*. Thus, the film is visible *as* its material body lived introceptively. Its visible existence is, indeed, its visual existence, and this existence is lived through as "*my* material body." Seen by others, rather than lived through, the film's "visual body" will appear as a purely objectified mechanical apparatus, made up of various discrete parts and functions.

What needs emphasis here is the difference between *living* one's body and *seeing* it.[53] Both modalities of perceptive and expressive experience are similarly dependent upon the body's material nature and existence in the world but are dissimilar in their respective rela-

---

[53] In *Phenomenology of Perception*, Merleau-Ponty writes that: "living (*leben*) is a primary process from which, as a starting point, it becomes possible to "live" (*erleben*) this or that world, and we must eat and breathe before perceiving and awakening to relational living, belonging to colours and lights through sight, to sounds through hearing, to the body of another through sexuality, before arriving at the life of human relations. Thus sight, hearing, sexuality, the body are not only the routes, instruments or manifestations of personal existence: the latter takes up and absorbs into itself their existence as it is anonymously given." (p. 160) For practical applications of this distinction between living the body and seeing it, see also Iris M. Young, "Pregnant Subjectivity and the Limits of Existential Phenomenology," in *Descriptions*, ed. Don Ihde and Hugh J. Silverman (Albany: State Univ. of New York Press, 1985), pp. 25–34; and "Breasted Experience: The Look and the Feeling," in Iris M. Young, *Throwing Like a Girl and Other Essays in Feminist Philosophy and Social Theory* (Bloomington: Indiana Univ. Press, 1990), pp. 189–209.

tions to that materiality. That is, for both the film and for us, living the body in its material existence as "mine," *as me* and *for me*, is not perceptively or perceptibly the same as living "one's body" in its material existence *for others*, or as I might see my body if it were *not* mine. One of the major differences between these material relations is that living my body introceptively I have a perception of its materiality which *exceeds* its visible presence as a "visual body" for others and even for myself. That is, the introceptive image I have of my body contains *more* than the *visual* experience of my arms, my legs, my head as they are reflected in a mirror.

Similarly, the film can look at and make visible to itself and to us an array of filmmaking apparatus presently connected to and enabling its very look, its present perception and perceptive presence. However, what we do not see in such a representation is that excess of the film's body which is materially, but not visibly, lived and experienced as significant. Perception of the lived-body by the same lived-body is synoptic and synaesthetic. It consists of more than visual reflection of the body's flesh or the latter's objective visibility. Whether seeing the cables that enable its present perception as well as their own visibility as cables, or whether seeing its sighted and mobile perceptive organ—the camera—reflected in a mirror, the film's perception of these anatomical parts of its body *exceeds* and *transcends* their material visibility in both scope and function. Looking at those parts of its visual body contained in its perception and figured as visible, both the film and its spectator are acutely aware of something "missing" but nonetheless there, something material and bodily that is *not present as visible* but is nonetheless experienced and sensible as a *visual presence*.

Insofar as it attempts to interrogate its own body as a material *object*, the film experiences the same relation to its material existence as we do when we interrogate the material nature of our own bodies. That is, the film's body can only stare and wonder at its incomplete visual and visible knowledge of itself, and at the strangeness of its estranged form. It can only stare and wonder at the "inhuman" mechanisms that invisibly and transcendently function together to inform that material body with animate life, with subjectivity, with the synaesthetic and synoptic coherence that constitutes the experience of consciousness and the consciousness of experience.

Seen objectively, the film's body presents itself as an apparatus that mediates the intentional realization of consciousness in the world as a *hermeneutic relation*. That is, for both the film and the human spectator of the visible body, the body's very visibility makes invisible its introceptive visual existence. It becomes not the body that is lived as the existential extension of intentional consciousness in the world (embodied consciousness), but rather the body that, like Ihde's rheostats and gauges, yields experience of the world indirectly, opaquely. Reflexively reflecting on the materiality of the body-object, the body-subject living that body-object as "mine" separates the coherence of embodied consciousness. The body becomes a privileged but nonetheless suspect "hermeneut." It becomes regarded as an unintentional machine that instrumentally enables unintentional consciousness and allows its experience of the world and yet exists problematically as situated *between* consciousness and the world.

The visible reflection of bodily reflexivity is not the only situation in which the material nature of the film's body exists in hermeneutic relation to the spectator (whether the human spectator or the film looking at its own body). As mentioned earlier, there is also a second situation in which the material nature of the film's body becomes problematic in relation to its perceptive and expressive function. A problem arises when the film makes no attempt to interrogate its mechanical materiality as a "visual body" but instead *assumes a material disguise* that is made *explicit* within the film's immediate perception of itself. That is, another kind of material body than the film's body is presented *in* the film's perception *as* the film's visual body enabling *all* its perceptions.

This is a disguise assumed not simply and unproblematically at the level of the film's narrative or representational function, at the level of *histoire*. Rather, it is a more radical disguise, one assumed at the level of the film's autobiographical and presentational function, at the level of its *discours*. Thus, I am not referring here to the occasionally introduced but extremely common "subjective perceptions" of characters *within* a narrative. Nor am I even referring to the explicit "persona" of a first-person narrator "outside" the narrated diegesis but still *within* the narrative (as in, for example, *Tom Jones* [Tony Richardson, 1963] or *Barry Lyndon* [Stanley Kubrick, 1975], where the omniscient narrators are never seen and only heard, but as human beings). These codings of "subjectivity" are stock-in-trade conventions of narrative cinema, and they are secondary to the more radical perception and expression subjectively performed by the film's materially nonhuman body.

A character, for example, may look in a mirror and see herself as a human body, but that character is not held perceptually responsible for enabling the totality and coherence of the perceptual correlations that are the film's activity and production of vision as visible. Because such subjective coding is discontinuous and relatively infrequent, or because it shifts from character to character within a single narrative, these perceptions are synthesized only by the temporal and spatial coherence of the film's own subjective perception as it takes shape before us. Thus, the film makes no claim that the character's material body is, in fact, its own.

In such instances, the film's body remains *implicit* in its materiality. It exists, as it usually does, as an anonymous and prepersonal subjectivity directing its perceptive and expressive activity outward toward the world from a "zero-degree" of orientation. Thus, only the character's body is explicit and visible in the character's subjective self-perception as it is seen and expressed by the enabling perception and expression of the film's *unseen* body. Indeed, as if to avoid any possible confusion and conflict between its material body and the character's, the film's body generally situates itself close to but behind the character's body in what is commonly called an "over the shoulder" shot. Thus, when a character sees himself in a mirror, the most common way we perceive his expressed perception is by seeing his visual body (or parts of it) *twice*: once in the mirror (as his viewed-view) and once in front of the mirror (in the activity of his viewing-view).

It is only occasionally that a single character appropriates the entire perceptual correlation from the film's body, and that appropriation is usually brief—for, as we shall see, if it is not, the difference between the material nature of the film's body and the character's (and actor's) human body becomes problematic in its sustained pretense of human self-reflexivity. (There is less of a problem when the character appropriating the film's perceptual correlation is not humanly embodied because we, as humanly embodied, have little experiential bases upon which to note a disparity between the two modes and materialities of embodiment. Thus, we could cinematically perceive the world through a mouse's body as happens in *Witches* [Nicholas Roeg, 1990] or through a cyborg's body as happens in *Robocop* [Paul Verhoeven, 1987] in a relatively transparent relation to the film's body. As we shall see, this is not so in the case of a human body.) Brief and discontinuous instances of human self-reflection are not particularly problematic. Presented briefly and discontinuously (figured against the ground of a broader, more sustained and coherent perception and expression), instances of human self-reflection and reflexivity are a perceptual correlation "bestowed" upon the character by the film, much as a prepersonal and anonymous narrator allows a character to refer to himself within that narration as "I." No claims are really being made about the materiality of the film's body or about its material equivalence to the human body. That is, in such instances, the film's body does not really set about "disguising" itself and then offering to visibility an inauthentic material presence.

The "disguise" of the film's material body in its relation to the human bodies of visible characters has been a frequent concern of contemporary film theory, particularly as it effects the construction and cohesion of "classical" narrative by "suturing" the text through a closed system of cinematic perceptions that are related, exchanged, and deferred but are always ascribed to participants *in* the narrative.[54] However, what is disguised within this system of visual and visible exchange is not the nature of film's *material* body, but rather the situation and location of the *act* of perception. That is, the system of suture has been discussed in relation to the way cinematic perceptions are connected throughout the entirety of the film's viewing-view/viewed-view so as to locate the *situated source* of the film's perceptions *within* the narrative, or diegesis. The aim of "classical" narrative is to cover the film's perceptual tracks, to disguise the "extra-diegetic" situation of the narrative's narrator, and so to transform an intentional and discursive *activity* (the viewing view) into the intended and produced *object* that is *histoire* (the viewed view).

"Classical" cinematic practice attributes perception to any number of characters within the narrative, and it does so in such a spatially shifting and "shifty" manner as to visually and visibly circumscribe and hermetically "sew up" narrative space. Thus the narrative world and events that take place within it are given to visibility as imma-

---

[54] The concept of "suture" is elaborated and discussed in the following seminal texts: Daniel Dayan, "The Tutor-Code of Classical Cinema," *Film Quarterly* 28 (Fall 1974), pp. 22–31; Stephen Heath, "Notes on Suture," *Screen* 18 (Winter 1977–1978), pp. 48–76; Jacques Alain Miller, "Suture (elements of the logic of the signifier)," *Screen* 18 (Winter 1977–1978), pp. 24–34; and Jean-Pierre Oudart, "Cinema and Suture," *Screen* 18 (Winter 1977–1978), pp. 35–47. Controversy about suture as a two-shot structure first emerged in William Rothman, "Against the 'System of the Suture,' " *Film Quarterly* 29 (Fall 1975), pp. 45–50.

nent, immediate, and present—rather than as generated, mediated, and represented by the film's presentation. Based upon such editorial structures as the shot-reverse shot, or a three-shot complex, the function of suture is to not merely *repress* the film's material existence and production of the visible narrative but also to *disguise* the film's perceptual presentation of a representation. That is, the function of suture is to appropriate the presentational function of the film's perceptive body for the narrative and thus to deny the narrative its dependent status as the expression of perception by a perceptual authority embodied outside the narrative.

It is important, however, to emphasize that the disguise of perceptual authority supposedly achieved through the system of suture is *not experienced as problematic*. Indeed, that it is unproblematic is the problem *with* the system, according to those who see its structure and function as homologous to the structure and function of ideology, and who would demystify and open the closed world the system posits as self-constituting, thereby proclaiming that world as not only real but also true. In experience, the disguise of the film's finite and situated perceptual authority afforded by suture works as effectively as it does precisely because *it avoids self-reflexivity*. The film generally does *not* refer to its material and bodily existence. Thus, the multiplicitous material forms that the film's perceptual authority usurps and assumes as its own remain uninterrogated. To *account* for the space and situation of the narrative (rather than to *recount* it), cinematic perception continuously and seamlessly shifts from character to character, visually gathering up and circumscribing the visible world so as to assure its seeming pre-existence and imperviousness to the perception discursively enabling it outside the narrative. Rendered seamless by the system of suture, such perceptual inconstance would be immediately exposed or troublesome were the *material authority* for each shift of perception made explicit *in* the perception *as* it was being perceived.

Thus, while accommodating the secondary subjective narrative coding previously discussed, in which a character self-reflexively confronts his or her (or even its) material body and assumes a temporary responsibility for the visible perception, the system of suture allows the film to *pretend* to a greater perceptual omniscience and authority than that enjoyed by any one character. However, for that pretense to work, the film's visual attention must be directed *away* from the many diverse *bodily* disguises its perception has to assume in order to visually possess and contain the total space of the narrative world. Authorial responsibility for a present perception is always presently deferred in its explicit materiality, its visual body, its visible form. That is, a character's body is made explicit before and/or after the perception it is supposedly responsible for enabling. Thus, the *material differences* among the bodies of various characters and narrative presences as they are *seen* are never in direct concert and confrontation with the present but materially implicit body that is *seeing* them or the visually habitable spaces of the narrative world. The system of suture, then, does not really problematize the material nature of the film's body within the film and its perceptive and expressive activity. Rather, along with the suppression of the film's perception as that perception which enables the narrative, the system of suture also suppresses interrogation of the film's body. In the activity of disguising its material and perceptual limitations and finite situation, the film never tries to *explicitly* disguise its material nature.

When, however, the film's body not only assumes a disguise, but that disguise is also made explicit within the film's enabling and visible perception, a major hermeneutic problem arises. The question that emerges in such instances is whether it is at all possible to reconcile the disguise of the film's body in its particular and *visible materiality* with the enabling and *introceptive perception* that is attributed to it as the *lived-body experience* of the film. Indeed, examples are notably rare and point to the difficulty of such a reconciliation of assumed bodily disguise and introceptively lived bodily behavior. The few cinematic instances of such an attempt demonstrate the difficulty of sustaining the disguise as *congruent* with the introceptive activity of perception and expression, the difficulty of inscribing an autobiography of visual experience through the instrumentality of a *false body*.

As already noted, in most cases where the film's body assumes the body of a human character, this assumption of a bodily disguise by the film and its revelation in the film's perceptual correlation as visible is used *conventionally* and *discretely* and makes no attempt to claim the "false body" as its own. Rather, the disguise is put forth as such: the *enabling narrator* enunciating the perceptual subjectivity of the various *enabled and narrated characters*. The "false body" in these instances is not so much false as it is "borrowed," for the film does not claim it as its own body. Rather, the film offers it to visibility as the character's "my" body, a body to which the film has the omniscient access that any narrator has to the characters whom s/he enables, constructs, and controls through the activity of narrating. This is quite a different kind of claim from the one in which the film asserts its very act of narrating, its enabling power, through a body that is not—in nature or material—its own.

This latter kind of claim is made through most of Robert Montgomery's *Lady in the Lake* (1946), a film that has become the paradigm for posing the hermeneutic problem of the film's body. With four brief exceptions (and they are significant exceptions, in terms of the problematic posed), *Lady in the Lake* insists that its inscription of perceptive and expressive activity is enabled by a *single human being* living his body *introceptively* as "mine" and having access to that body as it is simultaneously a "visual body" for others only in parts and through perception of its own reflection. In other words, with four exceptions, a character within the narrative is credited with the perceptive and expressive activity that radically originates in the film's body and claims the perceptual power of constituting the narrative as the *film's* autobiography inscribed through a *human* body.

The protagonist and perceptual autobiographer, detective Philip Marlowe, is predominantly visible only *in* the perceptual correlations of "his" (the film's) vision in the way that we appear materially visible to ourselves in our visual perception. That is, Marlowe sees himself *as* he sees only through his *visible reflection* in mirrors or other reflective surfaces. As well, he sees himself as directly and materially visible only in those *parts* of his body that are brought before his eyes—when, for example, the perceptual correlation makes visible a hand brought up to light a cigarette that hangs suspended from unseen lips. Otherwise, Marlowe is invisible to himself and to us but nonetheless constantly implicated as a *physically material* and *human presence* enabling the visible perception.

This constant implication of his presence as humanly embodied occurs because *visible human others address him as he sees them* and they act toward him and address him in his act of vision as having a *human character* and being a *human being*. (This is quite a different mode of address from a human actor's, character's, or actual person's direct address to the camera as a machine *through* which s/he addresses another human being—either the filmmaker or the spectator.) In *Lady in the Lake*, those human body-subjects *who are seen* intend toward the invisible perceiver identified as Philip Marlowe *as they see him humanly embodied*. And he, in turn, responds to them perceptually and introceptively as being human in material form. For instance, he is physically assaulted and responds by "passing out." The perceptual correlation loses focus and intentional consciousness *of* any/thing and fades into the obscure darkness of no/thing or unconsciousness. As Carl Macek and Elizabeth Ward note in *Film Noir*: "The subjective camera records Marlowe's impressions while he listens to a character speak. For example, as he is interviewed by Adrienne Fromsett, her alluring receptionist enters the room and Marlowe follows her every move while she answers his 'stare' with seductive expressions. . . . the camera's subjectivity . . . wanders tellingly about a room or examines a person inch by inch."[55]

What is here called the "camera's subjectivity" by Macek and Ward points to the hermeneutic problem of *Lady in the Lake* and to the strange discomfort, alienation, and disbelief experienced by the film's spectator. As accomplished by its mechanical organs of camera and projector, the film's visual subjectivity is offered to visibility as supposedly *identical* to the character's visual subjectivity, accomplished by its biological organ, the human eye. The film's body is emphatically posited (if awkwardly positioned) in Philip Marlowe's human situation, as Philip Marlowe's (and actor Robert Montgomery's) human body.

The film, however, has a good deal more difficulty disguising itself as a human body than the human actor has in disguising himself as a nonexistent human being. For reasons that will become evident, we, who are humanly embodied spectators, *know* and also can *see* the

[55] Carl Macek and Elizabeth Ward, *"Lady in the Lake,"* in *Film Noir: An Encyclopedic Reference to the American Style*, ed. Alain Silver and Elizabeth Ward et al. (Woodstock, NY: The Overlook Press, 1979), p. 166. A fascinating counterexample to this insistence on the equivalence of the film's vision and the human actor/character's, and thus on the isomorphism of their intentional interest in the world, occurs in Michelangelo Antonioni's *The Passenger*. During a conversation between the narrative's two protagonists (who are sitting mid-frame at a table in an outdoor restaurant), instead of immobily focusing on them and their interaction, the camera (and, by intentional extension, the film) seems to be more interested in the cars one can see on the street behind them. Keeping the protagonists in sight at all times, the film's glance moves laterally back and forth to directionally follow the cars driving by into and out of the frame, insisting on the film's own subjective interest in the world as different from ours (which is directed primarily toward the characters in the narrative.) What makes this particular example so compelling is that it suggests the interest of the technologically embodied film is evoked more by technological objects than by humanly embodied subjects.

film's body and the human body as distinct, different, and nonidentical in nature and materiality (if identical in perceptual function). Thus, disguised in human form in *Lady in the Lake*, the film's body and its perceptual experience is made explicit in its *inauthenticity* as a lived-body. That is, a visible incongruence emerges between the film's body in its realization of an informing "operative" intentionality and its attempts to realize the consciously willed intentional project of "being an other."

Most discussion surrounding *Lady in the Lake* has ascribed its lack of credibility to the problem the film poses in regard to the *human spectator's* process of *identification* with the film's *human protagonist*. For example, David Bordwell has pointed out how advertisements for the movie equated the film's disguised embodiment—and therefore its "human" subjectivity—with the spectator's lived-body experience of introceptive perception. The audience was promised the lived-body experience of the character: "YOU accept an invitation to a blonde's apartment! YOU get socked in the jaw by a murder suspect!"[56] As Bordwell goes on to ask, "Do we think we *are* Robert Montgomery?" Of course, the answer is that we do not. The reasons advanced as to why such an identification with the character (and/or actor) does not occur in *Lady in the Lake* are various, but they all have in common a focus on those relations that obtain between the *spectator's human body* and the *character's human body*. Thus, they neglect those possibly more crucial relations between the *film's technological embodiment* and the *character's human embodiment*. In some discussions, however, the issue of identification is seen to center less around a difference of bodily form or materiality than around the *visibility* of the character's body to the spectator. Jean Mitry, for example, quotes Barthélémy Amengual on the film. Amengual suggests that the spectator's assimilation of Marlowe's perception is impossible because of the "constant suppression of the image of the hero."[57]

---

[56] David Bordwell and Kristin Thompson, *Film Art: An Introduction* (Reading, MA: Addison-Wesley Publishing Co., 1979), p. 148.

[57] Barthélémy Amengual quoted from his "Le Je, le Moi, le Il au cinéma," in Jean Mitry, *Esthétique et psychologie du cinéma*, Vol. 2 (Paris: Editions Universitaires, 1965), pp. 66–67. Part of the text cited deserves quotation and comment:

Quand nous fumons, nous n'en voyons pas plus. La caméra est devenue l'acteur. Elle joue le drame: Et, comme elle est sensée être notre oeil—l'image n'étant plus chose regardée mais *regard*—(tous les protagonistes qui parlent au héros, regardent dans la salle, donc dans nos yeux) nous sommes sensés être Montgomery. Ce film manqué est intéressant

Edward Branigan echoes this argument in a note to an essay enti-
tled "Formal Permutations of the Point-of-View Shot": "The failure
of *Lady in the Lake* . . . has been attributed to the fact that in order to
internalize a character's look, one has to know the character. . . .
One cannot know a character from a purely personal narrational
stance (I, or I see) because psychology is an external construct which
depends upon the perspective of an *apersonal* narrational voice."[58]
Here Branigan's analysis affirms the necessary intersubjective relations that Merleau-Ponty works out in his system of four terms. And
yet his argument also denies that system's description of the intrasubjective relations by which we all, personally, connect our own
psyche with the *invisible* introceptive image we have of our own body
as it is lived, indeed, from a "personal narrational stance." This is to
say that we can and do know the character *of* the *film* from its "personal narrational stance," from its "I, or I see"; however, the film
cannot know the character of a *human body* without also knowing that
body as *visible*, because that human body and its character are the
film's visual *object*—and not the film as *subject*.

Jean Mitry focuses on yet another aspect of the problem. He sees
the failure of *Lady in the Lake* to convince the spectator that s/he *is*
Philip Marlowe as a failure based not so much on the invisibility of
the character's body as on real *bodily difference*. Mitry emphasizes the
difference between the spectator's body sitting relatively quiescent in

---

parce qu'il trace des limites à la subjectivité cinématographique. Cette assimilation totale
et impossible qu'il postule de nous avec les héros oublie que la participation esthétique,
imaginaire, exige une certaine complaisance de la part du spectateur. Cette suppression
constante de l'image du héros contrarie la vocation du cinéma qui doit permettre à
l'homme de *se voir*. Enfin, ce parti-pris de subjectivité se renverse curieusement en objec-
tivité. Interdisant au metteur en scène de recourir à des *équivalences*, le film est condamné
à montrer des scènes en plans d'ensemble, des portes, des plaques, des escaliers, bref et
uniquement de *l'extérieur*.

One could comment here that the "curious" reversal or transformation of what was
seemingly encoded as subjectivity to objectivity noted by Amengual is the result of
what, in effect, is a *double introceptivity* functioning as a *double negative*. The suppression
of the film's body and the character's human body from the perception results in an
emphasis on and positive foregrounding of the embodied nature of introceptive perception. Thus, the spectator's awareness of introceptivity as it is articulated by an invisible but lived body is heightened, and the differences among the lived-bodies of the
film, the human character/actor, and the spectator are underscored.

[58] Edward Branigan, "Formal Permutations of the Point-of-View Shot," *Screen* 16
(Autumn 1975), p. 62, n. 6.

a theater seat and the film's body invisibly living out, through the activity of the camera, a kinetic life and activity clearly not shared bodily by the spectator. Implicit in this argument is Mitry's agreement with what has been said here in earlier chapters regarding the relations between the film and the spectator. That is, although we, as spectators, may be sympathetic to cinematic perception and, indeed, may intentionally parallel the film's and/or character's bodily position and perceptual bias as it intends toward and inhabits a world, we physically and materially occupy our *own* bodies and space. The perception whose intentional interest we share belongs always to *another* perceiving and embodied subject, no matter how introceptively it is visibly presented as visual for us.[59]

Mitry articulates the problem of bodily difference in terms of human *character* and human *spectator*, and even in terms of human *actor* and human *character*. His discussion does not address the problem of bodily difference as it exists more radically between the nonhumanly embodied *film* and the *character/actor* whose human body the film would assume as its own. Mitry, however, is worth quoting at length

[59] Mitry, *Esthétique et psychologie du cinéma*, Vol. 2, p. 68. On our recognition of the other perceiver as other, Mitry says:

Poser le problème, c'est démontrer le même coup son absurdité.

D'autre part, ces sensations que nous éprouvons *en partage*, il nous faut pouvoir les attribuer à cet *autre* que nous devinons derrière de afin de les comprendre, ou, si l'on préfère, d'en connaître les motivations. Cet autre doit donc avoir une existence concrète pour que nous soyions en mesure de valider nos impressions en les reportant sur la qui les assume et doit le faire nécessairement. Affirmé comme n'étant pas *le nôtre*, ce "vécu" ne peut être évidemment que *le sien*. Or (en l'exception du miroir) nous ne le voyons jamais. Nous l'ignorons en tous qu'individu vivant et agissant. Nous ne pouvons donc plus objectiver les sensations que nous éprouvons et savons fort bien n'éprouver que pas personne interposée. Ce qu'on voudrait nous faire prendre pour un "vécu subjectif" s'évanouit de ce fait dans un *non-moi* vague et imprécis. Nous ne savons plus *qui* agit de la sorte. En place du "Moi" il n'y a plus que du vide, c'est-à-dire l'absence de celui qui, au cinéma, répond pour moi. Alors qu'en littérature je rapporte le "je" à moi, en cinéma c'est un "Moi" imaginaire ou intentionnel que je projette—un autre qui doit donc exister en tant que *lui*. On ne doit pas oublier que la participation nous procure une satisfaction symbolique et *fictive*. Il convient donc de faire coincider le sentiment, l'impression reçue, avec un comportement qui les justifie.

Mitry's words support the basic argument of this present work. The vague and imprecise "not-I" that spectators experience as they experience the introceptive experience as "mine" is precisely the film's prereflective subjectivity, the prepersonal and anonymous experience of consciousness lived not yet as an Ego but always as a body-subject.

because of what he has to say on the general issue of *bodily disparity* in *Lady in the Lake*. He tells us:

The impressions called subjective are *given* to me as all the rest: The camera advances down the street, I advance with it; it climbs the stairs, I climb with it. I therefore experience, in the moment, the *walking* and the *climbing* or, at least, everything happens as if I did. But the camera leads me, guides me; it communicates to me impressions which don't emerge from me. Moreover, these feet which climb the stairs and which I see in the scope of the image, they aren't *mine*; this hand which holds onto the bannister, this isn't *mine*. In each circumstance, I don't recognize *the image of my body*. Assuredly, therefore, this isn't me who walks and who acts this way, although I experience sensations similar to those which would be mine if I were acting thus. I walk, therefore, *with* someone, I share his impressions. And his face which appears in the mirror and which is different from mine emphasizes all that separates us. It can be justly said that this presence isn't mine but that of an *other* positioned objectively. Therefore, instead of my identification with his "subjective" images, I am increasingly detached because they result in making me conscious in a more precise way that although these impressions are felt keenly as mine, they aren't *seen* by me. I am not able, therefore, in any case, to believe myself "in him."[60]

Thus, the kind of identification that *Lady in the Lake* attempts to achieve between spectator and character fails. As Albert Laffay con-

---

[60] Ibid., p. 67. My translation from the following:

Les impressions dites subjectives me sont *données*, tout comme le reste: La caméra avance dans la rue, j'avance avec elle; elle monte les escaliers, je monte avec elle. J'éprouve donc, dans l'immédiat, *le marchant, le montant* ou, du moins, tout se passe comme s'il en était ainsi. Mais la caméra me conduit, me guide; elle me communique des impressions qui ne sont pas nées de moi. De plus, ces pieds qui gravissent les escaliers et que j'aperçois dans le cadre de l'image, ce ne sont pas *les miens*; cette main qui se tient à la rampe, ce n'est pas *la mienne*. En aucune circonstance je ne reconnais *l'image de mon corps*. Ce n'est donc pas moi, assurément, qui marche et qui agis de la sorte, bien que j'éprouve des sensations semblables à celles qui seraient miennes s'il en était ainsi. Je marche donc *avec* quelqu'un, je partage ses impressions. Et son visage qui vient d'apparaître dans le miroir et qui est différent du mien souligne tout ce qui nous sépare. Il dit justement que cette présence n'est pas la mienne mais celle d'un *autre* qu'il pose objectivement. Au lieu donc de m'identifier à lui ces images "subjectives" m'en détachent davantage puisqu'elles aboutissent à me faire prendre conscience d'une façon plus précis encore que ces impressions ressenties commes miennes ne sont pas *vécues* par moi. Je ne puis donc en aucun cas me croire "en lui."

cludes, "By pursuing an impossible perceptual assimilation, the film in fact inhibits symbolic identification."[61]

We might question, however, whether the "impossible perceptual assimilation" pursued by the film is, indeed, an assimilation of the spectator to Philip Marlowe, the character embodied by a human actor. Does the inhibition of symbolic identification have its radical origin in the exposed difference between the spectator's body and the character/actor's body? In the context of previous discussion, I would suggest that the film's lack of authenticity, its impossible perceptual pursuit of a *human lived-body experience in human form*, radically originates not in the impossibility of *bodily identification* between the *spectator* and the *character*, but in the impossible *bodily identicality* claimed between the *film* and the *character/actor*.

As eventually happens with any inauthentic existence that is recognized or experienced as such, disguise cannot be sustained for too long. Incongruities and gaps appear between the assumed form and its informing intentional behavior. Thus, in *Lady in the Lake*, the film's perceptual conduct and behavior are eventually visible and perceived as enacted by a body that seems to be *living falsely*. The human body the film pretends to possess and to be does not *consistently* converge with the film's own instrumentality, that is, its authentic perceptive and expressive behavior and way of "being-in-the-world" as the body it *is* beneath the disguise of the human body it assumes and *presumes to be*. Thus, a disparity or incongruence between the film's bodily disguise and the film's visible conduct emerges and is experienced by the spectator as behavior that "doesn't work," that is somehow inauthentic and false.

This disparity is initially not a problem in *Lady in the Lake*. The film begins with the radically anonymous but subjective action of its body living perception and its expression. That is, the film begins unremarkably as its own *unseen nonhuman body* looks at the *visible human body* of character Philip Marlowe (as it is inhabited by the human body of actor Robert Montgomery). This opening sequence of perceptions clearly belongs, then, not to Marlowe, but to the film that "sees" Marlowe as *directly visible*, as the *intentional object* of an anon-

---

[61] Albert Laffay quoted from his *Logique du cinéma* (Paris: Masson, 1964), pp. 94–97, in Christian Metz, "Current Problems of Film Theory: Christian Metz on Jean Mitry's *L'Esthétique et Psychologie du Cinéma*, Vol. II," trans. Diana Matias, *Screen* 14 (Spring/Summer 1973), p. 47.

ymous but intentional subject's vision. (There are only three other sequences in which we and the film see Marlowe positioned as the object of our perception rather than the subject of his own: Twice he is situated similarly to his position in the opening sequence, his function to sum up and to compress his experiential time, space, and action; and at the end we see him articulate his feelings to Adrienne Fromsett—an articulation that dramatically closes not only the case but also answers the narrative's romantic question.)

Marlowe is first seen sitting behind his desk as he discusses some of the more complicated elements of the "case" and invites his *unseen viewers* (both the film and the spectator as anonymous subjects) to help solve the mystery. However, to some degree, the nature of his direct address tends also to negate the film's vision as intentional. In his appeal to the human audience, he posits his relation to it *through* the mechanism of the camera, which stands in a *hermeneutic* relation to both Marlowe and the spectator. That is, as far as the narrative goes, Marlowe's direct address to the audience puts the camera *between* Marlowe and spectator—neither embodying it, each needing it to engage the desired intentional object. Given that most of the film will posit its vision as enabled by a *human body*, this first assertion of the film's body as merely *technologically instrumental* lays the ground for and further compounds the disparity and incongruence we experience in what quickly follows.

The film's opening, in which we and the film see Marlowe, serves also to preface and retroactively announce the film's subsequent assumption of a human body for its own as the *conventional* appropriation of a character's subjectivity by a narrator. Thus, the sequence posits a clear (if unarticulated) *distance* and opens a spatial and experiential *gap* between *the film's subjectivity* (its introceptive perception of the character as the intentional object of its perception) and *the character's objectivity* (Marlowe perceived as a human subject only by virtue of the visible intentional conduct his visual body displays to the film's subjective perception). This, of course, is the relation that radically constitutes the film as a film, and it is the ground of the film experience. In that this relation holds for every film, it becomes the background against which further relations can figure. It becomes invisible—unremarked upon and unremarkable. Thus, only a film like *Lady in the Lake* forces us to reflect *retrospectively* upon the radical relations that ground any film's visibility and intelligibility.

Although what perceptually and perceptibly follows the opening sequence as it is visible is narratively coded as enabled *only* by the character Marlowe living his human body introceptively and posing as the author of his own and present experience, what is *first* visible in the film is not Marlowe's vision but the vision of an other. This is an other who will soon after appropriate Marlowe's body and attempt to pass it off as its own, who will pose as a human character and pretend that the narrative is autobiography, that its own present discourse that narrates a history is, indeed, the discourse of a present human body in the process of living it. However, because the film initially (and subsequently) makes a visible distinction between the living of its own body as visually enabling perception and expression and the perception and expression of other bodies as visible, the pretense that occurs after this initial distinction is marked *as a pretense*— and it reverberates throughout the film's duration and is specifically echoed in the brief subsequent visions we have of Marlowe as visible.

For most of its duration, however, the film assumes a human disguise. It claims that Marlowe's body is *identical in material* and *isomorphic in situation* with its body. This identicality and isomorphism are posited by the film not as a mere temporary assumption of Marlowe's narrated point of view, that is, the brief "borrowing" of his body and situation by the film's lived-body narrating the narrative and, therefore, enabling the visible and controlling it. The claim to identicality and isomorphism the film makes in *Lady in the Lake* is problematic because it is based not on narrational appropriation but on *existential appropriation*. Marlowe's human body, once appropriated, is lived through for the duration of the film's expressed perceptions. But for three brief instances, there is no return to the anonymous but discursive other who began and begat the film's initial perceptive and expressive activity.

Thus, it is in the *temporal* and *spatial* continuity of this nearly constant existential claim to a *single human body* that the physical and material deception is both perpetrated and penetrated. However, it is precisely over time and in space that the disparity between the nature of the film's lived-body and the nature of the human lived-body emerges to mark the unwilled and reluctant self-exposure of the film as, in fact, in bodily disguise and existentially inauthentic. What might otherwise be comfortably assimilated within the narrative expression of the film's perception as the *secondary* coding of a "convention of subjectivity" becomes increasingly problematic as it is maintained over time and in space. Similarly, what might otherwise go unnoticed as a visible disparity between the film's introceptive visual experience and the introceptive visual experience of a human being is noticed, if not precisely marked, over time. The stress and strain of maintaining the human bodily disguise is eventually felt by the spectator watching the film's perceptual conduct in Marlowe's body, even if the specific pressures as they are visible are not named.

And, indeed, those pressures do become visible in the film's perceptive and expressive behavior. The disguise *as* disguise influences what is seen by the film and, as well, the film's act of seeing. For example, many times during *Lady in the Lake*, parts of the film's supposedly now-human body become visible as they enter its actually nonhuman perceptual field—a field that is supposed to be the perceptual field of a single human body and is, in fact, the perceptual field of the camera. However, these visible human body parts are not perceived as visible in quite the same way that we, living our human bodies, perceive the visibility of our body parts in perception. Pretending to Marlowe's lived-body, the film's body lights a cigarette while looking at a roomful of people and talking to them. Hands enter the introceptively experienced visual field, light a match, hold it to the end of a cigarette that is visible only in part as it disappears from the visual perception into Marlowe's supposed but unseen mouth. Also in sight is the room and its furnishings, and the various people toward whom Marlowe introceptively intends and who direct their intentions toward him as they converse and visually engage each other as similar beings in an intersubjectively shared space. And yet, as humanly embodied spectators, we sense something significantly "wrong" in the perception as it is supposedly enabled by Marlowe's human body.[62]

Previously, discussion has focused on the dialectical and dynamic nature of the humanly embodied and enabled visual field and on how what is visible *in* visual perception is not *equivalently* visible. Not only does the visible organize itself in concert with our intentionality into the nonequivalent relations of *figure/ground*, but the visible also

[62] For a lengthy and illuminating discussion of the inauthenticity and instability of this kind of subjective perception insofar as it is claimed as Marlowe's, see Chapters 5 and 6 (respectively, on *Murder, My Sweet* and *The Lady in the Lake*) of J. P. Telotte, *Voices in the Dark: The Narrative Patterns of* Film Noir (Urbana: Univ. of Illinois Press, 1989), pp. 88–119. Telotte's work is a parallel argument to the one here, because his concern is with the secondary construction of narrative coding and mine with a more radical cinematic ontology.

responds to the hierarchy of our intentional interest—to the *attention* with which we intend the visible. That is, in their relative importance as the *destination* of our attention, certain figures dominate other figures. Less dominant figures are still figures and visible as such, but they are less present in their visible presence in our vision.

There is, then, a certain latency in our visible perceptions—even at the level of figuration. As I type a manuscript, for example, the visible words and the paper are more dominant in their hold upon my attention than are the typewriter keyboard or the desk upon which the typewriter sits. While I can still see these latter objects, my intentional task and my attention are focused on the page and the words that I impress upon it. The point is that the desk and the typewriter keyboard *are* visible in my vision, if latent in my attention. And visible, they are *not* out of focus as if I had an astigmatism. It is their presence that is soft, not their visible form. Thus, the clarity of the words and the paper is not so much a condition of their being inherently *more visible* than the typewriter and desk as it is a condition of my being presently *more interested* in them.[63]

Returning to the film's appropriation of Marlowe's human body and perception, one of the things that is sensed as "wrong" in the perceptual conduct we see as Marlowe lights a cigarette is the visible *equivalence* of his vision. As he is supposedly directing his primary attention toward the people in the room, his hands and the cigarette loom large in his (and our) presence. Compare what would be visible in our vision to what is visible in "his." When we perform an unproblematic bodily action in which part of our body becomes visible in our visual field, our intention and attention, if directed elsewhere, subordinate our body's presence in its own vision. Insofar as we are attending toward the people who are visible in our vision, insofar as

---

[63] Of relevance here is a passage in Merleau-Ponty's *Phenomenology of Perception*, p. 369:

> I am thinking of the Cartesian *cogito*, wanting to finish this work, feeling the coolness of the paper under my hand, and perceiving the trees of the boulevard through the window. My life is constantly thrown head-long into transcendent things, and passes wholly outside me. The *cogito* is either this thought which took shape three centuries ago in the mind of Descartes, or the meaning of the books he has left for us, or else an eternal truth which emerges from them, but in any case a cultural being of which it is true to say that my thought strains towards it rather than that it embraces it, as my body, in a familiar surrounding, finds its orientation and makes its way among objects without my needing to have them expressly in mind.

our intention and attention are primarily and dominantly directed not toward our own simple activity of lighting a cigarette but toward the people with whom we are presently engaged, our hands visible before our eyes would lose a great deal of their presence for us. When I light a cigarette or sip a drink as I talk intently to another, my hands, the cigarette, the match, the glass, don't insist on their visibility as they enter my visual field. Rather, they are seen *through* and *beyond* without strain or effort or deliberation (unless, of course, I suddenly find my functional use of them troublesome). As well, in such circumstances, my *entire* lived-body relates the visual presence of my hands as they are visible to me to the remainder of my body that is invisible; and so the *dimension* of my hands as they are brought close to my eyes is not a function of abstract geometry and the laws of perspective, but rather of *my whole system of bodily being* and my relation at that moment with the world that I see and the others toward whom I intend with attention. Abstractly large as they figure in my visual field, my hands are relatively small in my attention because they do not usually *command* my attention abstractly. Rather, their size is determined by their unproblematic functioning and, in this circumstance, they make only a *small claim* on my attention. Marlowe's vision, however, does not respond to its visible figures in the same way. The material nature of the film's body, its difference from the human body, emerges to expose the film's pretense as pretense. Thus, the film's disguise cracks. Despite the film's similarly structured intentional interest in the visible world, and despite the similar function of its material body in accomplishing perception and its expression, the film's *intentional interest* and *perceptual accomplishment* are not identical to or isomorphic with those of the human body it is pretending to be.

In relation to differences between the film and the character's *intentional interest* in *Lady in the Lake*, the film's intentional interest is revealed as incongruent with Marlowe's because it is seen as *exceeding* Marlowe's. That is, the film is intent not only upon seeing *as* Marlowe sees but also upon *seeing Marlowe introceptively seeing*. Whereas Marlowe, the humanly embodied character, is less interested in watching his hands light a cigarette than he is in finding out information that will help him solve a murder, the film is interested not only in the mystery but also in Marlowe's perception. This discrepancy in intentional focus is revealed in the visible perception and sensed by the spectator. The *equivalence* given the visible as Marlowe lights a cigarette that has no special significance for him marks the film's perceptual intentionality as *exceeding* Marlowe's, rather than as being *contained by* Marlowe's perceptual intention. The film cannot relinquish its function and desire as narrator so easily as it might wish, nor can it easily live autobiographically within the perceptual constraints of the intentionality of its perceived human characters. And the same might be said of us sitting in the theater relating to the film's perceptual intentionality.

In relation to differences between the film and the character's *perceptual accomplishment* in *Lady in the Lake*, differences that cause the film's disguise to crack and make its pretense visible, the lack of co-incidence between the human body and the film's body is revealed as each instrumentally—and differently—realizes perception and its expression. By virtue of their respective material differences, even if the film and the humanly embodied character are intentionally iso-morphic (sharing the same interest and attending to the same inten-tional objects with the same emphasis), their *manner* or *means* of be-ing interested and attentive will differentiate them. That is, although the film's body and the human body it pretends to appropriate may be *identical in function* as they both realize the same intentional object, their *material differences* will constitute *visible differences* in their visual activity and the production of that object as visible.

This difference in material instrumentality suggests that the non-human visual equivalence the film gives to Marlowe's visual field as it pretends to Marlowe's human body, physical situation, and inten-tional directedness might be materially "corrected." The reference here is to the first problem and failure of the film's disguise insofar as it relates intentional interest to vision. That is, unproblematic parts of Marlowe's body and unimportant objects appear in "his" visual field as *equivalently visible* to those bodies and objects that, by virtue of their importance to his present intentional project, should domi-nate his visual field if, indeed, "he" were seeing humanly and the conduct of his body and the direction of his intentionality were con-gruent. This first failure of the film's disguise is a failure of *intentional congruence* of *two* bodies as they are seemingly conflated as *one*. In this regard, it might seem that the film's body could adjust its behavior to the human body, that it could realize the nonequivalence of the human body's intentional vision as it is visible. It might seem that the film's initial failure to achieve the exact coincidence of its vision with Marlowe's is correctable—were the film's body to use, for example, a lens that "sees" with variable discrimination, a lens with a shallow depth of field.

And, indeed, *Lady in the Lake* attempts such discrimination. In one sequence, for instance, Marlowe is speaking on the telephone and the part of the receiver that is visible in the foreground of his vision and close to his body appears less distinct in its visibility than do objects in the room that are farther away from him but more intended and attended to by his vision. The shallow depth of field makes the film's perception of the telephone receiver visible as somewhat blurred and out of focus as it simultaneously perceives other "more important" objects clearly defined and in focus. In regard to this directedness and movement of intention and attention, the film's material body could also realize coincidence with Marlowe's intentionality by changing its intentional directedness in concert with his. For example, the film's intentional focus could be reversed—"pulling" attention from background to foreground and back again, "shifting" the dominant and latent relations of the visible in congruence with the character's intentional directedness and motivation.

Clearly, in this case, the *intentional function* of the *film's body* would be *identical* to that of the character's *human body* as both organize the visible in the visual field hierarchically according to the intentional dynamics and dialectic of attention. However, in realizing an identical function, both bodies and their *perceptual accomplishment* of intentionality are nevertheless revealed as *different* in *material* nature. As previously noted, the human lived-body does not necessarily perceive figures as "blurred" or "out-of-focus" for them to exist as visible and yet latent in the visual field. There need be no blurring of the visible in my vision as objects slip from the grasp of my intention and attention. Thus, although the *function* of both Marlowe's body and the film's body is the *same* (i.e., to focus attention within a visible intentional horizon and express that perception as a viewed view), the *bodily means* through which that function is accomplished are *visibly different*—and dependent upon the different material nature of the respective bodies.

For the film's body to appropriate Marlowe's hands and to "see" them as its own in "soft focus" while simultaneously seeing the people in which he is more interested in "sharp focus" would be to *functionally express* human intentionality. But it would not *materially express* human intentionality. The film's cinematic means of achieving a human function would be different from human means. That is, the human lived-body does not attend to the world and realize its intentional projects of attention in the same visible manner as does the film's lived-body. In attempting to "correct" its visual field so that what is visible is *intentionally congruent* with the human lived-body experience, the film's lived-body is revealed as *materially and behaviorially incongruent* with the human lived-body it would assume as its own. *The achievement of intentional congruence between the embodied film and the embodied human would simultaneously expose the material incongruence between the film's body and the human body.*

In sum, as the film pretends to a human character's intentionality, it exposes its own difference from the material form in which that intentionality is embodied in existence. The success of the film's disguise at one level of its perceptive and expressive experience is the very failure of that disguise at another. Thus, the film cannot avoid the "double bind" that occurs when its present introceptive perception is expressed as that of a human other's. As the visible disparity between two material modes of realizing intentionality as behavior-in-existence, this "double bind" serves to demonstrate why the film cannot sustain a *human bodily disguise* even as it parallels the *human bodily experience* of an intentionally perceptive and expressive subject.

There have not been many films like *Lady in the Lake* that so problematize the differences between the material nature of the film's body and the human body by so insisting on their similarity of function. Indeed, the film was not meant to make the problem apparent, and its place as a relatively isolated oddity in film history points to its failed pursuit of an "impossible perceptual assimilation." As we have seen, that failure is grounded in the film's inability to *be* Marlowe's human body, and it is revealed in visible conduct as both film and Marlowe diverge in their styles of "being-in-the-world." This is nowhere more explicit than in the conflated viewing-view that makes visible Marlowe's hand opening a door seen from "his" bodily bias. This viewing-view produces a viewed-view that makes Marlowe's visible action (insofar as it is "his") a physical impossibility given the bodily situation from where "he" views it. Slightly "off" from the human body's visual situation in the world, the film's visual situation becomes a radical, if vague, disturbance in the perceptual assimilation experienced by the spectator.

Lady in the Lake also makes problematic another aspect of the failure of the film's body to disguise itself as human. While the film's lived-body is intentionally *directed toward* the project of making its perceptual correlations congruent with the human body's, it is *directed away from* realizing the *transcendent* aspects of its own embodied existence. That is, as the film's lived-body emphasizes its perception as grounded in a human body, it becomes a slave to that body, afraid to leave it for fear it will lose its already tenuous hold on its disguise. For the film's body, the human body exists not as *subjectively enabling* but as an *instrumental object*. The previous chapter pointed out the constrained way that women in our culture move and comport themselves insofar as that culture has placed them in a hermeneutic relation with their own bodies (the latter emphasized as an intentional object). We have seen that in such a hermeneutic relation with one's *own* body the body's transcendence as enabling is overwhelmed by its immanence, which generates the sense of being physically positioned and finite in worldly space, the sense of constraint.

In its attempts to maintain its human disguise, the film's body in *Lady in the Lake* exists in hermeneutic relation to itself and takes its own instrumental being as an object to be manipulated and overcome. Its intentional attention is riveted to the body-object and its behavior is informed by an overwhelming sense of the body's immanence. Thus, *Lady in the Lake* is peculiarly claustrophobic to watch. Its perceptive and expressive behavior is *curtailed* and *constrained* by bodily existence rather than *enabled* by it. Marlowe, and we as spectators of "his" behavior, are literally grounded and anchored in bodily existence, and we perceptually and expressively live the body through none of the other modalities of experience it enables: dreaming, imagining images, projecting situations, and temporarily assuming an other's situation as a subject. The fluidity, mobility, decentering, and discontinuity that are a condition of intentional existence as it is humanly embodied are extremely limited in Marlowe's visual and visible experience. As a result of this narrow conception of embodied vision as not only grounded in its material situation but as also chained to it, the visible world itself is seen to shrink. Indeed, it seems to exist only to accommodate and affirm the existence of Marlowe's body. In this regard what Paul Jensen says about the film's production is apposite: "The long, continuous takes forced the script to be constructed in a limited number of lengthy scenes. . . . Staging was likewise inhibited, as everyone had to relate to the lens, and the many camera movements limited the use of imaginative lighting. Although an interesting experiment, and probably a backbreaker to execute, . . . [the] approach was mistakenly literal and became a limitation rather than a challenge."[64] Overly insistent upon its "human body" and the humanly incarnate structures of physically relating to and in the world, the film loses the transcendent freedom that marks not only the human body but also its own body as both are lived physically and consciously. Whether the human body's or the film's, the "address of the eye" transcends its bodily situation and finitude, traverses space and time, visually inhabiting and constituting them as lived experience through reflection, imagination, memory, and dream. Similarly, the world transcends any single such visual address. It exceeds the situated and finite ground of any body's present intentional grasp and it cannot be constrained or contained by their vision.

The desperately felt "self-consciousness" of incarnate existence that *Lady in the Lake* belabors as the film's body strives to convince us of its bodily authenticity as human is an anomaly. Indeed, the careful concern with its "body" that overshadows and flattens its perception and experience is pathologically akin to that form of psychic pathology discussed by Merleau-Ponty in relation to his patient Schneider. Having lost the "sense" of his body, Schneider had to give it abstract orders to carry out various physical tasks because he could not spontaneously or "operatively" live his body as his own.[65]

For the most part, however, even as a film occasionally borrows upon the bodies and situations of the other subjects who inhabit its vision (as, in fact, we humans do also), a film inscribes its perception as the natural and easy result of an ambiguous and embodied visual consciousness. This consciousness looks at and visually produces its objects and is intentionally drawn toward them as things to be seen, the whole of its invisible bodily machinery doing what must be done to reach them perceptively, to express and bring them into visibility in vision. In its primary intentional directedness *toward the world*, the film turns *away from itself*. That is, it does not dwell on itself as literally or transcendently embodied, nor does it disguise itself. As well, its invisibility occurs from no inherent charlatanism, no invidious de-

[64] Paul Jensen, "The World You Live in," *Film Comment* 10 (November-December 1974), p. 24.

[65] See Merleau-Ponty, *Phenomenology of Perception*, pp. 103–109. For an anthology of cases in which neurologically damaged patients function in hermeneutic relation to their own bodies, see also Oliver Sacks, *The Man Who Mistook His Wife for a Hat and Other Clinical Tales* (New York: Summit Books, 1985).

sire to pretend an existence it does not possess—as does, on the one hand, *Lady in the Lake*, and on the other, certain purposefully "self-reflexive" films that offer up their visible mechanical parts as if they contained the whole of cinematic existence. Rather, the film lives its body and its vision not only *as a body* but also *in a world*. Its primary anonymity and invisibility, its radical lack of bodily self-consciousness as it visually lives in the world, results from the capacity of embodied vision to realize intentional consciousness as *extensional*.

Similarly functional to the human body in realizing perception and its expression, and yet different in material and means from the human body, the film's body is complex and ambiguous in its material existence as intentionality incarnate. Thus, when the film insists upon or accidentally expresses the nature of its embodiment as less complex and ambiguous than the expression of its vision suggests (either through reflexive reference to itself or through the inauthenticity of its bodily disguise), the film's perception expresses its own untruthfulness by becoming even more complex and ambiguous. It is in this sense that visual perception as visible expression might be said *to lie*.[66] To suggest that the film's perceptual correlations are completely enabled *either* by a partial and "objective mechanism" *or* a human lived-body is a *visible falsehood* that must be significantly sensed by the spectator, if not more precisely "found out." Each of these partial and limited expressions belies the ever-present "echo focus" that tempers both the spectator's and the film's visual and visible experience with the irreducible ambiguity of the relations *between* machine and human that inaugurated that experience. In other words, the film's body, as it is lived in the perceptive and expressive activity of that visual production we see as the "film," partakes of both the mechanical and the human.

The film's body, like our own, is a *subjective object*. It is an intentional instrument able to perceive and express perception, to have

[66] It has been often said that, unlike natural language, pictures can't lie. And it is through this capacity to lie that semiotic codes are established. See Eco, *A Theory of Semiotics*, pp. 6–7, 58–59. The perceptual and perceptible lie of the film's bodily appropriation of a character's human body thus becomes the code of narrative "subjectivity"—that is, cinematic perception communicated *as* the character's human perception because it is, in fact, marked as *unlike* human perception. For an empirical proof that human embodied vision—even when dysfunctional as focus—cannot lie, see the discussion of "binocular dislopia" in J. M. Heaton, *The Eye: Phenomenology and Psychology of Function and Disorder* (London: Tavistock Publications, Ltd., 1968), pp. 241ff.

sense and make sense. Seen only objectively, both our own bodies and the film's body are reduced to mere physiological visibility. Their *material nature*, whether human flesh or metal and celluloid, becomes strange as it is estranged, abstracted, and amputated from its *intentional function*. In sum, the body we objectify is finally not a *lived-body* for us—whether it be the film's body or our own. It is not the subject of experience, but merely an object for experience.

If we allow that we *are* our bodies and their visibly intentional conduct in the world, if we reflect upon our existence and understand that we are the subjects of our visual experience as well as visual objects for other visual subjects, then we cannot but recognize that the film's body and its visibly intentional conduct enjoy the same existential privilege. And if *enjoy* seems a peculiar or "unnatural" word to use in relation to a film, we should remind ourselves that *enjoyment* only exists in its intentional *expression*—that is, realized through bodily agency as a visible conduct, a "style" of being-in-the-world.

FILM'S BODY: A BRIEF INTENTIONAL HISTORY

In *Film as Art*, Rudolf Arnheim is cautionary about the technological advances of the cinema made by 1933: the advent of sound, the development of technicolor, the possibilities for stereoscopic (3D) cinematography. Less than sanguine about the fate of cinematic expression, he tells us, "The technical development of the motion picture will soon carry the mechanical imitation of nature to an extreme."[67] Convinced that such development would promote a literal realism antipathetic to aesthetic perception and its expression and would bring to a climax "that striving after likeness to nature which has hitherto permeated the whole history of the visual arts,"[68] Arnheim goes on to condemn what he calls the "complete" film: "The complete film is the fulfillment of the age-old striving for the complete illusion. The attempt to make the two-dimensional picture as nearly as possible like its solid model succeeds; original and copy become practically indistinguishable. Thereby all formative potentialities which were based on the difference between model and copy are eliminated and only what was inherent in the original in the way of

[67] Rudolf Arnheim, *Film as Art* (Berkeley: Univ. of California Press, 1957), p. 154.
[68] Ibid., p. 157.

significant form remains to art."[69] Arnheim was clearly afraid that technological invention would lead not to further possibilities for aesthetic sense and signification, but to a lazy reliance on the objects of perception, to a certain perceptual "automism" resulting from a pursuit of the world's meaning as it had already been posited.

On the other hand, years later Jurij Lotman in *Semiotics of Cinema*, taking an opposing view of the cinema's technological development, wrote: "The entire history of the cinema as an art is a sequence of discoveries whose aim has been to drive out automism from every element which can be subjected to artistic scrutiny. The cinema conquered motion photography, making it an active means for knowing reality. The world which it presents is simultaneously the object itself and a model of the object."[70] For Lotman, the development of cinematic technology is the active intentional realization of perceptive and expressive choice-making within the context of a world. The development of technology allows for more, rather than less, perceptive and expressive activity in its relation to an envisioned world, to a visible world, and to other visionary, viewing, and visible subjects. The result of this increased possibility for perceptive and expressive *choice* is an increased possibility for perceiving and expressing *meaning*, for *sign production*. Cinematic language is thus expanded in its paradigmatic and syntagmatic possibilities for selection and combination. In this sense, Arnheim's fears are unfounded in theory, if somewhat warranted by conventional practice. Indeed, one might argue that the "age-old striving" of the visual arts is less rooted in a facile realism and desire to *replicate* the world than it is in the desire to *know* the world, to *see* it, to *understand* it, and to *say* it. Thus, while the "age-old striving" of the visual arts has always been a *mimetic* striving, it is bent less on imitating the nature of intentional objects than on imitating the function of human intentional subjects who engage those objects as significant.

In some ways, of course, Arnheim's fear that technological advance would further the preeminence of the world's objects over the subject's world is justified—given that our Western philosophic and scientific heritage, until quite recently, has stressed empirical objects at the expense of intentional ones. Nonetheless, the technological de-

[69] Ibid., pp. 158–159.

[70] Jurij Lotman, *Semiotics of Cinema*, trans. Mark E. Suino (Ann Arbor: Univ. of Michigan Press, Michigan Slavic Contributions, 1976), p. 16.

velopment of the cinema has evidenced an intentional evolution that has pursued the project not only of realizing *visible objects* but also of realizing *visual acts*. Technology has afforded the cinema the means not only to perceive the visible world but also, and necessarily, to visibly express acts of perception. If, as Merleau-Ponty was earlier quoted as saying, "the movies are peculiarly suited to make manifest the union of mind and body, mind and world, and the expression of one in the other,"[71] then technological advance can only serve to broaden the expressed horizons of that union.

Thus, neither world nor lived-body is privileged or disadvantaged by technological innovation. Rather, as Lotman suggests, both benefit by the broadened context for choice-making and the production of significance. Indeed, technology and the instrumentality it affords the intentional project of perception and its expression (which is, after all, the primary project of both the cinema and human beings) is the cinema's sole means of *being-in-the-world*. Thus, cinematic technology allows both the world and visual experience their visibility. Simultaneously, cinematic technology enables the world of "nature" to visibly *impress* the film's viewed-view with its "significant form" and enables the film's viewing-view to *express* nature in a signifying act.

In this sense, the primary function of cinematic technology has been to allow the film both access to a world and existence in it. As emphasized throughout this chapter, cinematic technology has provided the film its matter and means of incarnation, has made substantial and visible its intentionality, its adherence to and in the world and with others. Technology has provided the film with an *enabling body* that can be considered "lived" in its activity and commutation of perception and expression. Thus, it does not seem completely cavalier to draw parallels between the development of cinematic technology and the development of the human lived-body from infancy to adulthood, because both are involved in the similar existential and intentional projects of perception and its expression. Both enable parallel inscriptions of increasing bodily proficiency and competence in the realization of signifying power and its possibilities. Thus, as Gary Madison says: "The desire to . . . celebrate the mystery of visibility will in the last analysis be Being which desires itself, which desires to get hold of itself, to re-flect itself, to see itself.

---

[71] Merleau-Ponty, "The Film and the New Psychology," in *Sense and Non-Sense*, p. 58.

And man, to the degree that he responds to this demand with a creativity and a metamorphosis which are peculiar to him, will be the com-prehension of Being—Being getting hold of and realizing itself: man will be the place where Being transforms itself into logos."[72]

The instrumental history of the cinema is a record of a medium striving to realize its perceptive and expressive intentions—first by consciously recognizing the possibilities of its "body" for action, then by refining its initially crude and clumsy activities, adapting its "body" to contingent situations and broadening its repertoire of possible responses to the world that it inhabits and expresses. Thus, the development of cinematic technology is not an abstract evolutionary phenomenon; rather, it intimately entails concrete performance and practice as both a function of perceptive and expressive competence and as constitutive and regulative of that competence. In this regard, the history of cinematic technology has emerged from and responded to the contingency of each individual film's situation in the world and with others (films and persons in the uniqueness and conventionality through which they constitute intertextuality and culture). The history of cinematic technology has also emerged from and responded to its need to exercise and practice its given means of vision and expression, and its need to grow in physical and intentional precision beyond whatever original competence it initially possessed. In other words, intentional necessity is the mother of cinematic invention, and cinematic exercise or praxis is its father—even as the latter sets up precedents that constitute convention and constrain invention by "law."

Although I am not suggesting exact correspondences between the development of the cinema and human lived-bodies, I am suggesting that there are certain broad similarities between them in their respective progress toward the perceptive and expressive realization of intentional existence in a world and with others. The human lived-body is born into a world with only the crudest motor skills and little control over and knowledge of its perceptive and expressive functions and potential. Initially, it is, to quote Lacan, "sunk in . . . motor incapacity and nurseling dependency."[73] And, to quote Freud, as a result of this physical helplessness, "the influence of the objective

---

[72] Gary Brent Madison, *The Phenomenology of Merleau-Ponty: A Search for the Limits of Consciousness* (Athens: Ohio Univ. Press, 1981), p. 95. Madison is here discussing the act of painting in relation to Merleau-Ponty's essay "Eye and Mind."

[73] Jacques Lacan, "The Mirror-Phase as Formative of the Function of the I," trans. Jean Roussel, *New Left Review* 51 (September-October 1968), p. 72.

world upon it is intensified."[74] The human lived-body develops through its progressive acquisition of self-control over its physical functions and, of course, in the knowledge of that control as enabled by its own intentionality. With exercise and experience, the lived-body becomes increasingly refined and precise in its movements and gestures. It becomes increasingly discriminating in its sensibilities and sense making. Eventually, it is able to articulate meanings and produce signs by controlling the body and its relations with the world and others in a systemic and systematic manner.

The film's lived-body develops similarly—in the progressive acquisition of and power over its motility and in growing awareness of motion as not only a quality of the viewed objects of the world but also as an activity possible to itself as a viewing subject. Its body becomes more discriminating with refinements in lenses and film stock, and in the development of its ability to perceive and express sound and to see in finer gradations of color. And even before these latter developments that afford it a variety of possibilities for nuanced perception and expression, the film's body learned to expressively organize the perceptual experience of consciousness. This organization was achieved not only in the prereflective activity lived through the camera in its immediate engagement with the world, but also in the reflective activity of association (editing) which expresses the consciousness of experience in a systemic and systematic fashion.

Like the infant's lived-body, the film's lived-body was sunk initially in "motor incapacity and nurseling dependency." Its gaze upon the world was first as fuzzy and ambivalent as its uncertainly directed intentional interest. At first that gaze was as objectively immobile as it was subjectively dynamic and active. Only objects in the film's gaze seemed to have the power to move themselves. Indeed, the motion picture camera was first carried about as a means of transporting its gaze. Like an infant, the camera was "perambulated" on various moving vehicles; at first, it had no knowledge of its own power to move and no knowledge that its gaze was, in fact, already charged with activity. As with the infant, the camera's physical helplessness and dependency on others to move it by means external to it resulted in the cinema's initial abjectness before the world as a sub-

---

[74] Sigmund Freud, *Inhibitions, Symptoms and Anxiety*, trans. Alix Strachey (London: Hogarth Press, 1936), pp. 139–140.

ject in it. That is, the objective world held dominant sway over the cinema's vision and seemed the source of all motility.

Eventually, however, and through gestures that only *after* their articulation were seen and selected as meaningful and functionally worthy of repetition, the film's lived-body moved itself—first, on the fixed axis of its immobile stance and later, with intentional purpose gained from its first control over its gaze, through the space carved out by the development of its own bodily mobility. In the beginning there was the static gaze in the earliest Lumière films. (Even when the camera was mounted on a boat, for example, it did not search the horizon but was carried past it.) Then there was the tentative turning of its vision to keep something in sight, as with the train robbers in Porter's *The Great Train Robbery* (1903). And next came the physical mobility of perception as a visibly dynamic expressive force in films such as Griffith's *The Birth of a Nation* (1915), the film's body and enabling technology acquiring greater and greater fluency in its intention to see and to show.

Camera movement becomes just the most obvious paradigm of the parallel development between the cinema and the human being in the appropriation and apprehension of one's own body and its power to become in the world. The infant controls the movement of its head before it controls the movement of its body, and it crawls and falls down and is clumsy before it walks and becomes so fluent in the latter activity that walking becomes an incorporated gesture, one hardly worth notice. In this regard, phenomenological psychologist Erwin Straus is particularly illuminating in his discussion of the way in which we first learn movement in discrete and clumsy "parts" and achieve fluency only when the "parts" are appropriated and incorporated as the *whole gesture of an intention to act*.[75] Constituted in its material nature from cinematic technology, the film's body has appropriated its gestures similarly. From the initially stationary camera with a fixed gaze at a world that moved, to the capacity of the camera to "liberate" itself from the paternal studio by virtue of its new-found portability, to the development from the awkward jerkiness of hand-held camera to the current invisible immediacy and appropriated fluidity of Steadicam, the technology of the cinema has

[75] Erwin Straus, *The Primary World of Senses: A Vindication of Sensory Experience*, trans. Jacob Needleman (London: The Free Press of Glencoe Collier-Macmillan Ltd., 1963), pp. 256–259.

seemed to respond to the intentional imperatives of the film's body as a series of perceptive and expressive tasks in need of performance.

The development of sound technology traces a similar project. Even before the Walkman, life was a moving sound track. Thus engaged and mobile in the world, the film intended not only the world's sounds but also its own audible expression of the world's emotional significance. From its initial introduction as external musical and/or verbal accompaniment to the film to its current and sometimes problematic all-surrounding presence in Dolby stereo, cinematic technology has progressed toward the incorporation of external and discrete aural mechanisms into physically synoptic and synaesthetic union with the film's visual organ, the camera, and its expressive organ, the projector. First, music was provided from a source completely external to the film's body, as dialogue and narration occasionally were (spoken from alongside of or behind the screen by human beings who were often unaware of or insensitive to the film's unfolding conduct and intentions). Then technological innovation and synthesis solved the problems of synchronization and amplification, and sound-on-disc emerged so that the film could more directly hear the world and emotionally color it with sound. Sound-on-disc, however, proved clumsy and limited and was only tenuously incorporated as part of the film's body; there were problems with maintaining synchrony with the film's more advanced visual fluency expressed by both the camera and projector. As well, individual expressions of the same film varied in the contingencies of projection, while the sound-on-disc did not and were therefore often "out of synch" with the rest of the film's body. Optical sound, or sound-on-film, literally achieved synaesthetic cooperation and bodily union with the film's primary perceptive and expressive organs. That is, technological synaesthesia between sight and hearing was accomplished through another bodily commutation of perception and expression: sound waves commuted to light waves that are recorded onto the film emulsion alongside the image and can be commuted back to sound waves simultaneously with the film's projection on the screen.

Optical printing also allowed all sorts of possibilities for the increased expression of the feel and flow of the film's perception: "freezing" the perception, "bleeding" it of color or infusing it with color, step-printing the perception so it occurs in linear or overlapping binary increments rather than analogic flow, and so forth. Optical printing and a myriad of special effects respond to the need of the film's body to realize its intentional existence in intentional acts that transcend the body's immanence—its immediate finitude and situation in a concrete world. That is, from the first in-camera "magic" performed by Méliès that "pixilated" objects and people so they appeared and disappeared from the perception according to no physical logic, to the current laboratory magic of rotoscoping or step printing, cinematic technology advances the possibilities for the realization of the film's *imagination*. In other words, effects technology allows for the film's actualization of its emotional impressions, for its capacity not only to see the world but also to transform, dream, and fantasize its world as a *possible* world.

Of course, it must be emphasized here that the intentional "teleology" of cinematic technology and its development is not necessarily more than materially or physically progressive. That is, it does not necessarily follow that the most physically advanced film's perceptive and expressive hold on the world is going to realize the most illuminating, sensitive, or significant situation and existence within it. Technological advance and the film's achievement of bodily fluency is no guarantee of the worth of its existence for others. Invention gave us, after all, the electric toothbrush. Simply, technological invention and syntheses emerge from the intentional need of the cinema to see and hear and imagine and dream with maximum physical and lived-body competence. The result of that competence may be a perceptual and intentional project that is as banal as it is physically fluent, recalling Heidegger's distinction of technology from the technological: "It is as revealing, and not as manufacturing, that *technē* is a bringing-forth."[76]

It is in this regard that Arnheim's caution about technological development usurping the cinema's imaginative development has a certain validity. The literalism that would emphasize the film's physical body and technological possibilities at the expense of its intentional existence and power to live that body transcendently could be seen as regressive rather than progressive. Such a physical cinema could be seen as comparable to the exuberantly physical adolescent: a kinetic joy to behold, but not necessarily interesting to talk to. Some films' engagement with their own bodies strikes one as merely autoerotic. Indeed, many current "special effects" movies are more about

[76] Heidegger, "The Question Concerning Technology," p. 295.

their physical bodies, their technologies, than they are about the complex relations between that body and the world, or about the cinematic imagination.

To celebrate technological advance and invention as the extension of the film's body and its progressive physical fluency is not necessarily to celebrate film history as increasingly more sophisticated or significant in those intentional projects of existence that inform seeing and hearing and imagining. There is no question that Erich von Stroheim's silent *Greed* (1924) expresses a perception that is at least as complex, interesting, and revealing of the world and the viewer (both film and spectator) as *Friday the Thirteenth, Part II* (Steve Miner, 1981). The point to be made is that there is no guarantee that technological extensions of the film's bodily powers of perception and expression will ensure the interest of its situation in the world to others. What this brief history of cinematic embodiment suggests, rather, is the intentional teleology of the film's body: its increased possibilities for perception and expression, for choice and action. Now the film may choose whether to attend visually to the world it physically inhabits or to a world it dreams, whether to move falteringly or smoothly, whether to hear or to close itself from the world's sound or the sound of its own feeling.

The teleology traced here is not deterministic and has no end. Commenting upon Merleau-Ponty's discussions of painting, Gary Madison illuminates the seeming paradox of a progress or development of expression that is infinite and nonhierarchical:

> The idea of a progress which would culminate in the perfect possession of . . . Logos is an impossibility, is nonsense. The history of painting does not make its way towards a perfect painting; and, in this sense, because there is no hierarchy among the different modes and periods of painting, there is no progress in painting. . . . In painting it is always the same adventure which is relived . . . , and painting never expresses anything other than the miracle of bodily existence—the miracle of visibility. Painting is not a succession of events in time but a series of advents—of Being. Painting does not copy anything whatsoever which exists before it; it expresses only visibility, that opening in Being: and an opening is nothing at all, merely the fact that something begins to appear.[77]

[77] Madison, *The Phenomenology of Merleau-Ponty*, p. 104.

In sum, the progress or development of cinematic technology has not determined anything. Rather, it has continued the advent of the cinema's being as an "infinite Logos,"[78] and also the possibilities for the further adventure of any single film's becoming. Advances in cinematic technology thus advance the film's bodily access to the world: They provide "openings" that are no/thing but that allow for the significant appearance of some/thing more. It is in this sense that the technological development of the cinema has increased the film's bodily possibility for "leaping over distances, piercing into the perceptual future, and outlining, in the inconceivable platitude of being, hollows and reliefs, distances and gaps—in short, a meaning."[79] Possibility, of course, is not practice. But possibility provides the horizons for practice (even as actual practice usually beclouds the horizon of possibility). Thus, it is in the possibilities it provides for outlining meaning that, along with Lotman, we can legitimately celebrate the technological progress of the cinema "as a sequence of discoveries whose aim has been to drive out automism from every element which can be subjected to artistic scrutiny."[80]

This brief celebration of the intentional history of cinematic embodiment in relation to any film's possibilities for signification may seem ahistorical. And, indeed, it is—if one thinks that the historical in its most dominant modality is what Merleau-Ponty has called "the empirical order of events."[81] In this mode, the historian "unites the moments" of cinematic perception and expression "as so many events which are external to each other."[82] Cinema "makes its way across time in an evolution which is sometimes hesitant, sometimes hasty, accumulating procedures and techniques which each generation augments in turn. Here there is but *succession* and *replacement*."[83] This mode of history is linear, phenomenal, visible—in short, thought only objectively, from "outside" the living encounters we have with what others have expressed before and for us. There is, however, another mode of historicity: a "secret, modest, non-deliberated, in-

---

[78] Ibid., p 105.

[79] Merleau-Ponty, *The Prose of the World*, p. 78.

[80] Lotman, *Semiotics of Cinema*, p. 16.

[81] Maurice Merleau-Ponty, *Signs*, trans. Richard C. McCleary (Evanston, IL: Northwestern Univ. Press, 1964), p. 68.

[82] Madison, *The Phenomenology of Merleau-Ponty*, p. 90.

[83] Ibid.

voluntary, and, in short, living historicity."[84] This living historicity is "cumulative"[85] and it emerges from the "order of expression,"[86] the "order of culture or meaning"[87]—and not from the empirical order of successive, dismembered events or from a series of displacements and replacements that progress toward an ideal state.

This living historicity is radical and, indeed, underlies and makes possible the construction of phenomenal history—not as some second system of causality, but rather as the in-formation of particular historical "events" with the generality of both bodily existence and the advent of meaning.[88] It is in this sense that we can regard the history of the cinema (and of the film's body) not merely as a series of technological and economic developments but also "as a milieu engendered by expression" which "establishes by virtue of its generality a recuperative or cumulative history."[89] This history of the adventure of expression and meaning, however, is not static nor recursive—even as it is integral and cumulative. There is, then, progress in the history of cinema and the film's body as there is in culture, but this is a progress conceived as having no beginning and no end but expression. Whatever the specificity of its enabling technology, each film "takes up and starts anew the entire enterprise" of cinematic expression.[90] It is in this sense that the history of cinema and its technology is "in principle a meaning in genesis," a history that "has always to be reconstituted."[91] Thus the lived history of films is, as Merleau-Ponty suggests, similar to the lived history of human beings, in that "it is the perpetual conversation carried on between all spoken words and all valid actions, each in turn contesting and confirming the other, and each creating all the others."[92]

The empirical history of cinema and of cinematic technology finds its source in the efforts of individual films to perceive the world and to express it, in "the continuous life, the integral and cumulative becoming" of each film within a context of other films and the human

[84] Merleau-Ponty, *Signs*, p. 62.

[85] Ibid., p. 60.

[86] Ibid., p. 64.

[87] Ibid., p. 68.

[88] Madison, *The Phenomenology of Merleau-Ponty*, p. 91.

[89] Ibid., p. 92.

[90] Ibid., p. 93.

[91] Merleau-Ponty, *Signs*, p. 69.

[92] Ibid., p. 74.

beings who enable them as visionaries and viewers.[93] Thus, as Gary
Madison says (quoting Merleau-Ponty), "It is in expression, in the
creative taking up of the native significance of his existence, that man
brings about the 'junction of the individual and the universal' . . . ,
joins up with 'a second-order value' . . . , and at once places himself in the field of History."[94] The history of the film's body is a history of intending bodies. And the history of cinema is the intentional
history of films justifying perception and its expression, actively
making their individual acts meaningful and apposite in the eyes
(and "I's") of others. Thus, if we can speak of something so unified
as a "history of cinema" at all, we must recognize its source in a unity
that is radical, that is, in "the simple fact" that all films (and all human beings) "do no more than take up and re-express their bodily
insertion into the world," giving symbolic form to "the signifying existence of the perceiving body."[95]

[93] Madison, *The Phenomenology of Merleau-Ponty*, p. 90.
[94] Ibid., p. 94.
[95] Ibid.

The Address of the Eye

THE AIM of the last two chapters has been to describe and thematize phenomenologically what it means to be both an embodied visual subject and an embodied visible object. This condition of existence is shared by filmmaker, spectator, and film. Indeed, experienced as and through the film, such commonality enables the filmmaker to signify visual experience as objectively visible, and the spectator to understand the objectively visible as visual experience. The aim of this present chapter is to interpret phenomenologically the implications of the double embodiment and reversible vision that dialectically structure the film experience as dialogic. In this regard, it becomes necessary to respond to the forceful but one-sided vision of that experience which, until very recently, has dominated contemporary film theory. The phenomenological reflections that have preceded and inform this chapter's interpretation of the film experience must lead one to reject the arguments that posit the spectator as, at best, merely an abject subject of the cinematic apparatus and the film's intentionality. Even as they articulate the desire to liberate both spectator and film from hegemonic cinematic practice, these arguments have tended to ground the film experience in structures that are essentially determined and monologic.

In order to understand the dialectical and dialogic structure of the film experience, it is necessary to remind ourselves again and again what much contemporary theory would lead us to forget: Both spectator and film are uniquely embodied as well as mutually enworlded. Both the spectator and the film are unique lived-bodies, each engaged in prospecting the world according to their particular materiality and their particular intentional projects. Each is also uniquely and particularly situated, each concretely enworlded not only in the different spaces they occupy but also on a bias, that is, with a unique perspective that gives particular meaning to the space that occupies them. Nonetheless, insofar as each engages the other in a world that exceeds either of them, the spectator and the film together uniquely negotiate and constitute the significance of visual and visible existence.

The spectator is never a merely "empty" visual body, nor is the film a "transcendentally" introceptive consciousness. However passive it may seem, the spectator's visual body is the visible side of an intending consciousness. And, however transcendent it may seem, the film's introceptive consciousness is the visible side of an intending and visual body. Both spectator and film commute perception to expression by means of their bodies and in the world, and both constitute vision intentionally, each act of perception visually realized as a viewing-view and visibly expressed in the production of a viewed-view. As well, both spectator and film are capable of reflecting upon their prereflective activity of vision and its visible productions. Both can and do transcend the immanence of their immediate bodily experience, generalizing and using their lived-bodies and concrete situation in the world to imaginatively prospect the horizon for future projects and possible situations and to re-member experience retrospectively.

Such visual transcendence in bodily immanence is what I have here called the "address of the eye." It is a visual address always housed in a situated body experienced as "mine" and yet always also able to extend itself to where that body is not. It is able to reflectively connect that body both with its own future and past situations and with the bodily situations of others. Thus, the "address of the eye" enables both the spectator and the film to fluidly and discontinuously redirect their visual address from the immanently actual to the possibility for action, and from their present "having of being" to "being re-membered." Both editors and re-viewers, the spectator and the film reflectively restructure parts of the whole *lived experience of consciousness* as the *consciousness of experience*—that is, as lived experience's significance. Just as crucially (and critically), the visual transcendence in bodily immanence that is the "address of the eye" enables both the spectator and the film to imaginatively reside in each other—even as they both are discretely embodied and uniquely situated.

What has been emphasized throughout the preceding pages is that the "address of the eye" is neither merely the immanent and visible material residence of vision that is the body-object (whether human or mechanical), nor is it merely the immaterial visual activity that visibly realizes the intentional consciousness of a disembodied and transcendental subject. The eye's address must originate in a body lived simultaneously and reversibly as an object for vision and a subject of vision. For spectator and film alike, the "address of the eye" is irreducibly both material residence and intending consciousness correlated in a world and with others. As it *enables* communication through its ability to transcendently project itself across the world's space toward other lived-bodies, the "address of the eye" must find hospitable abode elsewhere to *realize* communication. The "address of the eye" must be received, or it will return unrealized to its place of origin like a returned letter or an unanswered utterance. Thus, in the film experience, there must be two "material residences" and two "intending residents" for cinematic communication to take place and for its significance to be negotiated. The "address of the eye" demands two lived-bodies for its realization—as that subjective dialogue of vision which we too often reify as the objective cinematic "text."

Thesis and Antithesis: The Paranoia of Split Vision

Perhaps because of its remedial aims, its desire not only to describe the structure of cinematic signification but also to critique the hegemony of classical cinematic practice, most contemporary film theory has tended to neglect the double and dialectical nature of cinematic embodiment and the existential fact that both spectator and film are concretely and distinctly incarnate. Given the Lacanian grounding that informs most theories of cinematic identification and the general Cartesian orientation of those engaging in a "scientific" enterprise, it is not surprising that when film theorists do consider cinematic embodiment they consider it from "outside" embodiment. That is, they forget their own lived-body experience of vision as spectators and adopt an estranged and alienated position toward the film experience. Most usually, this position admits and considers only the film experience's "visible" aspects, greatly distrusting those "invisible" aspects of cinematic vision that trouble objective description. Although a major exception to this neglect of the "invisible" in cinema is a concern with "offscreen space" (a space that affirms the existence of the film's body, albeit somewhat problematically), the description of this "invisible" cinematic space is rigorously objective—and does not extend to or include the space inhabited by the spectator.[1]

Generally, then, the visible and invisible aspects of cinematic vision are perceived as antithetical. Vision is split in two, and with it so are the material body and intentional consciousness. Primacy is granted to the objectively visible, and the dialectical nature of cinematic embodiment (for both spectator and film as well as between spectator and film) is privileged in only one of its modalities. This focus on the objectively visible aspects of the film experience foregrounds the spectator's visible perceptive body (or to use Merleau-Ponty's term, the *visual body*) and the film's expressed and intentional vision. Outside the realm of the visible, both the spectator's expressed and intentional vision and the film's visual perceptive body are "ghosts in the machine" that produces cinematic meaning. They are phenomena that must be accounted for yet do not accommodate themselves to and are in excess of a purely objective account of their presence and function in the film experience. Indeed, their invisible presence provokes from those who privilege the visible and live vision from the "outside" what might be seen as a distinctly "paranoid" description.

In a provocative review essay appropriately called "The Anxiety of the Influencing Machine," Joan Copjec speaks to the kind of paranoia that informs a great deal of contemporary film theory as it alienates cinematic embodiment and wrestles with its objective entailments and descriptions of the spectator's passive body, the film's disembodied and godlike vision, and the cinema's active, secretive, and tyrannical "apparatus."[2] Copjec suggests that film theory that warns against the power of the cinematic apparatus and regards the spectator as victimized by it not only describes the film experience as paranoid in structure but is itself structured as a paranoid discourse. Thus, Copjec points out not only how Lacan's work (seminal in relation to contemporary film theory) suggests that "the formation of the subject's own ego from an image at a distance . . . structures all human knowledge as paranoid," but also how psychoanalyst Victor

---

[1] For a seminal discussion of off-screen space, see Noël Burch, *Theory of Film Practice*, trans. Helen R. Lane (New York: Praeger, 1973), and Pascal Bonitzer, "Partial Vision: Film and the Labyrinth," trans. Fabrice Ziolkowski, *Wide Angle* 4, no. 4 (1981), pp. 56–63.

[2] Joan Copjec, "The Anxiety of the Influencing Machine," *October* 23 (1983), pp. 43–59.

Tausk's work on paranoid delusions in schizophrenia "hypothesizes that the delusion begins as a projection of the patient's own body."[3]

This projection of the body, its alienating objectification rather than its productive objectivation, is precisely what occurs in most theoretical considerations of the film experience.[4] In terms of the spectator, the objectified and visible body has been regarded and recognized as visibly weak in its grasp on the world, tenuous in its position and situation. It has been seen as visibly immobilized and vulnerable, as infantile, as victimized, as subject-ed to the "kinesthetic unwindings" of the film's objectified and visible vision. In terms of the film, the objectified body has been recognized as visually powerful, alien, and insidiously self-effacing. In its objective mode as "apparatus," the film's body is perceived as bent on deluding and persecuting the spectator. Similarly, the objectification of the film's subjective mode as visible vision has granted the film transcendental power in the film experience. Resulting from the suspect work of a "negative" and "invisible" body that seems to have no presence and material form in the film experience, the film's visible vision is perceived as having the power to escape existential boundaries and to light in, appropriate, and tyrannize the defenseless spectator. Whereas in paranoid delusions, patients often hear their own objectified and displaced voices ordering them what to do, in the film experience the spectator sees an objectified and displaced vision ordering what they see. As one might instantly note, however, these are not really equivalent experiences, despite arguments to the contrary. In the case of the paranoid, the voices are the patient's *own*, whereas in the case of the film experience the vision is not the spectator's own but exists *in addition to* the spectator's vision.

As it visually enables the film experience but is not visible in vision, the film's objective body, its material presence, is considered both mysterious and monstrous. It is alien and other and exists in a negative incarnation. Objectively visible in this alien incarnation as "apparatus," the film's body is anatomized and analyzed by theorists like Jean-Louis Baudry in terms that evoke what Tausk terms an "influencing machine"—a major figuration of paranoid delusion. Describing the "influencing machine" as the patient's own body objec-

---

[3] Ibid., pp. 53–54.

[4] For clarification of the distinction between objectification and objectivation, the reader is directed to Peter Berger and Stanley Pullberg, "Reification and the Sociological Critique of Consciousness," *History and Theory* 4 (1965), pp. 196–211.

tified, alienated, and displaced, Tausk points both to its particularities and functions. The "influencing machine" is

> a machine of mystical nature. The patients are able to give only vague hints of its construction. It consists of boxes, cranks, levers, wheels, buttons, wires, batteries. . . . Patients endeavor to discover the construction of the apparatus by means of their technical knowledge. . . . All the forces known to technology are utilized to explain . . . the marvelous powers of this machine by which the patients feel themselves persecuted. The main effects of the influencing machine are . . . It makes the patients see pictures. When this is the case, the machine is generally a magic lantern or cinematograph. . . . It produces, as well as removes, thoughts and feelings by means of waves or rays. . . . In such cases, the machine is often called a "suggestion apparatus."[5]

Within the context of this description, it is illuminating to turn to Jean-Louis Baudry's "Ideological Effects of the Basic Cinematographic Apparatus," a seminal essay that carefully analyzes the work and effects of cinematic technology and has had great influence on contemporary film theory and its grounding.[6] However valuable its descriptions, Baudry's essay also clearly and effectively demonstrates the kind of suspicion, fear, and backhanded reverence that Tausk finds in the relation between the paranoid patient and the "influencing machine." The *manifest text* of Baudry's analysis of the basis of cinematic identification as it is an "effect" of the film's alien and influential body points to the spectator-subject as the "patient," subject and subject-ed to delusions and illusions caused by the cinematic institution. Baudry's *subtext*, however, points not to the spectator but to the theorist himself as the "patient"—his own explanations of cinematic technology and its process of self-effacement and visual persecution a demonstration of paranoia.

In describing the inaugural conditions for cinematic identification and their ideological information, Baudry describes the "influencing machine" as *ontologically* a tyrannical technology with an "evil eye." (His is a far more radical description of cinematic identification than those offered by theorists making *epistemological* claims about the

---

[5] Copjec, "The Anxiety of the Influencing Machine," p. 54, quoted from Victor Tausk, "On the Origin of the Influencing Machine (*Beeinflussungapparatus*) in Schizophrenia," *Psychoanalytic Quarterly* (1933), p. 157.

[6] Jean-Louis Baudry, "Ideological Effects of the Basic Cinematographic Apparatus," trans. Alan Williams, *Film Quarterly* 28 (Winter 1974–1975), pp. 39–47.

ideological functions of particular narrative forms, although many also rest upon the grounds provided by Baudry's ontological description of the cinematic apparatus.) Consider the following passage from the essay:

> What emerges here . . . is the specific function fulfilled by the cinema as support and instrument of ideology. It constitutes the "subject" by the illusory delimitation of a central location—whether this be that of a god or of any other substitute. It is an apparatus destined to obtain a precise ideological effect, necessary to the dominant ideology: creating a fantasmatization of the subject, it collaborates with a marked efficacity in the maintenance of idealism.
>
> Thus the cinema assumes the role played throughout Western history by various artistic formations. . . . Everything happens as if, the subject himself being unable—and for a reason—to account for his own situation, it was necessary to substitute secondary organs, grafted on to replace his own defective ones, instruments or ideological formations capable of filling his function as subject. In fact, this substitution is only possible on the condition that the instrumentation itself be hidden or repressed. Thus disturbing cinematic elements—similar, precisely, to those elements indicating the return of the repressed—signify without fail the arrival of the instrument "in flesh and and blood," as in Vertov's *Man With a Movie Camera*. Both specular tranquility and the assurance of one's own identity collapse simultaneously with the revealing of the mechanism, that is, of the inscription of the film-work.[7]

I have quoted Baudry at length here not only to illustrate the negative esteem in which the cinematic apparatus and its effects are held, and how Baudry's assessment of that apparatus parallels Tausk's description of the paranoid's assessment of the power and effects of his own objectified body that has become the "influencing machine." The passage also indicates quite clearly how the film's lived-body is bifurcated theoretically—reduced, on the one hand, to an alien and monstrous objectified apparatus and, on the other hand, to a disembodied, omnipotent, and transcendental visual consciousness. Baudry shifts his concern with the film's lived-body as it is visible from its alien and alienating form of materiality to the transcendental tyranny it exerts by means of its visible, and seemingly

[7] Ibid., p. 46.

disembodied, vision. Furthermore, in the latter instance, the invisibility of the film's body in its vision is taken as signifying that vision as *transcendental*, rather than signifying it as *introceptive visual experience*. It is not surprising that Baudry's objectivist approach privileges a reflexive cinema that would make visible the "flesh and blood" of the film's *objective* body to forestall its function as a transcendental signifier, and that he overlooks the way in which the cinema's "flesh and blood" also lives vision in a *subjective* modality.

Thus, Baudry not only remains "outside" the film's material incarnation (its intersubjective visibility as a "visual body"), but he also remains "outside" of the lived-body's experience of intrasubjectivity—the visual relation between "myself, my psyche" and "introceptive image" that is a modality of bodily perception in which visibility does not figure. Through a process of objectification, Baudry represses his own lived-body experience of vision in its entirety. He splits vision's intrasubjective and intersubjective modalities and ruptures the dialectical relations and reversible exchange that normally occurs between them. Disavowing his own lived-body experience as an active and visually signifying spectator, Baudry thus projects his own fragmented and alienated visual consciousness into the "influencing machine" that is the cinematic apparatus, and introjects the objectification of his visible (rather than visual) body as the empty shell that is the cinema spectator—what can be seen as the objective remains of Lacan's little "hommelette."

From this alienated, schizophrenic, theoretical perspective, the film's viewing-view/viewed-view is given to the vulnerable spectator as vision that has its origins nowhere, for it presents itself as detached from any "visible" body. And, having no visible body, such vision has the power to address itself anywhere and to reside in every body. It is to the point (and revelatory of a deep-seated logical contradiction) that Baudry talks not only about the operation and effects of the film's existential and material incarnation (the "apparatus"), but in the same essay also invokes Husserl's transcendental ego to describe the film's vision.[8] Within this framework, not only descriptive of but also structured by schizophrenic alienation and paranoid delusions of persecution and domination, the apparently "unintending" spectator is perceived merely as a body-object, an "apparatus" less powerful in its effects than the cinematic appara-

[8] Ibid., pp. 43–44.

267

tus—the film's powerful and monstrous body that possesses the power of invisibility. The spectator is thus commandeered and commanded by both the existential and material cinematic apparatus and the transcendental and immaterial visible visual intentionality of that apparatus. The spectator is more abject than subject before such power, is the effect of the film's vision rather than an active and potentially disputative collaborator in the production of the film experience's signification and significance.

The "influencing machine," according to Tausk, begins as a projection of the paranoid's own body. (Here, one might reread Baudry's barely metaphorical description of the "grafting" of new perceptual/mechanical organs onto the spectator to replace his "defective" or less powerful human ones.) So projected, the paranoid's human body is also transformed and alienated beyond all recognition. As Copjec says of the paranoid's body, "Through a replacement of parts, it gradually loses all its human attributes and finally becomes the typical, unintelligible, influencing machine."[9] And, indeed, in Baudry's schema, the film's perceptive and expressive body, a projection and objectification of the human perceptive and expressive body, loses all its lived-body attributes and becomes merely an "influencing machine." It is granted what seems the "special" power of invisibility, the power to operate "under erasure," the power to transcend its embodiment and "appear" as disembodied visual omnipotence.

Alienated from his own lived-body experience, Baudry forgets that this power of "invisibility" and "transcendence" is not at all special, that it is, in fact, one of the essential existential characteristics of lived-body experience. Objectifying and reducing vision and body in the film experience to only that which is visible, Baudry projects and mistakes the commonly experienced *transcendence of vision* (its power to prospect and traverse the world's horizon and thus extend the lived-body's existential experience beyond its material boundaries) for a *transcendentality of vision* (vision no longer bound by the material existence of the body that originates its address and sets the limits of its ability to exceed that body's concrete situation).

The hapless and helpless spectator posited by Baudry succumbs to the power of the "influencing machine" and its transcendental eye in a structure of identification that parallels the paranoid schematic

---

[9] Copjec, "The Anxiety of the Influencing Machine," pp. 54–55.

of ego development laid out by Lacan. Personally demonstrated as well as described by Baudry and others, paranoid delusion is held to account for cinematic identification. Weak in visible intention, the "empty-headed" spectator is seen to passively collapse and confuse his or her own visual activity with that of the film, and this conflation results in the *méconnaissance*, the false perception, of Lacan's Imaginary order. The film's viewing-view, supposedly freed from the constraints of a body, exerts a form of transcendental tyranny over the spectator who is subject-ed to it, who—in a paranoid regression to narcissism—confuses, rather than appropriates, the viewing-view/ viewed-view as his or her own and apparently has no choice but to submit to its vision. Baudry, of course, considers himself exempt from the spectator's visual confusion and delusion, at least enough to be able to write an essay on the subject. Yet Baudry is a spectator, and, although fearful of the influencing machine's total usurpation of the spectator's "empty" body, he disproves this usurpation in his very activity (however misguided) of acknowledging the film's vision as not *his* own.

Again and again in contemporary theoretical writing, it is presumed that because the film's body is invisible in its acts of perception and the production of expression, those acts are mistaken by the spectator as his or her own. Such objectivism and contempt for the spectator is, perhaps, nowhere so evident as in Christian Metz's "Story/Discourse (A Note on Two Kinds of Voyeurism)":

Spectator-fish, taking in everything with their eyes, nothing with their bodies: the institution of the cinema requires a silent, motionless spectator, a *vacant* spectator, constantly in a sub-motor and hyper-perceptive state, a spectator at once alienated and happy, acrobatically hooked up to himself by the invisible thread of sight, a spectator who only catches up with himself at the last minute, by a paradoxical identification with his own self, a self filtered out into pure vision. We are not referring here to the spectator's identification with the characters of the film (which is secondary), but to his preliminary identification with the (invisible) seeing agency of the film itself as discourse, as the agency which *puts forward* the story and shows it to us. Insofar as it abolishes all traces of the subject of the enunciation, the traditional film succeeds in giving the spectator the impression that he is himself that subject, but in a state of emptiness and absence, of pure visual capacity ("content" is to be found only in what is seen). . . . The regime of

269

"story" allows all this to be reconciled, since story, in Emil Benveniste's sense of the term, is always (by definition) a story from nowhere, that nobody tells, but which, nevertheless, somebody receives (otherwise it would not exist): so, in a sense, it is the "receiver" (or rather, the receptacle) who tells it and, at the same time, it is not told at all, since the receptacle is required only to be a place of absence, in which the purity of the disembodied utterance will resonate more clearly. As far as all these traits are concerned it is quite true that the primary identification of the spectator revolves around the camera itself, as Jean-Louis Baudry has shown.[10]

Thus, we are back to the power of the "influencing machine," its ability to make people/patients "see pictures," to produce as well as remove "thoughts and feelings by means of waves or rays." Alienated from his own embodied experience of viewing, and thus from both the spectator and the film, Metz schizophrenically regards the one with contempt and the other with paranoid suspicion.

SYNTHESIS: THE DIALECTICS OF DOUBLE VISION

The theoretical neglect of the introceptive aspects of the film experience for both spectator and film places theorists like Baudry and Metz in a position in which the act of vision is marked for the spectator only in terms of the visible. Baudry and Metz do not admit to the spectator's lived-body experience. That is, exempting themselves from the existential experience of vision, "looking" from a transcendental "position" at the "spectator-fish" watching the "film," they "see" that the spectator's body is visible and the film's body is not, and the film's vision is visible but the spectator's is not. Only the spectator's visible body seems to attend the movie theater. His/her "myself, my psyche" and "introceptive image" are apparently left at the door. It is merely a "body-object," an empty shell of flesh, which faces the awesome disembodied subjectivity on the screen. Thus, the "purity of the disembodied [visual] utterance" is apparently matched by the spectator's "purity" as a material receptacle, for images as well as popcorn. This sounds like a neat—if, for the spectator, an inequi-

[10] Christian Metz, "Story/Discourse (A Note on Two Kinds of Voyeurism)," trans. Celia Britton and Annwyl Williams in Metz, *The Imaginary Signifier: Psychoanalysis and the Cinema* (Bloomington: Indiana Univ. Press, 1982), p. 97.

table—trade-off. However, it does not describe the film experience as anything other than monologic, and it cannot account for the emergence of disjuncture, "rupture," and visual dialogue in the encounter between the spectator and film. Indeed, it cannot account for the individual bodily "autobiography" that the spectator and film's respective visions inscribe, nor for the entailment, argument, and negotiation that occur as these two autobiographies constitute the sense of temporal and spatial difference that structures consciousness as historical.

In the passages previously cited, Baudry and Metz not only deny the spectator's body an intentional life but also deny its synoptic and synaesthetic nature and function. For example, describing spectators (as fish) "taking in everything with their eyes, nothing with their bodies," Metz performs a peculiar theoretical dissection of the spectator's body and embalms it in an existential *non-sequitur*. In existence, the body and the eyes are not separate (in fish or in humans). The eyes are part of the whole body, and what the eyes take in, the body does also. As well, although the eyes are the body's access to a particular form of information, the body's other modes of access to its world always also inform vision—providing alternative sense and significance to it and coordinating its directed and prospective activity with the body's intentions as a whole.

In this regard, it is also unconvincing to speak of the spectator as "motionless" and "silent." Better description would at least suggest the spectator is not *visibly* or *audibly* active, thereby explicitly implicating the observer's own objective position "outside" the subject under scrutiny, and limiting the description's claims. As previous chapters have emphasized in relation to perception, and as we all know from our own experience of being viewers as well as of being visible, spectators are always in motion. Embodied beings are always active, no matter how "passive" they may be perceived from without. My vision is as active as the film's. What the film is doing visibly, I am doing visually. I prospect the film's viewing-view/viewed-view as energetically as it prospects the horizons of its world. In the specificity of its prereflective spatial situation and reflective temporal consciousness, my lived-body experience in-forms how and what I see, and I do not merely "receive" the film's vision *as* my own, but I "take" it up *in* my own, and as an *addition* to my own.

I am not a mere bodily receptacle for the film's visual address, but rather a hospitable host, allowing this *other* visual address temporary

271

residence in *my* visible address, in *my* body. My visible hospitality, however, in no way denies my own visual address, my own possession of the premises we both presently share so as to significantly negotiate meaning. Thus, although generally I appear to be a polite visual "listener" who seldom visibly and audibly interrupts or argues with my invited guest's narrative unless I am encouraged to do so by the form of her discourse, I am nonetheless actively engaged in an invisible and inaudible comparison of the guest's experience and performance with my own.

Visibly and audibly, I may seem to lack imagination and voice. I may seem, therefore, to "accept" everything I see and hear. Indeed, I may be seen from without by a third party as "passive" and silent— perhaps nodding in agreement and encouragement, at most interjecting my continued attention by demonstratively and audibly saying, "I see." And in fact I may "see" what my guest sees. I may become wrapped in his or her vision, a rapt listener whose consciousness of my own address and body fades beside the color and vividness of what I hear. As my interest in my guest's narrative or argument increases, the intentional direction and terminus of my consciousness locates itself there, in *what* my guest sees. I am, however, not really *where* my guest sees. I still and always am embodied Here. And both of us are located in this particular encounter at what is, after all, *my* address.

There are other times, however, when my guest provokes me to an active, visible, and audible response, a response that might be construed as rudeness if there are others about who may be more interested in some parts of my guest's discourse than I am, or when I am. I may, for example, interrupt and talk while the guest is talking. I may hoot in derision at what strikes me as a vision particularly incompatible with my own. I may comment out loud to myself or others about the content and the style of the guest's narrative. That narrative may bore me with its familiarity or lack of appeal to my particular interests, and I may shift it to the horizons of my vision and hearing, redirecting my attention to what I'm going to fix for dinner, or free-associating around a single word my guest uttered two minutes ago. In extreme cases, I may even audibly reject the guest and visibly refuse to see and listen to what I find ridiculous, offensive, or unintelligible.

If all of this sounds familiar, it should. This activity not only occurs in our living rooms with people but also in our movie theaters with films. If we reflect upon our own experience as spectators and listeners engaged in viewing and hearing films, we can hardly describe moviegoers as "motionless," "vacant," and "silent." Embodied and conscious, we are always engaged in forms of what Boris Eikhenbaum has called "inner speech."[11] All the "rude" activity in the movie theater these days merely makes overt that visual and aural dialogue with the film that generally occurs in an intrapersonal rather than interpersonal modality. Radical reflection upon and interpretation of the "natural attitude" of the general moviegoer in the theater reveals the way in which films are viewed in existence—even if such behavior is not usually admitted into theoretical discourse and indeed would constitute a challenge to those claims made about the passivity and emptiness of the spectator and the structure of cinematic identification. Indeed, such behavior demonstrates rather forcefully that the experience of watching even a single movie is hardly one of continuous and total absorption in or by the vision of an other.

Certainly, a form of absorption can and does occur in the film experience. But it is not a concrete absorption into the *body* of the other or the *consciousness* of the other. Rather, it is a mutual absorption in the *world*, a mutually directed interest that converges in the visible and its significance. This similar intentional directedness and interest is lived as a similar (but nonidentical) bodily style of being in the world. Thus, at moments, the spectator and the film may live their vision in concert, may seem to predicate it "identically," each absorbed by and in the other's predication. Merleau-Ponty tells us that this modality of dialogic experience has an "instructive spontaneity" about it: "To the extent that what I say has meaning, I am a different

---

[11] Boris Eikhenbaum, "Problems of Film Stylistics," trans. Thomas Aman, *Screen* 15 (Autumn 1974), pp. 7–32. See also Ron Levaco, "Eikhenbaum, Inner Speech and Film Stylistics," *Screen* 15 (Winter 1974–1975), pp. 47–58; and Paul Willemen, "Reflections on Eikhenbaum's Concept of Internal Speech in the Cinema," *Screen*, 15 (Winter 1974–1975), pp. 59–70. Eikhenbaum's concept of "inner speech" can be loosely related to some of Merleau-Ponty's discussions of thought and language as it is lived in intrasubjective dialogue. The concept is particularly useful in that it is differentiated from the intersubjective speech act, although it is based like the latter in the verbal and linguistic realms. (Here, Merleau-Ponty's description of the lived-body as nascent Logos helps reconcile the relations between the structure of inner sense and externalized signification.) In "Problems of Film Stylistics," Eikhenbaum emphasizes, "The internal speech of the film viewer is much more flowing and indefinite than uttered speech." (p. 16)

"other" for myself when I am speaking; and to the extent that I understand, I no longer know who is speaking and who is listening."[12]

Thus, whether through "speech speaking" or the "view viewing," subjectivity in the dialogic experience is lived not only in an intrasubjective mode as *inner* speech or vision but also in an intersubjective mode as *doubled* speech or vision. Therefore, the engagement of two body-subjects capable of perception and expression through speech or vision is a dialectical as well as dialogical process of making sense. Merleau-Ponty has described this dialectic and the interrogative nature of dialogue as it is constituted as both our own and an other's. In one pertinent instance, he speaks of such dialogic exchange and dialectical commutation in relation to the semiotics of bodily gesture. Within the context of the present discussion of cinematic spectatorship, it is particularly useful to think of gesture in the following passage as the gesture or conduct of the spectator and the film engaged together in their respective visual activity:

> The sense of the gestures is not given, but understood, that is, seized upon by an act on the spectator's part. The whole difficulty is to conceive this act clearly without confusing it with a cognitive operation. The communication or comprehension of gestures comes about through a reciprocity of my intentions and the gestures of others, of my gestures and intentions discernible in the conduct of other people. It is as if the other person's intention inhabited my body and mine his. The gesture which I witness outlines an intentional object. This object is genuinely present and fully comprehended when the powers of my body adjust themselves to it and overlap it. The gesture presents itself to me as a question, bringing certain perceptible bits of the world to my notice, and inviting my concurrence in them. Communication is achieved when my conduct identifies this path with its own. There is mutual confirmation between myself and others.[13]

A convergence of intentional directedness, an understanding of the gesture's meaning because it is one I could make toward the object intended by the other, an identification of the other's "path" or intentional trajectory with (not as) my own—all confirm the intersubjective (and social) relations between myself and others. However, they do not assert the identicality or conflation of our lived-bodies

[12] Maurice Merleau-Ponty, *Signs*, trans. Richard C. McCleary (Evanston, IL: Northwestern Univ. Press, 1964), p. 97.

[13] Maurice Merleau-Ponty, *Phenomenology of Perception*, trans. Colin Smith (London: Routledge and Kegan Paul, 1962), p. 185.

and unique situations in the world we both and always share. Merleau-Ponty clarifies these distinctions in a passage worth quoting at length. Again, in the context of a discussion of cinematic spectatorship, it is illuminating to see the author's relation to "Paul" in the following description as analogous to the spectator's relation to the film:

> The behaviour of another person, and even his words, are not that other person. The grief and the anger of another have never quite the same significance for him as they have for me. For him these situations are lived through, for me they are displayed. Or in so far as I can, by some friendly gesture, become part of that grief or that anger, they still remain the grief and anger of my friend Paul: Paul suffers because he has lost his wife, or is angry because his watch has been stolen, whereas I suffer because Paul is grieved, or I am angry because he is angry, and our situations cannot be superimposed on each other. If, moreover, we undertake some project in common, this common project is not one single project, it does not appear in the selfsame light to both of us, we are not both equally enthusiastic about it, or at any rate not in quite the same way, simply because Paul is Paul and I am myself. Although his consciousness and mine, working through our respective situations, may contrive to produce a common situation in which they can communicate, it is nevertheless from the subjectivity of each of us that each one projects this "one and only" world. The difficulties inherent in considering the perception of other people did not all stem from objective thought, nor do they all dissolve with the discovery of behaviour, or rather objective thought and the uniqueness of the *cogito* which flows from it are not fictions, but firmly grounded phenomena of which we shall have to seek the basis. The conflict between myself and the other does not begin only when we try to *think ourselves into* the other and does not vanish if we reintegrate thought into non-positing consciousness and unreflective living; it is already there if I try to live another's experiences, for example in the blindness of sacrifice. I enter into a pact with the other person, having resolved to live in an interworld in which I accord as much place to others as to myself. But this interworld is still a project of mine, and it would be hypocritical to pretend that I seek the welfare of another *as if it were mine*, since this very attachment to another's interest still has its source in me.[14]

[14] Ibid., pp. 356–357.

Indeed, as a spectator, I may have entered into a "sacrificial" pact with the film when I buy my theater ticket, "having resolved to live in an interworld in which I accord as much place to others as to myself." But that resolve is dis-solved in experience, by my lived-body situation in that "interworld" that is the "vision of the world" that both the film and I share in our mutual alterity. My resolve to yield my own experience and assume the film's is as impossible a resolve as the film's attempts to assume the lived-body experience of a human being. (Here, we might remember the example provided by *Lady in the Lake*.) In other words, "sacrificing" our vision to the film's, we are not ourselves blinded. Seeing as the film sees is still always *our* visual project.

Although Baudry and Metz describe those moments of the film experience in which we "forget ourselves" in our interest in another's vision of the world, they neglect those moments in which we grasp ourselves in the recognition that our vision differs from that of the other. They ignore the existential fact that we are, after all, uniquely embodied and situated even within our forgetfulness of that fact, and that embodiment and situation lived as "mine" always perceives the embodiment and situation lived by another not *as* mine, but as the *signification* of a lived-body experience *like* mine. As Paul Ricoeur suggests, "This transcendence of signification over perception, of speaking over perspective, is what makes the reflection on point of view as such possible: I am not immersed in the world to such an extent that I lose the aloofness of signifying, or intending, aloofness that is the principle of speech."[15] Thus my vision is sign-producing, even when it is most immersed in the signs produced by others or in the visible world. The significance that the film has for me as the visual expression and experience of the sign production of another is completely dependent upon my maintaining a visual aloofness, a situated perspective, in relation to its visible signification of vision.

In sum, as do others who follow their lead and/or ground further argument on their descriptions, Baudry and Metz suppress or deny the dialectical structure and dialogic nature of the film experience. First, they do not recognize the complex and dialectical nature of the human/machine relations structuring the film experience and discussed at length in the last chapter. They describe only a single em-

[15] Paul Ricoeur, *Fallible Man*, trans. C. Kelbley (Chicago: Henry Regnery Co., 1965), p. 48.

bodiment relation between the spectator and cinematic technology—not a doubled embodiment relation that simultaneously produces hermeneutic relations as well. Second, they do not acknowledge the dialectical relations of perception and expression in their intrasubjective and intersubjective modalities, both synthesized, however, as lived-body experience. Instead, they privilege only the intersubjective and visible aspects of perception and expression; the intrasubjective and invisible aspects of perception and expression are regarded either as nonexistent or as experientially repressed. Finally, given the determined oversight of the double embodiment and situation that constitutes the film experience as an experience of *two* viewers viewing and *two* acts of sign production, Baudry and Metz deny the film experience's dialogic nature. Although their descriptions are able to account for the agreement and congruence of vision that exists between the spectator and the film, they are unable to account for the difference, the rupture, the "aloofness" that differentiates the spectator's vision from the film's.

The second chapter of this present study described the commutation of perception and expression effected through the agency of the lived-body. This dialectical exchange synthesized in the person was seen to be the genesis of bodily sense as social signification. This dialectical exchange was seen also to existentially realize the intentional structure of consciousness in the world as both finitely directed and infinitely mobile. Directedness toward and away from, correlation between, consciousness of—all implicate not only the correlative and reversible structure of intentionality as it both links and distinguishes the intending body-subject to and from its intentional objects. All also implicate *movement* as that essential relation asserting and binding world and body-subject in an intentional structure that, by virtue of its existential constraints and diacritical motion, inaugurates meaning. Thus, for both the film and ourselves, motility is the basic bodily manifestation of intentionality, the existential basis for visible signification.

The film experience is predicated, therefore, on the *significance of movement*, on its activity of choice-making which is lived through the bodies of both the spectator and the film. It is the expressed bodily and intentional motility of the film's viewing-view that enables us as embodied and intentional spectators to understand the visual presence of the film's body to the viewed-view we see as visibly present. We understand that world we see projected before and for us as present *to* and *for* (not merely *in*) an embodied and conscious subject other than ourselves. Won from our reflection on the nature and function of our own vision, it is this understanding that confers upon the film the human capacity for perception and expression and infuses its performance of vision with meaning. We recognize the moving picture as the work of an anonymous and sign-producing body-subject intentionally marking visible choices with the very behavior of its bodily being. However, these choices are not initiated by the movement of *our* bodies or *our* intending consciousness. They are seen and visible as the visual and physical choices of some body *other* than ourselves, some body that possesses the vision more intimately than we do, some body for whom it counts as "mine." That some body is the film's body, and, however anonymously, our bodies experience it as a signifying presence in the film experience.

Phenomenological description reveals that our experience of cinematic movement is never merely of *one* intentionally structured and embodied consciousness signifying an individual relation to the world but is the relation of *two*. The spectator's significant relation with the viewed view on the screen is *mediated by, inclusive of*, but *not dictated by*, the film's viewing-view. The spectator's experience of the moving picture, then, entails the potential for both *intentional agreement* and *intentional argument* with the film's visual and visible experience. Indeed, if we attempt to thematize and interpret the imbricated and dialectical correlations that exist between the correlational structure of the film's intentional movement and visual activity and the correlational structure of the spectator's intentional movement and visual activity, *eight correlational possibilities* emerge as *primary*. Although other correlations can be derived from these eight that arise as original experience and constitute the "s-code" of cinematic communication, such correlations are *secondary*. For example, the film may signify that it is perceiving the perception of a character internal to the narrative by using various cinematic codes (such as shot-reverse shot). However, enabling that secondary code use is the original lived-body perceptual experience of the film as it is expressed to the spectator. Limited by the material and spatial conditions of the perceptive/expressive body, this original experience of intentional directedness and finite perspectivity sets the discursive boundaries and semiotic conditions that allow for the construction of secondary codes, such as those that communicate a character's subjectivity.

The eight possible correlations that structure the primary relations between the spectator and the film are diagrammed in Figure 3. They can be best illustrated, however, by offering a concrete example of a film's viewing-view/viewed-view as it is potentially seen within the spectator's viewing-view/viewed-view. Thus, let us begin with the cinematic vision of a stagecoach crossing Monument Valley, the film's viewing-view following it as it moves in the far distance. The film's visual organ, the camera, is intentionally and bodily *directed toward* the stagecoach as the *intentional object* of the film's perception. (See correlation "a.") This is the single and prereflective correlation most basic to the lived-experience of vision: Visual consciousness is the body's means of access to the world as visible, and, in this example, the stagecoach is the *noematic terminus* of the film's perception. This correlation of perception and its object would still hold, would still be operative as a commutation of perception and expression, even if I, the film's spectator, were not in the theater. Singular and intrasubjective, this primary correlation is that which is necessary to cinematic communication, just as my singular and intrasubjective correlation with the world is sufficient to cinematic communication, and, entailed with the film's correlation, makes the film significant as what it is.

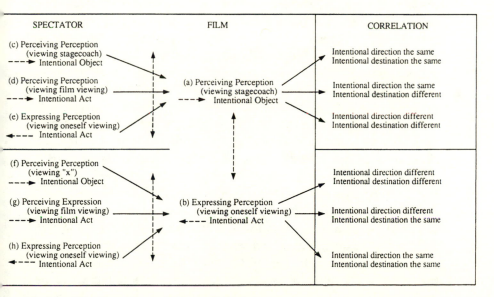

FIGURE 3. The Film Experience: Primary Correlations

end: Broken arrows indicate *intrasubjective* dialectic and direction.
Solid arrows indicate *intersubjective* dialectic and direction.

As the film's spectator, I also may direct my vision toward the stagecoach. Indeed, it is the directional trajectory or visual path of least resistance because the film's vision has prospected and paved the way for me. Following its visual lead, I am not aware of the camera's visual movement as such. In this instance, I am hardly aware of the camera's mediation at all, because I am intending my vision and directing my interest toward the *same* intentional object that occupies the film's interest. Thus, in this double correlation, I am perceiving *through* the film's perception, both of us visually outward bound from the address of our bodies toward a rendezvous at the noematic terminus that is the stagecoach. (See correlation "c"→"a" in Figure 3).

However, this visual enactment of the film's and my similar interest is not my only possibility as a spectator. Functioning as a film critic and faced with the same primary, intentionally directed correlation between the film and its perceptual object (the stagecoach), I may intentionally direct my interest and my vision *away from* the stagecoach that is the film's intended perceptual object, and *toward* the *mode* of the film's perception of the stagecoach, that is, toward its *intentional act* of perception and expression. Situated as a critic, I am no longer intending the same perceptual object (the stagecoach) intended by the film. I am no longer perceiving its perception (its viewed view). Rather, I am intending and perceiving its expressive activity (its viewing view). Although the film's intentional object is the stagecoach, my intentional object is the film's intentional act. My noematic terminus is the film's *noetic activity*. (See correlation "d" → "a.") In this instance, I am directed toward and aware of the camera's visual mediation of the world, its expressive activity of bringing the world to visibility, and its suddenly visible movement. Thus, in a certain modality of spectatorship, I am as likely to be interested in and directed toward the film's mode or "style" of expressing its perception as I am in the perception "itself."

Yet another possibility is open to me in relation to the film's visual and intentional directedness toward the stagecoach. As a film theorist bent on understanding and describing the way in which the bodily movement of the film is understood by me, I may intentionally direct my vision toward the mode of *my own* intentional act of perception. That is, I intend reflexively toward my own expression of perception, my own "viewing view." (See correlation "e" ← "a.") In this instance, both the film's intentional object and its intentional activity provide the *horizon* against which my own visual activity will emerge as *figure*. The film's intentional object and its intentional activity are still visible in my vision, but they are unintended and become equivalent as the general background of my vision whose noematic terminus is my own noetic activity of viewing.

Three other correlations are possible between the film and the spectator. These occur when the initial intrasubjective and prereflective experience of the film (its singular perceptual activity intended and directed outward toward correlation with a perceived object in the world) is transformed by the film through its own activity of *reflection*. In relation to the visual movement of the film's material body, this reflectiveness becomes visible as a *reflexive correlation*—that is, as a conscious self-reference, as the film's turn away from the world to fulfill its intention and interest in the noematic terminus of its own activity and materiality. This is the film's vision as it is *intentionally directed toward its own intentional activity* of realizing perception as expression. (See correlation "b.") Here again, some examples will be helpful. Consider the simplest and most obvious case, in which the film's visual organ, the camera, is visibly reflected in a mirror. A more complex example would be the sudden self-consciousness made visible by a hesitation in the film's visual movement as when, in a direct cinema documentary, the film miscalculates where the life drama in which it is interested is going to happen. Through its visible hesitations and corrections of its vision, its adjustment of its material and perspectival body, the film intends reflexively toward its own situation and acts of judgment. In frequently "mis-taking" where to anchor its "viewing view," the film has to move abruptly to "catch up" with the motor projects of its human perceptual objects—literally redirecting its bodily attitude or refocusing its attention. Here the film's vision becomes charged with a certain insecurity about its own anticipations and bodily reflexes and in so doing becomes self-conscious and reflexive not in relation to its own visibility but in relation to its fulfillment of its perceptual tasks.[16]

When the spectator visually encounters the film's primary reflective and reflexive correlation, three double visual correlations emerge from the encounter which parallel those three double correlations that occur when the film's primary correlation is prereflective and

[16] This issue is discussed in another context in my "The Active Eye: A Phenomenology of Cinematic Vision," *Quarterly Review of Film and Video* 12 (1990), pp. 33–34.

world-directed. The interactional results, however, are quite different. That is, when the spectator is interested in and visually intending *toward* the world and its objects (as in correlation "c"), but the film is intending *away from* the world and reflexively toward its own bodily activity (as in correlation "b"), the spectator becomes aware of the mediation of the film's lived-body, its hermeneutic presence between herself and the world she intends. Thus, a conflict of perceptual interest arises. Not seen *through*, the film's lived-body and activity are perceived by the spectator as *opaque*, and a hermeneutic problem emerges in the spectator's relation to the world as she intends it. (See correlation "f" → "b.")

Paradoxically, however, in a second correlational possibility, even though the spectator and the film intend their objects from *opposing directions*, there is no conflict of interest and no interpretive problem relative to the intended object. Here, the spectator is intentionally directed *toward* the world; that is, her intentional object is not her own body or activity but the film's noetic activity. However, the film in this instance of encounter is intentionally directed *away from* the world and reflexively toward its own activity of perception. Nonetheless, both spectator and film share a common interest, a common perceptual object, and thus they *intentionally converge* at the same noematic terminus. (See correlation "g" → "b.")

It bears mentioning here, however, that the film is not able to perceive its own perception of expression, although it can, as indicated, perceive and express perception. Only the spectator, who is outside the film's activity (though within her own), is privileged to "see" the film's perception of expression, and that occurs because her conscious experience *includes* the film's movement of perception and expression. This inclusion is not reversible. Whether film or spectator, we cannot physically stand behind our own backs. Indeed, René Magritte has aptly and wittily painted this impossibility. Suggesting the mystery of framing, inclusion, and infinite regress, his *La Reproduction interdite* (Not to be reproduced) presents to us the back of a man standing before a mirror mounted over a fireplace, his reflection showing us (and him) not his face, but—impossibly—his back. (See Figure 4.) As mentioned previously, within the *secondary* semiotic system of cinematic narrative, the film can signify that it is perceiving the expression of perception as it is intentionally realized by a character *within* the narrative. Thus, Magritte's painting is at once the representation of a perceptual impossibility for the lived-body who is

FIGURE 4. "La Reproduction interdite," René Magritte. Museum Boymans van Beuningen, Rotterdam

the original source of vision and the representation of an "over-the-shoulder" view common to secondary narrative expression, that vision included *within* the larger and inescapable perception that belongs to and bounds its enunciator.

Finally, the spectator and film may both intend in *similar directions* and yet never meet in interest or vision because they are intending *different intentional objects*, even as these objects may be similar in kind (that is, both the spectator and film's intentional objects are intentional acts). This is the case in the last correlation of spectator and film. In this instance, both spectator and film intend similarly away from the world's objects and toward their own acts of perception. But, because both are uniquely embodied and uniquely situated in the world, the terminus of each intention will differ in address from the other. (See correlation "h" ← "b.") Thus, when the film is reflecting upon or expressing its own acts of perception and the spectator is doing the same in relation to her own perceptual activity, there will be no cinematic communication at all, not even an argument.

As indicated in Figure 3, all these correlations are possible in the film experience, entailing the spectator and the film as each are engaged in the dialectical activity of intrasubjective vision, and as each encounters the visual intentionality of the other. Thus, the diagram also indicates the correlations between the *intentional directedness* of the spectator and the film—that is, whether or not they share the same intentional movement toward an intended object or toward an intending act or subject. And the diagram also indicates the correlations between the spectator and the film's *intentional destination* or terminus—that is, whether or not they share the same intentional interest at the same time. Finally, the diagram indicates also the dynamic and dialectical intrasubjective possibilities for both the spectator and the film to shift and reverse their intentional direction and destinations. Given these dynamic and reversible intrasubjective movements, the diagram as a whole indicates the primary possibilities for the intersubjective, dialogic, and dialectical movement of intentional convergence and divergence that occurs between the spectator and the film and constitutes the significance of the film experience.[17]

[17] These correlational possibilities and the diagram were first worked out and articulated in a previous article. See Vivian Sobchack, "Toward Inhabited Space: The Semiotic Structure of Camera Movement in the Cinema," *Semiotica* 41 (1982), pp. 323–325.

THE ADDRESS OF THE EYE

The Eye's Address

The dialectical structures and dialogic possibilities described in the previous section constitute the first part of a phenomenological interpretation of the structure of the film experience. This interpretation is meaningful only insofar as it emerges from our understanding of the film (and its intelligibility) as it is originally perceived by us in the film experience—that is, as an animate, conscious "other" who visually, audibly, and kinetically intends toward the world or toward its own conscious activity in a structure of *embodied* engagement with the world and others that is similar in structure to our own. Throughout this present work, the spectator's and the film's respective embodiments of perception and expression have been central to a re-cognition of the film experience as entailing two intentional acts of vision engaged in a negotiation, not only of their dialectical and dialogic relation to intentional objects of vision but also of their different material embodiments and enworlded situations. This is to say that the intelligibility and meaning of the film experience originates in the lived-body experience of perception and its expression, in the empirically concrete (as well as transcendent) "address of the eye."

Although it is contrary to our prereflective experience, we could argue (as others have done since the inception of film theory) that the viewing view/viewed view we see in the movie theater is always transparent like a window, or always opaque like the canvas, or always refractive and reflexive like the mirror—mediating, preventing, distorting, or giving us only illusory access to the material world we inhabit. We could argue this mediating viewing view/viewed view as merely instrumental, neither sentient nor spontaneously and autonomously active. If such were the case, however, the problematic conflicts of intentional direction and destination that commonly occur between the spectator and the film should not occur. Within the terms of this argument, the spectator, of course, would still be intentionally directed toward intentional objects and toward his or her own intentional acts of consciousness, but hermeneutic problems of understanding the directedness (the signification of significance) of the film's movement would not arise.

It is in moments of disjuncture and divergence that the film reveals itself most obviously to the spectator as an "other's" intentional consciousness at work. This other intentional consciousness has its own

285

projects of perception and expression which may differ from our own. If the cinematic experience were intentionally one-sided and we took the film's vision not merely *into* our own but *as* our own, there would be no moments of discontinuity and rupture, no need for hermeneutic activity—that conscious seeking to disclose what is understood as meant but whose meaning presently eludes us. It hardly needs pointing out that the film experience is dynamic. With every film we engage, we experience moments of divergence and rupture and moments of convergence and rapture.

In moments of rupture in the film experience, we are brought back from the film's and our mutual address of the world to the concrete address of our eyes: our differentiated and unique embodiments and our different and unique situations in the world whose horizons we share. At the same time that we, as spectators, intersubjectively understand the film as similar to ourselves and intentional in its mode of inhabiting space in the world and in its performance of commuting perception to expression, the ontological phenomenon of embodiment also clearly separates and delimits the spectator and film as singular lived-bodies, *different in their similarity*. As the condition of embodiment incarnates consciousness and situates it in the world, so it also makes each individual incarnation specific and unique in finitude and situation. Thus, although the spectator may identify with the film's effortless intentional and physical motility, with its modes of being in the world as both the material object and intending subject of conscious experience, the spectator does *not* identify with the film's singular embodiment even as it is presented in the modality of "mine." Thus, what is often taken to be the spectator's *identification* with the film's discretely embodied "address of the eye" is, in fact, the spectator and film's *identical directedness* toward the same intentional object. That is, the spectator and the film often share the same *interest* in the world. They do *not*, however, share the same *place* in the world, nor the same *body*. Their respective visual address *to* the world may, indeed, transcendently and intersubjectively converge in the world and its objects, but their address *in* the world is always discrete in its immanence and thus never the same.

As has been pointed out previously, the difference or differentiation between the spectator and the film is not necessarily nor merely related to the biological materiality of the one and the technological materiality of the other. Rather, this differentiation is the same as that found between any singular embodied consciousness perceived as "mine" and those "others" who are understood by me as intentional beings only by virtue of my own experience of myself while in the eyes of others and my resultant activity of inference. Whether a person relating an anecdote (whose "myself, my psyche" I infer from the conduct of her "visual" body as it resonates possible conduct for me), or a film expressing a narrative (whose "visual body" I infer from the intentional conduct of its "myself, my psyche" made visible through its "introceptive image"), all others are other than me and included in my experience—while I am myself, the experiencer. Possessing my body and living it means that I know it as uniquely "mine," as the Here where I am, where the world and experience bodily begin and end, where they are addressed and reside. Even though, as spectators, we perceptually engage the film's "eye/I" and follow its movement and orientation as it strives toward realizing its projects and becoming in the cinematic world, it finally remains always an "other" for us. We never watch a film as if, in fact, "we" as our bodies weren't engaged in the watching. Thus, although our interest may be dominantly and transcendently There, our bodies are also irreducibly and immanently Here. The film's Here, although it is always understood as such, always remains a There for us—for our Here is uniquely our own. It is where we are situated, where we're "coming from" as we intend toward the viewing-view/viewed-view we are watching and toward the intentional presence we feel constituting it for us in its particular significance.

The phenomenon of embodiment, then, both connects and separates our existence and address from that of others in the world we mutually share. Much as we may understand the embodied experience of the film as being structured like our own, because both the film and spectator are uniquely situated in the world, discontinuity and intentional conflict inevitably and commonly arise. The need to question and interpret a difference in interest, in focus, in perspective, in intentional projects, in the modes of prospecting the world, leads to the dynamic adjustments, movements, and negotiation in the film experience that also essentially characterize the shifts and reversals of existential consciousness as it engages a world and others. Both the problem and the pleasure of embodiment is that embodiment marks our differences as well as our similarities, that is— as we watch a film and its signifying and significant movement—we are suddenly, yet frequently, conscious of an implicit incarnation, an "other's" consciousness embodied both *like* and *unlike* our own, as a Here situated There upon the screen.

When the film inhumanely moves through carnage and seems impervious to the human blood and gore it sees, I will either share its inhumane interest (taking advantage of the curiosity of a technological body) or I will break my engagement with its gaze and stare at my lap, unable to share in a look that behaves with no subjective awareness of what it is to bleed or be in physical pain. When the film breaks a cultural taboo and tries to get a better look at something we regard as visually forbidden or disgusting, when it violates or looks upon the violation of another body-subject with prurience and pleasure, we may turn our own "eyes/I" away from the "eyes/I" of the "other." But then again, we may not. We may share the film's anthropological vision or feel titillated by its forbidden activity. If, given our own human bias, the film seems to move erratically in its interest, if it radically digresses from human subject matter or seems bored with its previous intentional objects (following, for example, a wire up a wall or moving out a window when something more central to the anthropocentric narrative it has been expressing is happening elsewhere), we become aware of the film's intentional and bodily difference from ourselves.[18] And, of course, as the film calls attention to itself and its embodied activity by moving rhythmically or jerkily or in some physically unusual way (mechanically, for example), we also become consciously aware that the Here on the screen is distinctly different from our own Here and that the invisible "other" implied by the movement is engaged in intentional projects that are marked off from, although included in, our own, and not completely disclosed to us in their purpose and significance.[19] In all these in-

[18] These two movements occur in Michelangelo Antonioni's *The Passenger*, a film that continually plays with the perspectival and finite nature of embodied experience—both on the level of plot and through its use of techniques to effect rupture between the spectator's and the film's intentionality.

[19] For example, although at the secondary, narrative level, it is meant to signify "physical involvement" in the action and to engage the spectator in a sympathetic physical experience, the jerky and mechanical quality of "hand-held" camera is so *unlike* our own general experience and sense of a physical movement such as running that we become aware of the physical difference and sudden presence of an intending, mobile "other." Our awareness of such difference leads us to hermeneutic activity: the "decoding" of what has become a fairly conventional *sign* of subjective physical immediacy and motor activity. (Since the advent of Steadicam, this sign has been used much more discriminately to express primarily disjunctive physical experience.)

stances in which difference between the spectator's materiality and situation and the film's materiality and situation becomes explicit, the spectator can refuse, partially share, or become rapt in the film's vision. I can look in my lap, peek through the fingers with which I cover my eyes, or fully engage the film's vision and the intentional and ethical interest and trajectory it takes in relation to a world and others. Thus, my experience of the film's different embodiment and situation may cause me discomfort. But this experience of difference can also be liberating. It can cause me to restructure my visual address, to transcend its present location in the reformulation and imagination of where it might locate itself in the future.

Insofar as we, as spectators, by virtue of our similar ontological condition of being embodied and situated, understand the film's intentional projects (what it is doing in the world and what it is making of space) and insofar as we share its interests, projects, and physical ease in the world, we will be directed *through* the film's different Here to our mutual There. As indicated in Figure 3, the direction and destination of the spectator's consciousness will be, in such an instance and at such a moment, the same as the film's. It is in this correlation that both Heres become transparent and the relationship between the spectator and the film is the most compatible and the least remarked upon. In other instances, at other moments (commonly in the same film experience), the spectator must adjust his or her own intending consciousness to the film's, must choose in that moment of perceived difference whether or not to shift intentional direction and destination in order to align it with the film's. On the one hand, that choice may be effortless and transparently made—the film's embodiment and intentional project perceived as "immediately" comprehensible and understood in the terms of our own lived-body experience of consciousness and its projects. On the other hand, that choice may be as difficult and self-consciously intended as the task of translating something from a foreign language of which we know only the rudiments of grammar and the most basic vocabulary. The ease and transparence of the one modality of our engagement with the film emerges because we not only know necessarily *that* the film's movement is meant (that is, intentionally and diacritically directed), but because we also know sufficiently *what* it means. The difficulty and opacity of the other modality of our engagement arises because we may know that the film's movement is meant but we must decipher what it means. In both modes of engagement with the film, however, there is no doubt *that the film means*, and that both its general and specific meanings derive from a primary semiotic code generated by the lived-body and its existential and intentional engagement in and with the world and others as animate gesture, as languaging, as intentional discourse.

TOWARD THE "INCORPORATION" OF SUBJECTIVE EXPERIENCE IN FILM THEORY

An accurate and responsive description and interpretation of the nature of existential vision and its rich and dialectical expression in the film experience must look not only to vision as it appears to others in its objective modality as the visible, but also to vision as it appears in its subjective modality: invisible to others who are not its subject. Cinematic communication and its dialogic "address of the eye" is possible and intelligible only insofar as the embodied spectator and embodied film are dually and simultaneously engaged in both the intrasubjective, introceptive, and invisible activity of visual perception and the intersubjective, projective, and visible activity of visual expression. Most theoretical description and interpretation of the encounter between spectator and film in the film experience has privileged this latter objective modality of vision—and, if not quite neglecting the former subjective modality of vision, has tended to regard it, too, in objective terms.

Vision is meaningless, however, if we regard it only in its objective modality as visibility. As phenomenological description reveals, both the spectator and the film function existentially not only as objects for vision, but also as subjects of vision. Both the spectator and film's visible bodies are lived also as visual bodies. They both are capable of commuting perception to expression and expression to perception. Thus, we must acknowledge subjective experience and the invisible as part of vision—that part which does not "appear" in it or to us, but which grounds vision and gives the visible within it a substantial thickness and dimension.

This inquiry into the radical relations between visibility and invisibility in lived-body vision and hence in the film experience is *not* posed in the currently fashionable terms of *presence* and *absence*. That is, visibility and invisibility have not been articulated here or elsewhere in this work as synonymous with presence and absence (nor, for that matter, have they been understood as within the context of the dualism and opposition of physics and metaphysics). Those contemporary theorists who practice Derridean deconstruction deny presence and assert that all is deferral and absence. Others, particularly those who follow upon Lacan's psychoanalytic theory, tend to conflate presence and absence. And those theorists who take a traditional positivist approach to phenomena deny absence any concrete presence. Unlike the various relations predicated between presence and absence by structuralist, deconstructionist, psychoanalytic, and positivist theorists, visibility and invisibility are articulated here as co-operative in the commutative and lived-body system of signification and interpretation that is vision. Visibility and invisibility are not opposed to each other. One is not privileged in existence over the other (even if one has been privileged in theoretical discourse). And they are not conflated; each maintains itself as a distinct modality within vision.

The terms *presence* and *absence* are also conceptually problematic. As the kind of terms they are, they repress interrogation of their existential use and the existence of their users. That is, they are *objective theoretical constructs* that do not acknowledge or call into question the *subjective existence and experience* of those who use them. Thus, they are both impossible and imprecise, articulating no concrete existential modality through which they might be experienced and explored. Indeed, they are informed by and implicitly articulate the philosophical and empirical tradition that falsely splits subject/object relations, mind/body relations, and the like.

Phenomenological reflection, however, has demonstrated that *visibility* and *invisibility* are concretely descriptive terms useful in illuminating the existential nature and function of embodied vision (be it human or cinematic). That is, they are terms related specifically to vision and they acknowledge the existence of enworlded and embodied subjects of vision and objects for vision. As such, they do not suggest some generalized and abstract state of presence or absence. As well, by their very delimitation, they implicate other modalities of access to the world and experience. For example, what is invisible or "absent" in vision might be audible or "present" in perception to inform the act and significance of seeing. Thus, what is concretely "sensed" as significant by the embodied subject may be invisible *in* vision or, as well, *to* vision but is still available to perception—of which vision is only a *single* modality (one synaesthetically informed by and synthesized with all one's other perceptual modes of access to the world).

Merleau-Ponty is instructive in this regard. Looking at a visible lamp, he says of his experience: "I grasp the unseen side as present, and I do not affirm that the back of the lamp exists in the same sense that I say the solution of a problem exists. The hidden side is present in its own way. It is present in my vicinity."[20] The back of the lamp is not absent. Rather, it is invisible. It exists in vision as that which cannot be presently seen but is yet available for seeing presently. It exists in vision as an *excess* of visibility. That excess charges the space around me (my vicinity) with dimension, and motor possibilities for re-vision. Thus, the visual image of the lamp is not reducible to a mere two dimensions, to "total" visibility as something without a "hidden side." Merleau-Ponty continues: "The classical analysis of perception reduces all our experience to the single level of what, for good reasons, is judged to be true. But when, on the contrary, I consider the whole setting [*l'entourage*] of my perception, it reveals another modality which is neither the ideal and necessary being of geometry nor the simple sensory event, the *percipi*, and this is precisely what remains to be studied now."[21]

The most forcefully felt "presence" of such invisibility in vision is, at one pole, the unseen world, the *off-screen space*, from which embodied vision prospects its sights and, at the other pole, the very enworlded eye/I, the *off-screen subject*, who enacts sight, revises vision, and perspectivally frames its work as a visible image. Prior to reflection upon itself, our vision synthesizes the world and our lived-bodies as a dynamic structure of reversible, chiasmatic relations between the visible and the invisible. Our vision constitutes both the world and our bodies in visible and invisible modalities, each commutable to the other.

In this regard, Jean Baudrillard tells us: "Looking requires that an object conceal and reveal itself, that an object suggest its own disappearance at any given moment, which is why the act of looking contains a kind of oscillating motion. . . . in which the visible parts ren-

[20] Maurice Merleau-Ponty, "The Primacy of Perception and Its Philosophical Consequences," trans. James M. Edie, in *The Primacy of Perception*, ed. James M. Edie (Evanston, IL: Northwestern Univ. Press, 1964), p. 14.

[21] Ibid.

der the others invisible: in which a kind of rhythm of emergence and secrecy sets in."[22] Or, as Merleau-Ponty elaborates, the visible object

is given as the infinite sum of an indefinite series of views in each of which the object is given but in none of which it is given exhaustively. It is not accidental for the object to be given to me in a "deformed" way, from the point of view [place] which I occupy. That is the price of its being "real." The perceptual synthesis thus must be accomplished by the subject, which can both delimit certain aspects in the object, the only ones actually given, and at the same time go beyond them. This subject, which takes a point of view, is my body as the field of perception and action [practique]—in so far as my gestures have a certain reach and circumscribe as my domain the whole group of objects familiar to me. Perception is here understood as a reference to a whole which can be grasped, in principle, only through certain of its parts or aspects. The perceived thing is not an ideal unity in the possession of the intellect, like a geometrical notion, for example; it is rather a totality open to a horizon of an indefinite number of views which blend with one another according to a given style, which defines the object in question.[23]

As they blend with one another and give dimension to worldly space and to visible objects, those invisible views also inscribe the horizons and domain of the viewing subject. They describe the motor possibilities for that subject and, ultimately, that subject's own visibility. Not only visual, but also visible, the subject's style of visual and bodily conduct is informed by these invisible and possible views and becomes a visible discourse on them.

Thus, we cannot depend upon an analysis of the objectively visible to tell us everything we want and need to know about vision. The visible is never the whole of vision. It is never experienced by us as complete. The content of our sight is never simply all there is for us. Correlatively, the world is never denied by or at the boundaries of our vision simply because the visible terminates at the material horizon provided by our eyes. In the prereflective experience of visual consciousness, invisibility penetrates the borders of vision and per-

[22] Jean Baudrillard, "What Are You Doing after the Orgy?" trans. Lisa Liebmann, *Artforum* (October 1983), p. 43.
[23] Merleau-Ponty, "The Primacy of Perception and Its Philosophical Consequences," pp. 15–16.

meates the visible. The content of our sight has spatial contours that suggest other possible views in excess of our present one, and the boundaries of our vision do not bring our existence and experience to a sensible end at the corners of our eyes. I always subjectively exceed my delimitation of the objectively visible in my vision, just as the objective world always invisibly exceeds my subjective visual de-limitation of it. As a modality of embodied (and, thus, expressed) perception, vision—whether human or cinematic—is constituted as the dialectic between the visible and the invisible, between the seen and the seeing, between embodiment in its objective and subjective expression. Existential vision is, in this sense, always an activity of re-viewing and re-vision (precisely the activity that defines and oc-cupies the film). In regard to this dialectic of perception and its mo-dality as vision, Merleau-Ponty is again worth quoting at length:

> Perception is thus paradoxical. The perceived thing itself is paradoxi-cal; it exists only in so far as someone can perceive it. I cannot even for an instant imagine an object in itself. As Berkeley said, if I attempt to imagine some place in the world which has never been seen, the very fact that I imagine it makes me present at that place. I thus cannot conceive a perceptible place in which I am not myself present. But even the places in which I find myself are never completely given to me; the things which I see are things for me only under the condition that they always recede beyond their immediately given aspects. Thus there is a paradox of immanence and transcendence in perception. Im-manence, because the perceived object cannot be foreign to him who perceives; transcendence, because it always contains something more than what is actually given. And these two elements of perception are not, properly speaking, contradictory. For if we reflect on this notion of perspective, if we reproduce the perceptual experience in our thought, we see that the kind of evidence proper to the perceived, the appearance of "something," requires both this presence and this ab-sence.[24]

This is not presence and absence set in opposition one to the other, but a pervasion of each in the other. The visible extends itself into the visibly "absent" but existentially and experientially "present." And the invisible gives dimension to the visibly "present," thicken-ing the seen with the world and the body-subject's *exorbitance*—their

[24] Ibid., p. 16.

concrete and empirical excess and transcendence of any single modality or act of being-in-the-world, of any individual situation. The visible, then, does not reveal everything to perception. Vision is not precisely coincident with enlightenment (even though historically it would seem that way). Indeed, the visible emerges in vision not only as revelation but also as concealment, as what Baudrillard calls secrecy. The visible always articulates itself as partially latent and partially unresolved. Correlatively, the invisible does not conceal everything from vision; it reveals itself as an active pressure upon vision and the visible—informing them, for example, with sounds that cannot be seen but are perceptible. Thus, existence disallows absolute "edges" to visual experience. Only in a coloring book or its adult equivalent can we secondarily abstract objects from the world with those intentionally insistent and hard black outlines that do away with the ambiguity of primary existence.

These dynamic and dialectical relations between the visible and invisible in visual experience articulate the cooperative and reversible nature of the *immanent* (what is directly given in and as existential experience) and the *transcendent* (what is indirectly taken from and as existential experience). Both ground and penetrate each other. As described here, the invisible is hardly transcendental, even if it is always ambiguous and mysterious in its transcendence of vision and visibility. Its mystery, however, is solved again and again in acts of perception—although, paradoxically, its transcendence both of and within any *single* act and work of visual perception demands that it be continually re-solved. Indeed, therein lies its mystery. But it is a mystery that is experienced daily by the lived-body being in the world. Not transcendental and beyond existence, the invisible is a transcendence *of* immanence *in* immanence. It is directly experienced by us as that which we cannot directly experience wholly or merely through sight.[25] Thus, the visible and invisible in-form each other, chiasmatically reversing and exchanging themselves in our most common acts of perception and expression.

The viewing-view and moving images that originate in both spectator and film in the film experience are not served adequately by

[25] For further discussion of "transcendence in immanence," see Gary Brent Madison, *The Phenomenology of Merleau-Ponty: A Search For the Limits of Consciousness* (Athens: Ohio Univ. Press, 1981), pp. 162–166; and Richard L. Lanigan, *Speaking and Semiology: Maurice Merleau-Ponty's Phenomenological Theory of Existential Communication* (The Hague: Mouton Press, 1972), pp. 90–93.

those descriptions that either ignore the existential, situated, and embodied nature of vision in the world and speak of an abstract and transcendental opposition of presence and absence or ignore those invisible aspects of vision that transcend the objective experience of vision but are immanent in its subjective experience. As a particular mode of grasping and expressing a world, vision *incorporates* both the visible and the invisible, and it does so always through and in relation to a *concretely embodied* and *contingently situated viewing subject*, be it the filmmaker, the film, the spectator, or even the film theorist.

It is not empirically accurate, therefore, to describe—as much as contemporary theory does—the moving image as marking only a visible absence, as merely (if powerfully) constituting visual desire and illusory satisfaction. It also is not empirically accurate to describe the viewing-view as marking only (if powerfully) a transcendental presence, a no/body. Finally, it is certainly not accurate to describe the spectator as either a passive and "empty" body-object, a vacant receptacle—or as an abstract structure whose trajectories of cinematic identification are severely limited and predetermined. It is grossly partial to assert that the spectator has no viewing-view and moving images of her own that engage those of the film in a dialectical and dialogic structure of visual communication. The spectator's own intentional visual activity and its constant co-production of signs and meaning in the cinema is ignored because it is invisible to the merely objective observer. Rather, what is visible to that observer is the spectator as body-object, apparently hosting the transcendental and intentional vision of no/body and submitting to subject-ion by a devious and invasive "influencing machine."

All of these problematic and partial descriptions of the film experience arise from consideration of cinematic vision and its productions solely as objective phenomena. That is, cinematic vision is looked at by theorists from *outside* the structure and experience of the human vision that constitutes cinematic vision and includes that vision within its own. Cinematic vision is regarded as if it were only what is visible in experience, rather than also that which is perceptible in vision and visual in experience. Those aspects of vision that are not visible in vision but that are perceptible to each individual viewer as s/he views are discounted in theoretical descriptions of the film experience, even as the theorist must subjectively *live through* those "invisible" aspects of his or her perceptual experience in order to see the images, imagining, and spectators s/he so objectively and partially describes.

Seeing, moving, hearing, sensually experiencing sensible and material being, imagining, remembering, dreaming, thinking, theorizing—all are the acts of a lived-body living its intentional existence in the world not only visibly for others but also invisibly for itself. Although the lived-body can reflect upon itself and "see" how it objectively appears as visible in the world, as it prereflectively lives and conducts its activity in the world and before others, it does not experience its conduct in terms of its objective visibility. It lives its behavior subjectively, invisibly, *introceptively*—as a body-subject engaging the world always and primarily as *my* experiencing of existence. Not objectively visible except in its already commuted and thus transformed objective expression as the body seen in its act of "looking," this introceptive aspect of vision has been "overlooked" by those theorists engaged in analysis of the film's objectively visible and moving images and the relations the spectator has with them.

This privileging of the visible in vision has led to a partial and pessimistic description of the relations between the spectator and the film in the film experience. Rather like the low-budget science fiction films of the cold-war and Communist-obsessed 1950s, the seminal theoretical scenarios of the film experience have the spectator's visibly passive body "taken over" by an alien visual consciousness, one that has no "visual body" of its own and is pure visual intentionality, pure "introceptive image" of an/other's "myself, my psyche." In the darkness of the theater, isolated from contact with the world of visible objects, physically confined and cushioned by a seat, the spectator's "visual body" (its introceptive perceptual and expressive activity invisible and forgotten) supposedly relaxes its active grasp on the world and is lulled into a state in which the body half-sleeps and loses sight of itself (as if, in fact, losing sight of ourselves isn't something we actively do all the time as we intend toward the world). In this unaware and unwary state, the spectator's body can be appropriated by the alien vision and turned into a simulacrum of itself. Objective analyses of cinematic identification evoke William Cameron Menzies's *Invaders from Mars* (1953) or Don Siegel's *Invasion of the Body Snatchers* (1956) and share their paranoid hysteria and fear of being "taken over," their anxiety about alien influence, co-option, subjection, and abjection.

If, however, the theorist recognizes and describes the vision that s/he and every other sighted body-subject *lives* rather than objectively *posits*, then the spectator is not simply the material ground for an alien visual invasion, nor does the film's vision mark the existence of a transcendental, extraterrestrial BEM (bug-eyed monster). The spectator lives through a vision that is uniquely her own even if it is invisible from without, and the film has a material and situated body even if it is invisible from within. In a full description of vision in the film experience, as elsewhere, the introceptive and invisible aspects of subjective embodiment cannot be overlooked—even if they cannot objectively be seen.

Paradoxically, it is the film's own expression of introceptive perception and expression and their commutation that brings these subjective and invisible aspects of embodied existence to the only objective visibility they have. However, given that it is not transcendental, omniscient, and disembodied, at the same time it makes introceptive vision visible, the film conceals from objective visibility what most usually mediates our knowledge of the subjective existence of others who are not "ourselves": its visible body. Unusually, except in our usual experience of ourselves, it is the film's visual and visible introceptive and intentional conduct—not its objectively visible body—that mediates our knowledge of the film's embodied and objective existence.

The cinema, then, is an astonishing phenomenon. Enabled by its mechanical and technological body, each film projects and makes uniquely visible not only the objective world but the very structure and process of subjective, embodied vision—hitherto only directly available to human beings as the invisible and private structure we each experience as "my own." Rather than merely replacing human with mechanical vision, the cinematic mechanically functions to bring to visibility the reversible and chiasmatic structure of human vision—the system "visual/visible" that necessarily entails not only enworlded objects but always also embodied and perceiving subjects. Indeed, through its motor and organizational agency, the cinematic inscribes and provokes a sense of existential and intentional "presence" that is situated and centered, yet mobile, self-displacing, and polymorphously modal. Phenomenological description and interpretation have revealed the cinematic subject (both film and spectator) as at once *introverted* and *extroverted*, as existing in the world as both *subject* and *object*. Thus, however much some might wish it, the film and the spectator are never experienced as completely self-possessed. The vision of both is always partially and visibly given over to the vision of others at the same time that it visually appropriates what it sees. As well, the very motility of vision structures the film and the spectator as always in the act of displacing themselves—if not in space, then in time; if not in time, then in attention and intention. Thus, because of and despite their existence as concretely embodied and finitely situated, the film and the spectator always elude their own (and our) containment and outrun their own (and our) determination.

Each film (as each spectator) exists as simultaneously presentational and representational, as viewing subject and visible object, as an embodied "presence" informed by the transcendent activity of retention and protention that grounds a reflection of time as past, present, and future. Each film (as each spectator) exists as a continuous "be-coming" that continually synthesizes the temporal and spatial heterogeneity of transcendent and immanent existence as the dialectical coherence of embodied and conscious experience. Informed by the heterogeneity of time, the space of each film (and each spectator) is both discontiguous and contiguous, lived from within and without. "Presence" is multiply located—simultaneously displacing itself in the There of accomplished ("past") and intended ("future") situations and orienting these displacements from the Here where the body is and lives. That is, as the multiplicity and discontinuity of lived temporality are synthesized and centered as a specific lived-body experience, so are multiple and discontiguous spaces synopsized and located in a particular material body. Articulated in each film as displacements of the viewing situation ("shots"), discontiguous spaces and discontinuous times are gathered together in a coherence ("scenes") whose reflection and signification constitute the significance of what can be called conscious experience. And (as with the spectator) that coherence is accomplished by the lived-body. The camera its perceptive organ, the projector its expressive organ, the screen its discrete and material occupation of worldly space, the cinema exists as a visible performance of the perceptive and expressive structure of lived-body experience. Viewing, re-viewing, revising vision as easily and transparently as one mechanically operates and the other biologically breathes, each film and each spectator separately live the advent of vision. Together, however, that advent becomes an always original—if always common—adventure.[26]

---

[26] The last part of this section is drawn from Sobchack, "The Scene of the Screen: Beitrag zu einer Phänomenologie der)Gegenwärtigkeit(im Film und in den elektron-

BECOMING AND CONCLUDING: THE END IS IN-SIGHT

The intelligibility and meaning of the film experience originates in the embodied experience of perception and its expression, in the empirically concrete (as well as transcendent) "address of the eye." If we are to understand how we understand the film experience, why it has significance for us, and why we care about it, we must re-member that experience as located in the lived-body. Indeed, at this historical moment in our particular society and culture (most often called postmodern, but more empirically described as electronic), the lived-body is in crisis. The lived-body's struggle to assert its differential existence and situation, its vulnerability and mortality, its vital and social investment in a concrete life-world inhabited by others has been recognized and articulated not only in the current popular obsession with "physical fitness" (the human body as lean, mean, and immortal "machine") and with moving images that show the human body being gouged and riddled with holes ("blown away"). Within the context of this crisis of the flesh, the human body has been also recently occupying a major amount of theoretical (if primarily objectifying) attention from a variety of scholars in the human sciences.[27]

It seems historically relevant to note, however, that this particular "crisis of the lived-body" has emerged coincidentally with our present culture's pervasive entailment of electronic mediation and simulation, and correlatively with what has been called a "crisis of the real." Postcinematic, incorporating cinema into its own techno-logic, our electronic culture has disenfranchised the human body and constructed a new sense of existential "presence." Television, video tape recorder/players, videogames, and personal computers all form an encompassing electronic system whose various forms "interface" to constitute an alternative and virtual world that uniquely *incorporates* the spectator/user in a spatially decentered, weakly temporalized, and quasi-disembodied state.

Digital electronic technologies atomize and *abstractly schematize* the

---

ischen Medien," trans. H. U. Gumbrecht, in *Materialität der Kommunikation*, ed. H. U. Gumbrecht and K. Ludwig Pfeiffer (Frankfurt am Main: Suhrkamp, 1988), pp. 416–428, in English as "Toward a Phenomenology of Cinematic and Electronic Presence: The Scene of the Screen," *Post-Script* 10 (Fall 1990), pp. 50–59.

[27] See, for example, "Fragments for a History of the Human Body," Parts I, II, III, *Zone* vols. 3–5 (1989–90).

analogic quality of the photographic and cinematic into discrete pixels and bits of information that are transmitted serially, each bit discontinuous, discontiguous, and absolute—each bit "being in itself" even as it is part of a system. As well, unlike the cinema, the electronic is phenomenologically experienced not as a discrete, centered, *intentional projection* but rather as a simultaneous, dispersive, and *neural/"neutral" transmission*. Thus, electronic "presence" as it is experienced by the spectator/user is at one further remove from previous referential connections made between the body's signification and the world's concrete forms. Electronic "presence" neither asserts an objective possession of the world and self (as does the photographic) nor a centered and subjective spatiotemporal engagement with the world and others accumulated and projected as conscious and embodied experience (like the cinematic). Digital and schematic, abstracted from *reproducing* the empirical objectivity of "nature" that informs the photographic and from *presenting a representation* of individual embodied subjectivity that informs the cinematic, the electronic constructs and refers to a "virtual reality"—a meta-world in which ethical investment and value are located neither in concrete things nor in human lived-bodies but in *representation-in-itself*. As Guy Debord has eloquently and succinctly put it, our electronic culture experiences its historical moment as if "everything that was lived directly has moved away into a representation."[28]

Living virtual reality in a meta-world (of computer simulations or contemporary global banking systems, for example), far removed in reference from the lived-body (that still bleeds, that still psychically and physically suffers when it is abused), the spectator/user may experience an exhilarating liberation from the physical (and moral) gravity of the real world the body inhabits and is marked by. The materiality of the electronic digitizes existential *durée* and situation so that a centered and coherent investment in the lived-body is atomized and dispersed across various systems and networks that constitute temporality not as an *intentional flow of conscious experience* but as an *unselective transmission of random information*. The existential, bodily situation of "being-in-the-world" becomes itself digitized, becomes a conceptual and schematic space that is both compelling and inhospitable. That is, the lived-body cannot intelligibly inhabit it. It is hardly surprising that our various narratives (academic and popular)

---

[28] Guy Debord, *Society of the Spectacle* (Detroit: Black and Red, 1983), n.p.

301

are dominated by attempts to re-cognize the biological body as informed by a techno-logic that will enable it to live in the spaces our electronic culture has constructed, spaces that have engaged our consciousness as they have refused our bodies. Cyborgs, androids, and replicants occupy our thoughts, arouse our emotions, and superficially drive our narratives while human bodies within them are repetitiously (compulsively) dis-membered and dis-integrated: riddled with bullet holes, slashed by knives, burned and melted by fire and toxic substances.

In an important sense, *electronic space dis-embodies*. The non-dimensional, fractal-dimensional, two-dimensional, poly-dimensional, and binary superficiality of electronic space transforms what, in the cinema, becomes a world of imaginative and potential bodily habitation. Electronic space at once disorients and liberates the activity of consciousness from the gravitational pull and orientation of its hitherto embodied and grounded existence. This is a space that cannot and could not be inhabited by our bodies *as they are*. This is a space that denies or prosthetically transforms the spectator/user's human body so that subjectivity and affect "free float" or "free fall" or "free flow" across a horizontal/vertical grid. In what has been called "paraspace," "virtual space," and "cyberspace," the "interface subjectivity" is at once decentered and completely extroverted, completely alienated in a phenomenological structure of sensual and psychological experience that seems to belong to *no-body*.[29] It is within this context of the cultural proliferation and popularization of electronic technology that contemporary film theory first emerged and distinguished itself from "traditional" or "classical" film theory. Thus, it is not surprising that, until very recently, the spectator's body *as it is lived* has been subject to oversight by most contemporary theorists or that cinema (and the spectator) have been extroverted and objectified, and theorists alienated from their own embodied, subjective, and intentional activity of vision. What has been forgotten by the excessive objectivism of dominant poststructuralist paradigms is the facticity of the lived-body and subjective experience—and through them the radical grounds not only of the individual but also of the collective agency possible and necessary for the transformation of conventional and repressive institutions.

[29] This discussion of electronic space is elaborated more fully (in relation to both photography and cinema) in Sobchack, "Toward a Phenomenology of Cinematic and Electronic Presence: The Scene of the Screen."

It has been the radical project of the present work to recover the cinema from this objectification and alienation—and to recover for the spectator her lived-body, her subjectivity, her intentionality, and some measure of existential freedom and the social and political responsibility that goes with freedom's possibility.[30] Indeed, informing this project has been the sense—based on my own experience at the movies which, I think, is neither atypical nor deluded—that there is originality and individual freedom as well as cultural constraint in the film experience, and that both the film and spectator are subjects of vision (as well as objects for vision) who have common existential bonds to the world but unique bodily and intentional investments in it and perspectives on it. This is an insight that is no less meritorious for being intuitive—or, for that matter, simple. However, given the dominant context and turn of contemporary reflection on questions of cinema, for others to share this insight with me required rigorous elaboration.

The desire to describe my possibilities for visual originality and freedom and to recover my lived-body in the film experience so that I, too, can claim the ability to respond and, thus, responsibility for what I see, has led me, through phenomenological reflection, to the cinema's originality and freedom and to a discovery and recovery of its lived-body. Existential phenomenology (particularly as it is articulated as a *semiology of embodiment* by Maurice Merleau-Ponty) has provided a philosophical context and a method of radical reflection responsive to the film experience as I live it in ways that dominant theory has not. In this regard, I feel something like the heroine of Sally Potter's *Thriller* (1979), who says she is "searching for a theory that would explain her life and death." Phenomenological description, thematization, and interpretation have literally and materially "fleshed out" and existentially "situated" those partial descriptions of the film and spectator previously provided by film theory based on assumptions and interpretations this work would both challenge and complement. What emerges suggests a radical "dialectical ma-

---

[30] In relation to this intersection of existential phenomenology as a philosophy and method and political theory and praxis, the reader is directed to the following recent volumes: Scott Warren, *The Emergence of Dialectical Theory: Philosophy and Political Inquiry* (Chicago: Univ. of Chicago Press, 1984); Douglas Beck Low, *The Existential Dialectic of Marx and Merleau-Ponty* (New York: P. Lang, 1987); and Kerry H. Whiteside, *Merleau-Ponty and the Foundation of an Existential Politics* (Princeton, NJ: Princeton Univ. Press, 1988).

terialism" that is not antithetical to neo-Marxist or feminist projects but also challenges theoretical determinism.

As a philosophy of embodied experience and a method of investigating its structures, existential phenomenology itself could be seen as the lost—and grounding—"body" of the contemporary philosophy of "undoing." In its various modalities of interrogating and denying "presence" and the integrity of the thinking "subject," the latter's project has been to deconstruct the Cartesian proposition "I think, therefore I am." Existential phenomenology, however, has reconstructed the proposition in a way that admits presence, subjectivity, and integrity as they are always qualified by a particular (and always social) lived-body "being-in-the-world": "I see, therefore I am embodied."[31]

As philosophy and method, existential phenomenology has returned vision from its abstraction to its status as a lived and embodied activity that is constituting as well as constituted. As well, existential phenomenology has responded to the "lost" and unacknowledged side or modality of vision in the film experience. It has provided the means and the vocabulary to describe, thematize, and interpret the film not merely as an object for vision, but also as a subject of vision—a subject whose body is generally "objectively" invisible in its own activity of perceiving, expressing, and realizing its intentional projects in the world not only as visual but also as visible. The film's body has been recovered and re-cognized as more than an inanimate mechanism, as more than a deceitful and self-effacing "apparatus" used to delude and dominate those who encounter its visual and visible work. The film's body has been seen also as a finite and situated body engaged in its sensing and sense-making work in the world. Like our own, it is a body that, living perception and expression visually from the inside as "mine," cannot simultaneously live it visibly from the outside—except through the eyes of others.

Similarly, phenomenological reflection has led us to locate the spectator as uniquely situated and intentionally active in the process and production of cinematic vision. Invisible from the "outside," the

[31] For those who think this emphasis on vision itself problematic, this reconstruction could read: "I hear/smell/taste/feel, etc." The point to be made is that in the Cartesian formulation, thought and being are abstracted from the material conditions of embodiment, conditions of materiality that make of every subject also an object and allow for certain forms of reversibility between subjects and objects not only in our perceptions, but also in our representations.

spectator's introceptive process and production of vision occupies what visibly appears as a "passive" body in the film experience. Regarded from the inside, from the perspective of the subject of vision, that body is not passive or "empty." It is a lived-body, informed by its particular sensible experience and charged with its own intentional impetus. Lived from within, rather than seen from without, it is not so openly or continuously available for "takeover" by the film's visible vision. It holds its own place and is informed with a certain (if always partial) integrity of experience that asserts its differences as well as its similarities in the enactment of its own vision.

This is to say that the signs and meaning, the signification and significance of vision, as they are doubly and reversibly articulated in the dialectic of the film experience, are constantly negotiable. What objectively looks like the "same" viewing-view/viewed-view is only the same as it is "objectively" looked at. As our embodiments differ and our situations change, so the film's activity of sign production and its meaning change for us in our differently situated activity of looking, in our different intentions toward it. Thus, while the sedimented significations and meanings of our historical and cultural context set the limits of both the film's and the spectator's activities of sign production and interpretation, our individual situation and contingency establish the possibilities of our semiotic and hermeneutic freedom.

The paradox of this freedom in constraint, this possibility of invention within convention, is founded in the "essential" claims that existential phenomenology makes: that is, the universal finitude and situated nature of the body in existence (a condition that enables the intersubjective and the social), and the uniqueness of each lived-body's concrete finitude, material situation, and intentional dynamic (a condition that enables the personal and the individual). Here, I am reminded of "Pierre Menard: Author of Don Quixote," Jorge Luis Borges's wonderful affirmation of historical consciousness and the difference that, in existence, always overtakes and transforms the identical.[32] Objective word for objective word, identical with Cervantes's tutor-text as quoted in the short story, Menard's "re-written" excerpt from his Don Quixote is newly written nonetheless—not only for Pierre Menard and the fictional critic/narrator evaluating his

---

[32] Jorge Luis Borges, "Pierre Menard, Author of Don Quixote," trans. Anthony Bonner, in Borges, Ficciones (New York: Grove Press, 1962), pp. 45–55.

work, but also for both the story's writer and its readers. All occupy different lived-bodies and life-worlds than did Cervantes and his readers, and the sedimented signs that were "his" words produce new meanings in new cultural and historical contexts and are irrevocably altered from their first inscription to become not only "our" words but always uniquely "my" words.

Umberto Eco is illuminating in regard to this revision of language as always also inaugurating originality and a plenitude of meaning. In *A Theory of Semiotics* (and just before his "Theory of Sign Production"), the very last note to his "Theory of Codes" speaks of what Eco calls a "freedom of decoding" (itself articulated as an act of sign production). Such freedom, Eco says, is derived from the finite and situated context and contingency of the recipient of the message: "biological factors, economic occurrences, events and external interferences which appear as the unavoidable framework of every communicative relationship." This complex of existential and contingent factors, Eco tells us:

> are almost like the presence of "reality" (if so ambiguous an expression is permissible) which flexes and modulates the processes of communication. When Alice asks: "The question is whether you *can* make words mean so many different things," Humpty Dumpty's answer is "The question is *who is to* be the master". Once this point of view is accepted, one might well ask whether the communicative process is capable of subduing the circumstances in which it takes place.
>
> Communicative experience enables us to answer positively, if only insofar as circumstance, understood as the "real" basis of communication, is also translated constantly into a world of coding while for its own part communication, in its pragmatic dimension, produces behavioral habits which contribute to the changing of the circumstances.
>
> But there is one aspect which is more interesting from a semiotic point of view, according to which the circumstance can become an intentional element of communication. If the circumstance helps one to single out the subcodes by means of which the messages are disambiguated this means that rather than change messages or control their production, one can change their content by acting on the circumstances in which the message will be received. This is a revolutionary aspect of a semiotic endeavor. In an era in which mass communication often appears as the manifestation of a domination which makes sure of social control by planning the sending of messages, it remains pos-

sible (as in an ideal semiotic "guerilla warfare") to change the circumstances in the light of which the addressees will choose their own ways of interpretation. In opposition to a *strategy* of coding, which strives to render messages redundant in order to secure interpretation according to pre-established plans, one can trace a *tactic* of decoding where the message as expression form does not change but the addressee rediscovers his *freedom of decoding*.[33]

This "freedom of decoding" is familiar to us all. It is, indeed, what film theorists and critics call reading "against the grain," even as they assume that they are privileged in such an ability. In existence, however, we all read against the grain, "see" against the grain, as our experience of the world differs from the experience of others who offer their vision to us. If we recognize our unique embodiment and situation in the world as well as the cultural world we were born into and historically share, seeing the vision of another from a perspective unintended by him is as much a fact of being as is attempting to share his vision and understand his perspective. Thus, we do not have to teach spectators to "see" against the grain. Rather, we need to offer to their attention and reflection the existential fact of what they already, and prereflectively, do.

What is at stake in recognizing the double embodiment and double intentionality operative in the film experience, and accommodating the introceptive and subjective aspects of vision in objective description, is the very possibility of dialectical and dialogic exchange between two viewing subjects who share the finite and situated conditions of objective embodiment and also share their uniquely situated and finite existence in a common, if contested, cultural world. In the context of current theoretical practice, it is not only optimistic but also responsible to recognize that the spectator's uniquely situated and contingent vision intentionally shapes the signs and meaning of the film's vision as much as the film's uniquely situated and contingent vision intentionally shapes the spectator's.

Entailing two lived-bodies engaged in perception and its expres-

---

[33] Umberto Eco, *A Theory of Semiotics*, p. 150. Although Eco makes no reference to Michel de Certeau's formulation of and distinction between *strategies* and *tactics* first published in France in 1974, the relation between his discussion of the freedom of decoding and the way individuals negotiate and make original meaning within and among the institutions of everyday life seems hardly coincidental. See Michel de Certeau, *The Practice of Everyday Life*, trans. Steven Rendell (Berkeley: Univ. of California Press, 1984).

sion in the presence of each other, the film experience enables the potential communication of experience from one uniquely situated lived-body to another. It brings together in a common encounter two acts of vision and their respective productions of signs and meaning, two differentiated viewing-views/moving images that meet but do not precisely merge. Two "I's/eyes" converge in the visual activity of the film experience, each a historical and cultural existence and each visually and visibly intentionally directed toward the world "on a bias" and with a differently invested interest in perceiving it and expressing its significance.

In sum, phenomenological reflection has recovered for us what was there all along but theoretically neglected: the film's lived-body and the spectator's uniquely situated and embodied consciousness. This was not an easy or brief recovery, but it was a crucial one, for its "fleshing out" and "filling in" the film experience challenges the common notion of what constitutes "objective" description of that experience. Indeed, such a recovery suggests that what currently passes for objective description is what Roger Poole has criticized as an *inadequate* objectivity.[34] Any objective description of the experience of phenomena cannot be truly objective unless it also accommodates the subjective mode of that experience and addresses the life-world in which we live as sensible and significant beings.

The negativity and pessimism that inform most contemporary film theory and circumscribe the limits beyond which it has not been able to go is born less from the frustration of a revisionary and utopian impulse meeting a recalcitrant film culture than from an inadequate objectivity that has blinded itself to existential possibility and the subjective and embodied grounds that enable personal and social responsibility. In "Machines of the Visible," Jean-Luc Comolli tells us, "The cinematic image grasps only a small part of the visible; and it is a grasp which—provisional, contracted, fragmentary—bears in it its impossibility."[35] But the visible cinematic image also grasps the invisible, and it is a grasp that—provisional, prospective, co-herent—bears in it its possibility (and the recognition of our own possibility) for extension, expression, communication, and insight. In this regard, cinema is a perceptive and expressive medium that remands us

[34] Roger Poole, *Towards Deep Subjectivity* (London: Allen Lane/The Penguin Press, 1972).

[35] Jean-Luc Comolli, "Machines of the Visible," in *Film Theory and Criticism*, 3d ed., ed. Gerald Mast and Marshall Cohen (New York: Oxford Univ. Press, 1985), p. 760.

to ourselves and our very conditions of existence as both immanent and objective material and transcendent and subjective consciousness. It reminds us of the dialectical nature of our "being-in-the-world" as both subjects and objects, both for ourselves and as we are for others. Thus, Karl Marx notes in his early writings: "A being which is not the object of another being . . . presupposes that no objective being exists. . . . To be sensuous, i.e., to be real, is to be an object of sense, a sensuous object, and thus to have sensuous objects outside oneself, objects of one's sense perceptions."[36] Cinema is a sensuous object, but it also comes—and becomes—before us a sensing and sensual subject and, in the address of its eye, allows us to see what seems a visual impossibility: that we are at once subject and object, the seer and the seen. The philosophical and interpretive insight we gain from this engagement with cinema is not that the film does not and cannot see us although we can see "it." Rather, the cinema provides us with a philosophical model that gives us concrete and empirical insight into and makes objectively visible the reversible, dialectical, and social nature of our own subjective vision. As Merleau-Ponty puts it: "As soon as we see other seers . . . henceforth, through other eyes we are for ourselves fully visible. . . . For the first time, the seeing that I am is for me really visible; for the first time I appear to myself completely turned inside out under my own eyes."[37]

Cinema uniquely allows this philosphical turning, this objective and subjective insight into oneself and, remarkably, others. In Ridley Scott's *Blade Runner* (1982), Roy Baty (the technologically produced "replicant" who objectively asserts his subjective status throughout the film) speaks to the man who genetically and quite literally made his eyes and says with an irony that resonates through the viewing audience even if it is not fully understood, "If you could only see what I've seen with your eyes." The perceptive and expressive medium through which we engage the articulation of this seemingly impossible desire for intersubjectivity is the very medium through which this desire is visibly and objectively fulfilled.

[36] Karl Marx, "Economic and Philosophical Manuscripts (1844)," *Early Writings*, trans. Rodney Livingstone and Gregor Benton (New York: Vintage Books, 1975), p. 390.

[37] Maurice Merleau-Ponty, *The Visible and the Invisible*, trans. Alphonso Lingus (Evanston, IL: Northwestern Univ. Press, 1968), pp. 143–144.

Selected Bibliography

BOOKS

Agel, Henri. *Le Cinéma et le sacré*. Paris: Editions du Cerf, 1961.

————. *Poétique du cinéma*. Paris: Edition du Signe, 1973.

Allen, Jeffner, and Iris Marion Young, eds. *The Thinking Muse: Feminism and Modern French Philosophy*. Bloomington: Indiana Univ. Press, 1989.

Andrew, J. Dudley. *The Major Film Theories: An Introduction*. New York: Oxford Univ. Press, 1976.

————. *Concepts in Film Theory*. New York: Oxford Univ. Press, 1984.

Arnheim, Rudolf. *Film as Art*. Berkeley: Univ. of California Press, 1957.

Ayfre, Amédée. *Le Cinéma et sa vérité*. Paris: Editions du Cerf, 1969.

Bachelard, Gaston. *The Poetics of Space*. Trans. Maria Jolas. Boston: Beacon Press, 1969.

Balázs, Béla. *Theory of the Film: Character and Growth of a New Art*. Trans. Edith Bone. New York: Dover Publications, 1970.

Barral, Mary Rose. *Merleau-Ponty: The Role of the Body-Subject in Interpersonal Relations*. Pittsburgh: Duquesne Univ. Press, 1965.

Barthes, Roland. *Elements of Semiology*. Trans. Annette Lavers and Colin Smith. New York: Hill and Wang, 1964.

Bauman, Zygmunt. *Hemeneutics and Social Science*. New York: Columbia Univ. Press, 1978.

Bazin, André. *What Is Cinema?* Trans. Hugh Gray. Berkeley: Univ. of California Press, 1967.

————. *What Is Cinema? Volume II*. Trans. Hugh Gray. Berkeley: Univ. of California Press, 1971.

Belsey, Catherine. *Critical Practice*. New York: Methuen Press, 1980.

Benveniste, Emil. *Problems in General Linguistics*. Miami: Univ. of Miami Press, 1971.

Bettetini, Gianfranco. *The Language and Technique of the Film*. Trans. David Osmond-Smith. The Hague: Mouton, 1973.

Biró, Yvette. *Profane Mythology: The Savage Mind of the Cinema*. Trans. Imre Goldstein. Bloomington: Indiana Univ. Press, 1982.

Brakhage, Stan. *Metaphors on Vision*. Ed. P. Adams Sitney. New York: Film Culture, 1963.

Branigan, Edward. *Point of View in the Cinema: A Theory of Narration and Subjectivity in Classical Film*. New York: Mouton, 1984.

Burch, Noël. *Theory of Film Practice*. Trans. Helen R. Lane. New York: Praeger, 1973.

311

Cavell, Stanley. *The World Viewed: Reflections on the Ontology of Film*, enl. ed. Cambridge: Harvard Univ. Press, 1979.

Cohn, Dorrit. *Transparent Minds: Narrative Modes for Presenting Consciousness in Fiction*. Princeton, NJ: Princeton Univ. Press, 1978.

Coward, Rosalind, and John Ellis. *Language and Materialism: Developments in Semiology and the Theory of the Subject*. Boston: Routledge and Kegan Paul, 1977.

de Certeau, Michel. *The Practice of Everyday Life*. Trans. Steven Rendell. Berkeley: Univ. of California Press, 1984.

de Lauretis, Teresa. *Alice Doesn't: Feminism, Semiotics, Cinema*. Bloomington: Indiana Univ. Press, 1984.

————. *Technologies of Gender: Essays on Theory, Film, and Fiction*. Bloomington: Indiana Univ. Press, 1987.

de Lauretis, Teresa, and Stephen Heath, eds. *The Cinematic Apparatus*. New York: St. Martin's Press, 1980.

Deleuze, Gilles. *Cinema 1: The Movement-Image*. Trans. Hugh Tomlinson and Barbara Habberjam. Minneapolis: Univ. of Minnesota Press, 1986.

————. *Cinema 2: The Time-Image*. Trans. Hugh Tomlinson and Barbara Habberjam. Minneapolis: Univ. of Minnesota Press, 1989.

Derrida, Jacques. *Speech Phenomena and Other Essays on Husserl's Theory of Signs*. Trans. David B. Allison. Evanston, IL: Northwestern Univ. Press, 1973.

————. *Writing and Difference*. Trans. Alan Bass. Chicago: Univ. of Chicago Press, 1978.

DeSaussure, Ferdinand. *Course in General Linguistics*. Trans. Wade Baskin. New York: McGraw-Hill, 1966.

Doane, Mary Ann. *The Desire to Desire: The Woman's Film of the 1940s*. Bloomington: Indiana Univ. Press, 1987.

Dreyfus, Hubert L., and Paul Rabinow. *Michel Foucault: Beyond Structuralism and Hermeneutics*. 2d ed. Chicago: Univ. of Chicago Press, 1982.

Dufrenne, Mikel. *The Phenomenology of Aesthetic Experience*. Trans. Edward S. Casey et al. Evanston, IL: Northwestern Univ. Press, 1973.

Eco, Umberto. *A Theory of Semiotics*. Bloomington: Indiana Univ. Press, 1979.

Freeman, Eugene. *The Categories of Charles Pierce*. Chicago: The Open Court Publishing Co., 1934.

Gadamer, Hans-Georg. *Truth and Method*. New York: The Seabury Press, 1975.

Ghandi, Ramchandra. *Presuppositions of Human Communication*. Delhi: Oxford Univ. Press, 1974.

Goffman, Erving. *Frame Analysis: An Essay on the Organization of Experience*. New York: Harper Colophon Books, 1974.

Habermas, Jürgen. *Communication and the Evolution of Society*. Trans. Thomas McCarthy. Boston: Beacon Press, 1979.

Hak Kyng Cha, Theresa, ed. *Apparatus*. New York: Tanam Press, 1980.

Heaton, J. M. *The Eye: Phenomenology and Psychology of Function and Disorder*. London: Tavistock Publications, Ltd., 1968.

Heelan, Patrick A. *Space-Perception and the Philosophy of Science*. Berkeley: Univ. of California Press, 1983.

Held, David. *Introduction to Critical Theory: Horkheimer to Habermas*. Berkeley: Univ. of California Press, 1980.

Holenstein, Elmar. *Roman Jackobson's Approach to Language: Phenomenological Structuralism* trans. Catherine Schelbert and Tarcisius Schelbert. Blooming-ton: Indiana Univ. Press, 1976.

Husserl, Edmund. *Ideas: General Introduction to Pure Phenomenology*. Trans. W. R. Boyce Gibson. London: G. Allen and Unwin, 1931.

———. *Cartesian Meditations*. Trans. Dorion Cairns. The Hague: Martinus Nijhoff, 1960.

———. *The Paris Lectures*. Trans. Peter Koestenbaum. The Hague: Martinus Nijhoff, 1975.

Ihde, Don. *Sense and Significance*. Duquesne Studies Philosophical Series, Vol. 31. Pittsburgh: Duquesne Univ. Press, 1973.

———. *Listening and Voice: A Phenomenology of Sound*. Athens: Ohio Univ. Press, 1976.

———. *Experimental Phenomenology: An Introduction*. New York: Paragon Books, 1979.

———. *Existential Technics*. Albany: State Univ. of New York Press, 1983.

———. *Technology and the Lifeworld: From Garden to Earth*. Bloomington: Indiana Univ. Press, 1990.

Iser, Wolfgang. *The Act of Reading: A Theory of Aesthetic Response*. Baltimore: Johns Hopkins Univ. Press, 1978.

Kawin, Bruce. *Mindscreen: Bergman, Godard, and First-Person Film*. Princeton, NJ: Princeton Univ. Press, 1978.

Keen, Ernest. *A Primer in Phenomenological Psychology*. New York: Holt, Rine-hart and Winston, 1975.

Kern, Stephen. *The Culture of Time and Space 1880–1918*. Cambridge: Harvard Univ. Press, 1983.

Kockelmans, Joseph L., ed. *Phenomenology: The Philosophy of Edmund Husserl and Its Interpretation*. Garden City, NY: Doubleday Anchor Books, 1967.

Kracauer, Siegfried. *Theory of Film: The Redemption of Physical Reality*. New York: Oxford Univ. Press, 1960.

Kuhn, Annette. *Women's Pictures: Feminism and Cinema*. London: Routledge and Kegan Paul, 1982.

Lacan, Jacques. *The Language of the Self: The Function of Language in Psycho-analysis*. Trans. with notes and commentary by Anthony Wilden. New York: Delta Books, 1968.

313

Lacan, Jacques. *Ecrits: A Selection*. Trans. Alan Sheridan. New York: W. W. Norton, 1977.

―――. *The Four Fundamental Concepts of Psycho-Analysis*. Ed. Jacques-Alain Miller. Trans. Alan Sheridan. New York: W. W. Norton, 1981.

Langan, Thomas. *Merleau-Ponty's Critique of Reason*. New Haven: Yale Univ. Press, 1966.

Lanigan, Richard L. *Speaking and Semiology: Maurice Merleau-Ponty's Phenomenological Theory of Existential Communication*. The Hague: Mouton Press, 1972.

―――. *Speech Act Phenomenology*. The Hague: Martinus Nijhoff, 1977.

―――. *Phenomenology of Communication: Merleau-Ponty's Thematics in Communicology and Semiology*. Pittsburgh: Duquesne Univ. Press, 1988.

Laplanche, J., and J.-B. Pontalis. *The Language of Psycho-Analysis*. Trans. Donald Nicholson-Smith. New York: W. W. Norton, 1973.

Lauer, J. Quentin. *The Triumph of Subjectivity: An Introduction to Transcendental Phenomenology*. New York: Fordham Univ. Press, 1958.

Lemaire, Anika. *Jacques Lacan*. Trans. David Macey. London: Routledge and Kegan Paul, 1979.

Linden, George. *Reflections on the Screen*. Belmont, CA: Wadsworth, 1970.

Lotman, Jurij. *Semiotics of Cinema*. Trans. Mark E. Suino. Ann Arbor: Univ. of Michigan Press, Michigan Slavic Contributions, 1976.

Low, Douglas Beck. *The Existential Dialectic of Marx and Merleau-Ponty*. New York: P. Lang, 1987.

Lowe, Donald M. *History of Bourgeois Perception*. Chicago: Univ. of Chicago Press, 1982.

Madison, Gary Brent. *The Phenomenology of Merleau-Ponty: A Search for the Limits of Consciousness*. Athens: Ohio Univ. Press, 1981.

Mast, Gerald. *Film/Cinema/Movie: A Theory of Experience*. New York: Harper and Row, 1977.

Merleau-Ponty, Maurice. *Phenomenology of Perception*. Trans. Colin Smith. London: Routledge and Kegan Paul, 1962.

―――. *In Praise of Philosophy*. Trans. John Wild and James M. Edie. Evanston, IL: Northwestern Univ. Press, 1963.

―――. *The Primacy of Perception*. Ed. James M. Edie. Evanston, IL: Northwestern Univ. Press, 1964.

―――. *Signs*. Trans. Richard C. McCleary. Evanston, IL: Northwestern Univ. Press, 1964.

―――. *The Visible and the Invisible*. Ed. Claude Lefort. Trans. Alphonso Lingus. Evanston, IL: Northwestern Univ. Press, 1968.

―――. *The Essential Writings of Merleau-Ponty*. Ed. Alden L. Fisher. New York: Harcourt, Brace and World, 1969.

―――. *Themes from the Lectures at the College de France, 1952–1960*. Trans. John O'Neill. Evanston, IL: Northwestern Univ. Press, 1970.

————. *Consciousness and the Acquisition of Language.* Trans. Hugh J. Silverman. Evanston, IL: Northwestern Univ. Press, 1973.

————. *The Prose of the World.* Ed. Claude Lefort. Trans. John O'Neill. Evanston, IL: Northwestern Univ. Press, 1973.

————. *The Structure of Behavior.* Trans. Alden L. Fisher. Boston: Beacon Press, 1983.

Metz, Christian. *Film Language: A Semiotics of the Cinema.* Trans. Michael Taylor. New York: Oxford Univ. Press, 1974.

————. *Language and Cinema.* Trans. Donna Jean Umiker-Sebeok. The Hague: Mouton, 1974.

————. *The Imaginary Signifier: Psychoanalysis and the Cinema.* Trans. Celia Britton, Annwyl Williams, Ben Brewster, and Alfred Guzzetti. Bloomington: Indiana Univ. Press, 1982.

Meunier, Jean-Pierre. *Les Structures de l'experience filmique: l'identification filmique.* Louvain: Librairie Universitaire, 1969.

Mitry, Jean. *Esthétique et psychologie du cinéma.* Vol. 1. Paris: Editions Universitaires, 1963.

————. *Esthétique et psychologie du cinéma.* Vol. 2. Paris: Editions Universitaires, 1965.

Munier, Roger. *Contre l'image.* Paris: Gallimard, 1963.

Münsterberg, Hugo. *The Film: A Psychological Study, The Silent Photoplay in 1916.* 1916; rpt. New York: Dover Press, 1970.

Nichols, Bill. *Ideology and the Image: Social Representation in the Cinema and Other Media.* Bloomington: Indiana Univ. Press, 1981.

Palmer, Richard E. *Hermeneutics: Interpretation Theory in Schleiermacher, Dilthey, Heidegger, and Gadamer.* Evanston, IL: Northwestern Univ. Press, 1969.

Penley, Constance, ed. *Feminism and Film Theory.* New York: Routledge, 1988.

Poole, Roger. *Towards Deep Subjectivity.* London: Allen Lane/The Penguin Press, 1972.

Ricoeur, Paul. *Fallible Man.* Trans. C. Kelbley. Chicago: Henry Regnery Co., 1965.

————. *Freud and Philosophy: An Essay on Interpretation.* Trans. Denis Savage. New Haven: Yale Univ. Press, 1970.

Roche, Maurice. *Phenomenology, Language, and the Social Sciences.* London: Routledge and Kegan Paul, 1973.

Sacks, Oliver. *The Man Who Mistook His Wife for a Hat and Other Clinical Tales.* New York: Summit Books, 1985.

Schmidt, James. *Maurice Merleau-Ponty: Between Phenomenology and Structuralism.* New York: St. Martin's Press, 1985.

Schrag, Calvin O. *Experience and Being: Prolegomena to a Future Ontology.* Evanston, IL: Northwestern Univ. Press, 1969.

————. *Radical Reflection and the Origin of the Human Sciences.* West Lafayette, IN: Purdue Univ. Press, 1980.

Schutz, Alfred. *The Phenomenology of the Social World*. Trans. George Walsh and Frederick Lehnert. Evanston: Northwestern Univ. Press, 1967.

Silverman, Kaja. *The Subject of Semiotics*. New York: Oxford Univ. Press, 1983.

Slade, Mark. *Language of Change: Moving Images of Man*. Toronto: Holt, Rinehart and Winston of Canada, 1970.

Spiegelberg, Herbert. *The Phenomenological Movement: A Historical Introduction*, 2d ed. 2 vols. The Hague: Martinus Nijhoff, 1965.

Straus, Erwin. *The Primary World of Senses: A Vindication of Sensory Experience*. Trans. Jacob Needleman. London: The Free Press of Glencoe/Collier-Macmillan Ltd., 1963.

————. *Phenomenological Psychology*. Trans. Erling Eng. New York: Basic Books, 1966.

Studlar, Gaylyn. *In the Realm of Pleasure: Von Sternberg, Dietrich, and the Masochistic Aesthetic*. Urbana: Univ. of Illinois Press, 1988.

Telotte, J. P. *Voices in the Dark: The Narrative Patterns of Film Noir*. Urbana: Univ. of Illinois Press, 1989.

Thévenay, Pierre. *What Is Phenomenology?* Trans. James M. Edie, Charles Courtney, and Paul Brockelman. Ed. James M. Edie. Chicago: Quadrangle Books, 1962.

Tyler, Parker. *The Shadow of an Airplane Climbs the Empire State Building: A World Theory of Film*. Garden City, NY: Anchor Books, 1973.

Warren, Scott. *The Emergence of Dialectical Theory: Philosophy and Political Inquiry*. Chicago: Univ. of Chicago Press, 1984.

Whiteside, Kerry H. *Merleau-Ponty and the Foundation of an Existential Politics*. Princeton: Princeton Univ. Press, 1988.

Wolff, Janet. *Hermeneutic Philosophy and the Sociology of Art*. London: Routlege and Kegan Paul, 1975.

Wollen, Peter. *Signs and Meaning in the Cinema*. New and enlarged ed. Bloomington: Indiana Univ. Press, 1972.

Wood, David, and Robert Bernasconi, eds. *Derrida and "Différance."* Evanston, IL: Northwestern Univ. Press, 1988.

Young, Iris Marion. *Throwing Like A Girl and Other Essays in Feminist Philosophy and Social Theory*. Bloomington: Indiana Univ. Press, 1990.

Zaner, Richard M. *The Way of Phenomenology: Criticism as a Philosophical Discipline*. New York: Pegasus, 1970.

————. *The Problem of Embodiment: Some Contributions to a Phenomenology of the Body*, 2d ed. The Hague: Martinus Nijhoff, 1971.

Articles

Allen, Jeffner. "Through the Wild Region: An Essay in Phenomenological Feminism." *Review of Existential Psychology and Psychiatry* 18, nos. 1–3 (1982–1983), pp. 241–256.

Altman, Charles F. "Psychoanalysis and Cinema: The Imaginary Discourse," *Quarterly Review of Film Studies* 2 (August 1977), pp. 157–272.

Anderson, Barbara. "Eye Movement and Cinematic Perception." *Journal of the University Film Association* 32 (Winter-Spring 1980), pp. 23–26.

Andrew, J. Dudley. "Film Analysis or Film Theory: To Step Beyond Semiotics," *Quarterly Review of Film Studies* 2 (February 1977), pp. 33–41.

———. "The Neglected Tradition of Phenomenology in Film Theory." *Wide Angle* 2, no. 2 (1978), pp. 44–49.

———. "Hemeneutics and Cinema: The Issue of History." *Studies in the Literary Imagination* 19, no. 1 (Spring 1986), pp. 21–38.

Baudry, Jean-Louis. "Ideological Effects of the Basic Cinematographic Apparatus." Trans. Alan Williams. *Film Quarterly* 28 (Winter 1974–1975), pp. 39–47.

———. "The Apparatus." Trans. Jean Andrews and Bertrand Augst. *camera obscura* 1 (Fall 1976), pp. 104–126.

Berger, Carole. "Viewing as Action: Film and Reader Response Criticism." *Literature/Film Quarterly* 6 (Spring 1978), pp. 144–151.

Berger, Peter, and Stanley Pullberg. "Reification and the Sociological Critique of Consciousness." *History and Theory* 4 (1965), pp. 196–211.

Bonitzer, Pascal. "Partial Vision: Film and the Labyrinth." Trans. Fabrice Ziolkowski. *Wide Angle* 4, no. 4 (1981), pp. 56–63.

Brinkley, Alan B. "Toward a Phenomenological Aesthetic of Cinema." *Aesthetics II, Tulane Studies in Philosophy*, Vol. 20 (New Orleans: Tulane Univ. Press, 1971), pp. 1–17.

Brunetta, Gian Piero. "Pour une sémiotique intégré des signes cinématographiques." In *A Semotic Landscape/Panorama sémiotique*. Ed. Seymour Chatman, Umberto Eco, Jean-Marie Klinkenberg. The Hague: Mouton, 1979, pp. 844–847.

Carr, David. "Maurice Merleau-Ponty: Incarnate Consciousness." In *Existential Philosophers: Kierkegaard to Merleau-Ponty*. Ed. George Alfred Schrader, Jr. New York: McGraw-Hill, 1967, pp. 369–429.

Casebier, Allan. "Representations of Reality and Reality of Representation in Contemporary Film Theory." *Persistence of Vision* 5 (Spring 1987), pp. 36–43.

Comolli, Jean-Luc, and Jean Narboni. "Cinema/Ideology/Criticism." Trans. Susan Bennett. In *Movies and Methods*. Ed. Bill Nichols. Berkeley: Univ. of California Press, 1978, pp. 22–30.

Copjec, Joan. "The Anxiety of the Influencing Machine." *October* 23 (1983), pp. 43–59.

Crawford, Larry. "Looking, Film, Painting: The Trickster's In Site/In Sight/Insight/Incite." *Wide Angle* 5, no. 3 (1983), pp. 64–69.

Crow, Bryan K. "Talking About Film: A Phenomenological Study of Film Signification." In *Phenomenological Research in Rhetoric, Language, and Commu-*

nication. Ed. Stanley Deetz. Doctoral Honors Seminar Proceedings. Southern Illinois Univ. at Carbondale, 1979, pp. 4–15.

Danto, Arthur C. "Moving Pictures." *Quarterly Review of Film Studies* 4 (Winter 1979), pp. 1–21.

Dayan, Daniel. "The Tutor-Code of Classical Cinema." *Film Quarterly* 28 (Fall 1974), pp. 22–31.

Dufrenne, Mikel. "Comment peut-on aller au cinéma?" *Revue d'Esthetique* 26 (1973), pp. 371–382.

Eberwein, Robert T. "Spectator-Viewer." *Wide Angle* 2, no. 2 (1978), pp. 4–9.

———. "The Filmic Dream and Point of View." *Literature/Film Quarterly* 8, no. 3 (1980), pp. 197–203.

Eco, Umberto. "Pierce and the Semiotic Foundations of Openness: Signs as Texts and Texts as Signs." In his *The Role of the Reader: Explorations in the Semiotics of Texts.* Bloomington: Indiana Univ. Press, 1979, pp. 175–199.

Eikhenbaum, Boris. "Problems of Film Stylistics." Trans. Thomas Aman. *Screen* 15 (Autumn 1974), pp. 7–32.

Habermas, Jürgen. "Systematically Distorted Communication." In *Critical Sociology.* Ed. Paul Connerton. London: Penguin Books, 1976, pp. 348–362.

Haraway, Donna. "A Manifesto for Cyborgs." *Socialist Review* 80 (1985), pp. 65–107.

Harrell, Jean C. "Phenomenology of Film Music." *Journal of Value Inquiry* 14 (1980), pp. 23–34.

Heath, Stephen. "Notes on Suture." *Screen* 18 (Winter 1977–1978), pp. 48–76.

———. "Difference." *Screen* 19 (Autumn 1978), pp. 51–112.

Heidegger, Martin. "The Question Concerning Technology." Trans. William Lovitt. In *Martin Heidegger: Basic Writings.* Ed. David Farrell Krell. New York: Harper and Row, 1977, pp. 287–317.

Ihde, Don. "The Experience of Technology." *Cultural Hermeneutics* 2 (1974), pp. 267–279.

Jarvie, Ian. "Philosophers at the Movies: Metaphysics, Aesthetics, and Popularization." *Persistence of Vision* 5 (Spring 1987), pp. 74–106.

Jenkins, Bruce. "Structures of Perceptual Engagement in Film: Toward a Technology of Embodiment." *Film Reader* 2 (Evanston, IL: Northwestern Univ. Press, 1977), pp. 141–146.

Kennedy, John M. "Pictures and the Blind." *Journal of the University Film Association* 32 (Winter-Spring 1980), pp. 11–22.

Kindem, Gorham A. "Pierce's Semiotic Phenomenalism and Film." *Quarterly Review of Film Studies* 4 (Winter 1979), pp. 61–69.

Klinkenberg, Jean-Marie. "Communication et signification: l'unité de la sémiologie." In *A Semiotic Landscape/Panorama sémiotique.* Ed. Seymour Chatman, Umberto Eco, Jean-Marie Klinkenberg. The Hague: Mouton, 1979, pp. 288–294.

Kockelmans, Joseph J. "Merleau-Ponty on Space Perception and Space." In

Phenomenology and the Natural Sciences: Essays and Translations. Evanston, IL: Northwestern Univ. Press, 1970, pp. 274–311.

Kristéva, Julia. "Ellipsis on Dread and the Specular Seduction." Trans. Dolores Burdick. *Wide Angle* 3, no. 3 (1979), pp. 42–47.

Lacan, Jacques. "The Mirror-Phase as formative of the I." Trans. Jean Roussel. *New Left Review* 51 (September-October 1968), pp. 71–77.

———. "Merleau-Ponty: In Memoriam." Trans. Wilfried Ver Eecke and Dirk De Schutter. *Review of Existential Psychology and Psychiatry* 18, nos. 1–3 (1982–1983), pp. 73–81.

Lanigan, Richard L. "Merleau-Ponty's Phenomenology of Communication." *Philosophy Today*, 14 (Summer 1970), pp. 79–88.

———. "Communication Models in Philosophy." In *Communications Yearbook III*. Ed. Dan Nimmo. New Brunswick, NJ: Transaction Books, 1979, pp. 29–49.

———. "The Phenomenological Foundations of Semiology." In *A Semiotic Landscape/Panorama sémiotique*. Ed. Seymour Chatman, Umberto Eco, Jean-Marie Klinkenberg. The Hague: Mouton, 1979, pp. 304–308.

———. "The Phenomenology of Human Communication." *Philosophy Today* 23 (1979), pp. 3–15.

———. "A Semiotic Metatheory of Human Communication." *Semiotica* 27, no. 4 (1979), pp. 293–305.

———. "Semiotic Phenomenology: A Theory of Human Communication Praxis." *Journal of Applied Communication Research* 10 (Spring 1982), pp. 62–73.

Levaco, Ronald. "Eikhenbaum, Inner Speech and Film Stylistics." *Screen* 15 (Winter 1974–1975), pp. 47–58.

Lewis, Brian. "Jean Mitry on Film Language." *SubStance*, 9 (1974), pp. 5–14.

———. "The Question of Cinematic 'Essence': A Phenomenological Model of Representational Film Experience." *Wide Angle* 4, no. 4 (1981), pp. 50–54.

Marx, Karl. "Economic and Philosophical Manuscripts." In *Early Writings*. Trans. Rodney Livingstone and Gregor Benton. New York: Vintage Books, 1975, pp. 279–400.

McCarthy, T. A. "A Theory of Communicative Competence." In *Critical Sociology*. Ed. Paul Connerton. London: Penguin Books, 1976, pp. 470–497.

Merleau-Ponty, Maurice. "What Is Phenomenology?" Trans. John F. Bannan. *Cross Currents* 6 (Winter 1956), pp. 59–70.

———. "The Film and the New Psychology." In *Sense and Non-Sense*. Trans. Hubert L. Dreyfus and Patricia Allen Dreyfus. Evanston, IL: Northwestern Univ. Press, 1964, pp. 48–59.

———. "The Experience of Others." Trans. Fred Evans and Hugh J. Silverman. *Review of Existential Psychology and Psychiatry* 18, nos. 1–3 (1982–1983), pp. 33–63.

Merleau-Ponty, Maurice. "Phenomenology and Psychoanalysis: Preface to Hesnard's *L'Oeuvre de Freud*." Trans. Alden L. Fisher. *Review of Existential Psychology and Psychiatry* 18, nos. 1–3 (1982–1983), pp. 67–72.

Metz, Christian. "Current Problems of Film Theory: Christian Metz on Jean Mitry's *L'Esthétique et psychologie du cinéma*, Volume II." Trans. Diana Matias. *Screen* 14 (Spring/Summer 1973), pp. 40–87.

Miclau, Paul. "Deux antimonies sémiotiques: immanent/transcendant, clos/ouvert." In *A Semiotic Landscape/Panorama sémiotique*. Ed. Seymour Chatman, Umberto Eco, Jean-Marie Klinkenberg. The Hague: Mouton, 1979, pp. 329–332.

Miller, Jacques-Alain. "Suture (elements of the logic of the signifier)." *Screen* 18 (Winter 1977–1978), pp. 24–34.

Mulvey, Laura. "Visual Pleasure and Narrative Cinema." *Screen* 16 (Autumn 1975), pp. 6–18.

Munier, Roger. "The Fascinating Image." *Diogenes* 38 (1962), pp. 85–94.

Olkowski, Dorothea. "Merleau-Ponty's Freudianism: From the Body of Consciousness to the Body of Flesh. *Review of Existential Psychology and Psychiatry* 18, nos. 1–3 (1982–83), pp. 97–116.

Oudart, Jean-Pierre. "Cinema and Suture." *Screen* 18 (Winter 1977–1978), pp. 35–47.

Ousley, J. Douglas, and Kolker, R. P. "A Phenomenology of Cinematic Time and Space." *British Journal of Aesthetics* 13 (1973), pp. 388–396.

Peritore, N. Patrick. "Descriptive Phenomenology and Film: An Introduction." *Journal of the University Film Association* 29 (Winter 1977), pp. 3–6.

Pontalis, J. B. "The Problem of the Unconscious in Merleau-Ponty's Thought." Trans. Wilfried Ver Eecke and Michael Greer. *Review of Existential Psychology and Psychiatry* 18, nos. 1–3 (1982–83), pp. 83–96.

Rothman, William. "Against 'The System of the Suture'." *Film Quarterly* 29 (Fall 1975), pp. 45–50.

Sesonske, Alexander. "Cinema Space." In *Explorations in Phenomenology*. Ed. David Carr and Edward S. Casey. The Hague: Mouton, 1973, pp. 399–409.

Silverman, Hugh J. "Merleau-Ponty's New Beginning: Preface to the Experience of Others." *Review of Existential Psychology and Psychiatry* 18, nos. 1–3 (1982–1983), pp. 25–31.

Skoller, Donald. "Aspects of Cinematic Consciousness." *Film Comment* 8 (September-October 1972), pp. 41–51.

Small, Edward S. "Introduction: Cinevideo and Mental Images." *Journal of the University Film Association* 32 (Winter-Spring 1980), pp. 3–9.

Sobchack, Vivian. "Towards Inhabited Space: The Semiotic Structure of Camera Movement in the Cinema." *Semiotica* 41 (1982), pp. 317–335.

———. "Inscribing Ethical Space: Ten Propositions on Death, Representation, and Documentary." *Quarterly Review of Film Studies* 9, no. 4 (Fall 1984), pp. 283–300.

————. "Postfuturism." In *Screening Space: The American Science Fiction Film.* New York: Ungar Press, 1987, pp. 223–305.

————. "The Scene of the Screen. Beitrag zu einer Phänomenologie der ⟩Gegenwärtigkeit⟨ im Film und in den elektronischen Medien." Trans. H. U. Gumbrecht. In *Materialität der Kommunikation.* Ed. H. U. Grumbrecht and K. Ludwig Pfeiffer. Frankfurt am Main: Suhrkamp, 1988, pp. 416–428, in English as "Toward a Phenomenology of Cinematic and Electronic Presence: The Scene of the Screen." *Post-Script* 10 (Fall 1990), pp. 50–59.

————. "The Active Eye: A Phenomenology of Cinematic Vision." *Quarterly Review of Film and Video* 12 (1990), pp. 21–36.

————. " 'Surge and Splendor': A Phenomenology of the Hollywood Historical Epic." *Representations* 29 (Winter 1990), pp. 24–49.

Spellerberg, James. "Technology and Ideology in the Cinema." *Quarterly Review of Film Studies* 2 (August 1977), pp. 288–301.

Spiegelberg, Herbert. "Husserl's Phenomenology and Existentialism." *The Journal of Philosophy,* 57 (January 1960), pp. 62–74.

Stern, Lesley. "Point of View: The Blind Spot." *Film Reader* 4 (1979), pp. 214–236.

Wild, John. "Existentialism as a Philosophy." *The Journal of Philosophy* 57 (January 1960), pp. 45–62.

Willemen, Paul. "Reflections on Eikhenbaum's Concept of Internal Speech in the Cinema." *Screen* 15 (Winter 1974–1975), pp. 59–70.

Wollheim, Richard. "The Cabinet of Dr. Lacan." *New York Review of Books,* 25 January 1979, pp. 36–45.

Young, Iris M. "Pregnant Subjectivity and the Limits of Existential Phenomenology." In *Descriptions.* Ed. Don Ihde and Hugh J. Silverman. Albany: State Univ. of New York Press, 1985, pp. 25–34.

UNPUBLISHED MATERIALS

Andrew, Dudley. "A Prolegomena for a Phenomenology of Indentification in Cinema." Society for Cinema Studies Annual Convention, San Francisco. March 1979.

Knee, Thomas Clark. "A Dialogical Investigation of the Phenomenon of the Human Body." Diss. Duquesne Univ., 1972.

Lanigan, Richard L. "Phenomenology and Semiotic Communication." Workshop on "Phenomenology and Communication Theory." Annual Conference of the Society for Phenomenology and Existential Philosophy, Pittsburgh. November 1978.

Oswald, Laura. "The Case for Subjectivity in First Person Cinema." Society for Cinema Studies Annual Convention, New York City. April 1981.

Peterson, Eric E. "Performing Art as Semiotic Play." Fourth Annual Meeting of the Semiotic Society of America, Bloomington. October 1979.

Index

"address of the eye": *See* eye: address of the

aesthetics, and cinematic technology, 248–50

Agel, Henri, xv, 29n

Allen, Jeffner, 148, 149

Amengual, Barthélémy, 232, 232–33n

Andrew, Dudley, 20

Antonioni, Michelangelo, 231n, 288n

"Anxiety of the Influencing Machine, The" (Copjec), 263–65

Arnheim, Rudolf, 248, 249, 255

attention, 71–72, 89–90, 240–41, 243–44

authority, perceptual, 228

autobiographical function of film, 168, 216, 225, 229, 230, 238, 271

Ayfre, Amédée, xv

Balázs, Béla, 112, 186

Ballet Méchanique (Léger), 209

Barral, Mary Rose, 64, 69

Barry Lyndon (Kubrick), 225

Baudrillard, Jean, 292–93, 295

Baudry, Jean-Louis, 169, 181, 264, 265, 269, 270, 271, 276–77

Bauman, Zygmunt, 23

Bazin, André, xv

Beauvoir, Simone de, 149

Benveniste, Emile, 270

Bergman, Ingmar, 188

Bergson, Henri, 30, 31

Birth of a Nation, The (Griffith), 253

Blade Runner (Scott), 309

blindness, 78, 79–80, 94–95. *See also* visual perception

"Body in Its Sexual Being, The" (Merleau-Ponty), 150

body. *See* Embodiment; film's body; human body; lived body

Bordwell, David, 232

Borges, Jorge Luis, 305

Brakhage, Stan, 90–91, 92, 96, 97, 98

Branigan, Edward, 233

Butler, Judith, 150–51

camera: as film's perceptive organ, 170, 183, 196, 206, 209, 222–24, 299; as mechanical eye, 184, 201, 202, 213; perceptive competence of, 22, 209; relation to filmmaker, 177, 183–84, 185, 186, 187, 193, 195, 196, 202, 203

camera-world hermeneutic relation, 195

Carr, David, 76, 77

Certeau, Michel de, 307n

character, in a film, 225–27

chiasmus, 4. *See also* reversibility

"Child's Relation with Others, The" (Merleau-Ponty), 115, 123

Cinema 1: The Movement-Image (Deleuze), 30

Cinema 2: The Time-Image (Deleuze), 30

cinema. *See* film

cinematic apparatus, 17, 18, 162, 167–71, 216, 219, 221, 265–66, 304; as the film's body, 203, 205, 206, 208–12, 218; function of, 215–16, 250; historical development of, 248–59; negative or reductive view of, 224–25, 266; paranoid descriptions of, 263–70; relation of filmmaker to, 215. *See also* camera; frame; projector; screen, cinematic

cinematic communication, 6, 8, 9, 13, 14, 15, 17, 20, 51, 262, 290; intersubjective basis of, 5; instrument-mediated, 168, 174; system code of, 278–84

cinematic embodiment. *See* film's body

cinematic finitude, 59

cinematic identification, 161, 232, 235–36, 262, 265, 269, 273, 286, 296

cinematic mediation, 191–203

cinematic perception, 193; double nature of, 4, 5, 10, 18–19, 23–25, 57, 172–73; phenomenological interpretation of, 260–62

323

gendered, 143–45; as ground of language, 41, 73–76, 104, 273n; history of, 251–52; "in pieces" (*le corps morcelé*), 111; instrumentality of, 213–14; and intentionality, 39–40, 63, 67; materiality of, xvi, 23, 220, 224; movement, 59, 64, 151–57, 161; as object, 153–58, 219n, 246; radical semiosis of, xv, 65; and sexual difference, 145–48; and spatial situation, 151–59, 210–11; as synaesthetic and synoptic, 76, 82, 83–85, 96, 210, 271; transcendent aspects of, 244–46

Lotman, Jurij, 249, 250, 257

McCleary, Richard, 42, 92
Macek, Carl, 231
"Machines of the Visible" (Comolli), 308
Madison, Gary, 250, 256, 259
Magritte, René, 282, 283f
Man Who Mistook His Wife for a Hat and Other Clinical Tales, The (Sacks), 78
Man With a Movie Camera (Vertov), 266
"Manifesto for Cyborgs, A" (Haraway), 163n
Marker, Chris, 60, 61n
Marx, Karl, vii, xvi, 309. *See also* neo-Marxist theory
Matter and Memory (Bergson), 31
méconnaissance, 109, 119, 123, 269
mediation, 18, 105, 114; cinematic, 10, 191–203, 285; in structure of consciousness, 33, 34; as structure of vision, 51–54
Méliès, Georges, 255
Menzies, William Cameron, 297
Merleau-Ponty, Maurice, xv, 3, 25, 122–26, 212–13; on attention, 71–72, 89–90; on cinema, 164; on cohesion of human experience, 22, 82; on consciousness, 40, 121; on the embodied subject, 116, 117, 118, 122, 213; on freedom, xix; on gesture, 274; on history, xix; on intentional directedness, 273–76 passim; on intentionality, 34–35, 65; on "other" as subject, 121–22, 126, 127; on perception, 69–70, 72–73, 77–78, 293, 294; on perspective, 95–96; phenomenological

method of, 42–48; on speech and language, 44; on synaesthesia, 77–78, 94–95; "system of four terms" of, 123–28, 136, 137; on transcendental reduction, 200; on vision, 86–94, 115, 118, 292–93, 294, 309. *See also* semiotic phenomenology
Metaphors on Vision (Brakhage), 90
Metz, Christian, 136, 269–70, 271, 276–77, 291
Meunier, Jean-Pierre, 30
Miner, Steve, 256
mirror, metaphor of the, 14, 17–18, 104
mirror stage: psychoanalytic, 105, 107–12, 114, 116; in semiotic phenomenology, 116–17, 118–21
Mitry, Jean, 5, 16n, 27, 29n, 232, 233–35
Montgomery, Robert, 230. See also *Lady in the Lake*
motion, cinematic, 60–61, 62, 205–8, 277–78, 299
Münsterberg, Hugo, 207

"natural attitude," 35, 36, 43, 46, 91, 97, 129, 160, 208, 211–12, 273
"natural perception," 31
Necker cube, 71
neo-Freudian theory, xv, 55–57. *See also* psychoanalytic theory (Lacanian)
neo-Marxist theory, xiii, xiv, xvi, 17
noema/noesis: defined, 34, 36

objective empiricism, 16
Oedipal phase, 105–6, 107, 108, 109, 113, 114
optical printing, 254–55
orientational center: of a film, 134; of a human body, 83–84, 159
Other, the, 42, 99, 103; in ego development, 108–16 passim, 118–21, 124, 126, 128; film as, 285–88; as subject, 120–21, 123, 126, 127. *See also* Self, the

parole parlante/parlée. *See* speech, speaking and spoken
Passenger, The (Antonioni), 231n, 288n
patriarchal culture, 157–58

Printed in the United States
94686LV00003B/9/A